INDIGENOUS SOCIAL WORK AROUND THE WORLD

Contemporary Social Work Studies

Series Editor:
Robin Lovelock, University of Southampton

Series Advisory Board:
Lena Dominelli, Durham University, UK
Jan Fook, University of Southampton, UK
Peter Ford, University of Southampton, UK
Lorraine Gutiérrez, University of Michigan, USA
Walter Lorenz, Free University of Bozen-Bolzano, Italy
Karen Lyons, London Metropolitan University, UK
Colette McAuley, University of Southampton, UK
Joan Orme, University of Glasgow, UK
Jackie Powell, University of Southampton, UK

Contemporary Social Work Studies (CSWS) is a series disseminating high quality new research and scholarship in the discipline and profession of social work. The series promotes critical engagement with contemporary issues relevant across the social work community and captures the diversity of interests currently evident at national, international and local levels.

CSWS is located in the School of Social Sciences at the University of Southampton and is a development from the successful series of books published by Ashgate in association with CEDR (the Centre for Evaluative and Developmental Research) from 1991.

Titles in this series include:

Globalization and International Social Work:
Postmodern Change and Challenge
Malcolm Payne and Gurid Aga Askeland

Revitalising Communities in a Globalising World
Edited by Lena Dominelli

Social Work in a Corporate Era:
Practices of Power and Resistance
Edited by Linda Davies and Peter Leonard

Forthcoming for 2008:

Social Work and Migration:
Immigrant and Refugee Settlement and Integration
Kathleen Valtonen

Indigenous Social Work around the World

Towards Culturally Relevant Education and Practice

Edited by

MEL GRAY
University of Newcastle, Australia

JOHN COATES
St. Thomas University, Canada

MICHAEL YELLOW BIRD
University of Kansas, USA

ASHGATE

Published by
Ashgate Publishing Limited
Gower House
Croft Road
Aldershot
Hampshire GU11 3HR
England

Ashgate Publishing Company
Suite 420
101 Cherry Street
Burlington, VT 05401-4405
USA

www.ashgate.com

British Library Cataloguing in Publication Data
Indigenous social work around the world : towards
  culturally relevant education and practice. - (Contemporary
  social work studies)
  1. Social work with indigenous peoples - Cross-cultural
  studies 2. Social work education - Cross-cultural studies
  I. Gray, Mel II. Coates, John III. Bird, Michael Yellow
  361.3'2'089

Library of Congress Cataloging in Publication Data
Gray, Mel, 1951-
 Indigenous social work around the world : towards culturally relevant education and
practice / by Mel Gray, John Coates and Michael Yellow Bird.
    p. cm. -- (Contemporary social work studies)
 Includes bibliographical references and index.
 ISBN 978-0-7546-4838-3
 1. Social work with indigenous peoples. 2. Social work with indigenous peoples--Study
and teaching. I. Coates, John, 1948- II. Yellow Bird, Michael. III. Title.

HV3176.G713 2008
362.84--dc22

2008015380

ISBN 978-0-7546-4838-3

Mixed Sources
Product group from well-managed
forests and other controlled sources
www.fsc.org Cert no. SA-COC-1565
© 1996 Forest Stewardship Council

Printed and bound in Great Britain by
MPG Books Ltd, Bodmin, Cornwall.

Contents

The key issue for social work in the twenty-first century is finding culturally relevant ways of knowing and helping.

Social work is best done by paying attention to particular persons in locally situated cultural contexts.

Social work is one of the few professions in a position to promote and engage in a sustained way with relationships at the level of local cultural practice. This is the ethical core of its work and the place where it can best sustain an ethical defense of its professional identity (Webb 2003: 202).

List of Figures and Tables

Notes on Contributors[1]

The Editors

Mel Gray
Professor and Chair of Social Work, Institute for the Advanced Study of Humanity (IASH), University of Newcastle, New South Wales, Australia. Mel's interest in culturally relevant – Indigenous – social work began in South Africa when, as the transformation drew nearer and with the change to a developmental welfare system, there were increasing claims that social work was not relevant. Having initially written about the relevance of social work to social development, she then realized that what was at the centre of the debate were questions about culture. There followed several papers written with a former sociology colleague at Newcastle that were published in the South African social work journal, *Social Work/Maatskaplike Work*. On moving to Australia in 1999, a totally different world of Indigenous social work was encountered, one into which it was very difficult for an outsider to enter. Mel worked with colleagues in *Wollotuka*, the School of Indigenous Studies, at Newcastle University, and Bruce Valentine in the NSW Office of Children's Guardian to develop out of home care guidelines for Indigenous childcare agencies. Two papers on this work have been published in *Illinois Child Welfare* and *Families in Society*.

John Coates
Professor, and former Chair, Department of Social Work, St Thomas University, Fredericton, New Brunswick, Canada. John is Chair and a founding member of the Canadian Society for Spirituality and Social Work, and helped establish the Mi'kmaq-Maliseet BSW Programme, a joint programme at St Thomas University and Dalhousie University. His recent publications include *Ecology and Social Work* (2003), Fernwood Press, Halifax; *Spirituality and Social Work: Selected Canadian Readings* (2007) (coedited with John R. Graham, Barbara Swartzentruber with Brian Ouellette), Canadian Scholars Press: Toronto; 'An "Ecospiritual" perspective: Finally a place for Indigenous Approaches' (2006) (with Mel Gray and Tiani Hetherington), *British Journal of Social Work* 36, 1–19; and 'Ideology and Politics: Essential Factors in the Path toward Sustainability' (2006) (with Terry Leahy), *Electronic Green Journal* 23. He has an active research agenda that includes research on trauma and youth homelessness, the political activity of social workers, spirituality and social work, and social work theory and practice related to environmental realities.

---

[1] Contributors are listed in order of chapter.

Michael Yellow Bird

Associate Professor and former Director of Indigenous Nations Studies, now Founder and Director of the Center for Indigenous Peoples' Critical and Intuitive Thinking at the University of Kansas, Lawrence, Kansas, USA. Michael Yellow Bird is a citizen of the Sahnish and Hidatsa Nations. He is the author of several articles, encyclopedia entries, and book chapters. His most recent book (coedited with Waziyatawin Angela Wilson) is *For Indigenous Eyes Only: A Decolonization Handbook* (2005). His research interests focus on the following topics related to Indigenous Peoples: critical and intuitive thinking, US foreign policy, oral histories of Native Vietnam combat veterans, the effects of colonialism and methods of decolonization, healthy masculinity, human rights, and political prisoners and prisoner rights. He has conducted research that has supported the empowerment of numerous tribal communities, served as a rapporteur for the health and human rights working group during the Indigenous Peoples' International Day at the United Nations, and has been a featured speaker, both nationally and internationally, on topics important to the well-being of Indigenous communities.

Contributors

James Midgley

James Midgley is Harry and Riva Specht Professor of Public Social Services at the School of Social Welfare University of California, Berkeley, USA. He has published widely on issues of social development and international social welfare. His most recent books include *Controversial Issues in Social Policy* (2003) (with Howard Karger and Brene Brown), Allyn and Bacon; *Social Policy for Development* (2004) (with Anthony Hall), Sage Publications and *Lessons from Abroad: Adapting International Social Welfare Innovations* (2004) (with M.C. Hokenstad), NASW Press.

Hilary N. Weaver

Hilary N. Weaver, DSW (Lakota) is an Associate Professor in the School of Social Work, University at Buffalo (State University of New York), USA. Her teaching, research, and service focus on cultural issues in the helping process with a particular focus on Indigenous populations. She currently serves as President of the American Indian Alaska Native Social Work Educators Association and President of the Board of Directors of Native American Community Services of Erie and Niagara Counties. Dr Weaver has presented her work regionally, nationally, and internationally, including presenting at the Permanent Forum on Indigenous Issues at the United Nations in 2005 and 2006. She has numerous publications including the recent text, *Explorations in Cultural Competence: Journeys to the Four Directions* (2005). Dr Weaver is currently funded by the National Cancer Institute to develop and test a culturally grounded wellness curriculum for urban Native American youth, the Healthy Living in Two Worlds programme.

Linda Briskman
Professor Linda Briskman is Dr Haruhisa Handa Chair of Human Rights Education, Curtin University of Technology, Perth, Australia. She works collaboratively with Indigenous communities in Australia on policy and practice issues and has conducted research in the areas of Indigenous child welfare and Indigenous housing. Her other human rights endeavours include asylum seekers and refugees. Books include *Social Work and Indigenous Peoples: Past, Present and Futures* (forthcoming 2007), The Federation Press and *The Black Grapevine: Aboriginal Activism and the Stolen Generations* (2003), The Federation Press.

Ling How Kee
Senior Lecturer, Social Work Programme, Faculty of Social Sciences, University Malaysia Sarawak. Her publications include: 'The Search from Within: Research Issues in Developing Culturally Appropriate Social Work Practice' (2004), *International Social Work*, 47(3), 336–45 and 'Drawing Lessons from Local Designated Helpers to Develop Culturally Appropriate Social Work Practice' (2003), *Asia Pacific Journal of Social Work*, 13(2), 26–44. Her doctoral thesis was entitled, *Towards Developing Culturally Appropriate Social Work Practice: Insights from a Study of Help-seeking and Help-giving Practices in Sarawak, Malaysia* (2000), University of Queensland, Australia.

Wheturangi Walsh-Tapiata
Senior Lecturer in the School of Sociology, Social Policy and Social Work at Massey University, Palmerston North, New Zealand. She has taught in a wide variety of areas including social work practice, Māori development, fieldwork, community development, and Māori issues in research. She is currently team leader of a three-year research study examining the health and well-being of Māori adolescents in her tribal organization Te Runanaga o Raukawa.

Tracie Mafile'o
Tracie Mafile'o is New Zealand born of Tongan (South Pacific) and Pakeha heritage. She is a social work lecturer in the School of Sociology, Social Policy and Social Work at Massey University in New Zealand. From 2007–09 she has taken leave from her substantive position to serve as Director of Counselling Services and Senior Lecturer at Pacific Adventist University in Papua New Guinea. Her teaching and research focuses on ethnic specific practice frameworks, Pacific peoples' well-being, and community work. Dr Mafile'o has published and presented internationally on Tongan social work, the subject of her PhD research. She has played a key role in advancing the well-being and development of diasporic Pacific islands peoples.

Michael Anthony Hart
Michael Hart, PhD, is a citizen of the Fisher River Cree Nation and an Assistant Professor, Faculty of Social Work, University of Manitoba, Canada, focusing on Indigenous social work thought, issues, and practice. He is the author of 'Seeking Mino-pimatisiwin (the Good Life): An Aboriginal Approach to Social Work Practice' (1999), *Native Social Work Journal*, 2(1), 91–112; *Seeking Mino-Pimatisiwin: An*

Aboriginal Approach to Helping (2002), Halifax, Canada: Fernwood Publishing; and 'An Aboriginal Approach to Social Work Practice', in T. Heinonen and L. Spearman (2006), *Social Work Practice: Problem Solving and Beyond.* Toronto: Nelson, pp. 236–59.

Jayashree Nimmagadda
Dr Nimmagadda is Professor, School of Social Work, Rhode Island College, Providence, USA. Her research interests have primarily centred on the transfer of social work knowledge from the West to the East (specifically India) and the process by which social workers indigenize this knowledge. Her publications include: 'Building Bridges through Indigenization' (2006) (with M. Bromley), *Reflections: Narratives of Professional Helping*, 12(3), 64–72; 'The Indigenization of AA: Interpretations from South India' (2006) (with K. Chakradhar), *Asian Pacific Journal of Social Work*, 16(1), 7–20; 'Indigenization of Social Work Knowledge: An Exploration of the Process' (2000) (with P.R. Balgopal), *Asian Pacific Journal of Social Work*, 10(2), 4–18; 'Cross-cultural Practice: Social Worker Ingenuity in the Indigenization of Practice Knowledge' (1999) (with C. Cowger), *International Social Work*, 42(3), 261–76.

Diane R. Martell
Diane R. Martell is Associate Professor, School of Social Work, Rhode Island College, Providence, Rhode Island, USA. She continues to support Southeast Asian communities in the development of culturally relevant programmes and is currently exploring the adaptation of social work knowledge with Cape Verdean people in southern New England.

Alean Al-Krenawi
Alean Al-Krenawi is the Chair of the Spitzer Department of Social Work and the Scientific Director of the Regional Research and Development Centre for Bedouin Society. He has completed a book on *Arab Ethno-psychiatry* and coedited a book on *Multicultural Social Work in Canada: Working with Diverse Ethno-Racial Communities* published by Oxford University Press, and is working on his third book, *Islam and Social Work* which will be published by Columbia University Press. The author of numerous book chapters and academic peer reviewed articles, recently published works appear or are due to appear in the *American Journal of Orthopsychiatry, British Journal of Social Work, Child Abuse and Neglect, Clinical Social Work Journal, Family Process, Families in Societies, Health and Social Work, International Social Work, International Social Psychiatry* and *World Health Forum*, among other professional journals. Alean and co-author John (below) have been collaborating since 1993 when they first met at the University of Toronto in Canada. Alean worked with the Bedouin-Arab of the Negev for 11 years in two settings: Primary health care and the Psychiatric Department at Sorkoka hospital.

John R. Graham
John R. Graham is Murray Fraser Professor and Director of the International Social Development Unit in the Faculty of Social Work at the University of Calgary,

Canada. Recent and upcoming Al-Krenawi/Graham books include *Multicultural Social Work with Diverse Ethno-racial Communities in Canada* (2003) Toronto: Oxford University Press; *Helping Professional Practice with Indigenous Peoples: The Bedouin-Arab Case* (2007), Hauppauge, New York: Nova Press; *Islam and Social Work* (forthcoming 2009), New York: Columbia University Press.

Rick Sin
Rick Sin is a lecturer in social work at McMaster University in Canada. His research is on the discursive formation of cultural boundaries, practices of cultural racism in diversity discourse, and Indigenous resistance in social work knowledge construction.

Angelina Yuen-Tsang
Professor Yuen-Tsang is Head of the School of Social Work at Hong Kong Polytechnic University. She has played an important role in introducing social work and social work education into China and has published widely on international social work. Her publications include: 'Chinese Communal Support Networks' (1999), *International Social Work*, 42, 359–71; 'Tensions Confronting the Development of Social Work Education in China' (2001) (with S. Wang), *International Social Work*, 45(3), 375–88.

Ben Ku
Ben Ku is Assistant Professor in the Department of Applied Social Sciences and Deputy Director of the China Research and Development Networks, at The Hong Kong Polytechnic University. He is also visiting professor at the Yunnan University of China. He has written extensively on the topics of cultural politics, social exclusion and marginality, social work education, and social development. His most recent books include: *Moral Politics in a South Chinese Village: Responsibility, Reciprocity and Resistance* (2003), Rowman and Littlefield Publishers; *Social Exclusion and Marginality in Chinese Societies* (2003), Hong Kong: Centre for Social Policy Studies, the Hong Kong Polytechnic University; *Research, Practice and Reflection of Social Work in Indigenous Chinese Context* (2004), Beijing: Social Sciences Documentation Publishing House; *Rethinking and Recasting Citizenship: Social Exclusion and Marginality in Chinese Society* (2005), Hong Kong: Centre for Social Policy Studies, The Hong Kong Polytechnic University.

Miu Chung Yan
Miu Chung Yan is Associate Professor, School of Social Work, University of British Columbia, Canada. Publications on international social work include: 'The Politics of Indigenization: Development of Social Work in China' (2006) (with K.W. Cheung), *Journal of Sociology and Social Welfare*, 33(2), 63–83; 'Searching for International Social Work: A Reflection on Personal and Professional Journey' (2005), *Reflections: Narratives of Professional Helping*, 11(1), 4–16; 'A Snapshot on the Development of Social Work Education in China: A Delphi Study' (2005) (with A.K.T. Tsang), *Social Work Education*, 24(8), 883–901; and two other co-authored articles with A.K.T. Tsang.

A Ka Tat Tsang

A Ka Tat Tsang is Associate Professor, Faculty of Social Work, University of Toronto, Canada. Publications include: 'Negotiating Multiple Agendas in International Social Work: The Case of the China-Canada Collaborative Project' (2000) (with M.C. Yan, and W. Shera), *Canadian Social Work Review*, 17(Suppl), 147–61; 'Chinese Corpus, Western Application: The Chinese Strategy of Engagement with Western Social Work Discourse' (2001) (with M.C. Yan), *International Social Work*, 44(4), 433–54.

Kwaku Osei-Hwedie

Kwaku Osei-Hwedie is Professor of Social Work at the University of Botswana, Gaborone. Publications include: *Indigenising Social Work: (Southern) African Perspectives* (forthcoming) (coedited with G. Jacques); 'Searching for Appropriateness in Social Work Education in Botswana' (2006) (with D. Ntseane and G. Jacques), *Journal of Social Work Education*; 'Indigenous Practice: Some Informed Guesses, Self-evident and Possible' (2002), *Social Work/Maatskaplike Werk*, 38(4); 'Culture as a Tool of Social Work Practice' (2000), *Social Work Africa*, 1(1); *A Search for Legitimate Social Development Education and Practice Models for Africa* (1995), Lewiston, NY: Edwin Mullen; 'The Challenge of Social Work in Africa: Starting the Indigenization Process' (1993), *Journal of Social Development in Africa*, 8(1), 19–30.

Morena J. Rankopo

Morena J. Rankopo is Lecturer in Social Work and coordinator of the Master of Social Work programme at the University of Botswana. He is actively involved in research on culturally relevant social work in Southern Africa, and is currently contributing two chapters, 'The Socio-cultural Basis of Indigenising Social Work in Southern Africa' and 'Problems of Indigenising Social Work in Botswana', to a German book project on the subject. Other research interests include community development, human rights, and HIV and AIDS. He has publications in the areas of Indigenous knowledge and community development. His current focus is on the development of Indigenous community development methods in Botswana.

Susan Gair

Dr Susan Gair is Senior Lecturer in the School of Social Work and Community Welfare at James Cook University in Northern Queensland, Australia. She manages a project within the School called Toward Critical Mass which seeks to recruit, support and graduate increasing numbers of Indigenous students. Her publications include: 'What's Stopping Them? Barriers Hindering Indigenous Students Completing a BSW at JCU' (2005) (with J. Thomson), *Advances in Social Welfare Education*, 7(1), 54–66; 'Reconciling Indigenous and Non-Indigenous Knowledges in Social Work Education: Action and Legitimacy' (2005) (with J. Thomson and D. Miles), *Journal of Social Work Education*, 41(2), 371–81; 'It's Very White Isn't It! Challenging Mono-culturalism in Social Work and Welfare Education' (2003) (with J. Thomson, D. Miles and N. Harris), *Advances in Social Welfare Education*, 5(1),

37–52; 'Honing Skills: An Evolving Model for Teaching Welfare Skills Appropriate to the North Queensland Context' (2002) (with R. Frangos), *Women in Welfare Education*, 5, 3–8.

Gord Bruyere
Gord Bruyere is Anishnabe and was born on Couchiching First Nation in Northwestern Ontario, Canada. He is currently the Coordinator of the Bachelor of Social Work programme at the Nicola Valley Institute of Technology in Merritt, British Columbia. He has worked in child protection, probation and parole and as an Aboriginal university student counsellor. Since 1995, he has taught, developed curriculum and coordinated Aboriginal programmes at seven mainstream and Aboriginal post-secondary institutions across Canada in Early Childhood Education, Indigenous Learning, Political Science, Aboriginal Law and Advocacy, and Social Work. His publication of book chapters and journal articles, and his national and international conference presentations, focus on issues of anti-racism and Aboriginal social work and education. His current research interests include Aboriginal culture-based approaches to helping, and Aboriginal educational approaches and curriculum design.

Erika Faith
Erika Faith (formerly Haug) is a Saskatoon-based writer, educator, and artist of Swedish and Norwegian ancestry. As a child of missionary parents, Erika spent 12 years growing up in rural Nepal. The themes of challenging and healing various forms of oppression, inequality, division, and imbalance, at the personal, local and global levels, inform all of her work. Erika holds a Master's degree in International Social Work from the University of Calgary, and is a sessional Lecturer for the Faculty of Social Work, University of Regina. Her publications include: 'Critical Reflections on the Emerging Discourse of International Social Work' (2005), *International Social Work*, 48(2): 126–35; *Writing in the Margins: Critical Reflection on the Emerging Discourse of International Social Work* (2001), unpublished MSW Thesis, Faculty of Social Work, University of Calgary, Canada.

Tiani Hetherington
Tiani Hetherington is a PhD Social Work student at the University of Newcastle, Australia. Thesis title: *A Cross-country Comparison between Australia (Hunter Region) and Canada (New Brunswick) of Indigenous Social Work Practice*. Her publications include: 'An "Eco-spiritual" Perspective: Finally a Place for Indigenous Approaches' (2006) (with J. Coates and M. Gray), *British Journal of Social Work*, 36(3), 381–99.

Preface

At the beginning of June 2006, all the contributors to this book participated in an international writers' workshop made possible by funding from the Social Sciences and Humanities Research Council of Canada (SSHRC), the Canada International Development Agency (CIDA), the Ministry of Indian and Northern Affairs Canada (INAC), the International Association of Schools of Social Work (IASSW), and St Thomas University in New Brunswick, Canada. Participants had been invited based on their prior work in writing about 'Indigenization' and 'Indigenous social work' around the world. While some individuals who were invited did not attend, the participants who attended were writing from their various locations about the 'Indigenization' of social work in China, Hong Kong, India, Malaysia, Africa, Australia, Tonga (New Zealand), the USA and Canada.

The original objectives of the workshop included reviewing the global trends impacting on the 'Indigenization' of social work, comparing the ways in which social work was being shaped by developments in specific countries, and the ways in which mainstream social work was positively influencing these developments, however, we quickly realized that these were naïve and inappropriate in light of current realities. The face to face discussions, the exchange of ideas, and challenges to different views forced all the participants to confront the complexities surrounding 'Indigenization', including issues of culture, politics, globalization, professionalization, internationalization and, not least, the varying use of terminology. Not only did 'Indigenization' and 'Indigenous social work' hold different meanings and significance in various cultures and contexts, we soon learned they were very different things; the first, a process of adapting Western social work to non-Western contexts and the other concerned with the development of social work among Indigenous Peoples of the world. Even the term 'Western' came under scrutiny, since for some it represented a too simplistic binary reaction to the world by placing Indigenous and non-Indigenous knowledges in two diametrically opposite spheres, which was regarded as unreasonable since there were many instances when participants observed the crossover of various bodies of knowledge, beliefs, values, and world views. Hilary Weaver (see Chapter 5) provided an important metaphor for these parallel processes, the story of the two *wampuns*, two canoes side by side and the wisdom of the chief that one cannot have a foot in both. One must choose. At the end of our lengthy discussions, heated debates, emotional wrenching, spiritual connecting and the camaraderie of being together as a diverse international group, we agreed that we would no longer use the word 'Indigenization' when writing about the development of culturally appropriate social work in our various contexts, especially since relevant, local, culturally sensitive, appropriate, localization, recontextualization and so on, were thought to be more accurate terms for what we were trying to accomplish. *Our common ground was that we were all in our own way trying to develop culturally relevant responses to our diverse local contexts* and the realization that, strictly speaking, Indigenous social work involves the Indigenous Peoples of the world.

Thus, those of us with our foot in the 'Indigenization' canoe soon realized that our prior writings had unwittingly furthered the ill-informed 'Indigenization' discourse which was deeply offensive to many Indigenous Peoples and struck at the very heart of their identity. For them, it was a misappropriation and misuse of both the term 'Indigenous' and the process of spreading social work from the west to the rest that was commonly referred to as 'Indigenization'. *We agreed that we were all concerned about the development of culturally appropriate social work to counter the juggernaut of western social work, and there was much discussion about this.*

This book is the collective accomplishment of a group of people who have taught one another a great deal. The participants at the workshop engaged in a process of clarifying misconceptions and developing a common and meaningful discourse on our subject matter. The face to face interactions, which were rich with various instances of Indigenous communication and relationship building protocols, apparent during the processes of questioning, getting across one's views, and the demonstrations of respect, were most important to working through differences, something that could not have been accomplished if we had been limited to emails and written correspondence. This positive outcome reinforces the value of such workshops for advancing knowledge development and the respect for Indigenous protocol, world views, and values. As Linda Briskman (see Chapter 6) said after the workshop, 'It was a unique forum. I wish there were more like it as it would make the world a better place.' It was a huge learning experience for all of us.

The proceedings began with Jim Midgley (see Chapter 2) revisiting his notion of 'professional imperialism in the third world' twenty-five years later. This provided an overview of the theoretical context, for far from being in a period when the colonial phase of human history is ending, colonialism and cultural imperialism are alive and well, and some would argue thriving, in numerous contexts around the world, not least in the lives of Indigenous Peoples. While we are particularly concerned with social work's response to Indigenous Peoples, and local cultures and contexts – call it anticolonialism or localization – 'professional imperialism' is a pressing concern given the internationalizing and globalizing mission of the Western social work juggernaut. So embedded is social work in some of the more virulent aspects of Western philosophy and Western world views that it must be seen, at least in its present form, as a Western cultural creation. This creates many tensions for universities seeking to expand their programmes and market share, for professors and professionals who seek to offer their skills in other cultures, and for local cultures and people who may be coerced by various means to conclude that 'what is west is best' and thus devalue their own local and Indigenous ways of knowing and helping. The workshop led us to conclude not only that social work must be very careful in all instances where the profession seeks to 'be helpful' in other contexts and cultures, but also that there are built-in challenges when social work moves outside its Western boundaries or works with people from non-Western contexts. These challenges arise from the fact that social work is a Western cultural creation and, as a product of modernity (Coates 2003) it does not deal with diversity very well. This book is the outcome of a workshop which brought together a group of scholars with a common purpose: to discuss the most significant global trends relating to the development of culturally relevant and Indigenous social work around the world.

Given its focus, this book is aimed primarily at a social work audience – researchers, academics, lecturers, practitioners, and students (both graduate and undergraduate). Additionally, however, the authors have a wider audience in mind given the growing understanding and development of Indigenous knowledge and practices in a wide variety of fields (for example, anthropology, psychology, counselling, ethnography, sociology, medicine, public health, community development, social development, media and cultural studies, business, and so on). For both audiences, social work's efforts to develop culturally relevant practices, and the varied array of case examples provided, provides a rich source of information. Moreover, as researchers and practitioners of international social work in all its varied forms, we are sure will find much to ponder and debate in these pages. It should be of special interest to social work educators aiming to give their students an understanding of social work around the world and of the importance of culture in social work practice.

Acknowledgments

This book would not have been possible without the support of many individuals and organizations. The contributors often put other work aside to meet our deadlines and were quite diligent in responding to our many editorial requests. While this book involved the contributions of many people, two of these individuals are particularly noteworthy. Background research was provided by Tiani Hetherington, a doctoral student at the University of Newcastle, Australia, and Stella Cooke, a social work student at St Thomas University, Canada, provided substantial assistance in preparing for the workshop, travel arrangements and helping to facilitate the smooth functioning of the workshop.

We wish to acknowledge the support received from The Wallace and Margaret McCain Faculty Research Award which enabled significant progress to be made in the completion of this book.

The editors are particularly appreciative of the financial support for the international writers' workshop from which this book emerged. Without this financial assistance, the book would not have come to fruition. We wish to thank the following organizations for their support:

Social Sciences and Humanities Research Council of Canada
Canada International Development Agency
Ministry of Indian and Northern Affairs Canada
International Association of Schools of Social Work
St Thomas University, Fredericton, New Brunswick, Canada

Structure of the Book

The book is divided into four parts. In Part 1 we examine 'Indigenization' as an outmoded concept. Beginning with Chapter 1, we explain the reasons for this and show how the real issue with which we are dealing is the development of culturally relevant social work practice and education around the world. We explain how claims to 'global' and 'universal' social work present a paradox for those concerned with social work's responsiveness to local cultural contexts. We argue that, in reality, social workers on the frontlines are mainly concerned with responsiveness to their local context, with most social work reaching, at most, to national concerns at a policy level, and that only a minority of social workers are directly concerned with international social work. Furthermore, most who are involved in international social work are mainly concerned with developing models of culturally relevant social work practice in local contexts, among cultures with varying degrees of *difference* from their own. There is far greater awareness now of the dangers of imperialism, and that 'Indigenization' is so associated with a response to colonization and missionary zeal that it cannot adequately reflect social work's contemporary efforts to deal better with diversity – being mindful of cultural sensitivity, competence, appropriateness, and relevance. Thus we believe that claims to 'global' social work are not only an exaggeration of the reach of social work but also deny the importance of nongovernment organizations, community and social development which play a far greater role in working with the majority of the world's population who are in need.

Social work is mainly an urban profession concerned with local and national issues. Claims to 'global' social work suit the political agenda of social work's international organizations which, in reality, have a limited reach. Its two main bodies, the International Association of Schools of Social Work (IASSW) and the International Federation of Social Workers (IFSW), respectively have just over 400 member schools in 55 countries and an estimated 80 member associations around the world representing 500,000 professional social workers. While not denying the importance of the work of these international organizations in promoting professional social work internationally, we believe that an uncritical acceptance of the globalization agenda is paradoxical in a profession which values cultural responsiveness and that concerns with cultural relevance force us to rethink the universals in social work and be wary of homogenizing processes like the search for international definitions of social work and global standards of social work education. These processes are political in that they are mainly concerned with professional interests and pushing a professionalization agenda. Cultural relevance is forcing us to entertain the idea of multiple social works and social work knowledges, rather than a universal profession with universal values. The latter amounts to a McDonald's-ization of social work, a one size fits all approach that is paradoxical in a profession which values and extols diversity. As we argue throughout this book, culture is central to Indigenous social work and to culturally relevant social work, which is responsive to local and national contexts worldwide. The nation state remains the central influence on welfare and the practice contexts in which social workers are found around the globe.

Chapter 2 warns us of the legacy of professional imperialism and shows that it is alive and well in social work. Though Jim Midgley focuses mainly on contemporary developments in the US, in revisiting professional imperialism twenty-five years on, there is much that resonates for the contexts from which our authors are writing and for many in developing countries. Good intentions in spreading social work internationally are not enough. Serious consideration must be given to local cultures and this involves respecting people's world views and cultural practices.

Having explored 'Indigenization' as an outmoded concept and replaced it with 'cultural relevance', in Part 2 we examine Indigenous social work as a just cause, and one on which international social work has remained largely silent. Chapter 3 aims to enhance our understanding of Indigenous social work and Chapters 4 and the Postscript invite us to pay closer attention to the language we use and its effect on this just cause. In Chapter 5, Hilary Weaver examines Indigenous social work in the United States demonstrating its cultural significance for First Nations Peoples. In Chapter 6, Linda Briskman, writing from Australia, looks at the political nature of Indigenous social work which is centrally concerned with 'decolonization', not only overcoming the worst effects of colonization but also resisting its continual onslaught in policies which deny Indigenous People their human rights, including their right to lands to which they are entitled. The dominant history of Indigenous People is one of dispossession and dehumanization and this history cannot be undone. It is part of the everyday life of Indigenous Peoples around the world. But it is not the only story. Increasingly, stories of the resilience of oppressed people everywhere are being told and these stories are rich with culture and narratives of resistance to colonization and territorializing agendas. More important for our purposes, they question the relevance of professional social work. It can never be forgotten that for Indigenous People it was their so-called *protectors* who took their children away and put them on mission stations and reserves. Those who ostensibly came to further their cause tried to deny them their Aboriginality, to take away their children, their land and their culture. Is universal social work still trying to do this today?

In Part 3, we examine several attempts to develop culturally relevant social work practices in Sarawak, Malaysia, among Māori and Tongans in Aotearoa/New Zealand, First Nations people in Canada, in India and among South East Asian people in the USA learning from the Indian experience, and among the Bedouin people of Israel and Palestine.

In Part 4, we explore culturally relevant social work education in a variety of contexts. In Chapter 13, Rick Sin takes a critical look at the construction of 'Chineseness' in social work literature. Chapter 14 provides a case study of the development of social work education in China by a group of educators from Hong Kong, while Chapter 15 takes a more critical look at these developments. Chapter 16 describes the experience of a group of educators in Botswana in attempting to develop a culturally relevant social work education programme in the face of pressure from university administrators for internationally competitive programmes. Chapter 17 is a reflection on an Australian experience in developing an Indigenous social work curriculum, and Chapters 18 and 19 recount experiences from Canada in developing social work education for First Nations people.

This varied array of case studies provides a rich source of information for practitioners of international social work in all its varied forms, and for social work educators aiming to give their students an understanding of social work around the world and of the importance of culture in social work practice. In Chapter 20, Gray *et al.* claim that Indigenous and local voices are being heard and it is hoped that they will continue to enrich our understanding as social work strives to embrace and value diversity.

Introduction

Mel Gray, John Coates and Michael Yellow Bird

Social work has been sought out or invited into many countries and cultures in efforts to develop ways to address personal and social problems, however, when social workers participated in the mass forced removal of Indigenous children from their communities, Indigenous Peoples knew quite well the culturally destructive side of the profession. The profession has made great efforts to develop effective methodologies that can be of benefit to First Nations or Indigenous Peoples, and minority populations, but despite holding significant roles in providing social services to people from different cultures and societies, social work has been slow to accept non-Western and Indigenous world views, local knowledge and traditional forms of helping and healing. As a consequence, social work education and practice, in regard to non-Western cultures, has struggled to develop and deliver services in an effective, acceptable and culturally appropriate manner. Often such efforts have been embedded in dominant Western paradigms and the results have proved inadequate in meeting the needs of diverse groups. A review of the literature in this area reveals a great deal of negativity around the world concerning social work's track record in working across cultures and with Indigenous and First Nations Peoples (see, for example, Hart 2002; Ling 2003; Nagpaul 1972, 1993; Nimmagadda and Cowger 1999; Tsang and Yan 2001; Yip 2004).

This is not surprising given that social work is essentially a modernist Western invention which has a history of silencing marginal voices and importing, into diverse cultural contexts across the world, Western thinking primarily from the UK and the USA. This technology transfer is the consequence of colonializing, Westernizing, globalizing and Americanizing forces. For cultural minorities, non-Western cultures and Indigenous Peoples, all these 'izings' reflect the 'rizing' of Western models and the sinking of local, diverse cultural wisdoms, knowledges and moralities.

Around the world Indigenous Peoples and cultural minorities are collectively asserting their rights to self-determination for political, economic, educational, and health benefits and these privileges cannot occur as long as entire populations or groups are disenfranchised. The 'self-directing potential of individuals' emphasized in Western social work is questioned in the face of such historical, social, cultural, economic, and political realities where self-determination concerns the liberation of entire populations. While not eschewing the value of a common discourse on and understanding about social work, we need to be mindful that there is a fundamental 'izing' – a domination – as certain destructive Western values are imposed from the top down: the globalization of knowledge and Western culture continues to reaffirm the west's view of itself as the centre and wellspring of knowledge. To many people, globalization[1] is just a new form of colonialism.

Cross-cultural, anti-racist and anti-oppressive practices are responses to the promotion and protection of diversity and have enabled social work to look more thoughtfully at the way in which it deals with these topics, however, much of this work appeared as adaptation rather than exchange since modernist social work has great difficulty welcoming and accommodating diversity (see Coates 2003; Haug 2001; Healy 2001). This lack of responsiveness occurred in dealings with local and Indigenous groups both within Western countries where 'the human services have contributed to the practices of colonization and dispossession' (Healy 2000: 61), as well as in countries where economic development efforts 'laid the foundation for intellectual colonization in which Western modernist scientific knowledge systems displaced previously established local, popular and indigenous knowledge systems' (Haug 2001: 44). A growing literature on the topic of diversity, written by Indigenous and informed non-Indigenous scholars, has been another response to offset the damaging aspects of modernist social work.

The modern Western context within which social work emerged and developed has been 'premised on the idea that there is a unified and identifiable set of critical practices' (Healy 2000: 125). These firmly held modern assumptions have contributed to social work's difficulty to take seriously the importance of local contexts in shaping practice (Coates *et al.* 2006). Western models of social work have been exported to other cultures and nations, and this process has led some writers to conclude that the profession has been a partner in intellectual, cultural and corporate colonization (Haug 2001; Nagpaul 1972, 1993; Zachariah, in Haug 2001). The development literature is replete with examples of the ways in which the homogenizing effects of universal aid has dramatically altered the security and sustainability of local socio-economic and cultural practices (Pearce 2001). The global education standards (IASSW 2004) can be seen to promote the damaging notions of globalization and to downplay the importance of local contexts (Gray and Fook 2004; Gray 2005).

This imperialistic direction has been supported by the advantages of academics from economically developed nations, primarily North America and Europe, whose access to money for travel has led to the dissemination and the dominance of Western academics and Western models of practice (Coates *et al.* 2006). For example, many professional schools were established by the British and North Americans (Haug 2005), and there is the preference for English in much international literature and at most international social work gatherings. Smith (in Hart 2002) identifies the implicit message in these educational processes as 'globalization of knowledge and Western culture (which) constantly reaffirms the west's view of itself as the centre of legitimate knowledge, the arbiter of what counts as knowledge and the source of "civilized" knowledge' (p. 29). Further, the assumption that expertise is based on formal academic training excludes the many 'social workers' in non-Western countries who lack professional qualifications (Haug 2001). The modern

---

1   We use globalization in the sense that it was used originally by Theodore Levitt (1983) as the changes in social behaviours and technology that allow companies to sell or market the *same* products worldwide.

assumption of universality and 'one best way' has hindered social work's effort to attend effectively to issues of diversity.

Social work and diversity

Social work's literature on cross-cultural practice has emphasized that the effectiveness of interventions depends on the social worker's acquisition of a particular body of cultural knowledge, values and skills (see Clark 2000; Devore and Schlesinger 1995, 1999; Lum 1996, 1999; Weaver 1998, 1999, 2000). According to Weaver, 'cultural competence' arises from a social worker's knowledge about the specific cultural group, as well as self-reflection and sensitivity to one's personal biases. The acquisition of culturally specific knowledge, values and skills leads to an understanding of other perspectives and cultures which can then be used by the social worker to understand the client's 'cultural frame of reference' (Clark 2000: 1). Culturally competent social work practice is seen to emerge from the integration of this knowledge and reflective understanding with practice skills, however, the assumptions that are foundational to Western models of practice – individualism, rationalism, objectivity and internal causality – lead some writers, for example, Hart 2002; Healy 2000; Prasad and Vijayaslakshmi 1997; Tsang and Yan 2001, to argue that micro-based cross-cultural models which emphasize rationalism and individualistic approaches are inappropriate in many non-Western cultures.

Coates *et al.* (2006) argue that the wealth of publications on cultural sensitivity, and cross-cultural, anti-oppressive and anti-racist practice, attest to social work's struggle with diversity. All are limited by the foundational beliefs of mainstream social work and, as a result, have had marginal success in working with, and incorporating, traditional, local, and First Nations' or Indigenous Peoples' perspectives and modes of helping and healing. These foundational mainstream beliefs include professionalism, rationalism, and reflexive individualism (Giddens 1991), to name a few, that run counter to the beliefs and values, such as respectful individualism (see Chapter 10), interdependence, connectedness and inclusion, of many non-Western and Indigenous cultures' beliefs.

A review of the social work literature exploring efforts to accommodate diversity reveals many trends, including multiculturalism, cultural and ethnic sensitivity, and cross-cultural, transcultural, and anti-oppressive practices. These approaches bring attention to, and attempt to counter, the ways that dominant cultures can marginalize and oppress minority cultures, but it can remain difficult for members of minority cultures to move beyond victim status and to rise above their situations (Ferguson 2001). Further, these practice models are constructed from the perspective of the dominant Western mindset wherein the emphasis on internal causality and individual work, dualism, and rational determinism, to name a few, tend to marginalize local and Indigenous knowledges. Frequently the emphasis on these universal criteria makes it difficult to attend to the needs of local communities and marginalized groups (Sjoberg and Vaughan 1993), however, since members of marginalized groups frequently experience similar realities, assisting one individual frequently demands that attention be given to collective rights and the empowerment of the entire population.

'The potential of individuals cannot be advanced without consideration of historical, social, cultural, economic, and political realities' (Coates *et al.* 2006: 384).

In social work's international discourse, the supremacy of the English language, the rigid expectation of formal academic training, dominant North American and European expertise, and the economic privilege of Western academics allowing them to travel and transport their ideas across the world, contributed to the dominance of Western social work values, theories, concepts, and methods in diverse contexts. Thus, says Haug (2001), the transfer of knowledge, by and large, has been from the west to everywhere else through the spread of professional schools established by the British and North Americans. Compounding this marginalization through professional training, according to Nagpaul (1993), is the tacit assumption in much professional training that 'the US social work philosophy is somewhat superior, and that principles and methods of US social work provide the only model which has universal applicability' (p. 217). English use is inseparable from a Eurocentric consciousness.

Current efforts to establish global standards for social work education threaten to continue the displacement of local ways of knowing and helping (Gray and Fook 2004; Yip 2004). While consistent with efforts by the Organization for Economic Cooperation and Development (OECD) to establish national and global vocational qualifications, rather than supporting dialogue among cultures, global standards threaten to continue the universalizing and homogenizing effects of globalization (Gray 2005). Firmly held modern presumptions have interfered with the acceptance of alternative, locally based practices. For example, the emphasis on rationality, dualism, individualization, individual self-determination and self-reliance, and therapy are frequently out of place in communal and traditional societies in which deference to the family and community is the priority. This negativity reflects the priority that has been assigned to globalizing and standardizing forces over the need and desire to work with people in the context of their local culture and place.

In the midst of this privileging of Western social work, criticisms about the inadequacy of exclusively Western methodologies are emerging. For example, Hart (2002), Prasad and Vijayaslakshmi (1997) and Yan (1998) argue from different contexts – Canada, India and China, respectively – that micro-based models, and an emphasis on rationalism and individualistic approaches, are inappropriate in the context of many non-Western cultures. However, we must be mindful that reasoning is part of all human communication and being rational does not necessarily equate to rationalism. Indigenous People have the same high expectations regarding well reasoned behaviour. Objections arise in many non-Indigenous societies regarding where Western notions of what is rational take us, and in what is promoted as appropriate, causing Indigenous beliefs and practices to be classified as 'uncivilized' or 'backward'. At the centre of Indigenous Peoples' objections to Western rationalism is the racism and imperialism it spawns. They object to the arrogance, intolerance and dominance of Western voices. Further, such concepts as individualism, objectivity and professional distance that are inherent in Western conceptualizations of social work practice are not as effective and may even be alienating in non-Western cultures.

From the west to the rest

These criticisms of the transferability of primarily Western models and interventions, together with challenges to universalism from post-premodernists, have rekindled interest in local and Indigenous social work rooted in local contexts and traditions which are consistent with the larger purposes of professional values and ethics. The discovery – or rediscovery – of the diversity and uniqueness of local cultures has led some academics and practitioners to question the relevance of applying Western models of social work practice to non-Western contexts (Haug 2001; Nagpaul 1972, 1993; Nimmagadda and Balgopal 2000; Nimmagadda and Cowger 1999; Walton and Abo El Nasr 1988). Hence, various authors have called for efforts to promote the 'Indigenization' of social work practice where 'Indigenization' or localization of social work was seen to refer to the processes through which traditional, Indigenous and local helping interventions were integrated into mainstream social work practices, and elements of mainstream approaches were adjusted to fit local contexts (Al-Krenawi and Graham 2003; Barise 2005). According to Shawky's (1972) early definition, 'indigenization' was essentially about '*adapting* imported ideas to fit local needs' (p. 2 emphasis added), as discussed in Chapter 1. However, as Ling (2004) notes, 'the quest for appropriate social work practice for non-Western countries and for non-Anglo-Saxon communities in Western countries has in more recent years moved from an Indigenization … approach to that of *authentization* or (a) culturally appropriate approach' (p. 336, emphasis added). The term authentization, which also means 'to become genuine' or 'to go back to one's roots to seek direction', was first coined by several Egyptian writers (Ragab 1982, 1990; Walton and Abo El Nasr 1988). The philosophical approach of authentization urges social workers in non-Western contexts to move away from simply adapting and modifying Western social work theory and practice to that of generating knowledge and practice models from the ground up, drawing on the values, beliefs, customs, and cultural norms of *local* and Indigenous helping practices. It is argued that through this process whereby local culture is used as a primary source for knowledge and practice development, social work practice can become culturally appropriate, relevant and authentic. Authentization may lead to a rethinking of what is really universal in social work by challenging the dominance of Western beliefs and values.

As a result, culturally appropriate social work practice, as well as social work among Indigenous and First Nations Peoples, are emerging in many parts of the world to deal with problems unique to individual cultural contexts. In the past decade, there has been increasing investigation, using qualitative and ethnographic research methods, into the lived experience of local cultures and the consequent emergence of Indigenous and culturally relevant social work practices in Western and non-Western countries and contexts. There is growing cross-cultural and Indigenous literature with case studies examining the everyday interactions and interpretations of what Indigenous and non-Western social workers on the ground are doing in practice. While this international literature remains largely unread by the majority of 'Western' social workers, and we suspect most Western academics, this literature is beginning to have an impact both nationally and internationally. As social work is developing in Indigenous communities and in non-Western cultures, *inter alia* in Australia, Canada, New Zealand (Tonga), China, Malaysia and India, the importance of using culture and local knowledges in the development of relevant and authentic social work practices is rising in importance. These case examples provide us with demonstrations of genuine, authentic social work practices as the cultural themes underlying these approaches are in consonance with the core values and beliefs of local peoples where there is a mutuality of world views (Bennett and Zubrzycki 2003; Cheung and Liu 2004; Hart 2002; Mafile'o 2004; Nimmagadda and Balgopal 2000; Nimmagadda and Cowger 1999).

These developments pose theoretical and practical challenges as social work is now confronted with efforts to develop culturally relevant and Indigenous forms of practice, that is, to provide professional services in a manner that is effective and consistent with local cultures and contexts – local knowledge, local traditions and local practices. This demand is arising from Indigenous groups and members of non-mainstream cultures in wealthy Western countries, like the USA, Canada, Australia, and many other parts of the world, as well as from people in non-Western countries which are undergoing economic modernization, such as China and India, where social work is seen as a means of providing assistance in the transition to a modern industrial economy (see Chapters 14 and 15).

The challenge is to acknowledge that mainstream social work is, at its core, a Western cultural creation and to recognize that 'good' and effective social work practice demands that we make culture explicit in thinking and practice. This is a substantial conclusion that emerged in our workshop, which brought together scholars from around the world to discuss the most significant global trends relating to Indigenous and cross-cultural social work. The chapters of this book review key theoretical, methodological and service issues and challenges confronting the development of culturally relevant social work. This includes demands to develop more effective practices in emerging economies by generating knowledge and models that use local cultural beliefs, values and traditions. It also involves demonstrating the way in which local knowledge can provide greater insight into more effective cross-cultural understanding and practice.

We learned that in many respects the profession, universities, and governments have been complicit in the process of expanding the realm of Western social work at the expense of local contexts and cultures. International social work can be seen to generate its own industry – perhaps hegemony – more bent on spreading social work's mission than on responding to people's problems in local contexts. This expansion is compounded by 'educational economics' – an industry without thought of outcome and totally unrelated to need (see Chapter 15). For example, some universities are accepting profitable contracts to establish social work programmes in contexts quite alien to Western social work methodologies. Such universities seem more intent on making money from 'advising' and exporting programmes than on assisting in the development of culturally relevant social work practices. In this regard, the emergence of social work in China is noteworthy. There are 200 social work programmes in China and they are training social work educators and practitioners when there are no jobs for graduates. The government sees the universities as competitors, professionalizing social work while they have a cadre of untrained bureaucrats and professors guarding their jobs. Further, the profession is complicit as global education standards and international definitions make little sense when viewed against the huge diversity of contexts in which 'social works' are being developed.

Each of our contributors was trying to use this thing called 'Western social work' as cloth from which to fashion something far more meaningful and useful for their own people and cultural context, but such is the reach of Western social work that we must first battle to remove its invasive threads from the cloth we are weaving. And for many, Western social work was not working in their context yet they persevered to fashion garments their people might wear (see Chapter 16). These tensions reflect the difficulty facing local and Indigenous groups as they look to social work as a vehicle to help resolve social and personal problems. In fact, many faculty members, even those who were raised in the local community, were educated in Western schools of social work and, as a consequence, must work through the culture shock of returning home to face the lack of relevance of what they have learned (see Chapter 8).

These examples demonstrate the complexities of the development of social work in non-Western contexts. These developments involve the use of local knowledge and traditions. Frequently, but not always, they involve the rejection of Western technology that is inappropriate and harmful, but is also motivated by political and economic gain. While some research points out that knowledge transfer has not been a one-way process from the west to the east (Nimmagadda and Cowger 1999) and has opened up the opportunity for the social work profession to benefit from a genuine exchange among cultures (see Chapter 11), mostly social work is so embedded in the norms and assumptions of Western thinking that developing genuinely helpful and culturally relevant social work is quite difficult.

Against this backdrop, several important themes emerged during the workshop and are discussed throughout this book:

1) *The relevance of Western social work for non-Western contexts is questionable at best* and the two discourses of 'Indigenization' and 'Indigenous social work' share some common intent about *making social work relevant to diverse cultural contexts*. There is agreement that culturally relevant social work is 'good' social work and *vice versa*. In both streams there is serious questioning of the relevance of social work itself and agreement that it is not working in certain contexts. In other words, the professionalized model of social work has limits in responding to the needs and issues within these diverse cultural contexts. For example, in Botswana where a large number of people are living with HIV and AIDS, social workers are being called upon as nurse aids or social carers. Such roles call into question much of the training students are receiving, however, the push within universities to meet dominant international expectations traps social work within its 'Western' garb even in 'non-Western' African societies like Botswana with its education programme built on the Euro-American model of professional social work (see Chapter 16). As we shall see throughout this book, social work is part of colonization and globalization and demands the realization that it is a product of 'the west' that is not easily transferable.

2) *'Indigenization' and 'Indigenous social work' are separate discourses*. There is a literature on 'Indigenization' in social work, which is essentially about importing social work from the 'west to the rest'. This literature spans just over forty years and is influenced by the United Nations' involvement in Developing Nations. Table 2 (see Chapter 1) provides an historical account of definitions of 'Indigenization' within social work literature. In the early 1980s Midgley (1981) raised the alarm about the risk of 'professional imperialism', a threat that continues in internationalizing trends within social work today (see Chapter 2). In much of this literature, social work appears to be more concerned with its own professional advancement than with responding to needs within local cultural contexts. Localization is the antithesis of internationalization as discussed in Chapter 1.

There is a separate literature on Indigenous social work that is essentially about the development of culturally relevant social work for, with and by Indigenous Peoples. It is particularly strong in North America and Australia where the term 'Indigenization' is seen as a misappropriation of the term 'Indigenous' and regarded as deeply offensive and outmoded – a euphemism for culturally relevant social work. 'Indigenization' is being used in the aforementioned literature when reconceptualization, localization and contextualization would be far more appropriate. In the course of this text the discussion of the 'Indigenization literature' is essential but, as stated earlier, we see this term as misappropriated from Indigenous social work.

The importance of language was an interweaving theme throughout our discussions. We became aware that we use similar terminology to mean different things. Sometimes we misuse or misappropriate terms, unaware of the implications of perpetuating certain themes in social work discourse. While 'Indigenization' might have made sense to Shawky thirty years ago, it is no longer appropriate (see Chapter 1).

3) *Parallel discourses exist but most social workers are unaware of them or fail to connect them or see the relationship between them*. What is most interesting is that along with the 'Indigenization' and Indigenous social work literature, there are other related but parallel discourses; though they discuss similar issues each seems totally 'unaware' of the others (see Table 1). It seems clear that the majority of social workers, and those in North America especially, do not generally read the international literature. Thus there is a fourth literature on international social work emanating from the UK and USA that seems oblivious of the 'Indigenization' and 'Indigenous social work' literature. This international social work literature is essentially about international exchanges and the adaptation of Western social work in Eastern Europe and Asia – mainly China at the moment. As is shown in Chapter 14, North American universities are eager to launch education programmes in China regardless of whether the country has the infrastructure to employ the graduates of such programmes. There are similar thrusts into Eastern Europe and Mexico.

Table 1 Parallel and related discourses in social work

Parallel and related discourses in social work					
'Indigenization' 'west to the rest'	Indigenous social work: Sovereignty, land, cultural, and human rights, and decolonization discourses	Cross-cultural; culturally sensitive; cultural competence, and 'rest in the west'	International social work	Emerging discourse on social work with immigrants and refugees	Anti-oppressive discourse on non-dominant and minority cultures

There is also an emerging discourse on social work with immigrants and refugees within Western contexts. And finally, there is a separate anti-oppressive discourse which talks about minority and non-dominant cultures, terms which have negative connotations for 'minority cultures' that do not approve of this label being attached to them (see Chapter 5).

4) *Culture is central to social work.* Not only is social work itself a cultural construction but wherever we are attempting to make social work responsive to local contexts we are fashioning it in a cloth that is culturally embedded. Closely related to culture is the relevance of spirituality and religion. Spirituality is important in the lives of all the cultures that are at odds with the secular nature of professional social work. Ceremonies, rituals and Shamanistic practices are an essential part of many people's everyday lives and are moulded and varied within particular cultures. As Michael Hart reminded us, spirituality is political for Indigenous Peoples (see Chapter 10).

The relationship between culture and religion, not only Eastern religions, like Buddhism, Islam and Hinduism, but also Western religions brought into these peoples' lives by colonization and the thrust to convert people to Christianity, could not be overlooked in the local contexts from which our participants came. Catholicism, for example, interweaves through peoples' lives even when they continue to practice their native religions. There is a sense in which people can move freely between religions, such as Catholicism and Hinduism, but the situation is very different within more fundamentalist religions like Islam (see Chapter 12). In these contexts secular social work has to be woven into peoples' daily lives as a foreign fabric, which has been imported with the same missionary zeal that brought Western religion. In a similar way, while efforts to enlarge social work are supported, the political orthodoxy of China is a constraint that influences the development of a culturally relevant social work.

5) *'Indigenization' and Indigenous social work are highly political.* Whether it involves interventions by governments, for example in China, or the struggle for land rights and self-government, as with Indigenous Peoples in North America and Australia, political realities are significant elements (see Chapter 6).

The chapters which follow are written by international scholars who were chosen not only for the quality of their scholarship but also because they share a concern about developing culturally relevant services and responses to their diverse local contexts. Throughout the chapters the major themes that influence the development of culturally appropriate social work are discussed, as are several examples that demonstrate the development of culturally relevant practices and education around the world.

PART 1
'Indigenization' as an Outmoded Concept

Chapter 1

From 'Indigenization' to Cultural Relevance

Mel Gray and John Coates

Our approach deliberately encourages a shift of focus away from the commonalities of the social work experience, to the differences experienced (McDonald, Harris and Wintersteen 2003: 192).

The globalization discourse in social work – with its exaggerated claims to social work's global influence – must be seen as further evidence of the profession's territorializing agenda. It follows hard on the heels of social work's colonializing past and continues its penchant for spreading itself with missionary zeal. This globalizing or internationalizing thrust has more to do with social work's professionalizing interests than its concern for people in local cultures and contexts. As Webb (2003) put it, '(the) burgeoning globalization agenda in social work is offering a very bourgeois model, namely the dominance of the concept (global systems) over the object (daily life). This mode of thinking provides for a liberal utopian politics, which is wholly out of sympathy with the realities of current practice' (p. 200).

As with many modern, Western professions, social work adheres to the globalization agenda by holding to certain universal views of social life which can be applied to all situations and contexts. Despite the profession's expressed concern for 'starting where the client is at' social work is following Western assumptions and beliefs and it seems unwilling to take seriously the realities of the social situation in which many people live their daily lives. The abundance of literature that critiques Anglo-American approaches, as reviewed in the Introduction, reflects the profession's proselytizing attitude and struggle to respond effectively in non-Western contexts.

Borrowing Deleuze's metaphor, globalizing social work is a 'war machine' – a force that seeks to territorialize – or to use the term most often found in the 'Indigenization' and Indigenous social work literature, to colonize. Like the 'war machine' (which has nothing to do with machines built for war) social work, like other professions, supports an industry that generates its own product. Thus, as professions establish themselves in countries and cultures around the globe and become increasingly international, they, like any business, seek to maintain control by centralizing their authority through their international bodies (Evetts, in Webb 2003).

Social work is no exception in forever being on the lookout for opportunities to reconstruct its identity and enlarge its role by, for example, its professionalizing mission, international definition and global education standards, with which the territorializing juggernaut overrides all other interests. By constructing itself as 'global social work' the profession claims more than it has credit for, as Webb (2003) and others eloquently argue (see, for example, Harris and Chou 2001; Harris and McDonald 2000; Pugh and Gould 2000). But more importantly for our purposes, it continues to fuel a crisis of relevance on at least two fronts – in relation to non-Western social work and to Indigenous social work; in other words, *in relation to contexts that are trying to develop culturally relevant social work practices*. On these fronts social work is clearly out of step with its practice reality and grossly missing its target. Instead it continues to promote professional and cultural imperialism by adhering to its particular universalizing ethical, ideological and political value biases. While less callous than the economic sanctions of the World Bank and International Monetary Fund, it is nonetheless imperialistic.

Rather than focusing on the primacy of client need, social work's line of attack is to champion its social mission – expressed in universal values, standards, definitions, methods, and theories – which claim to have relevance across diverse cultural contexts. International social work bodies promote a shared professional identity, and claim commonality in role and function, through *inter alia* an international definition of social work, global standards for social work education, and global ethical principles (see IASSW 2004). This 'essence' or 'common core' is said to make social work 'adaptable to different contexts' while at the same time enabling it to 'transcend context' (McDonald *et al.* 2003: 192). However, how can social work be culturally and context contingent while, at the same time, 'transcending context'? A profession serious about cultural relevance would surely want to highlight difference to reinforce its view of itself as culturally adaptable.

Instead social work is promoted as a modernist professional project with a universal core that fits well within modern Western democratic societies in the 'First World' where social work was born and remains 'a key instrumental expression of collective responsibility for individual citizens within a welfare regime authorized and legitimized by a liberal democratic regime of governance' (McDonald *et al.* 2003: 196) founded on a culture of human rights and social justice within specific nation states. While its international organizations claim a common universal professional identity, and advocate a definition of social work that states the 'profession promotes social change, problem solving in human relationships and the empowerment and liberation of people to enhance well-being and that, using theories of human behaviour and social systems, social work intervenes at the points where people interact with their environments informed by principles of human rights and social justice which are fundamental to social work' (IFSW 2002), in truth the settings in which most social workers work are not the types of places where advocacy for the rights of marginalized people is commonly practiced (and may even be discouraged) (see for example, McDonald *et al.* 2003).

In positing a unified identity and an enhanced global role for itself, social work belies the organizationally driven, bureaucratic and culturally contingent contexts in which most social workers work. In the Western nation states, social services are highly managerialist and frequently part of restrictive welfare reform regimes where empowering and liberating people is not the regular function being performed. Social workers on the frontlines of practice in the bustling downtowns of major cities and the isolation of remote rural villages would agree that 'the system' does not promote social justice nor hold human rights at the forefront of their work (see Carniol 2005; Mullaly 2007). Such realities led Webb (2003) to argue that the claims to international standards were 'pernicious to the harsh realities of their (social workers') everyday routine work' (p. 196).

When the realities of the local context are not the determining factor, as globalization leads social work into non-Western contexts, it has relied on a rights and justice foundation and, as a result, has great difficulty working across cultures. While 'the human rights framework works well in stressing our supposed common humanity to address inequalities between individuals' (Webb 2003: 198), it does not work well with differences and inequalities between groups or the uniqueness of any particular culture. More importantly for Indigenous contexts, social work's dominant modern foundation that includes individual rights, individualism, and materialism, cannot adequately deal with the responsibilities that membership in a particular community and place, relationship patterns, and/or longstanding cultural traditions require. For Indigenous Peoples – for whom relationship to community is experienced as part of the fabric of their identity – this denial of history and place has been immensely damaging and disempowering, and challenging it lies at the heart of Indigenous social work (see Chapter 10).

Indigenization must be viewed against the historical processes of globalization and colonization. As shown in Table 2, and discussed in the next part, we see the various interpretations that reflect the tensions for those trying to develop local, culturally responsive forms of social work practice that arose in response to social work's internationalizing agenda.

'Indigenization' over time

More than 30 years ago Shawky (1972), in the USA, referring to the development of social work in Africa, appropriated the term 'Indigenization' used by the United Nations in relation to modernization in the 'Developing World' to refer to the process of 'adapting imported ideas to fit local needs' (p. 2). Four years later Resnick (1976), also in the USA, reported on its use in the Fifth UN International Survey of Social Work Training to refer to the 'process of relating social work function and education to the cultural, economic, political and social realities of a particular country' (p. 22). In warning against professional imperialism, Midgley (1981) hailing from Africa and writing from the UK stated that 'professional social work roles must be appropriate to the needs of different countries and social work education must be appropriate to the demands of social work practice' (p. 170). Ragab (1982) in Egypt stressed the need to identify 'genuine and authentic roots in the local system, which would be used for guiding [social work's] ... future development in a mature, relevant and original fashion' (p. 21) and referred to 'authentization' as an aspect of 'Indigenization' by means of which social work practice becomes 'genuine', that is, involves 'the creation or building of a domestic model of social work in the light of the social, cultural, economic characteristics of a particular country' (p. 136). Prager (1985) in Israel noted that 'If helping, in all its nuances, is to be securely rooted in the cultural patterns and systems of the people to be helped, then education for the profession should be developed from within our border' (p. 136).

Walton and Abo El Nasr (1988), also writing from Egypt, then wrote a seminal paper in which they described 'Indigenization' as a three stage process involving adaptation of Anglo-American technology to the political and sociocultural patterns in the receiving country. Stage 1, *transmission*, involved the direct unquestioning transplanting of social work knowledge from Western to developing countries. This phase is similar to what Yip (2004) later described as a static model of uncritically importing Western social work models to non-Western countries. Stage 2, *Indigenization*, was the phase which usually began as a reaction to the lack of 'goodness of fit' between Western social work theory and practice to local culture, and the subsequent realization that Western social work concepts needed to fit with local values, needs, and problems. This phase was also similar to the concept of 'Indigenization from without' or what Yip (2004) later described as a passive model where receiving countries modified or extended the imported knowledge and practice to suit local culture. Stage 3, *authentization*, meaning 'to become genuine' essentially involved the creativity of local social work practitioners in developing their own strategies to address local problems and needs. This concept of 'Indigenization from within' emphasized that theories and practice methods should be developed using a bottom-up approach, wherein Indigenous information was a primary source of knowledge. At this point Ragab (1990) reiterated the need to 'go back to one's roots to seek direction' (p. 43). Cox (1991) in Australia, referring to the Asia-Pacific context, wrote that 'For reasons relating to relevance and context, it is incumbent on social work ... to produce, in each country a model that is consistent with the local culture, political, economic and social realities, while still hopefully retaining the core principles that give social work its distinctive character' (p. 9).

Since 1990 the 'Indigenization' literature is replete with authors from a variety of countries focusing on the development of culturally relevant social work using the concepts put forward by Walton and Abo El Nasr. For example, from Africa, Ghanaian born Osei-Hwedie (1993a) working in Botswana emphasized that 'Indigenization' 'should start from within' using local culture and helping practices as the primary source for knowledge, practice and development, so that social work practice is 'culturally appropriate and relevant' (p. 22). Later he claimed that Indigenization 'implies finding new ways or revisiting local ideas and processes of problem solving and service delivery. This involves understanding and articulating local indigenous resources, relationships, and problem-solving networks; and the underlying ideas, rationale, philosophies or values' (Osei-Hwedie 1996a: 216).

As Indigenization has emerged in China the importance of the local is emphasized. For example, Fei (1998) emphasized the importance of 'knowing oneself ... (and) one's own culture in its own context' (p. 3). Wang (1997) articulates this more specifically noting that:

> Indigenisation in the contemporary Chinese context means that we must consider the traditional Chinese culture, the impact of the market economy on people's livelihood, as well as the impact of collectivism and welfarism on the mentality of people ... Social workers must therefore seriously research the impact of the interplay of all these elements

on helping behaviours and on practice, so that we could eventually develop a model of social work practice which is appropriate to the needs of China (p. 10).

In relation to India, Nimmagadda and Cowger (1999) used the term Indigenization to 'reflect the process whereby a Western social work framework/or Western practice methodology is transplanted to another environment and applied in a different context by making modifications' (p. 263). Nimmagadda and Balgopal (2000) delineated six aspects of the Indigenization process: 1) *West is best* reflects the awkwardness of fit in directly applying a Western treatment model to another non-Western context; 2) *awareness of context* wherein good social work practice is about 'being where the client is' and issues relating to the 'goodness of fit' with service provision and the needs of clients; 3) the *cultural construction of social work practice* involves understanding that social work is a culturally constructed profession and the need to unpack this; 4) *learning by doing and using local knowledge* includes making pragmatic judgements as to 'what works' in applying knowledge in everyday practice. Nimmagadda and Cowger (1999) defined 'doing what works' as using local knowledge. They said, 'like sailing, gardening, politics, and poetry, law and ethnography are crafts of place. They work in the light of local knowledge' (p. 267); 5) *reflexivity* was defined as 'continuing reflection in evaluating both process and outcomes' (p. 276); and 6) the *thread of creativity* was woven by practitioners with intellectual inventiveness and imagination.

Tsang and Yan (2001) argued for the need 'to find a balance' (p. 435) between imported social work knowledge and local Indigenous conceptual frameworks and politics. They argue that the process of Indigenization involves four aspects of social work practice that needed to be noted in relation to the local environment: 1) *ideology* or the action oriented, value integrating and value legitimizing force that solidifies the community and defines their meaning and purpose; 2) *teleology* thus defined by ideology, dictated by the cultural context and concerned with the dual forces between individuals and society; 3) *epistemology* related to the search for relevant local knowledge as the main component in the Indigenization process, in learning of local needs, diversity and pluralism and developing practices that are culturally appropriate within local contexts; and 4) *technology* which need not be copied from the West as it is far more beneficial for professionals and academics to derive appropriate culturally friendly technology.

In the literature on Indigenization, although the degree of emphasis on integration, 'adjusting' (Barise 2005), and on 'creative synthesis' (Ling 2003) between the global and the local varies, the essentialness of attention to local culture, history and needs remained consistent throughout (see, for example, Al-Krenawi and Graham 2003; Bar-On 2003a; Forgey *et al.* 2003; Ling 2004; Mafile'o 2004; Tsang *et al.* 2000; Wong 2002). Osei-Hwedie (2001) expressed the sentiment found in much of this literature as he noted that 'Indigenization' referred to 'the idea that the theories, values and philosophies that underlie practice must be influenced by local factors' because 'indigenisation emphasises a cultural dimension, a cross-cultural aspect in and approach to social work' (p. 8). 'To be indigenous is to be relevant in an appropriate context ... all activities, ideas, processes and techniques must capture the socially constructed reality of a given society as it relates to its own

social experience, shared images, stock of knowledge, and institutional framework'
(Osei-Hwedie 2002: 314).

Thus we have concerns, continuing for well over thirty years, with developing
culturally relevant social work practices in diverse contexts where Anglo-American
social work has sought to supplant local cultural practices. Several writers presented
their own understanding or presented the stages or processes involved. In this
literature, however, the importance of using local knowledge, local customs and local
interventions for local benefit, is emphasized yet the colonizing trend continues as the
chapters in this book show. Similar tensions exist as social work struggled to deliver
effective services within Western contexts to people from diverse backgrounds.

Cultural relevance in Western contexts

Even in Western contexts social work is faced with the challenge of developing
culturally relevant practices among immigrant, migrant and refugee communities.
Even in countries that welcome immigrants and promote multiculturalism, these
communities most frequently remain on the fringes of mainstream society or there is
the expectation that they will adopt or, at least, fit into mainstream culture. Social work
has struggled to adequately meet the needs of immigrant and Indigenous cultures.
Part of this struggle relates to colonial attitudes, but it also relates to the profession's
difficulties in dealing with diversity. Cultural sensitivity, cultural awareness and
cross-cultural practices have each been shown as lacking in effectiveness, perhaps
nowhere more so than with Indigenous cultures where social work had earlier served
as an agent of cultural destruction and colonization (see Haug 2001, 2005). Cross-
cultural social work ventures with First Nations and Indigenous Peoples around
the world achieved largely negative results (Hart 2002; Ling 2003, 2004; Nagpaul
1993; Nimmagadda and Cowger 1999; Tsang and Yan 2001; Yip 2004). Social
work's efforts to deliver services in an effective, acceptable and culturally relevant
manner most often have relied on transferring dominant Anglo-American theory and
practice and, as a result, have been unable to accommodate diversity (Coates 2003;
Healy 2001).

This experience is mirrored somewhat in social work's efforts with immigrant
populations as cultural awareness and cultural sensitivity has proved generally
inadequate for effective service (see Introduction). The crisis of relevance relating
to the adaptability of Anglo-American social work to non-Western cultures in
Western contexts, is found in the cross-cultural literature while its relevance to
non-Western cultures in non-Western contexts is found more often in the literature
on 'Indigenization' (see Table 1 in the Introduction). A review of the literature
on 'Indigenization' – and cultural imperialism – reveals a connection between
Indigenous social work and these various areas described above. For the most part,
it seems that many authors are saying that Indigenous voices have been silenced
within Western social work, however, taking a different perspective, we suggest that
Indigenous cultures can and are beginning to enrich and add new discourses in social
work beyond the conventional, radical and postmodern (Coates *et al.* 2006). We
see the opening up of new ways of thinking about social work that are in tune with

Indigenous ways and suggest that perhaps the extent to which these perspectives are influencing social work discourse might reflect the extent of interaction between Western and Indigenous cultures. The literature on ecology and spirituality draws on Indigenous perspectives and offers a welcoming space for Indigenous voices. These sources appear not as knowledges for particular contexts but as knowledges with wider application, and in this respect they seem to differ from the social work literature on cross-cultural and culturally sensitive practice (Coates *et al.* 2006).

Dilemmas in international social work arise from the paradoxical directions and contradictory processes surrounding Indigenization, imperialism and universalism in social work. Cross-cultural dialogue and exchange is moulding and shaping new forms of social work – localized and culturally relevant – while social work is, at the same time, trying to hold onto some form of common identity – universalism. This is taking place at the same time as efforts toward internationalizing social work raise the specter of Westernization and imperialism. Put another way, localization raises challenges for universalization that are compounded by international efforts as these can quickly become imperialistic depending on what is proposed as 'universal' in social work. The dilemmas raised by Tsang and Yan (2001) in relation to the development of social work in China provide one example of the way in which considerations about culture can promote universality in social work while avoiding imperialistic applications of Western notions of social work. Gray (2005) proposes that culture is an important consideration that enables 'Indigenization', retains universals yet avoids imperialism.

Centrality of culture

Western social work has a penchant for formalization and standardization. Universalizing processes within the International Federation of Social Workers (IFSW) and the International Association of Schools of Social Work (IASSW) to find a global definition of social work and global standards for social work education are evidence of this. They are part of social work's attempt to find common ground for meaningful cross-cultural communication in international encounters (Gray and Fook 2004). Since social work, however, can only standardize the universals, *agreeing on the universals* is a key element in international social work, both in efforts to find global standards (if this is possible or desirable) and in the process of developing culturally relevant practice. But herein lies a paradox since cultural relevance challenges universal knowledge and the cultural hegemony of dominant discourses globally and locally (Wong 2002) and social work, overall, has been reluctant to grapple with these tensions (Park 2005). However, the 'Indigenization' literature is an effort to bring out multiple voices and ways of knowing that are *situated in particular socio-historical and cultural locations* so as to establish a solid local basis for localized social work practice. It questions simplistic, static definitions of culture and of Anglo-American social work for that matter, allowing for a deeper understanding of culture and the defense of local cultures in the face of intensified globalizing internationalizing forces. In such a world it can all too quickly be forgotten that people's lives are steeped in culture and that culture is not simply a set of competencies or defined characteristics one can learn and practice (see Chapter 3).

Culturally relevant social work is not only a professional concern with the appropriateness of imported knowledge (Midgley 1983; Nimmagadda and Balgopal 2000) but also 'a political position that asserts the intellectual and professional autonomy of ... social work academics and practitioners' (Tsang and Yan 2001: 435) *in particular contexts*. In such contexts, what is being sought is authentic social work practice 'from within' rather than adaptation 'from without'. In associating adaptation 'from without' with *appropriateness* and with 'adapting imported ideas to fit local needs' (Shawky 1972: 2), the idea is conveyed that it is a one-way process of technology transfer where certain knowledge is superior. The effort to achieve a *goodness of fit* between imported and local knowledge privileges the Anglo-American import. But there will always be tension generated by this approach as it results in practical difficulties for those involved in trying to develop culturally relevant social work practices. What is imported or adapted may not be useful.

There are other ways of gaining ground and this is what the 'Indigenization' literature speaks to. In efforts to overcome this attitude of superiority and one-way process, universalizing trends are out of place. The perspectives, theories, values and skills that inform social work practice must be influenced by local factors *including local cultures* (Gray and Allegritti 2003; Osei-Hwedie 2001). Our review of the Indigenous, Indigenization and internationalizing literature leads us to conclude that consideration of culture is essential for social work practice. So context bound is social work that 'any universal claim regarding the nature, purpose and method of the profession must be regarded with caution' (Tsang and Yan 2001: 448). As culture is seen as critical to effective social work it is important to think seriously about the way in which we use the term 'culture' in social work discourse and whether 'global' social work is feasible.

Understanding culture in social work discourse

There are a number of points we need to accept when we examine the use of the concept of culture in social work.

1) *Social work is itself a cultural construction, a product of modernity and Western thinking.* It developed in Anglo-American contexts to serve the needs and address the problems of industrializing democracies. It is modern and Western in its enduring search for empirical–rational knowledge foundations, professional status and universal values. Aspects of modernity, like colonization and more recently globalization, have had a lasting impact on diverse populations around the world and remain a constant memory and presence in their lives. Social work has played its part through transferring its technology, however unsuccessful, to non-Western contexts. Thus an historical perspective is needed to understand that social work is 'Indigenous' to Anglo-American cultures, and to have knowledge of both past and present influences like colonization and globalization on Indigenous Peoples, ethnic minorities and non-Western cultures.

2) *Culture is central to good social work practice.* The idea of a 'universal ethical code' in social work which continues its modernist thrust to operate from universal professional values and global standards of education and practice, runs counter to calls for local cultural expression. By way of contrast culturally appropriate social work emphasizes responsiveness to local contexts and cultures. Making culture central to social work forces the profession to question the primacy of Western (modernist) values and to *rethink just what is universal.*

The differences of cultures across diverse contexts is an integral aspect of culturally appropriate social work. Also relevant to the study of culture in social work is the emerging literature on work with immigrants and refugees, which historically goes back to the pioneering days of Jane Addams. The cross-cultural and culturally sensitive or ethnic sensitive practice literature has not fully explored the meaning of culture in social work.

Essentialist definitions of culture that identify people from their so-called core cultural attributes fuel the idea of 'fixed differences' such that we can learn people's cultural characteristics and become competent at identifying and working with them. Despite the best of intentions this is a pernicious form of stereotyping, especially when culture is used interchangeably with race and ethnicity as a marker of difference. Furthermore, static definitions such as this commodify culture such that it can become a classified 'body of knowledge which can be studied, disseminated, and acquired, however difficult those process[es] might be … [and at the same time] knowable and visible' (Park 2005: 24). To teach something we have to know or establish what it is. Thus social work reduces culture 'to the level of problems for which interventions [such as culturally sensitive practice models] … can be devised' (p. 25). In this way, otherwise objectionable problematic differences of race and ethnicity are made possible and palatable precisely because the intervention models are designed to ameliorate differences, however, the multiplicity of cultures and the dynamic subtle changes which accrue through multicultural, international contact and exchange make it impossible to devise objective knowledge relating to cultural attribution. It is especially undesirable where the goal is to identify difference when people are unable to adapt to normative society.

3) *We need to be mindful of critiques where culture is being used as a euphemism for racism in some contexts.* Park (2005) notes that in the social work discourse culture is 'inscribed as a marker for difference which has largely replaced the categories of race and ethnicity as the preferred trope of minority status' (p. 11). As such, 'the meanings social work assigns to "culture" are profoundly political, biased, and partial inscriptions' (p. 12). She notes its centrality in discussions of multiculturalism, diversity, social justice and the correlated issues of minority populations, including notions such as cultural competence even though 'neither the meaning nor the significance of the concept of culture has been sufficiently examined in social work' (p. 13). Thus the 'salience of "culture" and the efficacy of multiculturalism, its main paradigmatic support, remain uncontested and unexamined in social work discourse' (p. 14). Park supports her claim by reviewing and critiquing literature which seeks to define culture by looking at how it develops (Lieberman 1990); as a possession

(Green 1999; McPhatter 1997) and as a matter of identity and dignity which clients have (Sowers-Hoag and Sandau-Beckler 1996). Her review leads her to conclude:

> If culture, characterized as a kind of a personal and community resource, is of significance and relevance only to minority/underprivileged populations, then it must be understood also as a paradoxical measure of deficiency; that which marks one as being less than those without it, and simultaneously, that which one must strive to retain as a buffer against that very weighted differential (Park 2005: 19).

Here we find the 'paradoxical use of culture as both deficit and necessity' (p. 20) and the conflation of culture with race and ethnicity giving rise to a mix of labels such as 'minority', 'people of colour' and 'ethnic' as synonyms for the 'culturally different' or the 'culturally diverse' (Park 2005: 21). The equation of culture with minority races and ethnicities gives cause for consternation, especially when juxtaposed against 'the Caucasian mainstream, inscribed in its turn as the "culture-free" norm' (p. 21). Thus multiculturalism in social work is not without its problems and Park concludes that:

> Despite its insistent rhetoric of cultural relativism or multiculturalism purporting the sensibility that cultures are different but equal, social work constructs and deploys the central concept of culture as a device marking simultaneously that which is on the inside of the margins, and that which is outside (Park 2005: 22).

4) *Culturally appropriate practice calls for a critical and dialogical approach.*
Calls for culturally appropriate social work can be seen as a form of resistance and a medium for transformation from externally imposed to locally developed models of practice and solutions. Critical theory, anti-racist and anti-oppressive practice reminds us of social work's avowedly political nature. As Australian Indigenous author Tovey reminds us, to be born black or Indigenous is to be born political. However, we believe that conflict approaches have not served social work well in this respect, as they are always about labelling people as victims – as oppressed, marginalized, the butt of discrimination, intolerance and so on. While not denying these political realities we believe that there are positive developments and, not wanting to romanticize the situation, there are many stories of the survival of Indigenous cultures and their reascendence in many parts of the contemporary world. Further, Indigenous knowledges are re-emerging in spirituality with its inclusive approach, and in the growing environmental awareness where Indigenous People's closeness to the land, and the importance of place, is a sought after source of wisdom.

5) *Anti-oppressive practice discourse fortifies the inequities it purports to undo by constructing devices which simultaneously produce and preserve power inequities: oppressed and marginalized clients and the more powerful social worker advocating on their behalf.* Thus the very devices which define clients in deficit terms are also the devices for their progressive liberation. 'Culture-enforcing interventions, in this light, should be problematized as "power-obscuring", conciliatory measures that serve to both distract from and occlude out the mechanisms behind both the conceptualization of the problem and their proffered solution' (Park 2005: 27). Despite its avowed

mission to oppose and to dismantle oppression, social work remains entrenched in a paradigm which might well enforce it partly because inherent in its mission to mend the consequences of social problems is the professional necessity for determining and enforcing appropriate behaviour. At the same time, however, social work wants to argue that almost all behaviours are appropriate when viewed within their particular cultural milieu. Its relativist postmodern leanings are antithetical to its disciplinary and professional imperatives. The politics of social work (see Galper 1975, 1980) play a role here:

> Its existence as a viable profession depends on the maintenance of a paradigm which ensures that such troubling questions become concealed. The reification, or the commodification of culture and cultural traits is necessary to social work's professionalising project—the turf-claiming, identity-seeking enterprise which attempts to demarcate its incontestable purview apart from and on an equal footing with other disciplines ... Social work has claimed culture, particularly the practice of cultural competency, however precarious such a claim may be, as an arena in which it outstrips the competing disciplines. Perhaps more to the point, the reification of culture is maintained, since if social work cannot claim a body of objective, transmissible, and acquirable knowledge from which measurable outcomes and interventions can be built, it also cannot claim the legitimate disciplinary status in the academy it has long pursued (Park 2005: 28).

While social work's emancipatory discourse speaks of eradicating racial, ethnic and cultural inequities in society, we should not lose sight of the fact that difference makes for diversity. Difference equals dynamism. Life is structured by difference and would be singularly boring if we were all the same. Thus social work's tendency to seek 'one size fits all' universal or global standards, models and approaches is especially problematic when it comes to dealing with diversity. The modern Western context within which social work emerged and developed has been 'premised on the idea that there is a unified and identifiable set of critical practices' (Healy 2000: 125). These firmly held modern assumptions have contributed to social work's difficulty to take seriously the importance of local context in shaping practice (Coates *et al.* 2006). It is against this backdrop that we need to take a critical look at so-called 'global' social work.

'Global' social work?

Webb (2003) sees pretences to a 'global' social work as a 'neoliberal fantasy' that is completely misguided and 'little more than a vanity' (p. 191). Other writers also warn against social work's homogenizing tendencies and its uncritical acceptance of the globalization thesis (Harris and Chou 2001; Harris and McDonald 2000; McDonald 2006; Pugh and Gould 2000). While global economic forces might be shaping some aspects of welfare, there is still a great deal of diversity in local arrangements for work with diverse populations. Thus while social work practice shares some features across diverse contexts, it can hardly be seen as a global profession (McDonald *et al.* 2003) despite attempts at standardization (Anttonen and Siplila 1996; Pugh and Gould 2000). There is certainly no emerging unification of standard practices based on so called global influences; international social work is the exception rather than the rule:

> The majority of front-line practitioners have no involvement in the internationalized social issues that Khan and Dominelli suggest are increasingly dealt with in social work and there is no research to support this claim. Indeed, it would be very useful to gather accurate information on the amount of 'internationalized' work being carried out by social workers, although one suspects that overall it is a very small percentage (Webb 2003: 195).

Despite claims to the contrary, the nation state continues to be 'the basic unit of administrative responsibility for social work' (Webb 2003: 202) and social work remains context bound. As a result there is a great deal of diversity in the forms it takes across divergent sociocultural contexts. Responding to diversity creatively and imaginatively is new terrain for social work but it is the line of attack social work must take if it is to overcome its 'crisis of relevance' and remain viable and of service across diverse cultures.

Thus the globalization discourse in social work stands at odds not only with its claims to 'responsiveness to local contexts' and 'cultural relevance' but also its growing 'evidence based' thrust. Where is the evidence that the majority of social workers are bothered by, or even mindful of, this internationalization or globalization parlance? The majority of the world's people with whom social work is concerned, if it is serious about the poor, live in remote rural villages where the bulk of the population do not have televisions and computers with Internet access but still rely on battery charged radios. It is highly likely though that most social workers are urban-based with access to advanced technology and international literature but how many are aware of these debates and engage actively in discussions on social work's international role? It is also highly likely that those who do participate in them have a vested interest in promoting social work as having far more import and remit than it actually does. Thus politically it is in the interests of those who are involved in international social work organizations to claim that social work is 'global'.

We argue that the evidence would point strongly to the majority of social workers being locally-based workers trying to do their best with limited resources to respond to their local contexts advocating wherever possible, with local, municipal or national contexts for policy change. The global stage stands at odds with local practice and it is to the latter that our authors give their attention. Those writing about international social work tend to be people with expertise and resources at their fingertips; many are well known for their writing but less often heard are those working on the front line. Additionally, even the international literature has not adequately addressed the plight of the world's Indigenous Peoples. We hope that our collective attempt will redress this imbalance – or at least be a beginning in this direction – and lead to a greater awareness of the paradoxes implied in the idea of 'global' social work. Clearly, our goal is to stop talking of 'Indigenization' and to refer more appropriately to the need for culturally relevant social work. For us the central question is what is unique and different about these contexts and what type of social work is needed for an effective, culturally relevant response? This is a very different question from the 'Indigenization' model that we are trying to put to bed for good which asks how

I might apply social work to this local context and make it fit. The message we hear from our contributors is that very often it doesn't fit and, in fact, the pressures to make it fit come from university administrators wanting to attract international students rather than from clients wanting better services or social workers wanting more resources for their clients. International social work is caught between the proverbial Scylla and Charybdis – between the devil of globalization and the deep blue sea of local community need. There is no way to straddle this divide. As Hilary Weaver reminds us in her metaphor of the two *wampuns*, we have to choose: either we are going to develop local culturally relevant practice models or we are going to promote a universal social work and standardize practice regardless of context. This does not mean that we cannot *theorize* about what's universal in social work and that we cannot engage in discussion and debate about this (Gray and Fook 2004) and question whether or not social work is a global profession.

International social work is a reality but those working cross nationally are engaged in developing local models through dialogical processes and provide useful case examples of the nature of, and how we go about developing, culturally relevant social work education and practice embedded in and responsive to local contexts (see, for example, Nimmagadda and Balgopal 2000; Nimmagadda and Cowger 1999; Tsang and Yan 2001; Tsang *et al.* 2000; Yuen-Tsang and Wang 2002). We have several examples of this in Hart's (Chapter 10) and Bruyere's (Chapter 18) discussion of Indigenous social work practice and education, Nimmagadda and Martell's two-way exchange between India and the US (see Chapter 11) and Yuen-Tsang and Ku's work between Hong Kong and China (see Chapter 14). We thus have various examples of the development of culturally relevant social work education and practice from within and without which can add to the range of case studies on the diverse nature of international social work, which, we hope, will prove useful to practitioners and students alike. As Al-Krenawi and Graham remind us in Chapter 12, working from case studies is the way to go in exploring international social work which collectively comprises cases studies of culturally relevant practice from around the world!

Table 2 Definitions of 'Indigenization' in the social work literature (listed chronologically)

Author	Date	Country	Definition
Shawky	1972	Africa	'… adapting imported ideas to fit local needs' (p. 2).
Resnick	1976	USA	[The] 'process of relating social work function and education to the cultural, economic, political and social realities of a particular country' (Fifth UN International Survey of Social Work Training, p. 22).
Midgley	1981	England	'… professional social work roles must be appropriate to the needs of different countries and social work education must be appropriate to the demands of social work practice' (p. 170).
Ragab	1982	Egypt	'… identification of genuine and authentic roots in the local system, which would be used for guiding its future development in a mature, relevant and original fashion' (p. 21). 'Authentication of Indigenisation means to become genuine' and involves 'the creation or building of a domestic model of social work in the light of the social, cultural, economic characteristics of a particular country' (p. 136).
Prager	1985	Israel	'If helping, in all its nuances, is to be securely rooted in the cultural patterns and systems of the people to be helped, then education for the profession should be developed from within our border' (p. 136).
Walton and Abo El Nasr	1988	Egypt	Describe Indigenization as a three-stage process involving adaptation to the political and sociocultural patterns in the receiving country. 1. Transmission means direct unquestioning transplanting of social work knowledge from the Western countries to developing countries. This phase is similar to what Yip (2004) describes as a static model of the uncritical importing of Western social work models to non-Western countries. 2. Indigenization is the phase that usually begins as a reaction to the lack of 'goodness of fit' between Western social work theory and practice to local culture, and the subsequent realization that Western social work concepts need to fit with local values, needs and problems. This phase is also similar to the concept of 'Indigenization from without' or what Yip (2004) describes as a passive model where receiving countries modify or extend the imported knowledge and practice to suit local culture. 3. Authentization means 'to become genuine' and this phase essentially involves the creativity of local social work practitioners in developing their own strategies to address local problems and needs. This fits rather well with the concept of 'Indigenization from within' where theories and practice methods are developed using a bottom-up approach, and indigenous information is considered a primary source of knowledge.
Ragab	1990	Egypt	'… to go back to one's roots to seek direction' (p. 43).
Cox	1991	Asia-Pacific	'For reasons relating to relevance and context, it is incumbent on social work … to produce, in each country a model that is consistent with the local culture, political, economic and social realities, while still hopefully retaining the core principles that give social work its distinctive character' (p. 9).

Table 2 continued

Author	Date	Country	Definition
Osei-Hwedie	1993	Africa	Indigenization 'should start from within', whereby local culture and helping practices are used as a primary source for knowledge practice and development, so that social work practice becomes culturally appropriate and relevant (p. 22).
Osei-Hwedie	1996	Africa	'Indigenization implies finding new ways or revisiting local ideas and processes of problem solving and service delivery. This involves understanding and articulating local indigenous resources, relationships, and problem solving networks; and the underlying ideas, rationale, philosophies or values' (p. 216).
Wang	1997	China	'… being a practice oriented profession, social work cannot avoid confronting the task of indigenisation. Indigenisation in the contemporary Chinese context means that we must consider the traditional Chinese culture, the impact of the market economy on people's livelihood, as well as the impact of collectivism and welfarism on the mentality of people … Social workers must therefore seriously research the impact of the interplay of all these elements on helping behaviours and on practice, so that we could eventually develop a model of social work practice which is appropriate to the needs of China' (p. 10).
Fei	1998	China	'The foundation of cross-cultural communication begins with knowing oneself [and] … this is knowing one's own culture in its actual context' (p. 3).
Nimmagadda and Cowger	1999	India	Use the term indigenization to 'reflect the process whereby a Western social work framework/or Western practice methodology is transplanted to another environment and applied in a different context by making modifications' (p. 263).
Nimmagadda and Balgopal	2000	India	Six phases of the Indigenization process: 1. West is best: Reflects the awkwardness of fit in directly applying a Western treatment model for alcohol to another non-Western context. 2. Awareness of context: Awareness of the fact that good social work practice is about 'being where the client is' and issues relating to the 'goodness of fit' with service provision and the needs of clients. 3. Cultural construction of social work practice: Understanding that social work is a culturally constructed profession and the need to unpack this. 4. Learning by doing and use of local knowledge: This includes making pragmatic judgements as to 'what works' in the use of knowledge in everyday practice. Nimmagadda and Cowger (1999) define 'doing what works' as using local knowledge 'like sailing, gardening, politics, and poetry, law and ethnography are crafts of place. They work in the light of local knowledge' (p. 267). 5. Reflexivity: The importance of 'continuing reflection in evaluating both process and outcomes' (p. 267). 6. Thread of creativity: Practitioners need to have intellectual inventiveness and imagination.

Table 2 continued

Author	Date	Country	Definition
Tsang, Yan and Shera	2000	China	Argue for a 'discursive space' that needs to be created for the 'emergence of indigenous models' which involves an approach grounded in involving 'critical examination both of Western and local articulations' in order to establish a common basis for conceptual engagement (p. 149).
Tsang and Yan	2001	China	Indigenization is 'a political position that asserts the intellectual and professional autonomy of Chinese social work academics and practitioners' and they argue for the need 'to find a balance between importing social work knowledge and methods and the need to develop indigenous conceptual frameworks and structures for organising social work principles and practices' (p. 435). In the process of indigenization they outline four aspects of social work practice that need to be noted with reference to the local environment: 1. Ideology: An action oriented, value integrating and value legitimizing force that solidifies the community and defines its meaning and purpose. 2. Teleology: Ideology defines teleology and is dictated by cultural context. It is concerned with the dual forces between individual and society. 3. Epistemology: The search for relevant local knowledge is the main component in the Indigenization process, in learning of local needs, diversity and pluralism that are culturally appropriate within local contexts. 4. Technology: Technology need not be copied from the west, as it is far more beneficial for professionals and academics to derive appropriate technology that is culturally friendly.
Osei-Hwedie	2001	Africa	Indigenization refers to 'the idea that the theories, values and philosophies that underlie practice must be influenced by local factors' because 'Indigenisation emphasises a cultural dimension, a cross-cultural aspect in and approach to social work' (p. 8).
Osei-Hwedie	2002	Africa	'To be indigenous is to be relevant in an appropriate context … all activities, ideas, processes and techniques must capture the socially constructed reality of a given society as it relates to its own social experience, shared images, stock of knowledge, and institutional framework' (p. 314).
Wong	2002	China	Indigenization represents an epistemological position that challenges universal knowledge and the cultural hegemony of dominant discourses globally and locally.
Ling	2003	Malaysia	Indigenization is a 'creative synthesis between old (local and traditional) and new (Western social work) ways of helping' (p. 42). Advocates for integration between local traditional helping practices and social work practice.
Forgey, Cohen and Chazin	2003	Vietnam	American educators in Vietnam took 'a posture of not knowing … allowing for the indigenisation of course content … so that important ideas could be deemed relevant … and adapted to fit local needs' in the technology transfer of social work knowledge and practice (p. 152).

Table 2 continued

Author	Date	Country	Definition
Bar-On	2003	Africa	'Indigenous refers to physical and social traits inherently belonging to a people or place and so conjures up images rooted in history … [and if Indigenous] … social work is required then it can only be developed by Indigenous workers' (pp. 26–36).
Al-Krenawi and Graham	2003	Arab world	'Localization includes both the adaptation of imported ideas and practices … and the development of new ways or the revisiting of local ideas, processes and practices. [as well as]…developing new ways of incorporating local ideas, processes and practices' (pp. 78–9).
Mafile'o	2004	Tonga /NZ	Social work with diverse cultural groups 'requires theories and models for social work practice that are grounded in culturally appropriate worldviews in order for the Indigenisation of practice and ethnic-specific paradigms within non-Western cultural contexts' (p. 240).
Ling	2004	Malaysia	'The quest for appropriate social work practice for non-western countries and for non-Anglo–Saxon countries in more recent years shifted from an irdigenisation to that of an authentization or culturally appropriate approach' (p. 336).
Barise	2005	United Arab Emirates	Indigenization of social work involves dynamic, integrative, and primarily a bottom-up processes. 'Indigenisation or localization of social work refers to the process of mainly developing social work approaches rooted in the local context, but also adjusting mainstream social work to fit the local context' (online).

Chapter 2

Promoting Reciprocal International Social Work Exchanges: Professional Imperialism Revisited

James Midgley

Social work's global expansion over the last century owes much to international exchanges but, in many cases, these exchanges were unilateral resulting in the export of Western approaches to other parts of the world. In the profession's early years, formative training and practice models were diffused from Britain and other European countries to North America, Australia and South America. Subsequently, social work approaches originating in the United States became internationally popular. This was not surprising since they were theoretically sophisticated and enhanced the profession's academic respectability. After the Second World War, social work theories and methods from the United States, Britain and other European countries were adopted at the many new schools of social work that were being established in the newly independent nations of what was then known as the 'Third World'.

The founders of the non-aligned movement, who included many of the great nationalist, anticolonial leaders were committed to promoting the economic and social modernization of their nations and, for many, this meant emulating the achievements of the industrial powers. Industrialization, rapid economic growth, technological progress and the creation of modern economic, social and political institutions were given high priority. The governments of many developing countries sought to expand modern educational opportunities and to promote the adoption of scientific and technological knowledge. They were also amenable to the importation of Western innovations in fields such as health, education and the social services.

It was in this context that Western social work was widely adopted in the global south. Government officials in the metropolitan nations and staff at the international development agencies actively supported the diffusion of Western social work. Several Western governments and international organizations, such as the United Nations Children's Fund, sponsored technical assistance projects to facilitate the creation of social work training programmes in developing countries. Of course, social workers in the Western nations also supported these activities. They helped faculty members at the new schools of social work acquire professional credentials in the metropolitan countries and gave extensive advice on curriculum and educational policy.

Although the diffusion of Western social work to the global south was believed to be both helpful and appropriate, by the late 1960s and early 1970s some critics

(Almanzor 1967; Khinduka 1971; Shawky 1972) were questioning this assumption. They challenged the widely held view that social work was based on universal values and beliefs and that its practice methods were applicable to all societies. Instead, they argued that social work's universal values reflected a Western, liberal world view that was incompatible with the Indigenous cultures of developing nations. Accordingly, they urged the formulation and adoption of theories and practice methods based on Indigenous cultural realities. Another problem was social work's concern with individual and family dysfunction, and its historic commitment to remedial forms of engagement. While this focus might be relevant to the industrial countries, some challenged its relevance to societies where poverty and deprivation were widespread and where the need for economic and social development was paramount.

Concerns about the cultural and developmental relevance of Western social work to the needs of the developing world were more frequently expressed in later years, and the issue that conventional Western social work practice approaches could respond effectively to the massive problems of poverty and social deprivation that characterized the newly independent developing nations continues to be widely debated. As these concerns intensified, the need for a systematic overview of the arguments about social work's relevance to the societies of the global south became apparent.

The idea of professional imperialism

It was in this context that I undertook, in the late 1970s, a methodical review of the limited and fragmented literature that had previously been published about social work in the developing world. Descriptive accounts of social work education and practice in a number of developing countries were identified, and the views of social workers in both the Western industrial and developing countries on the issue of relevance were scrutinized. At the time, very few books about social work in the global south were available and most of the documentary information came from reports and journal articles.

In addition to surveying the literature, interviews were undertaken with a group of social workers in Ghana. They were questioned on a number of issues related to their experience of social work practice in their country. Most were employed in the public sector and much useful and interesting information about their work experiences, attitudes and opinions about the relevance of Western approaches was obtained. Those interviewed were extremely responsive and candid in their assessments of the challenges facing social work in their country. Using the findings of the literature survey as well as the interviews in Ghana, the study sought to systematize the arguments concerning social work's cultural and developmental relevance.

The study also sought to review attempts to identify what was described as 'appropriate' approaches to social work education and practice. For example, it documented the concept of Indigenization that had been formulated by some social workers in the global south to characterize the formulation of new and culturally relevant forms of intervention. It also noted attempts to link social work practice with developmentally relevant forms of intervention such as social planning and community development.

The study's findings were published as a book in 1981 under the title of *Professional Imperialism: Social Work in the Third World*. The title was suggested by Brian Abel Smith, my senior colleague at the London School of Economics (LSE). At the time, I was a member of the faculty at the School. Although some thought the title to be rather provocative, I used it in order to dramatize the need for social workers involved in international exchanges to critically examine claims about social work's universality, and respond to the problems of cultural and developmental relevance. Since many earlier proposals to address these problems were, in my opinion, unrealistic and unworkable, the book sought to identify feasible and 'pragmatic' approaches that could be used to enhance social work's appropriateness to the developing world. Its ultimate aim was to urge social workers everywhere to critically examine prevailing assumptions about social work's universality, to challenge unilateral transfers, and to engage in truly reciprocal international exchanges.

Conceptual influences

Professional Imperialism: Social Work in the Third World drew on wider social science debates about the nature of development and the relationships between the industrial and developing nations. It argued that social work exchanges in years following the Second World War had been influenced by the idea that the nations of the global south should adopt policies that promoted 'modern' economic, social, political and cultural practices if they wished to experience sustained economic and social progress. The view was systematically formulated in terms of the theory of modernization, which also offered clear policy prescriptions for development.

The modernization school's first policy prescription was to foster rapid economic growth. This goal could best be achieved by securing international capital to invest in new industrial enterprises that would draw labour out of the impoverished subsistence and informal economy and into the modern, urban industrial sector. This process, it was argued, would create new wage employment opportunities, raise incomes and reduce the incidence of poverty.

The second policy prescription dealt with social and cultural change. Modernization theorists argued that efforts to promote economic modernization were hampered by traditional cultural beliefs and practices that stifled innovation, individualism and self-improvement. The traditional culture needed to be replaced with modern values that rewarded competition, achievement, motivation, and ambition (Hagen 1962; McClelland 1964). Similarly, the cultural obligations imposed by the extended family on its younger members and preventing them from pursuing their own careers and relocating to places where jobs were being created, needed to be replaced with a Western nuclear family which was more conducive to modern lifestyles (Goode 1963). Economic development would also be more likely to take place if the authoritarian political structures that characterized the developing countries were replaced with modern, liberal democratic institutions (Hozelitz 1960; Lerner 1958). Some social work scholars, like William Clifford (1966), drew on these assumptions to argue that social work, based on Western theories and practice methods, could support the modernization process. However, most social work advocates of the diffusion of Western social work to the global south did not explicitly base their arguments on the modernization approach and instead were implicitly influenced by these ideas.

Professional Imperialism challenged the view that modernization theory offered useful prescriptions for the economic and social development of the global south. It also rejected the argument that Western social work should seek to promote social and cultural modernization. It drew primarily on the neo-Marxist, international structuralist or 'dependency' school to frame this critique. Andre Gunder Frank (1975) and other leading dependency writers, such as Walter Rodney (1972) and Samir Amin (1976), had vigorously criticized the notion that economic growth at the domestic level could solve the problems of poverty and deprivation in the global south. They argued that unless the exploitative, world capitalist system was ended, developing countries would continue to stagnate or otherwise, as some *dependistas* (Cardoso and Faleto 1979) argued, only experience limited, 'dependent development'.

A related normative influence came from the non-aligned movement, which was comprised mostly of nation states that had secured independence from European imperial rule in the post-Second World War period. The nationalist leaders of this movement hoped to create a 'third force' in world affairs that would challenge the perpetuation of 'neo-colonialism' in an ostensibly post-colonial world by opposing the hegemonic efforts of the Soviet Union and the United States – the world's two superpowers. It was at the non-aligned movement's conference in Bandung, Indonesia in 1955 that the term 'Third World' was first adopted and initially it had a geopolitical rather than economic or social connotation. The anticolonialism of the movement transcended political considerations to actively promote economic and social development since this, the movement's leaders believed, was a central goal of the struggle for independence and the realization of prosperity.

The dependency theorists and the 'Third Worldist' anticolonialism of the non-aligned movement offered a congenial intellectual framework for analysing international exchanges in social work. Using the insights of these two approaches, I argued that social work's notions of cultural universality and developmental relevance should be reconsidered, and that the unilateral transfer of Western approaches on the grounds that they were a 'modern' approach to development should be challenged. Local social work educators, practitioners and professional leaders should reject the importation of inappropriate approaches and should themselves formulate theoretical and practice approaches that were uniquely suited to the needs and economic, social and cultural circumstances of their societies.

This need not involve a total rejection of Western social work innovations. In formulating appropriate approaches, social workers in the global south can indeed learn from their Western colleagues but they should judiciously apply and, where relevant, adapt theories and practices that are suitable to their local situation. This idea was subsequently restated in my argument that social work in the industrial world had much to learn from colleagues in the developing world (Midgley 1990).

Although the dependency school provided useful insights for the analysis of professional imperialism in social work, its contention that authentic development could only take place if international capitalism were overthrown did not offer a realistic policy prescription for addressing the problems of poverty and deprivation in the developing world. Nor did it provide a viable framework for enhancing social work's relevance to the developmental efforts of the countries in the global south. Instead, I found that the policy proposals of the 'developmentalist' school offered more congenial and useful suggestions for how social work could engage effectively in the development process. The developmentalists, who included important economists such as Gunnar Myrdal (1970), Dudley Seers (1972), Keith Griffin (1978) and Paul Streeten (Streeten and Burki 1978; Streeten with Burki *et al.* 1981), were not only pragmatic but also optimistic about the prospect of achieving economic and social development.

While the members of the developmentalist school did not advocate the revolutionary overthrow of international capitalism, they challenged the orthodoxy of modernization theory. They urged that markets be carefully regulated and that planning be used to promote balanced economic and social development. They also recommended that efforts to address the twin evils of poverty and inequality be given high priority and that specific policies and programmes be adopted to ensure that the benefits of economic growth be redistributed towards the poor (Chenery *et al.* 1974). The developmentalists were explicitly committed to promoting social development through increasing social investments in education, health and social welfare and they urged that people's participation in community development projects be given high priority.

The book's proposals for enhancing social work's relevance to the development efforts and aspirations of the governments and peoples of the global south emphasized the need for state intervention and the use of both economic and social planning which would not only stimulate economic investments and improvement in production but ensure that the social goals of development effort were given priority. Largely through the efforts of Seers (1972), the idea that development should be measured through conventional economic output indicators, such as GDP per capita, was gradually augmented by a new emphasis on poverty eradication and improvements in living standards. The developmentalists, and Myrdal in particular, had also succeeded in persuading the United Nations and other development agencies to support the creation of social planning units within national planning agencies. Although I was then involved in teaching courses at the LSE on social development planning, my book placed relatively little emphasis on the involvement of social workers in national or sectoral planning and instead urged their deployment in community level development projects where their conventional skills could be combined with new, developmentally relevant forms of practice that addressed local needs in tangible ways. Much of my subsequent work on developmental social work and, more generally, on the theory of social development (Midgley 1995) was informed by examples of the innovative efforts of colleagues in the global south to identify developmentally relevant approaches to practice. These examples were culled from the literature and augmented by study visits to several African and Asian countries.

Reactions and responses

Although the uncritical transfer of social work theories and practice to the global south had been challenged before *Professional Imperialism* was published in 1981, it was the first to deal with the issues comprehensively and to offer a coherent set of proposals for addressing the challenges of cultural and developmental relevance that had previously been identified. As noted earlier, the book sought to catalogue and scrutinize the criticisms of unilateral exchanges in social work that had been formulated earlier and to offer concrete proposals for replacing culturally inappropriate and developmentally irrelevant forms of social work with pragmatic and workable alternatives.

The book received a decidedly mixed reaction. Generally, readers in the global south were positive and supportive. I received letters from several colleagues at schools of social work in developing countries expressing appreciation for articulating what several correspondents said were issues that had been of great concern to them for some time. They generously commended me for 'giving voice' to these concerns and for bringing the issues into the open so that they could be properly debated. On the other hand, some colleagues in the north were unhappy that my critique, and especially the rhetorical use of the term 'imperialism' in the book's title, seemed to impugn their motives. Some were openly hostile, and a few colleagues in the United States even accused me of being 'anti-American'. I was contacted by several social workers from Britain who had worked in the developing world during the colonial period. They were undoubtedly sincere in wanting to help their colleagues in developing countries expand professional education and practice opportunities, and they pointed out that they had acted with the best intentions. They rejected the idea that their efforts were 'imperialistic'. On the other hand, some Western social work colleagues who had been extensively engaged in international development work told me that the book raised valid and important concerns which should be fully debated.

Most journal reviews of the book were favourable and approved of its message. Some reviewers commended the systematic analysis on which the book was based and noted that it made a helpful contribution to the wider debates then taking place about the tendency to uncritically adopt Western ideas and practices in other fields. The problem was not confined to social work; similar tendencies could be identified in education, health, housing and the other social services. In addition to reviews in social work journals, reviews were published in development studies and other journals as well. The UK library journal *Choice* commended the book by listing it as one of the best academic books of 1981. Subsequently, in the mid-1980s, the book formed the theme for a panel debate at the Annual Programme Meeting of the Council of Social Work Education (CSWE) in the United States. Although I was warned that my ideas might receive a hostile reception, I was treated with respect by American colleagues who were attentive to my views and thoughtfully discussed the issues. Indeed, many agreed with my conclusions.

The issue of professional imperialism in social work has been widely debated during the quarter century since *Professional Imperialism: Social Work in the Third World* was published and the term is used from time to time in the literature. The book is still cited although, understandably, some younger scholars who write about international exchanges in social work are unaware of the origin of the term or the derivation of its arguments. The book has clearly resonated with colleagues in the global south who continue to criticize inappropriate professional transfers when they occur. Many colleagues in the north today are much more aware of the issues and receptive to the challenges of engaging in reciprocal exchanges.

Professional imperialism today

In assessing whether the issues identified in *Professional Imperialism* a quarter of a century ago have been adequately addressed, it is important to note that the book's analysis was framed by economic, political and social conditions that have changed significantly since 1981. Since the world is now a very different place, it is important to take these changes into account when attempting to assess whether progress has been made in addressing the issues of cultural and developmental appropriateness that were identified so many years ago.

In 1981, the European imperial epoch was coming to an end. Most of the territories that had been directly ruled by Britain, France and the other metropolitan powers had become independent nation states. There were obvious exceptions and even today colonial forms of oppression persist in Palestine, the Western Sahara, Dafur, Tibet and other places. In addition, the rights of Indigenous Peoples in many parts of the world that were settled by European colonists continue to be violated. Nevertheless, the political decolonization that began at the end of the Second World War has now, for all intents and purposes, been completed. Consequently, the book's intellectual debt to the 'Third Worldist' and anticolonial struggles of the time no longer apply and no longer provide a viable framework for analysis. But while the language of anticolonial 'Third Worldism' may have lost its relevance, imperialist forces in the world system continue to exert powerful pressures which have relevance for assessing the nature of international exchanges in social work.

Another major change was the collapse of the Soviet Union. This event had profound repercussions, dramatically altering world order. Although many hoped that the end of superpower rivalry would bring peace and greater cooperation between the world's nations, cosmopolitan ideals have not been realized – indeed, they have been actively challenged. Imperialist proclivities in the world system have resurfaced, initially in the guise of globalization and the vigorous export of liberal free market ideas, but more recently through the unabashed advocacy of unipolarism by neoconservative intellectuals and politicians in the United States.

When *Professional Imperialism* was published in 1981, the impact of radical right ideology in the United States, Britain, Germany, New Zealand and other Western countries had not yet been fully appreciated. Few would have predicted that the diffusion of neoliberal ideas and policies would significantly affect the world's economic system. The endogenous development models that were widely adopted by governments of developing nations in the 1950s lost their appeal, and instead trade, export led development, and economic liberalization has been emphasized.

Increased economic interdependence and the emergence of global markets have created new conditions for examining international exchanges in social work.

Another significantly different feature of the world system today is the influence of what has been called the 'New Imperialism' (Harvey 2003). Since the attenuation of the non-aligned movement and the collapse of the Soviet Union, the tripolar classification of the world nation states that prevailed in 1981 has lost its relevance. Instead, neoconservatives claim, current international relations are best characterized as unipolar in the sense that the United States has emerged as the world's only superpower. This entails a new global obligation on the government of the United States to maintain international peace and foster prosperity. Although neoconservatives urge the government to exercise this responsibility through what is called 'benevolent domination', they also insist that it should resist challenges to its global supremacy and crush those who seek to undermine its authority. It is this principle, and the cognate principle of pre-emption that legitimated the invasion of Iraq by the United States.

While many recognize that the earlier imperialism of European nations differs significantly from the way the government of the United States currently exercises military, economic and diplomatic power, the concept of imperialism is widely used to connote contemporary US foreign policy in academic and journalistic circles. However, it has been claimed (Frum and Perle 2003; Harvey 2003; Maier 2006; Mandelbaum 2005) that current US imperialism does not involve colonial settlement nor the installations of governors and imperial administrations in subjugated territories and it is for this reason that some writers characterize the international activities of the US government as 'hegemonic' rather than imperialistic. On the other hand, some believe that the term 'imperialism' has validity but, recognizing the differences between old-style European imperialism and current US practices, they prefer to use the term 'New Imperialism' instead (Harvey 2003).

The emergence of the idea of a New Imperialism reflects significant changes in social science theory since 1981. Dependency theory is no longer influential, and subsequent innovations with regard to world systems theory have been superseded by the emergence of globalization as an organizing concept for much social science endeavour in the international field. Other relevant conceptual innovations that have subsequently evolved and which provide insights into the issues raised in *Professional Imperialism* include Edward Said's (1978) writings on *Orientalism* and the work of the post-colonial school (Ashcroft *et al.* 1989; Guha and Spivak 1988; Young 2001).

Undoubtedly, an analysis of professional imperialism in social work today would draw on the insights of these approaches. In particular, the linking of globalization to imperialist tendencies in the world system would provide a useful conceptual framework for assessing international exchanges in social work. For some scholars, globalization is little more than the exercise of economic power by the world's powerful capitalist nations and transnational corporations which invariably act to secure their own advantage through exploiting the resources and peoples of the developing world (Agnew 2005; Hardt and Negri 2000; Wood 2003).

Although these conceptual innovations offer new insights that could be used to assess the extent to which professional imperialism persists in social work, the systematic use of the theory of New Imperialism would facilitate an analysis of the issues, providing an incisive tool for analysing the current situation. Accordingly, its insights will be employed to assess the extent to which professional imperialism has been challenged and to determine the extent to which truly reciprocal exchanges have emerged.

The following account draws on these insights to discuss three aspects of the question of whether professional imperialism in social work has been adequately addressed. First, an attempt will be made to examine the extent to which the overt and uncritical exportation of Western social work to other parts of the world has ended. This will include a discussion of definitions, standards and the notion of international accreditation, considering whether these promote uniformity. Secondly, the extent to which the social work profession in Western countries imports and adapts insights and innovations from other cultures and societies will be considered. Finally, the chapter will seek to determine the extent to which social workers have challenged the hegemonic influence of imperialist attitudes and beliefs, refusing to accept the normality of unequal professional encounters. In addressing these issues, it is important to point out that the narrative is written from the perspective of someone living and working in the United States. It is to be hoped that scholars in other societies will also contribute to the debate from their own perspectives.

Exporting Western social work: Changes and continuities

As noted earlier, the issues raised in *Professional Imperialism* have been widely debated in the social work literature, and social workers in the United States and other Western countries are today much more aware of the problems of cultural and developmental appropriateness discussed in the book. Many are now aware that international exchanges in social work should be based on a careful assessment of the nature of these exchanges and an understanding of the needs and interests of partners. Also, the notion of reciprocity is now more widely understood and respected.

A wider appreciation of the issues raised by the book reflects an increasing interest in international issues among social work educators and practitioners in the United States and other Western nations. When *Professional Imperialism* was published, international social work was regarded as an exotic specialism and the literature on the subject was extremely limited. Few courses on the subject were offered and generally only a few faculty members at American and European schools of social work were engaged in international activities. Today, the situation has changed significantly. Textbooks and courses on international social work have proliferated and many more social work educators and practitioners attend international meetings and conferences, travel abroad on study visits and collaborate with colleagues in other parts of the world. Today, international social work is increasingly regarded as a mainstream activity.

This extremely positive development has been accompanied by specific efforts to promote mutual international exchanges in social work. In addition to continuing references in the literature to the problems of professional imperialism, manuals on how to foster reciprocal exchanges in international social work have been published and case study material documenting successful international exchanges is now available (Healy *et al.* 2003). Several projects designed to develop and implement joint innovations in social work between schools of social work in the industrial and developing nations have been established.

These developments are indicative of the considerable progress that has been made over the years to reduce unequal, unilateral exchanges in social work and to promote reciprocity, however, it cannot be claimed that these old school exchanges have ended. Indeed, several examples of the perpetuation of unilateralism can be given. In some cases, this involves the well intentioned and unwitting transfer of inappropriate social work approaches. In others, the transfer of Western social work approaches to other countries is planned and intentional. Sometimes, this involves the active collaboration of colleagues in the recipient country (see Chapters 14–16).

Many schools of social work in Western countries have established academic exchange agreements with their counterpart schools in universities in the global south. In addition to hosting student exchanges, faculty members are encouraged to spend their sabbaticals at counterpart universities and to collaborate on joint research projects. In addition, these exchanges often involve sharing curriculum content and it is here that problems frequently occur (as the case of Botswana in Chapter 16 shows). Although faculty members at many schools in the United States and Europe intend these activities to be helpful, they promote unilateralism and perpetuate professional imperialism. It is for this reason that collaborative efforts between schools of social work in the north and south, however well intentioned, should be subjected to critical scrutiny to determine exactly what the proposed exchanges will involve and whose needs and interests will be served.

As noted earlier, social workers in industrial and developing countries sometimes enter into exchanges that are specifically intended to foster unilateral transfers. One example is the practice of offering social work degree programmes from universities in Western countries to students in developing countries. In this case, students in the recipient country do not actually attend the provider university but are taught at a local site, however, they receive exactly the same curriculum as their counterparts in the Western country and little, if any, effort is made to include local cultural or other appropriate curriculum content. Generally, recipients of these 'extension' programmes welcome an opportunity to acquire a professional education from a Western university. A foreign degree is often regarded as more prestigious than a local one and is more likely to enhance employment or promotion opportunities. In some cases, it may also facilitate opportunities to migrate to the country providing the extension programme. But while students receiving a social work education through an extension programme may benefit from the opportunities it provides, they receive totally inappropriate professional training. In addition, extension programmes undermine local social work education and the efforts of local social work educators to enhance the quality as well as the cultural and developmental relevance of their own educational offerings.

Although the practice of offering extension courses of this kind is not widespread (examples can be given primarily from the United States), it is highly likely that similar programmes have been established by universities in other Western countries and that more programmes of this kind will be offered in the future, particularly by private universities. The availability of new information technologies, the ease of travel and the growing international prestige of North American and European schools of social work will, in all likelihood, facilitate the spread of these programmes. Equally relevant is the need to generate revenues. As education budgets in Western countries shrink, and as educational programmes are compelled to find new sources of income, extension programmes in social work are likely to expand (as the case of China today shows, see Chapters 13–15).

International extension programmes in social work were not being offered when *Professional Imperialism* was published and the fact that now they are should cause concern. While progress has obviously been made in discouraging the export of inappropriate Western social work approaches, the use of extension education internationally reveals the extent to which the problem of professional imperialism still needs to be resolved.

Definitions, standards and international accreditation: Promoting uniformity?

The prestige of Western educational qualifications has also encouraged some schools of social work in the global south to seek accreditation from accreditation organizations in the industrial countries. A recent request of this kind to the Council of Social Work Education (CSWE) in the United States was initially viewed favourably as presenting an opportunity to be helpful to colleagues in the developing world. However, the proposal was fiercely resisted by members of the organization's Global Commission who explained that this would require educational programmes in developing countries to conform to the curricular requirements prescribed for American schools. Obviously, this would result in the inappropriate replication of the US curriculum. It was heartening to hear that the proposal was resisted and has been shelved. It was also heartening to hear that the term 'professional imperialism' was used on several occasions during the discussions to dramatize the issue.

The possibility of enhancing the prestige of local social work schools by securing their accreditation with the Council on Social Work Education or another accrediting body in the north raises the question of whether international accreditation by a body such as the International Association of Schools of Social Work (IASSW) would be desirable. Although it is likely that an effort to establish international accreditation would be resisted, steps have already been taken to promote the international standardization of social work education in terms of what some regard as a predominantly Western world view. The publication by the IASSW and the International Federation of Social Workers (IFSW) of the standardized international definition of social work elicited a vigorous response from some critics who contend that it provides a distinctly Western interpretation of social work that is unsuited to the cultural realities of other societies (Gray 2005; Gray and Fook 2004; Yip 2004). Although efforts had been made to consult widely and secure international agreement, this did not ultimately achieve the objective of formulating a universally acceptable definition of social work.

Nor is it likely that recent efforts to formulate international global standards for social work education will achieve the goal of identifying a universally applicable set of standards that schools of social work throughout the world should adopt if they are to be regarded as offering an authentic professional education in the field. Although this may be a well intentioned goal, a cursory glance at the new standards reveals their dependence on Western and particularly American accreditation requirements. Accordingly, the adoption of the standards will do little to promote diversity in curriculum and educational approaches. Indeed, it may impede efforts to maintain the cultural appropriateness of curricular offerings at schools of social work in the global south and instead foster the diffusion of an approach to social work education that is essentially Western in character. The introduction of formal accreditation by an international body, which could be a logical next step in the process of standardizing social work education around the world, would ensure that social work everywhere conforms to a Western model.

At the time that *Professional Imperialism* was being written, the prospect of using accreditation in another country to enhance the standing of a social work programme in the global south was unheard of. Although many universities in the former colonial territories initially awarded degrees through universities in the metropolitan countries, this was an interim measure designed to assist the development of their own higher education. Efforts to secure international accreditation, and to promote a standardized international definition of social work, as well as the promotion of international educational standards based on a Western model, suggests that the challenges identified in the book many years ago still need to be addressed.

Using innovations and insights from other societies

The promotion of truly reciprocal exchanges in social work not only requires that the approaches exported from Western countries to the global south be culturally and developmentally appropriate, but that relevant innovations from the global south be imported into Western countries as well. This rather elementary proposition was unheard of when *Professional Imperialism* was published in 1981 and it was not discussed in the book. It was only during the 1980s that the issue was raised in social science literature and only in 1990 that it was first discussed in a social work journal (Midgley 1990). Today, however, it is common to hear that innovations originating in the developing world have been adopted in the United States (Hokenstad and Midgley 2004). In child welfare, for example, family group conferencing and kinship care are imported interventions that have now been mainstreamed in Western social work. Another example is the use of micro-finance and micro-enterprise in community-based programmes serving low income clients. These approaches were developed in the global south and offer a developmentally relevant approach that is increasingly regarded as a viable alternative or supplement to conventional income transfer approaches (Midgley and Livermore 2004).

However, it would be an oversimplification to conclude that innovations from the global south are routinely being imported into social work education and practice in the Western world. Imported innovations have only had a limited impact and much more needs to be done to promote truly reciprocal exchanges. An indication of the problem is the limited use of curriculum content suited to the social and cultural needs of the diverse clients and communities that have immigrated to the United States and other Western countries. Many social work educators and administrators are only too aware that culturally relevant curriculum content needs to be enhanced if students are to be adequately prepared to practice with clients from these immigrant communities, however, few schools of social work in the United States can claim that they have adequately responded to this challenge.

Although efforts have been made to include appropriate cultural content in the curriculum and even to offer language training, few schools of social work in the Western nations have sought to collaborate with counterpart educational institutions in the countries from which immigrant communities originate. Consultations as well as exchanges of faculty members and students could create new opportunities to understand immigrant culture, establish links with local immigrant leadership and significantly improve the appropriateness of the curriculum.

While some schools have sought to employ new faculty members from other countries to help enhance diversity and promote culturally competent professional training, more use of international linkages designed specifically to draw on the expertise of colleagues in other countries could be made. This would have the added advantages of reversing the conventional flow of expertise from north to south and promoting reciprocal exchanges.

Unfortunately, there are barriers to promoting international exchanges of this kind. In addition to logistical problems, conventional prejudices about the possibility of learning from the global south need to be addressed. Some social workers with considerable expertise and experience in international social work find it hard to accept that they can learn from colleagues in what are sometimes described as 'underdeveloped' countries. They are used to providing expertise to colleagues in these countries and the idea that they should also learn from them and adopt their innovations is, to say the least, implausible.

The problem exists at the institutional level as well. Accreditation standards and the almost sacrosanct status of the American Master's (MSW) degree makes it difficult for schools of social work to recruit faculty members from other countries. A few years ago the Council on Social Work Education was embarrassed by an article in the higher education newspaper, *The Chronicle of High Education*, reporting that it had required the newly appointed head of an American school of social work, who happened to be European, to enrol at another university to obtain an MSW degree on a part-time basis. He was told that his school's accreditation would be jeopardized unless he complied. Although this decision was subsequently rescinded, it reveals the extent to which discriminatory attitudes towards colleagues from other countries are institutionalized. This is a pity because social work education in the United States has much to learn from colleagues who come from abroad. Of course the experience of the United States is to some extent mirrored by developments in other industrial countries.

Challenging the hegemony of imperialist assumptions

Human beings are socialized to function within a cultural as well as social, economic and political environment. An acceptance of this environment is functionally necessary if social life is to acquire a sense of normality and be sustained over time, however, the legitimacy of this environment is frequently challenged by individuals or groups who identify injustices within the system and seek to change it. While slavery, the subjugation of women, the exploitation of labour and discrimination against people of colour is now deplored, these practices were previously regarded as perfectly normal. As in other fields of human struggle, many years of campaigning were required to undermine their legitimacy. Similarly, while European imperialism is today much criticized, it was also sustained by widely held assumptions that had to be challenged and overturned. Assumptions about the benevolence of European imperial rule and the advantages that accrued to subjugated peoples were widely shared in the nineteenth and early twentieth centuries and legitimated imperialism as a normal and desirable form of governance. Violent struggles, as well as peaceful campaigns, waged over many years by nationalist and other anticolonial movements and their supporters in the metropolitan countries finally eroded the institutionalization of European imperialism as an acceptable way of organizing world order.

New arguments designed to legitimate the New Imperialism are also being formulated today. As noted earlier, neoconservative writers have articulated a set of arguments about the proper role of the United States in international affairs that seeks to institutionalize unipolarism. Many books (Ferguson 2004; Lal 2004; Mandelbaum 2005) celebrating the virtues of US imperialism have now appeared, and they claim that the spread of American-style individualism, liberal democracy, capitalism and consumerism throughout the world will usher in a new era of global peace and prosperity. Although they urge the American government to use its economic, diplomatic and even military power to promote these ideals, some such as Michael Mandelbaum (2002, 2005) contend that American ideas have already conquered the world, and that the United States has already emerged as the world's *de facto* government. This, he claims, has been achieved with the consent of the great majority of the world's peoples who accept that American hegemony will bring stability, peace, and prosperity.

Although claims about the desirability of the *Pax Americana* are hotly contested in academic circles, they are regularly reiterated by leading neoconservatives in the current Bush administration and indeed by the President himself. Claims that the government of the United States is actively spreading democracy, promoting free enterprise and engaging in nation building are frequently reiterated in the media and accepted by many citizens in the United States and by the conservative media in many other countries as well. Claims about the flowering of democratic practices in Egypt, Iraq and other countries under American tutelage are widely circulated while the government's hypocritical reaction to the democratic election of the Hamas government in Palestine is seldom mentioned.

It is in this context that social workers involved in international activities need vigorously to assert their historical commitment to cosmopolitanism and actively challenge the institutionalization of the New Imperialism and with it, assumptions about the superiority of Western and specifically American social work. As efforts are being made to normalize imperial subjugation by securing its acceptance and legitimation, social workers and their professional associations need purposefully and vigorously to challenge the new hegemony. Edward Said (1978) argued that the conscious rejection of the idea of empire is an essential step in the struggle for emancipation. Social work scholars have made similar arguments with regard to racism, patriarchy, homophobia and other forms of oppression. They need now to extend these ideas to challenge current efforts to normalize the idea of empire.

Steps need also to be taken to address the tendencies towards professional imperialism that have been identified in this chapter. Although much progress has been made, it has been shown that unilateral exchanges have not ended. These exchanges sustain inequalities between professional colleagues in different parts of the world and must be challenged. The profession must commit itself to fostering mutuality and reciprocity. By sharing the intellectual and practice wisdom that has emerged around the world, social work will be enriched and its commitment to addressing injustice and oppression will be enhanced.

PART 2
Indigenous Social Work:
A Just Cause

Chapter 3

Towards an Understanding of Indigenous Social Work

Mel Gray, Michael Yellow Bird and John Coates

The social work profession's involvement with Indigenous Peoples has frequently been viewed through the same lens as work with people outside these cultures. Not surprisingly, the social work literature views its work with Indigenous Peoples from cross-cultural, anti-oppressive or structural perspectives. While recognizing their marginalization and colonization by colonial, non-aboriginal governments, and despite the efforts of some to adapt social work education programmes to better fit their needs and cultural traditions (see Gair, Chapter 17), the profession has not developed its knowledge or approaches in tandem with Indigenous Peoples. Instead, its general focus has largely relied on adapting its therapeutic modalities to deal with problems that arise among Indigenous populations. For example, child welfare and corrections, which focus on individual pathologies rather than reforming the oppressive system, stand out as institutionalized vehicles through which this has taken place. In short, social work has largely attempted to 'Indigenize' social work in the same ways it has attempted to export its Anglo-American methodology to non-Western nations (see Chapter 1).

Not only have the efforts of social workers, and others, been proven to be largely ineffective, the profession has not stood out as being at the forefront of advocacy efforts to expose or combat the rampant poverty, the 'third world conditions' and the human rights abuses, nor has it been a major supporter of efforts to uphold land claims and treaty rights. The profession has been largely absent from these political realities and this absence is a direct result of the dominant modern paradigm under which social work has developed, which has more often than not, been ineffective in dealing with the needs of Indigenous Peoples. Mainstream social work has seen 'the other' culture as an aberration, as a technological problem, where effective intervention is a matter of finding the right theory or technique, rather than seeing its lack of effectiveness as resting in the profession's world view and its inability to shift from its Eurocentric, Anglo-American assumptions and values. Indigenous social work has arisen in the context of the vacuum created by the social work profession's inability (along with that of government and other professions) to engage in the political and cultural realities confronting Indigenous People.

Indigenous social work has arisen, by and large, as a response to the lack of effectiveness of Euro-American social work approaches and as part of broader efforts to develop effective relevant interventions with the understanding that a great many of the personal and social problems encountered are a direct consequence of the decades of mistreatment and exploitation that have taken place under various government policies aimed at colonization (see Chappell 2001). Indigenous social work is deliberately political and framed within the discourse of human rights and social justice with contemporary manifestations marked by the ever present memory of Indigenous Peoples' unjust treatment under colonialism (see Briskman, Chapter 6).

Such a perspective enables us to seek to understand the situation of Indigenous Peoples, to place the development of Indigenous social work in the context of past and current efforts at colonization and to identify some of the distinguishing features that make Indigenous social work unique. In this chapter, we discuss Indigenous Peoples' experiences and outlook on the world beginning with a discussion of their history. We next focus on the continuous loss experienced by Indigenous Peoples, the importance of the connection between land, environment and livelihood, the importance of Shamanism, negative portrayals of Indigenous Peoples and the need for culturally relevant responses. We conclude suggesting that Indigenous social work must inherently be political and that there exists a critical language in Indigenous social work that demands a new critical theory.

The importance of history

One of the most prominent aspects of Indigenous social work is an understanding of the history of these groups, which does not begin with colonialism. Indigenous Peoples inhabited and civilized their worlds long before the various waves of colonial invasion. Chronicling a time before invasion, Ronald Wright (1993) dispels the myths that Indigenous lands were vacant, undeveloped and lacking in civilization before the arrival of whites. Observing the Americas before Christopher Columbus he writes that Indigenous Peoples '… had developed every kind of society: nomadic hunting groups, settled farming communities, and dazzling civilizations with cities as large as any then on earth. By 1492 there were approximately 100 million Native Americans – a fifth, more or less, of the human race' (Wright 1993: 3–4).

Many contemporary Western writers have chosen to ignore this history before their arrival. Indeed, most write a biased story about the world before the documented Western, Eurocentric history begins and the events that marked these changes (Abram 1997; Berman 2000; Diamond 2005; Fernández-Armesto 2000, to name a few). Many writers hold Indigenous Peoples as rooted in a time before history and thus over romanticize 'oral cultures' and their connection to the land (Abram 1997; Berman 2000). According to these writers, all cultures progress in different ways through history, with the exception of Indigenous Peoples who have been regarded as frozen in time with respect to their development.

Colonialism had a devastating effect on Indigenous Peoples. Settlers and their governments took away Indigenous Peoples' control of their lives by robbing them of their land, livelihood, and traditional lifestyles, by bringing diseases to their nations and by concerted efforts to eliminate their culture. Not only is colonialism a living memory for Indigenous Peoples, it is also a contemporary reality – a lived present – as non-Indigenous society continues to push Indigenous Peoples to the margins where they are found living on unprofitable land which no one wants, without services and support. In this context we can better understand why anthropologist Hugh Brody says that 'the history of the world is inseparable from the fate of indigenous peoples ... [and] the morality of our world is also bound up in their fate' (in Hughes 2003: 5). History's treatment of Indigenous Peoples should be a moral concern for everyone.

Loss is a central feature of Indigenous Peoples' lives

Characteristic of this lived history of Indigenous Peoples around the world is the memory of ancestors murdered brutally, women raped and children stolen; of people stripped of their land, culture and heritage; people in search of their family; mothers grieving for their lost children; and fathers robbed of their dignity. First contact with Europeans most frequently resulted in death and disempowerment for Indigenous and local peoples, as the colonizers were the aggressors who systematically restructured the landscape, seizing land, establishing new boundaries, dividing people along ethnic lines and even pitting people from the same language and cultural group against one another. Colonizers established systems of government that no longer recognized Native rights and commandeered control of natural resources. Social institutions like the church became instruments for colonial territorialization.

Most damaging was forcing people off their land – their spiritual source of survival – onto reserves and vigorously attempting to assimilate them into mainstream society by taking their children into white foster care or sending them to government run boarding schools, which resulted in numerous instances of neglect, rigid rules and physical and sexual assault. Such experiences have directly and indirectly traumatized generations of Indigenous Peoples and left a legacy of cultural loss and psychological and spiritual damage. In fact, many groups still continue to recover from these deeply traumatic experiences.

Numerous conquering colonialists, lauded as heroes in Western history, mowed down Indigenous Peoples with brutal military force. When Captain Cook invaded Australia he waged war upon its rightful owners (Aboriginal Peoples) claiming the eastern seaboard for the crown which then banished convicts to this remote land that had been home to six to seven hundred clans, each with its own territory, political system and laws, for 60,000 years (Hughes 2003). In observance of these one-sided outcomes, Darwin narrowly and simplistically concluded a 'strong' eliminating the 'weak' paradigm which helped give rise to his racist evolutionary theory, which was supported by generations of scientists and used by colonialist policy makers with damaging effects.

Besides war, disease brought by colonizers severely reduced Indigenous populations. Hughes (2003) reports that Australian Aboriginal people decreased from over a million to thirty thousand by the 1930s; Māori from a quarter of a million to forty-two thousand by 1890; Polynesians on Tahiti from forty thousand to six thousand between 1769 and 1840; eleven million Indigenous South Americans died over the eighty years following the Spanish invasion of Mexico; in Brazil alone Indians fell from two and a half million to two hundred and twenty-five thousand after the Portuguese conquest; more than eight million Incas perished in the Andes;

and the number of native North Americans fell from eight million to eight hundred thousand by the end of the nineteenth century. Slavery too decimated Indigenous populations with an estimated eleven million Africans sent to America, though many died en route. Indigenous Peoples were also dispersed by a system of indentured labour and labour gangs and army conscription as the west capitalized on local resources, including people.

Following the explorers were the missionaries who were not only set on converting Indigenous Peoples, whom they considered heathens, to Christianity but were also driven by the same sense of cultural superiority that led them to support the efforts to 'improve' Indigenous Peoples through a compelled European education and socialization which they believed would expunge Native culture and language and enfranchise them into 'mainstream' society. Through their efforts Indigenous Peoples were forced to wear Western dress, taught the colonial language and force-fed a diet of religious dogma in a Western language. While some missionaries protested the treatment of Indigenous Peoples most found little value in Indigenous world views, customs and culture and believed that the education, religion and languages that they were administering was done so with 'good intentions' and for the sake of salvation.

The links between land, the environment and livelihoods

For Indigenous Peoples, land and nature are inseparable and the spiritual, social and material are inextricably entwined. Everything is connected. The environment is sacred and people are expected to live in harmony with nature as the nurturer of all life. Land shapes their cultural identity and well-being. This is a social and economic reality. Indigenous People have a special relationship to the land and their traditions prompt them to work at being good environmentalists, which is an expertise of benefit to all lands and peoples. Many people in mainstream society who intimately understand the delicate balance in which the earth hangs cite the importance of Indigenous religious and material relationships to the earth and look to model sustainable practices upon Indigenous beliefs, values and practices (Hughes 2003; Suzuki and McConnell 1997). Hughes (2003) writes that the displacement of Indigenous Peoples from their lands is 'all the more poignant ... [f]or loss of land usually means the loss of the possibility to be themselves. They rely on the territory: where ancestors have nurtured the earth, cared for the animals, [and] propitiated the spirits' (p. 6). Most were left on their original lands only if it were deemed of little or no value to the colonial conquerors. For those whose original lands were taken from them, minimal or no compensation was received and some were herded onto reserves in the remotest areas of their nations.

For Indigenous Peoples, place constitutes life in the highest ontological sense. The land and nature lie at the heart of identity and culture and shape the view of the world wherein human life mirrors nature flowing in cycles, circular rather than linear time (see Zapf 2005, 2007). For example, 'Aboriginal people [in Australia] relate totally to the earth, derive their spiritual power from it, and draw from the Dreamtime their ideas about how best to look after the environment. They believe the spirit of life exists forever, and manifests itself in the landscape' (Hughes 2003: 46). Indigenous Peoples have an intimate knowledge of the environment, treating it as endowed with human moods and emotions. Thus the environment must be managed if it is to sustain them and, most importantly, it must not be tampered with in a way that threatens its fragile ecosystems. Indigenous Peoples' survival flows from their ability to harmonize with the land. By adhering to the traditions of their ancestors, they learned how to find sustenance and healing remedies in extremely harsh environs where few could survive. However, due to colonialism many such traditions, which should have been passed to many Indigenous People today, are in minimal use or non-existent.

In contemporary society we are witnessing a renewed respect for oral modes of sensibility and awareness with the realization that 'the coherence of human language is inseparable from the coherence of the surrounding ecology, from the expressive vitality of the more-than-human terrain. It is the animate earth that speaks; human speech is but a part of that vast discourse' (Abram 1997: 179). There is an increasing appreciation of 'ethnoecology' or 'traditional environmental knowledge' much of which, especially the curative potential of certain plants, is finding its way into major drug companies frequently without compensation. As a result of this 'biopiracy', many Indigenous groups are taking steps to patent 'local knowledges', such as local wisdom about plants, not only to protect their knowledge base but also to control and protect their environment and many are working cooperatively with scientists to this end. The close connection with nature is frequently expressed in the role played by Shamans in many Indigenous cultures.

Long a subject of anthropological study, Indigenous Peoples have endured outsider misunderstandings of their cultures, 'ripping off their knowledge in the name of scientific development' (Hughes 2003), appropriating their stories, and researchers and academics reinterpreting and reconstructing their lives in a form of 'bibliopiracy' which persists today. This has led to Indigenous Peoples' mistrust of the interests and intentions of those who come to study their lives.

Along with their knowledge of the curative power of many plants, Indigenous stories have been appropriated and commodified by Western writers, poets and academics from myriad disciplines, like sociology, anthropology, political science, history, philosophy and social work. Many have prospered from this stolen knowledge. Some spiritual entrepreneurs in Western society have highjacked Indigenous spiritualities, as well as Eastern religions, to fashion a New Age culture that feeds the emptiness of secular, de-traditionalized, modern, Western culture. For instance, Abram observes:

> New Age spiritualism regularly privileges pure sentience, or subjectivity, in abstraction from sensible matter, and often maintains that material reality is itself an illusory effect caused by an immaterial mind or spirit … [thus it] perpetuate[s] the distinction between human 'subjects' and natural 'objects', and hence [does not threaten] … the common conception of sensible nature as a purely passive dimension suitable for human manipulation and use (Abram 1997: 67).

This form of spiritual idealism is no different from scientific determinism. It makes human subjectivity pivotal and all else subject to human ends, and thus in the translation loses the Indigenous sensuous connection to nature as inseparable from 'human nature'.

Ecotourism profits from eco-ethnicity where the lifestyles, cultures, dress and abodes of Indigenous Peoples attract money from tourists wanting to see the exotic. People are gaped at and photographed like zoo animals and spoken about disrespectfully as though they don't understand Western languages. Corporations appropriate local herbs and healing remedies which for centuries have been part of Indigenous wisdoms borne of Indigenous Peoples' close relationship with the earth.

Shamanism in Indigenous cultures

Many Indigenous cultures practice some form of shamanism while others, who have experienced high levels of colonization and Christian conversion, condemn such practices. Some Indigenous groups do not use this term and instead prefer a name in their own language to acknowledge and describe their spiritual leaders and healers. For many groups a Shaman must exhibit a great deal of integrity and successful treatments in order to be taken seriously as a healer. Indigenous shamans (*dukuns* in Indonesia, *dzankris* in Nepal and *nyanga* or *ngaka* in Southern Africa) are natural phenomenologists experiencing the world directly, sensuously; for them all life forms, organic and non-organic, from diminutive insects to giant rocks and mountains are alive, necessary and impact on the human senses. They are part of the body's sensuous experience (Abram 1997).

Shamans are both magicians and healers – curative artists – who, like Western psychotherapists and physicians, 'work with the malleable texture of perception' (p. 5). But this is not their central role in the community nor do they position themselves at the heart of the village but on its periphery, at its edge, where they mediate '*between* the human community and the larger community of beings upon which the village depends for its nourishment and sustenance' (p. 6).

Western researchers, especially anthropologists, make a great deal of the shamans' supernatural powers, often overlooking the ecological dimensions of their craft. Abram (1997) believes that this is because they are viewing shamanism from the Western perspective that 'the natural world is largely determinate and mechanical, and that that which is regarded as mysterious, powerful, and beyond human ken must therefore be of some other, nonphysical realm *above* nature, "supernatural"' (p. 8) rather than a natural extension of their attunement with nature. Western philosophy separated human beings and nature and made people 'special', more valuable than non-human nature. It reduced nature to an *object* of study and control. All else was there to serve the human subject. Indigenous cultures 'experience their own consciousness as simply one form of awareness among others' (p. 9). It is this that defines the shaman.

> ... the ability to readily slip out of the perceptual boundaries that demarcate his or her particular culture—boundaries reinforced by social customs, taboos, and most importantly, the common speech or language—in order to make contact with, and learn from, the other

powers in the land. His magic is precisely this heightened receptivity to the meaningful solicitations—songs, cries, gestures—of the larger more-than-human field (Abram 1997: 9).

In this sense it is the experience of existing in a world of multiple intelligences and having the intuition that every form one perceives is an *experiencing* form, an entity with its own predilections and sensations which are very different from a non-aboriginal world view. It may be that the loss of this sensuous connection to this external more-than-human world is the source of the 'inner world' conflict in non-Indigenous psychological or spiritual experiences, which prompts the need for religion and the desire to feel connected to something larger than oneself. In seeing the world as controllable and explainable the only refuge for the ineffable and unfathomable is to retreat to some form of supernatural or metaphysical experience to quiet the spiritual dissonance of Western reductionism.

Acknowledging the connection between all things, the shaman turns inward to his personal psyche and also moves laterally and outward into the landscape and its many voices. Such an approach is consistent with contemporary physics which 'sees the universe as a vast, inseparable web of dynamic activity ... whole and undifferentiated, a fathomless sea of energy that permeates every object and every act' (Kehoe 2002: 2). We can then understand why Indigenous Peoples do things to acknowledge nature and all its connections through prayer, ceremonies and rituals. These practices have become entwined with religious practices as civilizations have blended with one another. For example, in Balinese culture Indigenous animism has become thoroughly intertwined with Hindu rituals to Hindu gods and goddesses. For most oral cultures 'the enveloping and sensuous earth remains the dwelling place of both the living *and* the dead' (Abram 1997: 15). Hence bodies must be buried so they can decompose and return to the earth from which they were born and integrate with ancestors and Elders who went before.

Today shamanism has come to connote an alternative form of therapy with an emphasis on the curative power of nature and personal insight. For Indigenous Peoples the land is ever watchful, watching human action: 'The country knows. If you do wrong things to it, the whole country knows. It feels what's happening to it' (Koyukon elder, in Abram 1997: 70). Similarly, the ancient Upanishad believed, 'When a blade of grass is cut, the whole universe quivers' (Kehoe 2002: 2).

This is another respect in which Western social work stands at odds with Indigenous world views for it pursues a universal model of secular professionalism even though, on its fringes, there is a growing spiritual movement which invites a relativistic particularity. Indigenous social work cries out for social work models and knowledges that value the particular and the local, as well as the diversity of the world's cultures.

Negative portrayals of Indigenous Peoples

Because non-Indigenous cultures misunderstand Indigenous cultures in their fullness, Indigenous Peoples are dogged variously by negative or racist attitudes or romanticized, poetic references and images, like 'noble savages' that result in governments' and nations' failure to realize and accept the legitimacy of their causes.

In the modern world, the ways some Indigenous Peoples of the world still live – pastoralism, hunter gathering and subsistence agriculture – are seen as 'uncivilized', 'backward', 'undeveloped' or evidence of a 'lack of progress' as Social Darwinism continues to hold sway. Imperialist attitudes continue to shape social policies related to Indigenous Peoples in contemporary society and the world is impoverished as a result.

The need for culturally relevant responses

As noted in earlier chapters, development does not have a good track record with Indigenous Peoples and, far from helping them, has often done more harm than good since it was 'usually misplaced because indigenous peoples did not … ask for it. It was (and still is) often driven by racism and the belief that indigenous peoples [a]re backward and therefore obstacles to national development' (Hughes 2003: 120). Efforts to force development upon them has frequently forced Indigenous Peoples to assimilate into societies through forced urbanization, resettlement, relocation and removal while national development encroached on their homelands introducing inappropriate technologies in the name of progress (see, for example, Hofrichter 1993; Latouche 1993; Pulido 1996). It forced alien religious, political and other ideologies onto Indigenous Peoples, thereby undermining their traditional languages and cultures and supporting strong ethnic groups over weaker ones. It supported men while ignoring women and children's rights. Despite Indigenous Peoples' natural affiliation with nature and the environment, it gave wildlife management and conservation over to Western bodies.

Thus many Indigenous communities continue to 'take control of their own development and speak for themselves' (Hughes 2003: 120). Tired of external top-down control dominating them, they want bottom-up grassroots approaches so that their voices can be heard. They want their collective rights recognized, especially their rights to land, natural and social resources and healthy living environments; however, because of the relative lack of support of these groups and the overwhelming power of the colonizer they vacillate between models of self-reliance and negotiation with the state and others who try to exploit them. But mostly they are wary of outsiders even though some believe that it is their 'separateness' that places them at risk. Hughes (2003) believes that if Indigenous Peoples wish to be separate this choice must be respected. This is more easily done when Indigenous Peoples live in isolated communities away from the mainstream but in modern societies there is a mixing of cultures due to past assimilation policies and the paradox of the benefits and catastrophes of modernization. Indigenous Peoples struggle in such contexts to retain and sometimes even to regain their traditional cultures and thus resist outside intervention (Gray and Allegritti 2002, 2003), however, with the numerous challenges that they encounter, many actively seek outside help. In urban environments, especially, rather than maintaining a 'separateness', people have to find ways to live together harmoniously.

Social workers need to be sensitive in such environments to the colonialist and imperialist thrust of international forces that threaten local, culturally relevant responses. They need to avoid paternalism, ethnocentric attitudes, dubious power brokers and top-down strategies. Instead they must recognize Indigenous Peoples' skills and knowledges, work with them at their own pace for their own ends rather than just giving handouts and support all Indigenous groups, not just those who are well organized and vocal. They need to engage in what Hughes (2003) calls 'good development' which includes the provision of resources for self-management and enabling strategies which promote Indigenous Peoples' just causes and secure them legal and political representation. They need to promote understanding, meet real needs, restore confidence and allow plenty of time to build consultation on and participation in development. They need to prioritize causes rather than trying to solve all the problems at once while supporting women and children's rights.

To accomplish these tasks social workers must work collaboratively and in partnership with other organizations. Social work needs to contribute to the broader goals of social development, finding its niche within a multidisciplinary environment which might variously involve mobile health services, housing development, water provision and electrification, infrastructural development, micro-enterprise development, job creation, jobs skills programmes and training in diverse areas like numeracy, literacy, management, advocacy and political engagement. Hence the first lesson is that social work has to find a niche in Indigenous social development where cultural relevance and political justice is more important than professional interests. Indigenous Peoples are wary of professional social workers and are more concerned with relevant responses than with social work's territorializing agenda. Indigenous Peoples must be convinced that social workers support their just causes for land security, appropriate education and health and welfare services, *self*-representation, *self*-development, *self*-government and *self*-determination, and that they place the interests of Indigenous communities at the centre of their activities. They must recognize and work with Indigenous community organizations and engage in community advocacy. They must work in the background facilitating local peoples' community and social development initiatives.

The political nature of Indigenous social work

Indigenous Peoples are fighting back and struggling for self-rule in many parts of the world (see Hughes 2003: 53–107). They 'ask that their voices be heard, [that] their stories be told and that they take their place, on their own terms, in their own lands' (Brody, in Hughes 2003: 6). Thus implicitly Indigenous social work is political and asks that social workers:

1. Engage with Indigenous Peoples' 'right to develop on their own terms and at their own pace' (Hughes 2003: 120) including claims for land rights, nationhood or sovereignty, self-determination and, in some contexts, self-government. An overriding issue is the desire 'to own, manage and control their lands' (Hughes 2003: 20) and later we shall see how this is central to Indigenous culture.

2. Shape and enforce policies that help Indigenous Peoples achieve the entitlements to which they have legitimate claims.

3. Facilitate access to resources since Indigenous Peoples are among the most disadvantaged and impoverished in the world, have high health needs and high rates of addictions, violence and suicide as remnants of colonization.

4. Engage in advocacy. Indigenous Peoples are fighting back. They are engaging in activism at an international level. They have formed international alliances and have a permanent presence at the United Nations. Social workers can align themselves with Indigenous Peoples' movements worldwide.[1]

5. Develop service delivery models and theoretical frameworks that are relevant to local cultures and contexts.

6. And most importantly, work with colonizing peoples and governments to ensure that they take responsibility for their encroachments into the lives of Indigenous Peoples, live up to their agreements (treaties) with Indigenous Peoples and give proper restitution for their damages to these groups and their lands.

A critical language in search of a new critical theory

Though the language people use is 'critical' in nature – such as anticolonialism, imperialism, power and resistance – most social workers are not living it from an expressly critical paradigm. Linda Briskman calls for the return of anti-racism to our discourse for the matters raised in many nations are deeply embedded and woven with intolerances toward races, ethnicities, other cultures, religions and gender. Michael Yellow Bird speaks of 'terms of endearment', by which he refers to terms more relevant to the experiences of Indigenous Peoples which must be incorporated into the everyday actions and lexicon of social workers; terms that articulate, conceptualize and operationalize the need for justice and truth on behalf of these groups (see Postscript). Michael Hart (Chapter 10) and Gord Bruyere (Chapter 18) talk about Indigenous values like harmony and balance, which do not sit well with the conflictual nature of critical social work. This raises the challenge of developing theoretical frameworks that can accommodate diversity but identify what is shared among social workers in different contexts. Hughes (2003) says, 'Often, too much emphasis is put on victimization and not enough is said about the way [Indigenous] people have fought back' (p. 9). We believe this is true of the anti-oppressive practice in social work that does not pay enough attention to the resistance and resilience of Indigenous Peoples around the world. Rather than continuing to label them as 'marginalized', the profession needs to recognize that Indigenous Peoples are becoming 'more visible and audible' (Hughes 2003: 9) but their issues remain marginalized in most societies. Thus they have yet to make an impact at national levels where national governments continue to problematize Indigenous issues rather than accepting them as a matter of national responsibility.

---

1   See <www.cwis.org/fwdp/Resolutions/WCIP/wcip.txt>.

Chapter 4

Indigenous People and the Language of Social Work

Michael Yellow Bird and Mel Gray

The social work profession is guilty of false advertising when, to paraphrase its international definition, it claims to promote social change and to empower and liberate people to enhance their well-being at the points where they interact with their environments through promoting principles of human rights and social justice (IFSW 2002). One would be hard put to find a more general mission statement for a values-based profession, which ostensibly promotes respect for diversity and culturally relevant practice responsive to local contexts. Thus as an afterthought, in revising this misleading definition, Hare reports that:

> The term 'indigenous knowledge' ... refers to the critical importance of shaping social work to suit economic and cultural realities, particularly in developing countries. Indigenization implies 'adapting imported ideas to fit local needs' ... and modifying social work roles to become appropriate to the needs of different countries ... For example, (North) American practitioners must develop cultural competence in serving First Nation clients ... and others in its diverse society; and in contemporary China indigenization means considering traditional Chinese culture, the impact of the market economy on people, and the impact of collectivism and 'welfarism' on people's mentality and on helping behavior ... (Hare 2004: 415–6).

Clearly, Indigenous Peoples and the social work profession do not speak the same language, for as we show in this chapter and throughout this book, the very term 'Indigenous' as used above is offensive to Indigenous Peoples. The Western cultural construction of social work does not fit the sociocultural realities of many of the world's cultures no matter how vigorous the attempts to 'adapt imported ideas to fit local needs'. If the truth were told, this is what accurate advertising for Indigenous social workers would look like:

JOB DESCRIPTION

Wanted: Social workers to assist Indigenous Peoples

Indigenous Peoples are seeking highly motivated social workers to serve their communities' drive for self-determination, empowerment and complete return of their lands and other resources illegally stolen by colonial societies. The social worker will be required to develop aggressive programmes of decolonization that can be used to enlighten and reform members of mainstream society.

Required qualifications:

- Graduate degree from the Leonard Peltier School of Social Work.

- A complete belief in the sovereignty of Indigenous Peoples and an ability to successfully assert it on their behalf.

- Has been jailed at least four times for standing up for the rights of Indigenous Peoples.

- Can speak the language of the Nation they want to work for.

Preferred qualifications:

- Successful completion of formal accredited programme in decolonization.

- Success at getting territories, rights, and dignity returned to Indigenous Peoples.

Review of applications will begin immediately; however, the position(s) will remain open until filled with qualified individuals.

The fact that Indigenous Peoples and the social work profession do not speak the same language is not surprising since the colonizers and the colonized have developed and possess vocabularies based on the status, privilege, respect and power they are or are not accorded in society. It is not unreasonable to believe that terms such as *vulnerable*, *power*, *social justice*, *empowerment*, and *self-determination*, to name only a few of the concepts used in the everyday lexicon of professional social work, vary in their meaning for those who represent and support the colonizers and those who struggle against them, Indigenous Peoples. Indeed, some of the language of this discipline may be appropriate and applicable in various contexts when social workers work with Indigenous Peoples, however, in other situations, especially those that pit the cultural and political interests of Indigenous Peoples against those of the colonial state, many of these terms and concepts become blurred and meaningless. As Professor Churchill makes clear, colonizers are adept at introducing and using 'euphemisms' that distort, to their advantage, an accurate reality of the relationship between the colonizers and the colonized.

> ... US propagandists have contrived a whole new set of terms to mask the nature of US-Indian relations. These have centred on semantic conventions that the US, rather than occupying and colonizing Native America, has assumed a permanent 'trust responsibility' over Indian land and lives, a responsibility imparting 'plenary (full) power' over native poverty. The employment of such euphemisms has allowed projection of an illusion that federal interactions with Indians, while embodying a number of errors and excesses during the 17th and 18th century settlers' wars, has long been and remains benevolent, well-intended and ultimately for the Indians' own good (Churchill 1991: 6–7).

The language of social work is not only imprecise when applied to Indigenous People, it is also misleading and lacks 'truth-in-advertising'. Individuals who enter the profession believe that they can truly make structural changes to accommodate the needs of the oppressed, which are in opposition to the needs of the privileged in society who benefit from the oppression of others. For example, if a large transnational corporation wants to build on First Nations' land, it will be very difficult for social workers to stop this because: 1) social workers have little power to do so; 2) corporations possess significant levels of power to resist such actions; and 3) social workers rarely get involved in such actions. Instead, social workers are more likely to help by giving these workers referrals for better paying jobs, or getting them into employment training programmes to increase their skills so that they can earn more money, or locating services that help supplement the food, housing and child care needs of these workers. Each of these actions of the social worker occurs within the existing system and not one constitutes structural change.

The language of social work is enticing and misleading since it promises young, idealistic people that they will be trained to 'empower' others, to learn how to effectively promote and secure 'justice' for vulnerable peoples, and to imaginatively create opportunities for 'self-determination' for the marginalized. Of course the chances of these events occurring will vary in direct proportion to what will support or threaten the colonial *status quo*; colonial society, not social work, will determine just how much empowerment, justice and self-determination is good for the client. The code of ethics and mission of social work, like the aforementioned international definition of social work, contains several euphemisms that are vague in their meaning and function. For instance, the mission of social work in the US is to 'enhance well-being and help meet the basic needs of all people, with particular attention to the needs and empowerment of people who are vulnerable, oppressed, and living in poverty' (NASW 1999: 1). After reading this mission one is left wondering what the authors of this and similar statements meant by 'well-being'. To what extent were they thinking about Indigenous Peoples when they were using this term? Did they wonder whether there was one standard for all human beings? What did they mean by 'basic human needs' and who has defined what constitutes 'basic' needs? What did they mean when they used the term 'empowerment' and were there limits on the level of empowerment that social workers were willing to help clients achieve? Perhaps Hare can provide an answer.

> Promoting the empowerment and liberation of people are important social work processes, both in newly-industrializing countries and in more developed societies … Since its inception, social work has been particularly concerned with people who are poor, vulnerable and oppressed, as well as those who are coping with the problems and vicissitudes of living. The goal of empowering people to handle their lives more effectively has in recent times become more prominent in social work thinking … There are many definitions of empowerment … the process of increasing personal, interpersonal or political power so that individuals, families, and communities can take action to improve their situations. It is a means of addressing the problems of powerless populations and the role powerlessness plays in creating and perpetuating social problems in both developing and developed societies … The concepts of empowerment and liberation have been greatly influenced by the theories of Paulo Freire, the famous Brazilian educator (1921–97) (who *pace* Marx) … emphasized the process of conscientization, which 'refers to learning to perceive social, political, and economic contradictions, and to take action against the oppressive elements of reality' … This represents a 'critical consciousness', which enables people to reflect on their everyday experience not just in personal terms, but also with the awareness of the

social and political environments which influence that experience. According to Freire, this empowers people to take action to overcome oppressive social conditions ... Many social work writers have emphasized the importance of Freire's work for social workers internationally ... For example, he exerted a strong influence on social work in Chile and other countries in Latin America ... and ... Africa (Hare 2004: 413–4).

Missing entirely from this empowerment discourse is any critical understanding of the colonial forces that shaped the lives of the people of Latin America and Africa as well as Indigenous Peoples everywhere in the world. The claim that 'attention to the environmental forces that create, contribute to, and address problems in living' (NASW 1999: 1) is central to the profession's mission yet does little, despite this simple but powerful language, to explain or clarify what constitutes these 'forces' and says little about social work's association with colonialism and imperialism (Midgley 1981; see also Chapter 2) and the invasion, murder and dispossession upon which Western society is built. While this analysis might appear shocking for those who wrote this language, it remains appropriate for the language of the oppressed, the subject of this chapter.

The purpose of this chapter is to provide an overview of some key issues that are routinely overlooked, not known, or avoided by social workers, agencies and policy makers when providing services to Indigenous Peoples. In the Postscript, Yellow Bird discusses appropriate language relevant to the experience of Indigenous Peoples as this is one of many strategies that will help continue the process of *de*colonizing social work. Failure to do so will continue to mask the relations and understanding of language between the colonizers and the colonized as suggested by Professor Churchill above. What we are seeking here in terms of language and in the Postscript on 'terms of endearment', is a lexicon that is culturally sensitive and reflects a deep understanding of, and respect for, Indigenous Peoples and non-Western cultures of all stripes.

Lesson one: The decolonization of social work history

A first step in changing the language of social work is to acknowledge the Eurocentric history of its development. Long before colonizing populations passively or calculatedly invaded the territories and disrupted the lives of Indigenous Peoples in different parts of the world, there existed innovative formal and informal systems of support, welfare and helping that were developed and maintained by various Indigenous Peoples, nations, confederacies, tribes, villages, clans, societies and families. The concept of social work is, thus, not new by any means despite claims by US Americans that such helping practices began in the United States through the influence of the English Poor Laws used by Jane Addams, who is often referred to as the Mother of social work, to give birth to this profession.[1] This colonial narrative, like that of many of the 'discovery' narratives of colonizing peoples, weaves the

---

1   See the Lincoln Library of Essential Information, Frontier Press Co. (1924) as reported at <www.lkwdpl.org/wihohio/adda-jan.htm> and also the Hull House Museum's website at <www.wall.aa.uic.edu:62730/artifact/HullHouse.asp]>.

myth that social work – as a discipline that employs specific strategies and laws to help the less fortunate in society – is a white European innovation and 'proof' of this is offered in textbook after textbook in professional social work schools as one reviews the development of social welfare in the United States and elsewhere.

In fact, very few social work scholars who examine and teach the development of this profession include an analysis or a mention of the existence and genius of Indigenous forms of social work prior to, or after, the invasion phase of colonization by their forebears. Such omission is not benign by any means and, in fact, contributes to the notion of white supremacy and Indigenous inferiority, especially when social work students in the classroom or policy makers in colonial governments openly debate the competence and readiness of why each nation or race of people may or may not possess the competency to 'adequately' care for the members of its nation, tribe and/or community. When a people cannot care for themselves, as is the case of many Indigenous groups following the events of colonization and domination, they are labelled as vulnerable, deprived or disempowered. There is never a question of what is meant by 'vulnerable' or what makes them so.

Rarely do social work texts or scholars employ a 'fierce critical interrogation' (hooks 1993) of the history and contemporary harm that social work has inflicted on the rights, sovereignty and well-being of Indigenous Peoples. Even rarer is an analysis acknowledging that the colonial societies that now control and occupy the lands of Indigenous Peoples are often regarded by these groups as oppressive invader, settler societies, rather than civilized bodies of people interested in true democratic reform and fairness with respect to Indigenous Peoples' rights and well-being. Failure to have this discussion has two major consequences: First, it violates the mission and code of ethics of social work and makes nonsense of its international definition. Second, it prompts social work students, in these institutions, to actively or passively endorse these colonial myths rather than gain a clear objective understanding of the destructive effects their profession had and, in many ways continues to have, on Indigenous Peoples and local cultures. Third, it prevents social workers from learning what could be effective and culturally relevant interventions for First Nations people. In order to expose social work students and schools of social work to this important discussion, one has to travel outside the parameters of social work scholarship to fields such as Indigenous Nations Studies, Native Studies, American Indian Studies, Ethnic Studies or specific fields such as Hawai'ian Studies. For instance, in her book *From a Native Daughter: Colonialism and Sovereignty in Hawai'I*, Native Hawai'ian professor Haunani-Kay Trask states:

> Modern Hawai'I, like its colonial parent the United States, is a settler society; That is, Hawai'I is a society in which the indigenous culture and people have been murdered, suppressed, or marginalized for the benefit of settlers who now dominate our islands. In settler societies, the issue of civil rights is primarily an issue about how to protect settlers against each other and against the state. Injustices done against Native people, such as genocide, land dispossession, language banning, family disintegration, and cultural exploitation, are not part of this intrasettler discussion and are therefore not within the parameters of civil rights. This is true whether we are speaking of French settler colonies like Tahiti, New Caledonia, and Algeria or British colonies like Australia, New Zealand, and India or Portuguese colonies like Brazil, Angola, and Mozambique or Dutch colonies

like South Africa and Indonesia or the strange Spanish, French, British amalgam called the United States of America (Trask 1990: 25).

Lesson two: If you want something done right you have to do it yourself

Mainstream social work scholarships rarely provides such a realistic, courageous and unapologetic view of the relationship between colonizers and Indigenous Peoples. Experience has taught that such writings and views must be promoted by Indigenous social work scholars with the understanding that the messenger will often be regarded as having a personal agenda that accomplishes nothing but an unwarranted attack on innocent people – social work students who are trying to help – who had nothing to do with the historical oppression of Indigenous ancestors by non-Indigenous ancestors. Fierce critiques of US policies toward Indigenous Peoples by Indigenous activists, intellectuals and academics are generally not known or promoted by mainstream schools of social work, however, when social workers are given the opportunity to hear or read such appraisals first-hand, it is not unusual for them to respond with shock, denial, sadness, bargaining, hostility and/or helplessness. Social work has yet to reach the stage of accepting the oppressive colonization activities of the US, and perhaps other countries, such as Canada and Australia, as well. In fact, the post-9/11 US still believes that the attacks of this day in 2001 were unprovoked. Fierce defence of US foreign policy in the Middle East, and the rest of the world for that matter, has resulted in extremely hostile responses from mainstream citizens toward those making or writing statements critical of the US. For instance, when the lead singer of the Dixie Chicks (a country and western musical group) criticized US President Bush for his invasion of Iraq, she received death threats and her group's music was banned from many radio stations. Further, Professor Ward Churchill, an Indigenous Ethnic Studies professor suggested in an article entitled the *Justice of Roosting Chickens* that 9–11 attacks were likely due to inhumane US Middle East policies that have killed millions of innocent Iraqi and Palestinian babies, toddlers, children and adults. For this and other statements critical of the US, Professor Churchill has endured death threats, was forced to step down from his position as Chairman of Ethnic Studies at the University of Colorado at Boulder, and has been under investigation by his university for academic misconduct. Recently, the investigating committee found that he was guilty of five charges levelled against him by the university (Denver Channel News 2006).

Social work does not regularly advance concepts that correspond to the experiences and needs of Indigenous Peoples. It is rare to find terms and readings that openly require social work students to undertake a serious and systematic investigation of how terms such as invasion, genocide, murder, occupation, takeover, imperialism, colonialism, decolonization, dispossession, reparation, apology, responsibility, justice, white supremacy, suppression, land and resource rights, spirituality, Aboriginal title, sovereignty and monetary compensation apply to Indigenous Peoples.

Lesson three: The hidden world of colonialism embedded in social work

A major shortcoming of social work is that neither the mission nor code of ethics, which are central to the profession, was fully or partially conceived of by Indigenous Peoples nor, it seems, was the expanded international definition of social work (Hare 2004). As is often the case between the colonizer and the colonized, rarely is there a period of consultation when policy makers sincerely encourage or allow Indigenous Peoples an opportunity to provide serious, meaningful input into the development of key societal institutions or processes. Of course the exception occurs when Indigenous Peoples, who have become trusted members of the colonial state, are given positions in the system in order to give the appearance of the interests of Indigenous communities being taken seriously and provided for. While many Indigenous Peoples who become a part of the system do fight for the rights of their peoples, many serve in their role as neo-colonizers for the colonial order.

While there are many reasons for the exclusionary behaviour of colonizers, perhaps the two most common are: 1) in the process of invasion and conquest, colonizers purposely did not regard Indigenous Peoples as possessing civilization, nor did they view them as human beings with comparable intelligence and worth. As a result they thought that they had to bring civilization and enlightenment to these primitive groups; and 2) exclusion ensured that colonizers would protect their own interests and not lose their status and control over Indigenous Peoples, nor would they risk losing their ability to continue dispossessing Indigenous Peoples of their territories, resources, language, and culture (Hughes 2003).

Social work was formed on a foundation of colonization and exclusion of the well-being of Indigenous Peoples and is, therefore, not significantly different in its assumptions and protections of the colonial *status quo* than other mainstream organizations or institutions that maintain the interests of the colonial state. Perhaps the most obvious evidence of this condition is found in social work's codes of ethics. For example, those who wrote the National Association of Social Workers' Code of Ethics (NASW 1999) were clever enough to include a disclaimer stating that 'some of the standards that follow are enforceable guidelines for professional conduct, and some are aspirational. The extent to which each standard is enforceable is a matter of professional judgement to be exercised by those responsible for reviewing alleged violations of ethical standards' (p. 1). While the code does not identify 'those responsible', it does become clear in standards 1.01 Commitments to Clients and 1.02 Self-determination, that the interests of the colonial state or colonialism are pre-eminent.

The first standard states: 'Social workers' primary responsibility is to promote the well-being of clients. In general, clients' interests are primary. However, social workers' responsibility to the larger society or specific legal obligations may on limited occasions supersede the loyalty owed clients, and clients should be so advised' (p. 7).

Lesson four: Social work is colonization

The problems associated with fulfilling the above standard with respect to Indigenous Peoples are numerous. For instance, picture the following interaction between a community of Indigenous Peoples – the client – and a social worker, clearly one who believes that she is qualified for the position described at the outset.

Social worker: I just graduated from a fully accredited school of social work that was recently rated in the top ten graduate social work schools in the United States by the US *World and News* magazine's 2006 annual ratings of the 'Best Universities in America'. I have been trained in the strengths perspective and resilience theory and have taken advanced standing graduate social work courses in ethics, diversity, community organization and participatory research. I believe in our social work code of ethics and even had one African-American and one Native American professor as instructors. Oh, excuse me, I meant to say 'I had one Indigenous professor'. I also had one gay professor who helped me round my confusion on the sexual orientation thing. Just to reassure you of the diversity of my experiences and my commitment to diversity, I chose to do my practicum placements in two agencies whose directors are people of colour. During my classes I read a great deal about social justice and I believe that I am culturally competent enough to help your tribal situation. What can I do for you?

Indigenous Nations: Well, it seems that your people and society do not understand that they illegally stole our territories and resources and have been occupying our lands, without our consent, for the past five hundred and fourteen years. They also made several treaties with us on a government-to-government basis and promised to live up to the terms of agreement in these treaties, which they have not. As part of the deal we agreed to give your people a great deal of our lands through these treaties; now we want them back because your people have broken every agreed to obligation yet force us to live up to what our ancestors agreed to. Somehow this doesn't seem fair or, as you social workers say, 'socially just', especially since both our nations signed these treaties with an understanding that we had a legal obligation to do what we said we would. In fact, the Supreme Court has stated on more than one occasion that 'treaties represent the supreme law of the land'.

Your society has also used its state and federal courts to diminish our sovereignty and keep us under a perpetual state of domination where our concerns and rights are trivialized, ignored and/or censored. However, while your government sometimes refers to us as sovereign nations, it still controls and limits our sovereignty. Because your nation has declared your US Congress to have plenary – absolute – power over us, they can pretty much do what they want. For instance, for more than 200 years your society has asserted its claim to having a 'trust responsibility' over our nations, stating in writing and in your courts that you are bound by US law to protect our interests and ensure our well-being. Well, your people haven't done such a good job at this trust thing. In the last two hundred years, it seems you've stolen, given away or misplaced more than $200-billion of our money that was earned through the leasing and selling of our tribal lands, forests and other resources. If you're not familiar with this case you can *Google* it on the Internet; it's called Cobell versus Norton.

And there's …

Social worker: Excuse me but I'm not familiar with everything you're talking about. No disrespect intended but are you sure this really happened to Indigenous Peoples? I don't remember reading or discussing these issues in my social work classes and it would seem to be a major social justice issue.

Indigenous Nations: Sure it did and a lot of it is still going on today. Take the Cobell case for instance; it's going on right now. Didn't your Indigenous professor teach you about this stuff?

Social worker: Well, if he did I either wasn't listening or I missed that particular diversity lecture. The stuff you're telling me about is very troubling.

Indigenous Nations: Yeah, we know what you mean. We're beginning to feel your pain. Hey! Isn't that what you social workers refer to as 'empathy' or 'getting in the shoes of another?' Or is that what you call 'starting where the client is?'

Social worker: Well, yes it is. It's all of them I think.

Indigenous Nations: Good! So, now that you know where we are, what are you willing to work on first for us and when can we expect some changes?

Social worker: Before I begin I'd like to talk with my supervisor and look at our professional code of ethics. I'm sure there's something in there about what our commitment is to our clients and how I can help you.

Indigenous Nations: Great.

[The next day]

Social worker: Well, I checked with my supervisor who said your demands were very unreasonable and that I was crazy to think that we could ever get our society to live up to the treaties we made with you because that was all in the past. He said I was even crazier thinking we could get our government to live up to its trust responsibility by giving you back the $200-billion we stole, lost or gave away. He said the only kind of groups that get that kind of handout are US multinational corporations who get no-bid contracts for nations we destroy.

Indigenous Nations: Hmm. What else did he say?

Social worker: He said he doesn't know much about sovereignty but thought you guys were conquered nations so you don't have sovereignty anyway.

Indigenous Nations: Conquered you say?

Social worker: Yes, I think that's the word he used. Maybe he said 'conjured' or 'conjugal'. I'm not sure.

Indigenous Nations: So, what did he say about helping us get your people off our lands and getting our land back?

Social worker: Well, I'm sorry to say but he laughed most at that issue. In fact, he was laughing so hard that I thought he was going to choke or have a heart attack.

Indigenous Nations: Really? He thought it was that funny, eh?

Social worker: Yes, and unreasonable too.

Indigenous Nations: Really? That's strange. Did he attend the same social work programme as you? Does he have the same training in ethics, empowerment and diversity?

Social worker: Yes, in fact, he took the same courses and graduated with high distinction in his class and is a member of *Alpha Delta Mu*, the graduate social work academic honour society. So he knows his stuff.

Indigenous Nations: He's that smart, eh? Well did you tell him the part about illegal stuff, breaking your own laws and treaties and trust responsibility?

Social worker: I told him everything you told me, practically word for word.

Indigenous Nations: And he still didn't think you could do anything?

Social worker: No, in fact, he said I should reread the NASW mission and the code of ethics to more clearly understand what my responsibilities are to my clients.

Indigenous Nations: And did you reread them?

Social worker: Yes, I did. The mission statement is fairly general but the first ethical standard, section 1.01 Commitment to Clients, seemed the most relevant to your request.

Indigenous Nations: Great. What part?

Social worker: Well, I quote, 'social workers' responsibility to the larger society or specific legal obligations may on occasions supersede the loyalty owed to clients, and clients should be so advised.

Indigenous Nations: Interesting. So are you saying the rights of the people who stole our lands and money, broke the law and failed to live up to their legal obligations supersede ours?

Social worker: Well no, I'm not saying that. At least I don't think I am. All I'm trying to do is be sensitive to your cultural needs and make sure I honour my professional responsibilities to the broader society. So, I have to advise you that I cannot help your nation because your interests, despite your valid claims, are in direct conflict with my obligations to the larger society. And, if I put your interests above those of our society I will lose my job and end up in jail.

Indigenous Nations: Well, we don't want you to lose your job or end up in jail. But, tell us, what do you mean by larger society? Who are you talking about?

Social worker: I think you know who I mean: the people, the mainstream, those whom we referred to as the 'dominant society' in our diversity classes.

Indigenous Nations: You mean white people?

Social worker: Not necessarily. I believe there are many people of colour who are key members of our larger society. Take Condoleezza Rice for example. But I don't have time to get into this. Let me tell you how I can help you. My supervisor says, if some tribal members qualify, I can provide them with bus tickets, job referrals, childcare services, meals on wheels or coupons for your children so they can 'super-size' it at McDonald's.

As we claimed at the outset and demonstrated in the interchange above, clearly Indigenous Peoples and the social work profession do not speak the same language and social work, if its international definition and code of ethics is anything to go by, is guilty of false advertising for it is both unwilling and unable to fulfill its promises to the Indigenous Peoples of the world. If it were serious, it might adopt a lexicon to endear itself to the most marginalized peoples living today. This is the topic of the Postscript, which we have called 'terms of endearment'.

Chapter 5

Indigenous Social Work in the United States: Reflections on Indian Tacos, Trojan Horses and Canoes Filled with Indigenous Revolutionaries

Hilary N. Weaver

This chapter examines the concept of Indigenous social work as it exists within the United States. Here, as in many countries around the world, the social work profession is one of the core helping professions. In particular, social workers' mission is to serve disenfranchised and vulnerable populations. This often includes people from various ethnic minority groups, as well as Indigenous Peoples, some of whom have been trained as social workers and apply social work skills and values in their own work with these groups. The mere fact, however, that Indigenous Peoples are serving as social workers should not be taken to mean that the work that they are doing is 'Indigenous social work'. In fact, it may or may not differ from social work services offered by any other social worker. This reminds me of an old joke which poses the question, 'What makes an Indian taco Indian?', the answer to which is 'The chef'! However, I do not believe it is that simple. Anyone who has eaten an 'Indian taco' would recognize that the ingredients and the way they are served do vary from what would constitute a taco in a non-Indigenous context. Therefore, as we move forward with an examination of what constitutes Indigenous social work in the context of the United States, I take the position that the identity of the social worker is not enough to make social work 'Indigenous'.

Indigenous social work is an interesting concept. Social work as it is practiced in the United States, and perhaps throughout the world, is essentially a profession grounded in a Eurocentric world view and value system. In one way of thinking, this might make the term 'Indigenous social work' an oxymoron like 'jumbo shrimp' or 'a good war'. A different way to conceptualize 'Indigenous social work' would be to ensure that social work practices are locally relevant, in spite of the fact that social work itself may be borrowed from another culture. It is the oxymoronic conceptualization of Indigenous social work that will be wrestled with in this chapter. Indeed, much has been written on the way in which social work's methodologies are in conflict with Indigenous ways of knowing, doing and being. In his classic article, 'Native American non-interference', Indigenous social worker Jimm Good Tracks clearly articulates how some of the most basic social work techniques are perceived as intrusive and disrespectful by Native American clients (Good Tracks 1973). For example, making eye contact and a firm handshake may be seen as engaging by a social worker but may feel intrusive to a First Nations client. The very idea of an 'intervention' may be perceived as invasive. Likewise, it has been suggested that social work educational practices are likely to make Native American students less culturally competent and less employable when returning to work in Indigenous communities (Voss *et al.* 1999).

Clearly there is a social work presence in Indigenous communities. Some of these social workers are Indigenous while others are not. We cannot assume that the social work done in Indigenous contexts is any more 'Indigenous' than that performed in other contexts. Indeed, an Indigenous social worker from the Great Plains region of what is now the United States may know little about how to work appropriately with an Indigenous client from one of the southwestern Indigenous nations. Thus it is worthwhile to raise the question, what would Indigenous social work look like? Additionally, it is worth questioning whether helping practices truly guided by Indigenous principles, values, beliefs and ways of life could appropriately be called social work. The terms social work and social workers are associated with a profession that many Indigenous People experience as oppressive. Thus, even when Indigenous social workers are applying social work principles and skills in 'culturally appropriate' ways with Indigenous clients and communities, they may be reluctant to own the label 'social work'.

As we move forward with our inquiry into what would constitute Indigenous social work it is helpful to look at the history of the social work profession and use that as a framework for examining where we are in terms of an Indigenous social work, where we might want to go, and whether it is possible to get there. Additionally, information on Indigenous ways of helping, a comparison of Indigenous and social work value systems, and reflections on Indigenous social workers and academics inform this line of thought.

This chapter is written from the perspective of a Lakota woman. The Lakota are one of the five Indigenous groups in the United States with populations over 100,000 (Ogunwole 2002). Traditionally we lived in the Great Plains region and *tatanka* or buffalo were central to our existence. I now live in Haudenosaunee territory, western New York State, where I have been adopted into the Seneca Beaver Clan and married into the Seneca community. This dual Indigenous background, Lakota and Seneca, along with my professional training in social work provide the foundation for the following reflections.

The evolution of the social work profession in the US

The profession of social work as we know it today can be traced to the development of Settlement Houses and Charity Organization Societies that were initiated in England in the latter half of the nineteenth century. The first Charity Organization Society was founded in London in 1869 and was followed by similar developments in several former British colonies. The first US Charity Organization Society was founded in Buffalo, New York and was based on the London model (NASW 1995). Likewise, the first Settlement House was founded in London in 1884 and its first counterpart in the US was initiated in New York City in 1886 (NASW 1995). Charity Organization Societies and Settlement Houses quickly took hold in northeastern and mid-Western urban areas across the US. As these organizations spread, they carried with them a value system grounded in Anglo traditions and a Judeo-Christian belief system, emphasizing individualism and personal responsibility.

Early social workers in Settlement Houses and Charity Organization Societies had little interaction with Indigenous Peoples since these groups had a limited presence in urban areas at the time. It was primarily missionaries who took it upon themselves or were charged by the federal government to interact with Indigenous Peoples during the first centuries of European presence in what became the United States. Because of the government-to-government relationship between the US and the Indigenous nations within its boundaries, the federal government exercised significant oversight and involvement in Indigenous communities. Additionally, states like New York developed a position of 'Indian Agent' with oversight of programmes designed to promote the health and welfare of Indigenous People. It was not until the federal government's Bureau of Indian Affairs (BIA) relocation programmes of the mid-twentieth century that First Nations Peoples had a large urban presence in the US. The BIA relocated 33,466 Native Americans to urban areas by 1960 (Newberry Library 2002).

Social workers, however, did sometimes play roles in implementing various assimilationist policies of the federal government. In particular, social workers played primary roles in the removal of Indigenous children from their families and communities through foster care and adoption programmes. By the mid-1970s between twenty-five and 35 per cent of all Indigenous children in the US were being raised in substitute care, usually by non-Indigenous People (Mannes 1995). These removals were sometimes due to charges of neglect related to the limited resources of severely impoverished families. Another cause of child removal was the abuse rendered by Indigenous parents who had experienced and learned abusive practices when they themselves were children in 'Indian' boarding schools. Additionally, a continuing philosophy of assimilation practiced by the federal government that believed that Indigenous children would be better off if they were raised in a dominant society environment was an underlying factor in large-scale child removals. Social workers also played a role in the coercive sterilization of Indigenous women. Sometimes women were threatened with the removal of their children if they did not consent to sterilization (Lawrence 2000; Torpy 2000). Other times they were sterilized without their knowledge when hospitalized for other procedures. From 1970–76 between 25 and 50 per cent of Indigenous women of childbearing age in the US were sterilized under the auspices of the federally run Indian Health Service (Dillingham 1977; Jarvis 1977; Larson 1977).

As this brief recounting of the history of social work with Indigenous People in the US reflects, social workers have often been involved with 'doing things to' Indigenous People, such as removing children or preventing the birth of future children. The federal government in general, often with social workers acting as its agents, is also well known for its paternalism and 'doing for' Indigenous People who, at times, have been considered wards of the federal government incapable of acting in their own best interests. In a recent example of federal paternalism, the

American Indian Probate Reform Act of 2004 (PL 108–374) (in John 2006) which went into effect on 20 June 2006, requires that all 'Native Americans' with land on reservations have wills (John 2006). No other population in the US is subjected to this level of federal oversight. If social work is to live up to its value system and potential for truly helping Indigenous People, social workers will need to move toward 'doing things with' Indigenous People as their allies. In particular, social workers are well trained to work with Indigenous People to diminish federal oversight and paternalism. But will they do this?

Indigenous ways of helping

Indigenous ways of helping existed since long before the birth of the social work profession. Indigenous communities have their own types of healers who are knowledgeable about how to use various medicines and ceremonies to insure the well-being of Indigenous Peoples and communities. These medicinal and spiritual interventions often have to do with achieving, restoring or maintaining a balanced life. Additionally, some Indigenous People filled roles that included responsibility for the social well-being of their people. These might be Clan Mothers or other individuals vested with the responsibility for settling disagreements and counselling those in need of advice for a variety of issues, such as marital problems or guiding unruly children. On some level, all people in an Indigenous community shared responsibility for the well-being of the group. Reciprocal relationships and responsibilities existed across age groups as adults cared for infants and Elders taught youth. This social symmetry and reciprocity included balanced and reciprocal gender roles that contributed to the well-being of all individuals as well as Indigenous societies (Mankiller 2004).

Compatible value systems

We have always had ways of providing assistance to those in need. As noted above, some of the functions that social workers perform, such as assisting families through transitional times and helping individuals access resources, have existed in Indigenous communities since time immemorial. These traditional functions continue, to a greater or lesser extent, depending on the Indigenous community. The values that support these helping functions can be found in both Indigenous cultures and the helping professions.

What is valued varies among Indigenous Peoples. Likewise, colonization has shaped the ways that Indigenous Peoples operationalize and fulfil their values. This being said, I believe it is still worthwhile to examine some of the core values commonly held by the Indigenous Peoples of what has become the US while recognizing that not all Indigenous individuals espouse these values to the same degree. In particular, some of the values found in both social work and Indigenous cultures in the United States are respect for the individual, the importance of the society or social environment as a shaping context, individual responsibility and self-determination, interconnectedness, caring for others and social justice.

Respect is one of the key desired values found among many of the Indigenous groups in the United States. People are deserving of respect simply for being. There is dignity and respect accorded to all life forms. Additionally, respect can come from achieving certain deeds, particularly if they benefit the community or from attaining a certain age. There is typically tolerance for those who are different in some respect as long as the way that difference is expressed does not harm others. For example, an Indigenous person with a mental illness may behave in ways that are perceived as unusual but that person is still deserving of respect and remains a valued member of the community. Likewise, respect is a key value of the social work profession. Much of the National Association of Social Workers' Code of Ethics (1999) emphasizes the need to respect each and every client even when that person's values, beliefs and lifestyle may differ from that of the social worker. A difference exists, however, in that in many Indigenous societies the respect accorded to the individual does not supersede the needs and desires of the group. Respect for the community is not found to the same extent in the social work profession or in the highly individualistic US society. For example, a social worker might have difficulty understanding how the rights of an Indigenous nation can take priority over the expressed interests of an individual parent under the Indian Child Welfare Act. Under this Act an Indigenous nation may prevent the finalization of the adoption of an Indigenous child by a non-Indigenous family even though the birth mother may have selected the prospective adoptive parents.

The importance of the community is one of the defining characteristics of Indigenous societies. In fact, we often find it natural to use the term community to define ourselves as Indigenous People even when we live in urban areas and not in close geographical proximity. Being part of a community is a core element of Indigenous identity that goes beyond physical location. Even long-term urban dwellers will identify the reservation to which they are connected when introducing themselves. Additionally, the natural environment has a key shaping influence. As 'people of the land' or Indigenous People, the environment shapes our spirituality as well as our lifestyles. In one particularly poignant example, Griffin-Pierce (1997) describes how Navajo college students often experienced profound feelings of dislocation when attending universities outside the boundaries of their sacred mountains, to the point of not being able to complete their studies. An interesting parallel can be found in the emphasis that the social work profession places on the social environment. Various schools of thought within the profession emphasize a systems perspective, ecosystems or ecological perspective, or the person-in-environment (PIE) as conceptual frameworks for social work practice influenced mainly by sociological and biological – developmental – theory. All of these models emphasize how clients can only be understood fully by taking into account their context or social environment. While it is clearly understood from an analytical perspective that problems can exist within the person, within the environment or in the interaction between the two, generally social work interventions draw on psychodynamic interpretations of human behaviour and have an individualistic focus. Thus while the basic tenets of social work might appear to be compatible with Indigenous perspectives, social work tends to define the environment narrowly as only the *social* environment, while Indigenous conceptualizations of environment are often inclusive of a variety of entities beyond other human beings and systems created by humans. Only recently has this broader environmental perspective been recognized in emerging theories influenced by Indigenous knowledges and broader environmental awareness, such as Coates (2003) ecosocial perspective and Coates, Gray and Hetherington's (2006) ecospiritual perspective.

Responsibility is a key value found in Indigenous communities across the United States. We have responsibilities toward our families, our communities and to all of creation. These responsibilities lead us to a variety of roles that include being good caretakers of the environment for the sake of all living beings, the generations to come and for the continuance of the world. Responsibility is also emphasized in social work but typically in more individualistic and human-centred ways. Clients are encouraged to take responsibility for their actions or inactions and the ensuing consequences. This perspective is reflected in US social policies that expect clients to 'pull themselves up by their bootstraps' and not to be dependent on either social programmes or other individuals. While colonial influences have led some Indigenous Peoples, including many leaders, to adopt similar perspectives, traditionally the responsibility emphasized in Indigenous communities promotes social responsibility rather than individualism. Indeed, interconnectedness is seen as necessary for physical, mental, spiritual and community well-being. While social workers have some understanding that the well-being of individuals is connected to the well-being of communities or, more accurately as outlined above, the *social* environment, this is not emphasized to nearly the same degree among social workers as it is among Indigenous People. For traditional Indigenous People individual well-being is understood in the context of the well-being of the whole community.

Caring for others is a key part of what it means to be a respectful and socially responsible Indigenous person. While social workers typically build their careers around caring for others, this type of caring is not held in high esteem in US society. Indeed, in the United States, those who make a career out of caring for others are typically underpaid and constantly put in the position of defending their career choices. The profession of social work, which emphasizes the impact of the social environment far beyond what other helping professions such as psychology and psychiatry do, is particularly undervalued, even among caring professions. Thus, while the social work profession shares some common values with Indigenous People, members of this profession are penalized and ostracized for doing so within the US societal context.

Self-determination is another value held in common by Indigenous People and the social work profession, but these two groups express this value somewhat differently. Among Indigenous People in the US, self-determination is associated with non-interference. No one has the right to tell another what to do or think (Good Tracks 1973). Although the social work profession emphasizes self-determination as a key value, many Indigenous People would accuse most social workers of constantly telling Indigenous People what to do and think (Good Tracks 1973). Additionally, for Indigenous People in the US, self-determination is closely tied with sovereignty or the right to be self-governing and politically determine for ourselves what type of education and services are appropriate in our own communities. While some social workers have supported Indigenous Peoples in making our own choices for our own communities, this has rarely been the case and generally social workers do not get involved in Indigenous political issues. In particular, many social workers have no understanding of the meaning of sovereignty or how this can exist for Indigenous People in contemporary times while living within the boundaries of the United States.

Indigenous helping professionals

A significant number of Indigenous People in the US have been trained in the helping professions such as social work. While these people work in a variety of settings, many of them are employed in tribal entities or urban First Nations agencies. It is worthwhile to examine the work that they do. To the best of my knowledge, no studies have been conducted to identify what differences may exist between the work done by Indigenous social workers in Indigenous settings and the work done by other social workers in non-Indigenous settings. One might suppose that there may be substantial differences but that is something that needs to be closely examined. It is also worthwhile to question whether the people who are implementing culturally-based programming in tribal entities or other Indigenous settings are social workers. It may well be that the people who are implementing culturally-based programming are those who have not been educated in a Eurocentric tradition-like social work.

It is also important to look at the work that is being done by Indigenous social workers in Indigenous settings. What models and theories are they using to ground their work? If they are drawing on their social work education they may well be applying mainstream models even though they themselves are Indigenous and are working within an Indigenous context. Just as many populations experience internalized oppression, Indigenous People often continue the process of colonization by internalizing the colonizer's ways of knowing, doing and being. Further, Indigenous social workers who are knowledgeable about their own cultures and try to apply this in their practice are often hindered by powerful external mandates. Indigenous social services are often financially dependent on grants that require that programming meet current dominant society standards. For example, terms like 'evidence-based practice' and 'measurable outcomes' are as common in Indigenous agencies as they are in other agencies. Perhaps some of the wealthiest tribes will be able to fund their own services and thus escape the need to meet these external, Eurocentric standards. It is plausible, however, that the wealthiest tribes are the ones that have adopted, at least to some extent, a mainstream capitalistic way of operating and thus may have fewer cultural resources to draw on in implementing distinctively Indigenous ways of delivering social work services. While accountability to Indigenous clients and communities is of vital importance, it seems that it would be most appropriate to use Indigenous measurement standards, whatever those may be, within a particular Indigenous context, rather than adopting external standards.

Social work and Indigenous models

There are numerous theories and models of social work practice. Indeed, new ones are being developed on a regular basis and social work continues to borrow knowledge from other disciplines. In this context, it seems that it would be reasonable for an Indigenous model or perhaps multiple Indigenous models of social work to emerge in the mainstream social work literature for, as the chapters of this book show, there have been numerous attempts to develop Indigenous practice models. But are they truly Indigenous? A truly Indigenous model would arise directly from an Indigenous context *rather than be an adaptation of a model from another cultural context.* It would be developed by Indigenous social workers for Indigenous social work practice in a specific local context and, as such, would be more than a model of culturally competent social work practice. However, having said this, in spite of the significant tensions and conflicts between social work and Indigenous ways of doing things there may be some social workers who are able to provide helping services grounded within Indigenous ways of knowing and being. It is not clear to what extent they incorporate their social work training or, if perhaps, they are able to ground their work in Indigenous ways in spite of their social work training. It is my belief, however, that this type of work exists primarily at the *local* grassroots level and has not become established or visible to the point of constituting a specifically Indigenous model of social work practice recognized within the mainstream literature. Additionally, it is important to keep in mind the vast diversity that exists among Indigenous groups within the US, and elsewhere, is likely to result in many different approaches to helping that are regionally and/or tribally specific.

If we are to move in the direction of establishing an Indigenous model of social work practice it would be worth our while to see what can be learned from Afrocentric models. Until recently, African-Americans were the largest population of colour in the United States and they have long been disproportionately represented in social services, such as substitute care and juvenile justice. Many African-American social workers came to feel that mainstream ways of helping were ineffective and inappropriate with this population and indeed, replicated their experiences of domination and oppression in US society (Schiele 2000). Afrocentric social work services have been applied in many areas, such as HIV prevention (Randolph and Banks 1993) and juvenile justice programmes (Harvey and Coleman 1997). Afrocentrism is based on the guiding principles of *Umoja* (unity), *Kujichagulia* (self-determination), *Ujima* (collective work and responsibility), *Ujamaa* (cooperative economics), *Nia* (purpose), *Kuumba* (creativity) and *Imani* (faith) (Gavazzi *et al.* 1996; Harvey and Rauch 1997). Perhaps there is something that Indigenous social workers can learn from these efforts. Additionally, there is much that can be learned from social work on the international scale.

The voices of Indigenous social workers

Much rests on the shoulders of Indigenous social workers. Will we transform the social work profession? Will we develop our own Indigenous models of social work and make sure that they are filtered into the mainstream social work literature? Will we apply mainstream social work practices even when working in Indigenous contexts? And most importantly, can we apply Indigenous ways of knowing and doing without blending these with social work?

In fact, Indigenous social workers have raised their voices and identified the specific components of culturally competent social work (Weaver 1999). These social workers identified that culturally competent service provision with Indigenous People in the US requires that social workers be knowledgeable about the diversity, history, culture and contemporary realities of their Indigenous clients. They must have strong general skills and in particular be able to apply containment skills like allowing silence and listening patiently. Additionally they must value helper wellness and self-awareness, display humility and willingness to learn, be respectful, open-minded, non-judgemental and value social justice (Weaver 1999). While all these principles are important, perhaps the last element is the most crucial in framing appropriate social work practice with Indigenous Peoples. Social justice must be the fulcrum on which social work turns if we are to truly escape the oppressive legacy of past social work practice with Indigenous Peoples in the context of colonialism within the United States and elsewhere (see Chapter 6). The elements identified here are important in developing culturally competent social work with Indigenous Peoples in the US; indeed many of these traits are integral to competent social work practice with any type of client. Still, identifying elements of culturally competent social work remains quite different from developing an Indigenous model or anything that could truly be called Indigenous social work.

Indeed, the educational process that Indigenous People go through to become social workers socializes them into Eurocentric ways of thinking, doing and believing. This process is often experienced as alienating and devaluing of Indigenous cultures (Voss *et al.* 1999; Weaver 2000). Indeed, the very process of becoming a social worker is likely to take someone away from Indigenous models of helping. A crucial question is whether the socialization process inherent in higher education in the US necessarily changes Indigenous students. It might be that some students are able to go through this process without diminishing their Indigenous values and perhaps even being able to bring about changes in academia. On the other hand, the power imbalance between higher education in the US and the few Indigenous students in its midst favours compromise on the part of the students rather than the institutions (see Chapter 17).

The role of Indigenous social work academics

Indigenous social work academics find themselves in a potentially pivotal position. On the one hand, they are ideally positioned to shape the profession and make it more welcoming to Indigenous ways. Social work academics write books and articles, as well as deliver presentations and conduct research; all of these activities have the potential to steer the social work profession in ways that are new and creative. We serve in key professional organizations like the National Association of Social

Workers and the Council on Social Work Education. Even as a small minority within our profession there is significant power in our voices should we choose to use it.

On the other hand, most social work academics are products of a Eurocentric educational process and are members of a profession with strong roots in an Anglo tradition (Weaver 1999). It may be that to survive in these contexts we have compromised or left behind our Indigenous ways to such an extent that we are no longer capable of transforming the social work profession in ways that make it more compatible with Indigenous cultures.

People of the Haudenosaunee confederacy tell the story of when the Europeans first began to arrive on the east coast of North America. The Indigenous Elders met in council to decide what to do about the newcomers. Should they be destroyed? Should they be welcomed into Haudenousaunee communities? A decision was made that they would be allowed to stay but that their ways and beliefs were so different that it would not be possible for them to successfully co-mingle with Indigenous People. This understanding was commemorated in a Two Row Wampum Belt. This beaded belt depicts two straight lines that do not cross, symbolizing parallel ways of life or communities. The Haudenousaunee have one canoe or way of life; the Europeans have another. They are equally valid and deserving of respect but it is not possible to travel with one foot in each canoe. The person who tries will fall in the water. An Indigenous person may choose to travel in the European canoe or *vice versa*, and that is fine, but one person cannot do both. I wonder about the position of Indigenous social work academics. Which canoe will we place our feet in? In the past, in order to survive academia, we needed to have our feet in the European canoe. Is that still the case? This story depicts a clear dichotomy. Is there perhaps another way that can be used to understand surviving culturally as an Indigenous person while successfully functioning in social work academia?

To borrow a story from another culture, might we ride into social work academia in the belly of a Trojan horse, remaining undercover long enough to survive but remaining true to our Indigenous values in ways that would lead us to transform the social work profession and perhaps develop truly Indigenous models of social work? Is there a way to remain firmly in the Indigenous canoe and be vital participants in a profession with such strong Eurocentric roots?

Reflections on the current state of affairs

As I reflect on the current state of affairs, I fluctuate between optimism and pessimism. Part of me would like to think that Indigenous social workers and social work academics can hold strongly to Indigenous ways in spite of our professional socialization and that ultimately we can transform the profession. I am, however, aware that our history has often shown that we are more likely to be transformed by the profession than to transform it or perhaps those who go on to succeed in higher education have already adopted dominant society ways, to some extent. I think that we have made inroads into developing definitions of culturally competent social work practice with Indigenous People and that is an important step for the social work profession. We can continue to identify Indigenous practices that can be infused in social work practice as we raise our voices to shape our profession.

I also know that social work is not the only way that Indigenous People get help or find balance in their lives, nor should it be. There have always been Indigenous ways of helping and these will remain as long as there are Indigenous People. There is no need to incorporate this or subsume it under social work practice: Indigenous ways of helping have their own legitimacy without the need for professional sanction. The part of me that strives to live my life in the Indigenous canoe would say that perhaps these Indigenous ways of helping might, in fact, be more legitimate than professional ways that we have learned from those outside our cultures.

Perhaps the most successful models for combining Indigenous ways and the best of mainstream helping traditions are happening at the local, grassroots level and may or may not be connected with social work. When I visit Indigenous communities across the US, I often hear of creative ways of helping that are strongly grounded in the traditions of those communities, such as empowering women to leave domestic violence relationships by teaching them tribal history and the traditional power attributed to women in some Indigenous societies. These programmes are rarely publicized in journals or spoken about at conferences. Indigenous helpers, not necessarily social workers, quietly go about providing needed services in culturally appropriate ways.

Conclusion

I struggle with describing Indigenous social work in the US because there are so many different ways that it could be defined. I reject the 'Indian taco' model that just because an Indigenous person is providing social work services that it automatically leads to an Indigenous model of social work. I fantasize that Indigenous social work academics will rise up as revolutionaries from their Trojan horse and declare that they are, in fact, in the Indigenous canoe, although I will not hold my breath. I believe that we are moving toward models of culturally competent social work that are meaningful for Indigenous People in the US, although I still would not call these Indigenous models of social work. These models come from people like myself who are and always will be products of generations of socialization in dominant society educational systems. My comfort lies in the fact that our Indigenous ways of helping persist in many communities in spite of often having gone underground. Indigenous ways of knowing, being and doing persist and can continue to shape how people are helped, with or without social work.

Chapter 6

Decolonizing Social Work in Australia: Prospect or Illusion

Linda Briskman

An oft quoted statement by Australian Aboriginal activist and educator Lilla Watson (in Riggs 2004) says, 'If you have come here to help me you are wasting your time ... but if you have come because your liberation is bound up with mine, then let us work together'. From a social work prism this statement represents a plea to support the liberation project of Indigenous Peoples and a call to liberate social work from its modernist and oppressive shackles.

I am a non-Indigenous woman raised and educated in ignorance of the history and oppression of Indigenous Peoples, the Aboriginal and Torres Strait Islanders of Australia. I am now aware of my unwitting perpetuation of the colonial process, which was previously masked through blindness to my race privilege and acceptance of the Eurocentric tenets of social work. Newly emerging interpretations of colonialism have presented challenges to social work, with moves to challenge the received knowledge from which many social workers uncritically enact their practice. A decolonizing approach to practice requires workers to recognize their race privilege, validate Indigenous wisdom, acknowledge Indigenous rights and discard the power they exert in the name of professionalism. Social work educators have paramount responsibility to ensure that social workers leave academic institutions with appropriate understandings and practice tools so as not to perpetuate the harm that has been caused and to challenge dominant paradigms in theory and policy domains. This is particularly necessary within the current neoconservative context where political ideologies are antithetical to Indigenous rights and in the light of organizational policies that silence social work challenges to dominant ways of thinking.

A key question that arises is: How can social work amend its ways and contribute to social change when most social workers choose not to recognize the political dimensions of their practice and when political activism is not expressly advocated through social work professional bodies? Dominelli (1998) points out that the role and purpose of social work has been contested since its inception. Although dichotomies are problematic, there remain two broadly distinct positionings for social work: 1) the more conventional, derived largely from psychology and applied to direct practice where the majority of social workers are employed, and 2) a more progressive revisioning where social work practice is overtly linked to the political domain and challenges the idea that existing social structures are fixed or even desirable. It is only with such revisioning that anticolonialism, social justice, and emancipation can be at the forefront of practice.

In this chapter, I take a critical social work perspective that embraces a range of emancipatory positions linking people's experiences with the dominant ideologies of society. My analysis draws on structural social work, anti-racist approaches and a broad postmodern perspective that emphasizes difference and points to the part played by language and discourses in constructing social reality (Pease *et al.* 2003). Although taking some leads from the post-colonial literature, I do so with reservation as this literature has limited application to colonized people of the fourth world (see <www.en.wikipedia.org/wiki/Fourth_World> and wrongly implies that the colonial project has ceased. The interconnected range of theoretical underpinnings enables me to grapple with the issues, to decentre my own position and to examine Western dominance that remains unquestioned and unrecognized by the majority population of Australia. In so doing, I acknowledge that I have been fortunate in having my own world views challenged through immersion in Indigenous communities and organizations and through my work on collaborative endeavours. Employment in an academic setting provides some privilege in being able to exercise voice without organizational constraint. The pressing quest is to find a pathway through which the majority of social workers can contribute to the decolonizing project, engage with the political dimensions and discard some of the theoretical and practice frameworks that are irrelevant and harmful to Indigenous People. Alongside this is the issue of tactics, where social workers have to find ways of moving through the constraints they face as organizational agents.

The context

Before examining the place of social work, it is necessary to identify the ongoing impact of the British invasion of 1788 as social workers can only fully understand their roles by having an acute understanding of the history/policy nexus. There is little doubt that the legacy of policies of oppression, the most enduring being protectionism and assimilation, has resulted in Indigenous People remaining at the lowest rung of the socio-economic ladder. In summary, they have not yet experienced the gains evident in some other fourth world settler nations particularly in the spheres of health, education and economic status. Aboriginal and Torres Strait Islander peoples have poorer health and, on average, live twenty years less than other Australians. They experience high rates of substance abuse, poor nutrition and inadequate housing and infrastructure. Unemployment rates are three times the national average (Department of Immigration and Multicultural and Indigenous Affairs 2002). Children and young people are vastly over-represented in the child protection and juvenile justice systems, and this is followed by over-representation in the adult criminal justice system, including prisons. The scandal of Aboriginal deaths in police cells and prisons was investigated by a Royal Commission that in 1991 brought down a far-reaching report that looked to the broader issues of self-determination and public education as well as the systematic and deliberate disempowerment of Aboriginal people (Johnson 1991). All of these socio-economic indicators contravene Article 25 of the 1948 Universal Declaration of Human Rights where everyone 'has the right to a standard of living adequate for the health and well-being of himself and of his family, including food, clothing, housing and medical care'.

The latest national census results from 2001 clearly outline the extent of Indigenous disadvantage when compared with other Australians. For example, 35 per cent of the non-Indigenous population had a post-secondary qualification compared with less than 15 per cent of Indigenous People; almost 22 per cent of Indigenous males over the age of 15 years were unemployed, with the corresponding non-Indigenous figure at 7.7 per cent; the median family income for Indigenous People was slightly more than one-half of that for non-Indigenous People; and in remote areas, 19 per cent of Indigenous houses needed major repairs (Australian Indigenous Health InfoNet 2006). Paradoxically, as one of the world's wealthiest nations, Australia, along with New Zealand, Canada and the United States, has Indigenous People as the poorest citizens. And furthermore the wealth of these countries has been substantially built on resources taken from Indigenous Peoples, whose poverty is a relatively recent creation (Cornell 1999).

Exacerbating the disadvantage is evidence that there is severe under-funding or mis-spending by government in Indigenous spheres. This is despite a common and highly inaccurate community perception that Indigenous People receive benefits over and above the rest of the population. In health, for example, expenditure does not match the urgent need and flies in the face of healthy federal budget surpluses and one of the most effective health services in the world (Oxfam Australia 2006). The peak health organization in Australia, the Australian Medical Association (2006), has called for an inquiry into the under-funding of health and education in Aboriginal communities.

The social conditions of Indigenous People contradict the most basic conditions for true citizenship and full humanity. In just over 200 years since the white invasion, the colonizers have endeavoured to strip Indigenous Peoples of their cultures, their lands, their spirituality and their autonomy. The historical processes and the reasons for ongoing disadvantage are ill understood by the wider community and by the majority of social workers, yet they are important to know about as social workers, the state and Indigenous Peoples meet and clash at the sites of formal institutional arrangements in such spheres as child welfare, education, employment, housing and health. Social workers have two broad choices: To collude with the apparatus of the state or to resist and embrace the ideologies and struggles of Indigenous social movements and work collaboratively for the realization of Indigenous rights.

Deconstructing social work

A necessary precursor for transformation is for social work to examine manifestations of continuing racism and the need to combat this blight to redress the past and build the future. Adopting a whiteness perspective, I posit that the responsibility for social change rests in large part with the majority non-Indigenous population, with the first steps being a transformation in thinking and acting. What I present is a somewhat harsh depiction of the place of social work in contributing to, perpetuating and failing to respond to Indigenous issues. But of course there are many social workers who have challenged the status quo, and joined in social movements for change. For example, during the official reconciliation process that took place for a decade from the early 1990s, social workers were among those who worked with their local communities and organizations to facilitate relationships. Yet there are other social workers who are unreceptive to the cause of change and are co-opted into continuing to practice in ways that are unquestioningly taken for granted; Bourdieu's (1990) notion of *habitus*. Margolin (1997) speaks of how, with the advent of social work, people became vulnerable to judgement. This is shamefully evident in the contact between social workers and Indigenous communities and has caused great hardship, misunderstanding and ongoing oppression. This has resulted in a relationship between social workers and Indigenous groups that is confrontational rather than collaborative. It is difficult but essential for social workers to challenge the racism that underpins their practice frameworks for, as Australian Aboriginal activist Gary Foley (2000) aptly states, the real problem confronting Indigenous People is one that exists in the white community. He argues that the most important role for white 'helpers' is within their own communities where it is necessary to challenge the ignorance and fear that prevail.

The building blocks of racism in Australia were derived from Social Darwinist ideologies that in earlier times were enacted through official legislative and policy instruments. These included the White Australia Policy that discriminated against Asians and protectionist and assimilationist policies targeted only at Aboriginal people. Now the racism that social workers are likely to encounter is often unacknowledged, unrecognized and embedded in policy, organizational practices and the way in which dominant groups, including the professions, exercise power over others. This reflects the views of the wider society where racism is characterized by the indifference, distortions and harassment, which characterize the relationships between Indigenous and non-Indigenous citizens (Groome 1995).

Insidious, invisible racism is evident in the array of policy documents and in the practices of government where the construction of practice remains largely within an Anglo-Australian lens. Here the values, beliefs, meanings and practices from the dominant culture are the benchmarks against which other values and meanings are measured, and those outside these mainstream constructs are deemed as inferior (Quinn 2003). One example is white feminists who benefit from colonization, having key roles and constituting the norm and the standard of womanhood in Australia (Moreton-Robinson 2000). Another is the way in which terms such as 'capacity building' have currency, implying a deficit that needs rectifying. Here the assumption is made that non-Indigenous knowledge can be effectively channelled into Indigenous communities that are seen as having limited or absent capacity. In these formulations, concepts of sovereignty, self-determination, collectivity and rights do not feature. Furthermore, contemporary manifestations of racism include indifference to remediation of suffering, the failure to commit adequate and appropriate resources, and the refusal to acknowledge the wrongs and injustices perpetrated on Indigenous People (World Conference against Racism, Racial Discrimination, Xenophobia and Related Intolerance 2001). Despite good intentions, social work schools have, according to Carniol (1990), generally lacked an appreciation of the impact of past and present racism on clients and communities and continue to ignore Indigenous values of extended family, Elders, and the community in their over-emphasis on individual cases.

In the current political context we are witnessing a revival of calls for assimilation and a rejection of those who do not conform to the re-emerging monolithic view of what it means to be Australian. Despite lauded policies of multiculturalism the reality is that plurality, alternative allegiances and different ways of life are not espoused; nor is diversity affirmed. It is not so long ago that immense damage was done to Indigenous communities through assimilation policies that resulted in the removal of Indigenous children from their families and communities and that legacy remains through subsequent generations. Reminiscent of the past, there are continual calls by sections of media and government to remove Indigenous children from communities where disadvantage and violence prevail 'for their own good'. Regrettably, anti-racist theorizing is not always at the forefront of social work. In recent years there has been a slide into a broader anti-oppressive framework that masks constructs of racism and makes it more difficult to challenge the prevailing ideologies. Recognition of covert and overt racism is an essential first step in the transformation of social work to Indigenous centeredness.

Ongoing colonialism through knowledge control

There has been very little movement in Australian society, or in the professions, to affirm Indigenous knowledge. The dominance of Western knowledge has caused great harm to Indigenous People. Indigenous knowledge has been seriously overlooked in the past and has been subjugated and given an inferior status alongside the privileged place given to 'expert professional knowledge' (Trevithick 2005: 23). The disparity between the two knowledge systems is the crux of the problem of social work with Indigenous Peoples. The failure to recognize and incorporate Indigenous notions of spirituality and healing which encompass holistic ways of seeing the world and oneness with nature is a form of cultural arrogance. Moreton-Robinson (2000) explains that knowledge is never innocent or neutral but is a key to power and meaning and is used to dominate and control.

Eliminating colonialism requires a social worker to overturn the dominant ways of seeing the world to avoid perpetuating colonial values (McLeod 2000). This requires social workers to cease imposing their values on others and to promote the interests of those with whom they are working and not their own self-interest (Ife 2001). This is not always easy as prospective social workers do not enter social work education as 'blank slates' but come with their own cultures, values and belief systems (Weaver 2000). Colonialist practice is often not overtly visible and not challenged. Most practitioners would deny that we operate within colonial structures and implicitly believe we are operating in a post-colonial era. But as New Zealand academic Linda Tuhiwai Smith (1999) so compellingly tells us, naming the world as post-colonial is, from Indigenous perspectives, to name colonialism as finished business. Even though the colonizers may have formally left the institutions, the legacy remains.

Revisioning social work and challenging racism requires us to listen and to take heed from the adherents of a whiteness framework. Critical studies of whiteness inform us that being white is not interrogated as it is the standard against which everything is measured. This is at the core of the persistence of non-Indigenous dominance and the imposition of Western knowledge as the accepted orthodoxy. The lack of inclusion of whiteness studies in most social work training programmes results in many graduates being unaware of the power they continue to exercise, for whiteness is hidden and most non-Indigenous social workers do not recognize their race privilege. If we accept different world views, this challenges our preconceptions about practices that do not adhere to dominant ways, such as different approaches to child rearing. This can threaten the very basis of professionalism and is hence resisted. Macedo and Bartolome (1999) speak of the invisibility of whiteness and point out that only when we see white as a 'colour' we can begin to interrogate the false assumptions that strip white people of their ethnicity. In Australia thinking about whiteness is increasingly taking hold in academic circles (see, for example, Holt (1999) and Moreton-Robinson (2000)).

Contemporary manifestations

Current mainstream ways of presenting Indigenous affairs is through a white lens. In April 2006 the media began a concerted campaign of reporting on Indigenous 'dysfunction' with sensationalist headlines and commentary resulting in moral panic by governments and others in Australian society. Among the matters that drew media attention were violence against women and children, including sexual violence, youth crime and substance abuse. Rarely was there a critical analysis of historical causes, policy problems or lack of expenditure or goodwill on the part of governments. Predictably the federal government reacted harshly, calling on the states to tighten law enforcement measures and asserting the failure of self-determination which, in effect, has never been part of the government's platform. Alongside this it continued to advocate for the sinister policy of removing service development and provision from Indigenous responsibility. Contradicting the picture of ineptitude presented by governments, there was a parallel call from governments to employ Indigenous People from remote communities for tourist 'infotainment' in city hotels. Understandably, Indigenous People reacted strongly against this new form of paternalism and cultural abuse. I recently attended a meeting where Indigenous People expressed despair, commenting that they had done nothing to provoke such harsh responses.

The media activity and government responses have built on repressive and patronizing policies that fit within the individualistic and market driven policies of the current conservative federal government, where responsibilities take precedence over rights. The harshest and most reprehensible of these policies that are framed by an ideology of 'mutual obligation' are Shared Responsibility Agreements in which Indigenous communities are required to demonstrate behavioural changes before having access to services and programmes that are considered rights for other

Australian citizens. A former federal minister for Indigenous affairs went so far as to name small Indigenous communities as 'cultural museums' thus questioning their continuity and sustainability.

Coinciding with the demonization of Indigenous culture and communities was the abolition of the Indigenous governance structure, the Aboriginal and Torres Strait Islander Commission (ATSIC), with the government now consulting hand-picked rather than elected leaders. ATSIC was created by the federal government in 1989 and, at that time, was seen as a bold experiment in transferring a degree of decision making and responsibility to Indigenous communities. The disbanding of ATSIC in 2004 was the first structural signal of the mainstreaming of Indigenous affairs. Without consultation, the Government abolished ATSIC in its entirety replacing it with a government appointed National Indigenous Council. Although ATSIC had been subject to considerable criticisms by Indigenous People, particularly as it was a structure imposed by governments, there was even more rugged criticism of its abolition without consultation or without endeavours to deal with its flaws. ATSIC's abolition was followed in 2006 by the transfer of the Indigenous ministerial and bureaucratic portfolio to a mainstream family and community services portfolio.

Aside from the more formal structures, Indigenous community organizations are also subjected to ongoing assaults by the federal government. This is far removed from the vision that established these organizations in the spheres of health, law and education from the 1970s onwards when Aboriginal people and their supporters saw them as the drivers for emancipation. Although the roles overlap, most of these spheres have national bodies with broad policy and advocacy roles, supported by state and regional bodies that focus on service delivery, reflecting the Australian federal system under which such bodies have been established. One example is in the child welfare arena where a national body, the Secretariat of National Aboriginal and Islander Child Care (SNAICC) is the national Indigenous policy advocate for the well-being of children and families. It supports and works alongside the state and regional Aboriginal and Islander childcare agencies (AICCAs) to facilitate their shared visions often through rugged negotiations with federal and state governments. Under the close scrutiny of governments, these bodies constantly have to justify their existence and can have their funding diminished at whim. They express frustration at the lack of will from bureaucrats and service providers to consult meaningfully and to transfer decision making authority to Indigenous organizations (Briskman 2003).

The current reactionary environment contributes to the difficulties confronting social work practitioners, with the move to mainstreaming and service integration through 'non-ethno-specific' agencies likely to result in ill-equipped social workers delivering services. If Indigenous People are not employed by these organizations, their knowledge may be lost. And if they are so employed they may well struggle with their community obligations in a non-supportive work environment where white privilege abounds. The policy climate is exacerbated by a culture of managerialism and corporatization within community organizations, many of which, Indigenous and non-Indigenous, have been forced to comply with restrictive requirements in order to maintain their funding base. For Indigenous organizations this has meant acquiescence at the expense of cultural imperatives, including operating within narrow programme requirements rather than in a holistic, Indigenous-centred manner.

Why are these factors important for social work? First, because they are incompatible with tenets of self-determination that are espoused by both Indigenous groups and social workers even though interpretations may vary; second, because they raise the prospect of a shift back to social control rather than the liberation spoken of by Lilla Watson (1988); and third, because social workers have been tardy as advocates and in working collaboratively with Indigenous People for change. In rising to these challenges, social workers need to be vigilant in determining which voices predominate in influencing the policy domain; too often it is the media or right wing commentators. When Indigenous People speak out or conduct their own research those in positions of power, including the professions that flaunt their expertise as if it were sacrosanct, often thwart their endeavours.

Reconstructing social work

Social work cloaks itself in fine rhetoric; empowerment, social justice, redressing disadvantage and social change are but a few examples. But the reality of social work is that it is a form of practice that reinforces colonialism in the name of helping. Faith (see Chapter 19) admonishes social work for being part of the imperialist project of assimilation that replaces traditional social structures with European systems. This clearly is the case in Australia where governments have always imposed policies and dictated the manner in which governance structures and funding operate, and always at the expense of Indigenous ways of being. Being located within the state, social work reinforces ongoing colonialism despite a myth of being a helping profession. Social work has also become so professionalized that it perpetuates its own survival. As pointed out by Michael Yellow Bird (in Postscript), the rise of social work rarely mentions the existence and genius of Indigenous forms of social work that existed before and after colonization. Similarly, Hilary Weaver (in Chapter 5) speaks of how Indigenous ways of helping existed long before the birth of social work, evidenced by traditional healers who conducted medicinal and spiritual interventions to achieve, restore or maintain balance in life.

The ongoing problems facing Indigenous communities and the harsh government responses to them can have a paralyzing effect on social workers. There are a number of ways in which social work can rethink and redevelop its practice to truly decolonize itself. Indigenous spirituality, and its centeredness in Indigenous ways of life, is often discarded. In the past, I too have tended to see a disjuncture between the political realm and the spiritual, which in a Western world view have been considered as two separate spheres. This is a position of ignorance for, although I am not sufficiently arrogant to profess an understanding of Indigenous spirituality, there is the clear connection of nature, oneness with the world and a holism that encompasses all spheres of life. During the Fredericton conference, I was awakened to the connections, when one Native participant pointed out that the 'spiritual is political'. Here I can see a place for critical and political social work in melding the two aspects. After all, as Gray and Coates (2006) point out, drawing from the work of Noel Tovey, to be born black or Indigenous is to be born political.

Placing human rights in the forefront is a way of moving beyond the idealistic and somewhat nebulous rhetoric of social justice that appears, without explanation, in professional social work and organizational policy documents. A human rights discourse is still lagging in social work practice although in recent years, inspired by the work of Australian academic Jim Ife, there have been nascent endeavours to redress this. Yet social work remains largely needs-based rather than rights-focused and this, in its essence, reifies professional knowledge at the expense of Indigenous rights. In advocating a human rights approach it needs to be recognized that Indigenous Peoples around the globe have asserted their rights in many ways and in a range of forums, including the United Nations (1948). Not only do human rights provide social workers with a moral basis for their practice (Ife 2001) but they also lend social work practice to a range of modalities that discount the emphasis on responsibilities, something that is imposed only on oppressed groups.

How do social workers inform themselves about Indigenous perspectives and world views in order to advance their practice? This can be achieved in a variety of ways including experiencing Indigenous literature, music, film, theater, painting and sculpture. Oral histories are a powerful medium for bringing Indigenous perspectives to the forefront, but in the current 'positivist' environment, oral histories are often belittled and maligned. When the report into the 'stolen generations' was released by the Human Rights and Equal Opportunity Commission in 1997, Indigenous voice through oral history was discounted and right wing commentary viewed this methodology as negating 'truth' and not providing hard evidence. Similar debates have occurred with the construction of history, resulting in Indigenous People and sympathetic white historians supporting alternative ways of speaking about the past. Social workers can adopt similar alternative approaches by questioning the way policy and practice frameworks are usually developed with limited or selective consultation and even more limited interpretations. Hearing people's life stories directly or indirectly provides great insights. Schaffer and Smith (2004) point out that it is through life narratives that people tell of human rights violations as stories demand that readers attend to histories, lives and experiences often vastly different from their own. They point out that such narratives have become one of the most potent vehicles for advancing human rights claims.

Social workers need to examine and overturn their part in perpetuating stereotypes. Far too often Indigenous People are portrayed as victims, denying agency and ignoring resilience, cultural richness and supportive family structures. A focus on strengths contributes to negating the prevailing discourse that views Aboriginality as a 'problem'. This means that social workers must heed their use of the language they use and not be co-opted into populist ways of presenting concepts. In so doing, the adoption of a position of humility would question the premises on which normative lifestyles are defined. Social workers need to abandon some of the theoretical and practice creeds that do not accord with a view that different forms of knowledge and different ways of being are important for social well-being. Part of this involves understanding the nature of Aboriginal healing and not imposing Western counseling and mental health paradigms. Immersion in Indigenous cultures when the opportunity arises provides a way of learning to challenge dominant world views. An obvious example is to draw on Indigenous concepts of family and the value of extended family, including the care of the young, the old and people with disabilities and illnesses. Alongside this is a deep respect for Elders. Surprisingly, concepts of extended family and the obligations and deep care that they entail are discounted in a discourse that speaks of overcrowding in housing, neglect of children who move seamlessly between family members and harsh criticism of time away from employment to deal with family obligations.

Knowledge and interpretation of history is foundational to social work's understanding of the plight of Indigenous People today and for constructing ways to move forward. Gilbert (2001) states that social workers cannot expect to work effectively with Indigenous communities without having a sound understanding of the history of Australia and the experiences of Indigenous People with government authorities. She continues, 'Working with Aboriginal people requires soul-searching, forgiveness and preparedness to challenge our potential for racism' (p. 46). Similarly Aboriginal leader, Pat Dodson (2005) tells us that it is not possible to sustain true reconciliation without recognizing and righting past wrongs. Part of this understanding is an examination of competing views of history that traverse the dominant views and the underbelly of the oppressed. This is not an easy task as the federal government today seeks to acclaim heroic versions of history and to disclaim the importance of the history of oppression, genocide and suffering.

Alongside understandings of history is the ability to critique and analyse social policy and to keep abreast of changes and debates. Social workers need to hear what Indigenous People have to say and work together with them to try and influence changes in public policy. Social workers in public welfare may not see themselves as having either the authority or the expertise to challenge dominant policy dictates and their underpinning ideologies. Yet it is these very social workers who can see the effect of policy on those they work with and it is essential to move beyond addressing individual needs to influencing broader change.

Organizational constraints deter many social workers from speaking out and joining social movements for change. Aboriginal activism is strong in Australia and abroad and many social workers are hesitant to understand their place in fighting for Indigenous rights across the spectrum, including sovereignty and land justice that underpin the Indigenous quest for rights. Non-Indigenous social workers do not have the right to speak *for* Indigenous People, but they do have a duty to speak out against injustice in collaboration with those non-Indigenous support groups that are held in high regard by Indigenous People. Even though non-Indigenous social workers have not experienced the racism and exclusion facing Indigenous People, they can empathize with the treatment meted out as they observe its consequences. Being an advocate requires recognition that the current social arrangements are not natural and inevitable. This means that given the political will, a social order can be developed that promotes human welfare and in this quest social work cannot be politically neutral (Mullaly 1993).

Conclusion

Indigenous affairs cannot be the sole responsibility of Indigenous Peoples. Adopting an anticolonialist stance does not equate with the abrogation of responsibility by non-Indigenous social workers for the past, present and the future. Although respecting the need for Indigenous groups to 'go it alone', social workers need to be open to providing support and resources in a way that they suggest will be useful (Fraser and Briskman 2005). The transformation project of social work is by political and practical necessity the responsibility of both Indigenous and non-Indigenous Peoples working in collaboration. An acknowledgment of one's own value base, a reflective approach and an open heart are some of the essential ingredients for working towards social change. To be truly pre-colonial, social workers must question their role within the constrictions of the nation state and work with others to discard previously sacrosanct notions of professionalism, knowledge and power. Acknowledging shame about what has happened to Indigenous Peoples is a starting point. As stated by Gaita (1999), 'Shame is as necessary for the lucid acknowledgment by Australians of the wrongs the Aborigines suffered at the hands of their political ancestors, and to the wrongs they continue to suffer, as pain to mourning' (p. 92).

PART 3
Towards Culturally Relevant Social Work Practice

Chapter 7

The Development of Culturally Appropriate Social Work Practice in Sarawak, Malaysia

Ling How Kee

Ever since Western social work methods were exported into non-Western developing countries at the end of the Second World War, their relevance and appropriateness to these non-Western contexts has been questioned and debated. Two recurring themes can be identified. The first concerns the misfit between social work methods or models of practice and the nature of social problems in these developing countries (Bose 1992; Gangrade 1986; Hodge 1980; Midgley 1981; Rao 1990; Robertson 1980; Sanders 1980) and the second, the incompatibility of Western social work principles and values with non-Western cultures and philosophies (Chow 1987, 1996; Ejaz 1989, 1991; Ngan 1993; Prager 1985; Ow 1990a, 1990b, 1990c; Silavwe 1995). Cautions against professional imperialism (Midgley 1981), cultural imperialism (Hodge 1980; Ngan 1993; Prager 1985), cultural oppression (Graham 1999), professional colonization (Husband 1990; Meemeduma 1993) and professional encapsulation (Pedersen 1984; Sanders 1980) have been fervent topics in social work academic writing and conferences. Concomitantly, the last five decades have seen the significant mushrooming of writings advancing diverse approaches and the development of culturally specific models of social work practice (Devore and Schlesinger 1999; Lum 1996; Lynn *et al.* 1998; Mokuau 1991).

As a social work educator with thirteen years practice experience in my homeland of Sarawak, Malaysia, the development of culturally relevant social work strikes a chord with me. While my social work training in Australia had been a 'culture shock', on returning to Malaysia I committed myself to developing relevant social work theory, which could respond to the multicultural reality of Sarawak despite the huge discrepancies between the professional education I had received and the local sociocultural milieu. My homecoming was something of a 'reverse culture shock' for the divergent world views and cultures of my own people made the dominant social work practice frameworks seem ill-equipped to deal with this diversity and multiplicity.

In this chapter I first introduce Sarawak to provide an understanding of the context, and then discuss the challenges in developing a multicultural practice theory by highlighting the divergence between local world views and cultures and those that underpin mainstream social work theory, while emphasizing the diversity and multiplicity of cultures across and within local cultural groups. This multiplicity of cultures raises critical questions: How do we begin to develop practice theory grounded in local cultures? How do we honour commonality while embracing differences and acknowledge continuity while addressing change? It seemed to me that honouring diversity required a rethinking of social work, specifically the way in which culture is understood and conceptualized, and the intricate relationship between culture, research and ways of knowing to inform locally-based practice. Relevant social work theory development needs to begin by unravelling the epistemological base of professional social work as a cultural construction in its own right. Culturally-based methods of inquiry enable us to see the centrality of culture in regard to ways of knowing in mainstream and locally-based knowledge. I conclude with a proposed culture centric methodology for developing and researching culturally appropriate social work through the creation of a borderland, an intercultural space from which culturally relevant research and practice can emerge.

Sarawak: The context

Located in the northwestern part of Borneo and constituting one of the thirteen states of Malaysia since 1963, Sarawak has its own unique history, geography and ethnic composition. With a population of 2.2 million comprising about 35 *Bumiputra* groups (meaning Natives or literally 'prince of the earth') and non-*Bumiputra* of mostly Chinese and less frequently Indian origin, Sarawak is noted for its cultural diversity. The Native communities of Sarawak consist of the Iban (the largest group), the Bidayuh, the Malay, the Melanau and many other smaller groups, including the Kayan, the Kenyah, the Kelabit and the Penan collectively referred to as the *Orang Ulu* (the Interior People). This ethnic diversity is further accentuated by rural urban differences, and a trend towards increasing urbanization and industrialization.

Sarawak's colonial history began with the reign of three successive white Rajahs (James, Charles and Vyner Brooke) from 1841 to 1941. The 'era of Brooke' has been variously described as a mix of adventure and battles, of pioneering and entrepreneurship, of rebellion and resistance (Chew 1990; Pringle 1970; Turnbull 1989). It has, however, laid the foundation for a Western-based system of administration further strengthened when it was ceded to the British Crown in 1946 after the Japanese occupation between 1941 and 1945.

The war years (1941–45) resulted in massive disorganization, such as destitution, illness and malnutrition, and crime and delinquency prompting the then colonial government to establish the Advisory Committee for Social Welfare in 1948. This led to the formation of the Sarawak Social Welfare Council in 1950. A glimpse of the list of organizations which developed during the 1950s and 1960s, many of which still exist today, indicates their Western origin; for example, the Salvation Army Children's Home and Boys' Hostels, the Sarawak Cheshire Home, the Catholic Relief Society and the Red Crescent (Cross) Society. Other organizations that have sprung up include those involved with the care of elderly persons, outreach services for children with disabilities, and organizations in the medical welfare fields such as associations targeting tuberculosis, leprosy rehabilitation, family planning and mental health. Since the 1980s there has been a sporadic emergence of a number of self help, rights-based groups, such as the Association of the Blind, Parents of Intellectually Disabled Children's Association and Sarawak Women for Women Society.

The government social welfare department also provides an array of services, including financial aid to the poor; relief schemes to victims of natural disasters; care, protection and rehabilitation of children, elderly persons, disabled persons, homeless persons; and reformatory services for young offenders and underage girls involved in prostitution. Family and counselling services are also provided for couples experiencing marital discord and adolescent problems. In more recent years, community-based rehabilitation programmes for children with disabilities and community development projects for the rural poor and women have been introduced in line with the Malaysian National Welfare Policy (1990) aimed at promoting community development (Kandiah 1991). Prior to the establishment of the social welfare department, the administrative officers in the divisional and district offices were charged with the responsibilities of handling interpersonal and family matters, such as marital problems and adoption matters, and in many rural regions they continue to play an important role in welfare provision.

Informal forms of helping and natural social support systems have been in existence much longer than these formal services that accompanied post-Second World War colonization. In fact, helping and welfare activities are related to informal social organizations of the various ethnic groups. For example, the activities undertaken by religious and ethnic-based organizations in catering for the needs of destitute and elderly persons in the Chinese immigrant community in the early 1900s reflected the non-Western origins of self help and philanthropic organizations in China (Chin 1981; Tien 1953). The role of the village heads and community leaders in helping with problems and mediating conflicts continues to be of importance. The *bomoh*, *manang*, and *sinseh* (names for shaman, witch doctor or temple medium in Malay, Iban and Chinese respectively) are a popular source of help. Another important source is legal pluralism in which civil and criminal law, Islamic Syariah Law[1] and the *Adat* (Native customary law) function side by side. All these features of Sarawak make locally-based multicultural social work a pertinent topic for consideration!

Understanding culture

Anthropologists define culture as a distinctive way of life that is reflected in the mundane practices of everyday living (Rosaldo 1989). Culture shapes our world view; the way we relate to people, the way we communicate, the way we engage with nature, our perception of human nature, our conception of knowledge, our beliefs about what can and cannot be known and the way we view life and existence. Often, a static definition of culture is used in terms of which categories are formulated based on fixed cultural characteristics that tend to be prescriptive, limited and limiting. Based on such definitions, we have been led to believe that Western social work

---

1   Also referred to in other contexts as 'Sharia Law'.

practice theories are adaptable and applicable to non-Western cultures, that through a process of Indigenization Western social work theory can be adapted to fit the world views and cultures of local people.

Others have tried to emphasize the dynamic nature of culture. For example, Green (1982) uses the term 'transactional understanding' which affects the way we come to know, how we behave and how we interpret experience (see also Barth 1995; Keesing 1981). Conceptualizing culture in this way reminds us that it permeates our way of being in the world. Yet when social work theorists in non-Western countries propose local models, they often overlook the multicultural nature of their society alongside the heterogeneity within particular ethnic groups. Hence some argue that the heterogeneity and diversity of cultures is often not recognized nor is the changing and dynamic nature of culture acknowledged (Martinez-Brawley and Brawley 1999; Sanders 1980, 1984). They point to the diversity even within ethnic groupings, for example, the Chinese have different dialects and religions that vary in terms of their rural or urban location and thus are not culturally homogenous. Assumptions of cultural homogeneity can pose a danger when one cultural group seeks to dominate another even within cultures. Thus it is more helpful to view culture as always plural, always hybrid and always heterogeneous and to recognize that social work – itself a cultural construction – sees itself as 'being able to transcend cultural and national boundaries' (Sanders 1980: 9). For those of us committed to developing culturally relevant social work practice there is a need to explore and respond to cultural diversity and local knowledges.

Uncovering local knowledges

Research is one way in which we can uncover local knowledges and the way people think about knowledge as well their ways of knowing. From her postmodern stance, Hartman (1990a) argues that there are 'many ways of knowing' (p. 4). Culture shapes our ontological, epistemological, and value assumptions, which shape our world view and, in turn, reflects and expresses our culture. For example, the dominant (Western) research methodology is itself culture bound, rooted in a way of knowing based on a particular world view. Knowledge produced and institutionalized within a Western paradigm not only limits the uncovering of important local knowledge but has misrepresented or distorted many local cultures (Asad 1986; Clifford and Marcus 1986; Geertz 1973, 1983; Smith 1999).

The problem of language is one that confronts researchers in non-Western contexts. Concepts and theories transplanted from a Western frame of reference are inappropriate when conducting studies with people of different languages and cultures in developing countries. Concepts, such as time, modernity, family planning, self-esteem and independence are culturally-based and are either alien to or differently interpreted in different cultures (Alatas 1972; Awa 1979; Gold and Bogo 1992). When culturally-based norms are brought into a study and administered or imposed on the research participants, the findings are open to question. For example, in Sarawak the term 'social work' has no equivalent in local languages. When conducting my research with non-social workers, I decided to present social work as a 'way of helping'. This facilitated the uncovering of local knowledges and the meaning behind local help seeking patterns and practices. It enabled me to develop a definition of helping as interwoven with kinship responsibilities and obligations, the local concepts of *tolong-menolong* (mutual aid) and *gotong royong* (organized group community activities). Had I used the term 'social work', it would either not have been understood, or it would have been perceived as charity, as understood among people embedded in a colonial tradition who speak English. The value of any data would have been severely limited by this understanding of social work.

While language and culture are inextricably bound together, so are communication processes and styles. A researcher who studies a community needs to be aware of the community's communication patterns and processes. There may be issues of what can or cannot be asked, and who can ask what of whom, that must be taken into consideration when designing research methodology (Briggs 1986). For example, awareness of cultural sensitivities or taboo subjects in certain cultures resulted in my hesitancy to broach the subject of unmarried pregnancy with a community leader in a Malay Muslim community, whereas the subject was openly discussed by community leaders of Iban and Chinese backgrounds without any prompting.

A second example is that one to one, open, and direct communication, typical of research methods and social work interaction, was not the norm among some of the cultural groups in Sarawak. In some situations, indirect communication as well as the use of a 'go between' or 'mediator' may be a more appropriate way of interacting. In other situations, it is much more acceptable for participants or clients to have the information gathering or interviews conducted in a group, family or neighbourhood setting. In doing research in a village setting, it is common to conduct interviews in the open, with family members or neighbours coming and going freely. A typical experience was an interview with a woman which lasted three hours, starting with her – and her elderly mother and two young grandchildren – continuing with two neighbours, then her sister who lived a few houses away, followed by her nephew who worked in the local district office.

Third, in Western research, the researcher–participant relationship is predicated on the Western assumption of professional relationships between people being individualized and contractual. In Sarawak, relationship is not individualized, but governed by one's social position and roles in an interconnected network. The social roles expected of younger and older persons in a community partly define social interaction patterns. For example, in interviews with older community leaders and elders, I intuitively listened, allowing them to steer the direction of discussions and asked fewer questions than was necessary in interviews with younger people. This is similar to the experience of Briggs (1986) who, as an unmarried, nineteen-year-old Anglo-American youth doing research in a Mexicano community in New Mexico, found himself having to learn from the elders, and speaking only when directly addressed. Thus research interviewing in such contexts can be a very different experience than researcher directed Western interviews.

The notion of a 'contractual relationship' is alien to many non-Western cultures. I found that it was difficult for people, particularly those from rural backgrounds, to approach and relate to a 'stranger in an office'. When a social work relationship is established, it is either perceived as short-term by the clients or, if longer-term, there is an extension of friendship on the part of clients and the expectation of mutual exchange and reciprocity. Some social workers report that they feel 'less professional' and have to eliminate the professional–personal divide common in Western models. The simultaneous emphasis on relationship and professional detachment is paradoxical and out of sync in a culture that values mutuality and reciprocity.

The relationship between culture and ways of helping and knowing draws attention to the epistemological base of social work practice. Local knowledges can only be uncovered through the development of a research paradigm grounded in local world views and ways of knowing. This means social work researchers and practitioners need to break free of their 'professional encapsulation' (Pedersen 1984; Sanders 1980) and intellectual imperialism in order to uncover local ways of knowing and helping (Alatas 1972, 2000a, 2000b). Ethnographic and grounded approaches seem most suited to the development of knowledge and theory relating to local experiences. Below I discuss the local knowledge I uncovered through my research relating to help seeking patterns and help giving practices, and living in 'multicultures'.

Help seeking patterns and help giving practices

The family and extended family is generally the first source of help. This is partly because a great deal of importance is attached to the concept of *malu* or shame, not just to the person, but to their families, which contributes to people's reluctance to seek help from outside the family. This concept of *malu* is manifested in the way individualism is downplayed and self-expression is not encouraged; in fact, little importance is attached to the 'self'. Familial interdependence has implications for individualized Western social work approaches. Self control is extolled and people are expected to exercise restraint in the expression of feelings and emotions. To an outsider this may be seen as a tendency to understate or hide the seriousness of problems. The marked contrast of these cultural realities to Western social work's emphasis on freedom of choice, uniqueness of the individuals, independence, self assertion and expression of feelings underscores the importance of developing culturally appropriate social work practice approaches.

Besides family, the two main sources of help are the local helpers, specifically community leaders and traditional shamanistic helpers. The approaches of local and traditional helpers with their emphasis on collectivity, group consensus, cooperation, harmony and control of feeling, are consistent with the cultural values of the help seekers. In addition, the traditional helpers or *bomoh*, *sinseh* and *manang* (shamanistic healers) who see problems – whether 'interpersonal', 'relationship problems', 'problems related to unmet needs' or 'problems of dysfunctioning' – as related to supernatural or spiritual forces, are also popular among the local people. This poses a challenge to social work's concept of 'person-in-environment' as in this case the help seekers' perception of the environment extends beyond the physical and social. What may be interpreted by social workers as a reluctance to confront problems head on is, in fact, related to the belief in fate, *karma*, and in the 'natural' as well as the supernatural. Spiritual explanations of mental illnesses are seen as culturally acceptable (Crabtree 1999; Crabtree and Chong 1999; Razali *et al*. 1996). Often these beliefs are a means of coping with stress and adversity, and remove blame and stigma from sufferers and their families.

Living in multicultures

The help seeking and help giving experiences of local people and their diverse cultures and world views clearly demonstrate the need for a locally grounded culturally appropriate social work practice. Yet there is a need to take into account the diversity and heterogeneity which exists within as well as across cultures, and in terms of rural–urban divides and religious differences. Furthermore, a person can move between cultures and be multicultural; as a result such a person might hold divergent world views and contradictory perspectives and values. This may include individuals who synthesize different blends of traditional spirituality and formal religion; who are of mixed heritage; who converted from one religion to another; or who are influenced by different cultures within and/or outside of Sarawak. The result of this 'pluralization' of the 'life world' means that it is unlikely that a particular culture exists as a neat and discrete category in a multicultural world.

A culturally appropriate practice model, therefore, needs to be open to this multiplicity and diversity. It needs to allow for multiple understandings and ways of working with clients, including respect for their choice of helping strategies or modalities. It should be open to an individuals' interpretation of their culture rather than in accordance with prescriptive or stereotypical interpretations of ethnic or religious affiliations.

Taking the concept of culture further, social work and other ways of helping can be considered as distinctly cultural, if we define a cultural group as those 'who spend much of their time in unique contexts that foster and reward remarkably distinctive assumptions, values, beliefs and rules for behaviour' (Koegel 1992: 1). Social work is at once a Western cultural construction with a distinctive set of implicit values, a recognizable language, a body of knowledge and received traditions, and its own set of institutions and activities that maintain its professional identity (Green 1982) which entreats social workers to see *multiculturalism* not only as a way of life but also as a way of working. Every social work encounter is an intersection of different cultures; the social worker is embedded in a Western professional culture as they work with clients from a different culture. In developing culturally appropriate social work, it can be considered as a culture of helping that must not only be aware of, but also learn or draw lessons from other non-Western cultures of helping as in the case of Malaysia (Ling 2003).

Developing culturally appropriate social work through an open cultural space

Culturally appropriate social work should include an understanding of the role and significance of the family and extended family network, and a theory of human development which emphasizes the way in which an individual's sense of self evolves and is shaped not only by the family and community, but also by culture, religion and spirituality. Ethnographic methodologies enable us to ground research in local world views and cultures, and engage culture and social diversity at the community, group, family and individual level. It enables us to engage with commonalities across cultures as well as the multiplicities and differences between and within groups so that the two are mutually enriching. The social worker is guided then neither by the culture of the 'dominant' majority nor the overlooked 'minority', but by an engagement with all cultures. This enables social work to be open to what is effective within diverse cultures and helps guard against the prescriptive use of research and helping strategies. Therefore, a culture centric methodology for developing culturally appropriate social work through the creation of a borderland – an intercultural space – is proposed as the way forward.

The creation of a borderland or 'third' cultural space facilitates the application of the principle of cultural relativism without slipping into moral relativism. It points to the possibility of social workers appreciating cultural differences without being removed from the moral implications of their work. It allows for the inclusion of what are considered universal principles to be used as guiding principles for practice (Gray 1995; Taylor 1999). For example, applying the principle of cultural relativism may lead social workers to view so-called 'oppressive' practices against women as part of a culture and, therefore, to condone or even accept them as such, however, the universal principle of respecting human dignity and maintaining harmony between people opens up a way of viewing oppressive practice as detrimental to the well-being of the women which is bound up with their families. The mutual engagement of cultural relativism and universal principles can, therefore, guard against one extreme of a worker's inaction in the face of oppressive actions on the grounds that it is cultural or, at the other extreme, they run the risk of imposing their ethnocentric judgement. Social workers can respect clients' traditional beliefs and at the same time provide direction and vision.

The creation of the borderland or the 'third' cultural space is also relevant when we consider whether social work should be developed as an alternative way of professional helping, or as a way of strengthening local helping systems. Informal helping systems play an important role in people's lives in Sarawak, however, in more recent years, urbanization has seen many emerging needs and issues that could not be adequately met by informal support systems, resulting in additional burdens to the family (Crabtree 1999). There needs to be a balance between recognizing the strength of informal and existing helping systems, but not romanticizing these helping systems as a panacea for all needs, nor should social work take away the role of traditional helping networks. For example, lessons can be learned from the changing role and subjugation of village *bidan* (midwife) as a result of the Western-based health system. Social work must guard against itself co-opting other helping systems that usurp the central role played by traditional healers and support networks, relegating them to a minor supplementary role.

The potential is present to create a dynamic balance between strengthening traditional ways of helping and developing professional social work. Achieving this dynamic balance involves recognizing the strength of local helping systems, building on or further developing them while simultaneously developing social work or social services to supplement or complement the gaps in traditional systems. An example of this dynamic balance is the present social work services in the field of community-based rehabilitation and early intervention programmes.

Culturally appropriate social work can also be developed by drawing lessons and borrowing techniques from the traditional helping practices. It can incorporate some of these approaches in terms of presentation and methods of service delivery; for example, the integration of community support used in some shamanistic rituals could be a valuable lesson for social work. Social work can also learn and incorporate the *rondeng* (negotiation) process of the community leaders and the *gotong royong* (mutual aid) activities of the people. On the other hand, local helping systems are also undergoing transformation; for example, village leaders are being introduced to counselling courses and shamanistic healers are adopting the service delivery approach in response to changing help seekers' perceptions. Local helping systems are also embracing change, thus enriching and reinventing themselves. There is, therefore, potential for mutual learning and enrichment between mainstream social work and local helping approaches through the creation of a 'third' cultural space between them (Ling 2003).

Conclusion: Research and educational implications

There is a need for more research to develop grounded and contextual knowledge about help seeking and help giving in Sarawak to contribute towards the development of culturally appropriate social work practices, however, if research is to generate knowledge and construct theory to guide practice, then its relationship with culture and ways of knowing needs to be clearly understood. Social work research has to engage in different ways of thinking about knowledge and other ways of knowing in order to uncover valuable local knowledges (Barth 1995; Ling 2004, Martinez-Brawley 2000; Martinez-Brawley and Brawley 1999; Stanfield 1993, 1994). Our ensemble of knowledge and our ways of knowing can be enlarged and enriched by opening up possibilities for culturally-based epistemologies to emerge and be further developed (Asante 1987, 1988; Collins 1991; Scheurich with Young 1997).

The creation of a borderland or intercultural space implies that help seekers, people who engage in other ways of helping, local social workers, together with researchers, are all partners in the knowledge generation process, not just to generate knowledge itself, but also to uncover and develop local ways of knowing. Social work research and knowledge building should be carried out in partnership with disadvantaged people and communities in a dialogical relationship, in such a way that local cultural knowledge is embraced.

Social work education curricula in Sarawak need to incorporate local knowledge within a multicultural approach. Social work students need to develop a dialogical understanding of diversity. A continuing challenge for social work education is to develop knowledge and learning relevant to local values and cultural practices by engaging in a dialogical process of mutual enrichment while debating universals. Professional education should strive to instil in students the confidence to work with complex varieties of persons-in-situations, to dialogue with differences, to share knowledge and develop the humility and willingness to learn from others and to form collaborative relationships with clients. Their education and training needs to provide students with a sense of professionalism that is creatively tailored to the nature of the relationship between them and their clients, to the local cultural ways of interaction.

Chapter 8

The Past, the Present and the Future: The New Zealand Indigenous Experience of Social Work[1]

Wheturangi Walsh-Tapiata

Tena koutou katoa, greetings to you all, from the Land of the Long White Cloud – Aotearoa or, as most of you might know it, New Zealand. Aotearoa is the name that the Indigenous People have for our country and as the Indigenous population of that country we call ourselves the *tangata whenua* – people of the land.

In this chapter I look at how social and community work has impacted on the Indigenous People of Aotearoa. We have a saying that goes something like 'by acknowledging the past and laying down the foundations for the future, past, present and future are brought together in one space' (Marsden 1990: 5). Weaver also says that the First Nations people of North America:

> ... have a sense of existing in a time continuum with both ancestors and children of the future having relevance for everyday life. Our ancestors planned for the well-being of people who exist today and those of us who are alive now have a responsibility to ensure the well-being of native people and communities in the future (Weaver 1990: 180).

According to Maybury-Lewis (1997), as Indigenous Peoples we carry a sense of marginality, much of which has been the result of colonization by groups who have conquered peoples who are racially, ethnically or culturally different from themselves. Indigenous Peoples have therefore been marginalized as a result of conditions created by those who claim 'jurisdiction' or privilege over them by others. As Tucker (in McIntosh 2005) asserts, marginalization can find any group, 'ignored, trivialized, silenced, rendered invisible and made other' (p. 40). Many Indigenous Peoples find themselves as 'periphery dwellers, living in a liminal space where stigmatization and exclusion are part of a lived reality' (p. 40).

There are significant differences between Indigenous Peoples but it is possible nonetheless to identify shared realities, comparable patterns of development and common aspirations for the future. For many Indigenous Peoples, the journeys have been similar in that for a long time they lived in tune with their natural environment. This was then unfortunately followed by an abrupt change in direction, namely

---

1 First published in the *Social Work Review*, Summer 2004, pp. 30–37 based on a keynote speech given at the Global Social Work Conference of IASSW and IFSW held in Adelaide, October 2004 and adapted for this book.

colonization. With colonization came, 'economic reform, education, new technologies and new foodstuffs, but also dispossession, high death rates, deculturation, and disease' (Durie 2003: 183).

For social workers who work with Indigenous populations, it is critically important that they have a 'correct' understanding of the history of that Indigenous population, recognizing the impact that history has had on them, much of which is still evident today. Personal troubles cannot be separated from public issues and social workers need to understand how they have historically contributed to the colonization process, but also how they can also play key roles as agents for positive social change. Social workers should ask themselves these questions: Are you an agent of control, an agent of compliance or an agent of positive social change? Do you perpetuate oppression or attempt to overcome it? These questions might appear simple in the asking but require considerable analysis and self-reflection for social workers who find themselves working with Indigenous Peoples.

The past

Looking at the past enables us to confront the issues of today in order to build platforms for tomorrow (Durie 2003). The narratives of my ancestors tell us that some of us travelled from Hawaiki to settle in Aotearoa, while others say that we have always lived here. There are many stories about the various migrations and settlement in the new land. This was followed by the arrival of a new wave of settlers from the west which led to confrontation. They brought new technologies and home comforts, 'but as the numbers grew, and the hunger for land increased, so too did the novelty wear off' (Durie 2003: 19). Hence began a period of extreme deprivation. By 1857 the population had declined from an estimated 250,000 to around 56,000. Changes of diet and new infectious diseases, such as measles, tuberculosis and influenza contributed to a swift and relentless decline in the population as mortality rates soared. The survival of the Māori population was under threat. Alongside this, there was large-scale confiscation of millions of acres of Māori land under the guise of government policy introduced during the land wars (Orange 1987; Walker 1996). By 1900, out of nearly 27 million hectares, only 4.5 million hectares remained in Māori ownership.

Policies of the day sought to 'modernize' a 'backward' people in need of development. Land was redefined; a communal culture was converted to an individualistic one, new forms of leadership were encouraged, and education focused on removing from them their Māoriness. All of these ideas were influenced by colonization and assimilation (Department of Social Welfare 1988).

The New Zealand Herald (1874) was so convinced of the inevitability of the Māori demise that they wrote: 'The fact cannot be disguised that the natives are gradually passing away; and even if no cause should arise to accelerate their decrease, the rate at which they are now disappearing points to their extinction in an exceedingly brief period' (Durie 2003: 19–20). Statesmen of the day talked of 'smoothing the pillow of the dying race'.

To contextualize these facts from our past, Māori and other Indigenous communities often use narrative as a way of explaining their situation. In my *whanau* (family) we tell the story of my grandmother who was born in the early 1900s. She talked of being sent to school where the only language was English. For her this meant years of corporal punishment every time she spoke Māori, including having to scrub the floors with a toothbrush. Eventually she learned to speak very good English and because her parents – heavily influenced by the Church – also believed at the time that English 'was the bread and butter language', she lost the ability to speak her own language and her own dialect.

My nanny was also known in her family as a *matakite* (a person who could predict events), however, due to the Tohunga Suppression Act (1907), these practices were frowned upon and went underground, all but disappearing. Consequently this meant that she did not speak to us about her abilities until much later in her life. Sadly therefore such attributes have not been passed down through the generations.

My nanny also spoke of the loss of land when communal ownership of property moved to individual title. People lost their land, selling it to pay for rates, funeral expenses and bills, among other things. Large portions of land were also confiscated after the Land Wars and under the Public Works Act, taken to build roads and other public amenities. Land or *whenua* is seen as a life source for Māori. A person without land is lost. Legislation even attempted to eradicate small shareholders of their land holdings, but my nanny would say that while she owned even a blade of grass she would not sell because her land was her identity. Unfortunately in some areas of the country our family like many other families no longer have any land.

In defiance of predictions, the demise of Māori did not occur but the effects of colonizing policies and laws of assimilation continued to dramatically affect the Māori population. By 1936 the population had increased to 82,000 and by 1996 to 579,800 (Durie 2003). Māori now comprise approximately 14 per cent of the New Zealand population of four million. Similar to other Indigenous communities, despite a legacy of cultural loss and violence, these communities have not been eradicated (Weaver 2001).

Many of the upheavals of the nineteenth century would, however, lead to Māori becoming increasingly dependent on the state, a state that was essentially committed to policies and programmes to assimilate Māori into the prevailing systems of colonial New Zealand rather than respecting their diversity and difference. Such policies and practices have continued to the present day in an attempt to 'domesticate' Māori people and Māori culture.

Throughout this period of history social work practice (though it may not have been called this) with many of our Indigenous communities maintained and upheld the practices of the government of the day. It is little wonder that Weaver (2001) says that the image of a social worker in many First Nations communities is that of a child snatcher. This is a concept familiar to many Indigenous communities in the world. It should come as no surprise that many Indigenous Peoples are suspicious and distrustful of social workers and others associated with helping systems. Social workers must build trust with Indigenous communities before any work can be accomplished. From a structural perspective, we cannot remove ourselves from the fact that many of the social problems in our communities have roots in colonization, oppression, and internalized oppression.

> Until we are willing to look at these larger issues, we will only be putting bandages on festering wounds. This is not to say that it is not important to address problems such as poverty, violence and substance abuse, but, in order to work on these issues, we must address their fundamental causes (Weaver 2001: 185).

Social policy as it has been practised in Aotearoa New Zealand has relied excessively on the norms of the majority falling well short of incorporating Māori needs and aspirations (Durie 1998; Ihimaera 2004). Disease, alienation from the land, a changing economic climate, and a loss of political control and authority marked our history as Māori leading into the twentieth century while, more recently, urbanization and government assimilation policies have further undermined marginalized communities like that of the Māori. Such approaches have been particularly harsh on tribal structures and the fundamental social structure of the *whanau* or family. Historically the Indigenous Peoples of Aotearoa were identifiable by their *whanau* (family), *hapu* (sub-tribe) and *iwi* (tribe) and yet the impact of colonization would attempt to annihilate such structures and call them all 'Māori'.

The present

The extent of disadvantage within society is inevitably a reflection of government policies. Compared to other New Zealanders, Māori experience higher levels of unemployment, are more likely to leave school with no qualifications, have lower standards of health and housing, lower incomes, higher suicide rates, higher adolescent pregnancy rates, higher conviction rates and a higher likelihood of joining gangs (Durie 2003: 190) and this is the story about Māori people most often promulgated in the public media.

However, Durie (2003) and McIntosh (2005) support Weaver (2001) believing that it is far too easy to look at these statistics and assume that Māori and other Indigenous communities are immersed in problems, and that we need to assert a positive and empowering image that erodes such stereotypes. While such problems should not be ignored or minimized, it is important to assess the context in which they occur. For generations those in the helping professions have imposed their models of practice on those they are helping, influenced by their values and understanding of the world and, from our Indigenous communities' perspective, with minimal success. Many of these approaches have used a deficit theory approach, effectively silencing Indigenous approaches, relegating them to the periphery or bringing them out of the cupboard only for cultural celebrations (Lynn 2001).

Indigenous writers from Australia, North America, the Pacific Basin and Aotearoa all state emphatically that social work theory and practice has much to learn from peoples about the ways in which they help their own (Durie 2003; Lynn 2001; Mafile'o 2004; Weaver 2001). Mafile'o asserts that, 'if social work is to facilitate social change then it must encompass the social constructions of diverse cultural groups' (p. 240). She adds that if this were to occur then, 'ethnic minority peoples will move beyond being objects of social work and become active participants in achieving social justice' (p. 240).

Such statements are now being strongly supported by various Indigenous communities with solutions to many of their issues evolving from within their own communities. There is now recognition that Indigenous communities have their own strengths and solutions to issues that derive from within their own traditional contexts (Munford and Walsh-Tapiata 2001). Of course, colonization has ensured that, in many instances, traditional knowledge has all but been lost and so the validation of these approaches comes with considerable struggle. Strengths within Indigenous communities have enabled them to survive despite the many social problems that they are faced with (Weaver 2001).

Tino rangatirstanga (Self-determination)

Self-determination is viewed as a fundamental principle in social work but what needs to be clearly postulated here is the different understandings of self-determination from different cultural perspectives (Ewalt and Makuau 1995). While the Western perspective of self-determination in the social work context places emphasis on the ramifications of client self-determination, much of which is reflected in the literature, such an approach supports the prevailing middle-class North American ethic of individualism.

Within many Indigenous cultures, however, the emphasis of the collective perspective over the individual perspective on self-determination is paramount. Ewalt and Makuau (1995) use the case of cultures in the Pacific region where self-determination is defined by values of collective affiliation rather than by individualism. While 'the Pacific' region is incredibly diverse, it can also be acknowledged that there is a common emphasis on the group and, in terms of self-determination, this may mean fulfilling group obligations, not necessarily ridding oneself of them in this cultural context. The importance of community contributes a great deal to the well-being of the group. This is possibly why Indigenous People see themselves as primarily members of groups (for example, clans, communities and nations) rather than as individuals (Weaver 2001). When working with clients towards an aspect of self-determination as a goal, actions that are inclusive of the extended family are most desirable. Often self-determination denotes the fight for self-governance of entire communities.

Indigenous models

Indigenous models of practice are now beginning to be acknowledged within some countries as well as at an international level. South Africa, Canada, Australia and Aotearoa New Zealand, in particular, are developing models in the area of collective decision making and partnerships with families in child and family welfare, youth justice and corrections, all of which are showing some signs of success in informing and transforming social work practice as the chapters of this book show. In this sense there is recognition of cultural difference as a strength rather than a weakness, as a resource rather than a problem. There is, however, still considerable distance to go before Indigenous forms of social work practice are more fully recognized and valued as theory and practice that can inform and transform Western social work practices and not simply be relegated to the 'other' as Nimmagadda and Martell show (see Chapter 11). There is still the tendency to compare these models against Western models of practice, when potentially these models should simply be accepted for their appropriateness to certain contexts.

One effective way in which Indigenous models are being created and strengthened in Aotearoa is in the development of social services created by *iwi* (tribal) and Māori organizations. Weaver (2001) says that similar developments have been happening in North America since the 1970s. While State organizations have still been major providers of social services for Māori people, there is now a growing recognition that in order to produce positive outcomes for Māori families it is necessary to work collaboratively with tribal and Māori organizations who often have the insider networks and practices necessary to work effectively with their own people. For example, non-verbal behaviour is culturally determined and can be misconstrued by people unfamiliar to that culture. The same goes for the use of narrative as a guiding form for teaching children (Weaver 2001). Such examples are indeed strengths that derive from our cultural communities but can be overlooked by well meaning outsiders who may only see the problem and not the solutions. As Weaver puts it, 'while the extent of cultural tradition that remains varies across Native nations as well as within those nations, much still exists of these cultures once targeted for annihilation' (p. 186). As well, cultures are not static; they change and grow over time and we should see this as exciting because we are adapting to the ever changing context in which we find ourselves.

Lynn (2001) on the other hand voices some concern that while the approaches to practice have ranged from adapting Western concepts to local relationships and behaviours to building specific Indigenous practice theory from their core values, beliefs and practices, such knowledge still primarily remains as local knowledge for a particular context rather than having a wider application. She appropriately reflects that there is still some distance to travel in seeing such approaches to practice validated alongside other social work approaches. Learning about the models being developed among other Indigenous communities contributes to a critical mass which gradually leads to a wider acknowledgement of these models of practice.

Our Māori communities are now actively developing their own models of practice, with some of them being adaptable across a variety of contexts. Many of the models recognize traditional cultural practices based on *whanaungatanga* (relationship building or connectedness). Such approaches respect the person's cultural and ethnic identity, language and religious or ethical beliefs and the importance and significance to the person of his or her ties to *whanau, hapu and iwi*, all factors that contribute to a person's well-being (Ihimaera 2004). From our cultural perspective the contributions to group interests ultimately strengthen the person as well as their cultural continuity in that community. Ewalt and Makuau (1995) make similar statements from a Pacific Island perspective where they say that an essential element of their cultures is the 'affiliative nature of relationships' (p. 4). The person is a locus of shared biographies and the relationship defines the person not *vice versa*. It is therefore this connectedness and the pronounced value of group identity and cohesiveness that is a major value and something that permeates their lifestyle practices. These values cannot be emphasized enough as core components of this cultural context and a genuine understanding of this in terms of the social work practice is necessary in order to work effectively in these communities. An appreciation of these aspects can be acquired via the literature and learning at an educational institution, but only living and becoming intimately involved in these communities will give a social worker a close understanding of these perspectives. 'Knowing' the other as an Indigenous person before 'doing' is what leads to positive long caste-term social change and Lynn (2001) suggests that this can only come about by being intimately connected to that community and, in some instances, to that experience. Cultural continuity and traditions are important strengths that provide guidelines for living that have served our Indigenous community well for thousands of years. A focus on how Indigenous People help their own opens up possibilities for social work practitioners to think differently, to see the world differently and perhaps even feel differently.

Narrative

Many of our Indigenous stories have all but been erased from the landscape of social welfare work. Minimized to positions of 'myth', much of the detail of our history has been lost and yet, as oral cultures, this was our means of transferring knowledge between generations. Now, as a part of revitalizing our cultural contexts, our stories are being retold, rewritten and consequently recognized in terms of their importance as tools in the social work arena. Within the stories are traditional methods that could positively influence our social work practice. These stories need to be a recognized and respected, not misappropriated and relegated to mere myth. Lessons emerge from these stories. They contain the voices, authority and visibility that ensure Indigenous Peoples are a part of the landscape of social welfare work as participants in the dialogue about their own future (Moore, cited in Lynn 2001; see Chapter 20). Storytellers are important in our country as they are the repositories of knowledge carried through the generations. It is important, therefore, that we think creatively about how it is that we transfer knowledge.

Empowerment, like sovereignty, is inherent and an internal strength, something that cannot be given by an outside entity despite what our governments might say. It is something that only those in their local communities can collectively work toward. Nonetheless, empowerment is critical for confronting the continuing impact of colonization (Munford and Walsh-Tapiata 2001).

Current state for Māori in Aotearoa, New Zealand

Comparing Māori living standards with those of non-Māori gives some indication of the gaps between Māori and other New Zealanders. There are no surprises. For almost any indicator, such as health, education, employment, offending, home ownership and income levels, Māori performance is substantially worse. However,

Durie (2003) warns that measuring Māori progress by using *Pakeha* New Zealand as a benchmark does not really capture the dynamic state of Māori society and, therefore, the hugely significant gains that have been made. Certainly suicide rates for young Māori are high, and a large number of Māori children are brought up by single parent families. While such negative images would presume that we are in a state of crisis, the strengths that characterize *whanau* (family) in modern times are hidden. It is our skills and strengths that have allowed us to survive more than 160 years of colonization (Durie 2003).

Māori language revitalization is higher now than it has been for more than five decades. In many Māori communities there are local positive initiatives enabling Māori to have a strong sense of who they are and the positive contributions that they can make to their communities. Māori are living longer, can look forward to a standard of living which would be the envy of their parents, and many make up substantive numbers in the sporting and entertainment industries.

Of note to social work is also the increasing number of Māori who are now training to be social workers and who are insistent that their cultural reality is the foundation of any programme. Many educational institutions overtly appear to support such a focus, though some Māori still remain sceptical about the true intent of including cultural issues in any curriculum. In other words, it is one thing to teach students about how to greet in Māori and to learn a *waiata* (song), but where is the necessary critical analysis giving students an understanding of the broader structural issues at various levels, if social workers are to be true agents of change? The increasing number of *iwi* (tribe) and Māori organizations that are evolving also offers a new and vibrant contribution to social work practice in Aotearoa.

The introduction of the Social Work Registration Act (2003) in Aotearoa New Zealand offers a new set of issues for Māori social workers, many whom have worked much of their lives in their communities but who may not have a recognized social work qualification. This legislation has resulted in an influx of Māori undertaking a social work qualification with registration increasingly being seen as a requirement for social work positions or of social service contracts. A new set of challenges arises with this legislation around best practice models and standards of competency to practice with Māori clients. This legislation has also resulted in an increasing number of Māori social workers becoming members of the Aotearoa New Zealand Association of Social Work (ANZASW), though recently there have been some preliminary considerations about the development of an Indigenous Association. The question still remains, however, about whether this registration legislation will necessarily improve the plight for Māori.

Future

So what is the direction for Māori and social and community work in the future? We need to begin by having our own people define our reality, inclusive of both the strengths and challenges of our communities. Too often, others looking from the outside have made determinations about our needs and problems, failing to see the potential that is evident within. A major challenge is to understand the context in which our people live and to transform it. It is not just about surviving any more; it is about how we can be leaders of today and tomorrow. In Aotearoa this means that we, as Māori, need to reclaim our identity. I am not sure that we ever completely lost it, but the impact of colonization is such that many of us have felt lost from many aspects of our culture. One of the most obvious ways in which this reclamation is occurring is by learning our own language, ensuring that future generations are able to not only maintain the Māori language but also its various dialects. Imagine living in a nation where the language has all but been lost and to then have your children and grandchildren dreaming and talking in their sleep in their own language. The introduction of immersion education over two decades ago with Kohanga Reo and Kura Kaupapa is now producing generations of young people with a strong sense of who they are, with strong links with their families and tribal communities, and who are making positive contributions to New Zealand society. Cultural legitimacy of Māori knowledge and values are being transposed into everyday practice, and while many social workers from Aotearoa might question whether there has been substantial change in our Māori communities, I am hopeful that there is now more than a glimmer of light. Social work classrooms are starting to see a trickle of students who come from such backgrounds, and an increasing number of Māori practitioners who have a strong cultural identity are effecting changes in practice across a range of the helping professions. These approaches are not ours alone, as other Indigenous nations in other parts of the world are also reclaiming their cultures and passing them on to their children. I learned Māori as a second language but I am proud to say that my children's first language is Māori. They speak Māori exclusively to each other, their friends and connected adults, including people of our grandparents' generation who are still the repositories of our traditional knowledge. Traditional values, far from being outmoded, can be a major source of strength in contemporary times.

Such developments are, however, very fragile and can still be easily marginalized. It is important not to further devalue those whose voices have been absent. We need to continue to develop new discourses and to recognize ways in which we might celebrate our diversity while still maintaining our respective cultures. There are ways in which Maori communities can reach out to the wider world without returning to the imposition of monocultural constructs or the formulation of a universal approach, as if all New Zealanders were part of a homogenous population. If Māori aspirations materialize, then we too will not be able to ignore the realities that characterize the modern New Zealand or the global influences that impact on all peoples (Durie 2003).

We can reflect on the millennium just past, but we need to consider the new millennium that we are part of. We have real opportunities and need to maximize them. We cannot always wait for the State to catch up with us – because let's admit it, they don't want to – but we can continue to develop the grounds well of positive change in our respective communities. Our past does inform our future. What we have learned is that no matter how many challenges have been put before us we are still able to determine our own destiny and the way we live our lives. This is our present challenge and the challenge for those who will follow in our footsteps – *mo ake tonu atu* (for ever and ever).

Chapter 9

Tongan Social Work Practice

Tracie Mafile'o

Tonga is part of Oceania, a 'sea of islands' (Hau'ofa 1994) which provides a rich source of learning about the diverse nature of social work practice. Western 'professional social work' is not part of the culture of most South Pacific Island nations though there are social and community support systems based on *Pasifika*[1] knowledges and cultural practices. These culturally embedded helping systems and institutions perform what those in the West might regard as 'social work functions'. Western professional social work among Pacific Peoples emerged as a result of colonialism within Oceania and the migration of Oceanic Peoples. Thus Tongan social work, the subject of this chapter, provides an example of a dynamic interface between an Indigenous world view and a Western context, providing a cross-cultural space for building social work theory and knowledge.

'Transnational' Tongans

Historically and culturally, Pacific nations comprise migratory peoples who have navigated the ocean swells in search of development and well-being; contemporary *Pasifika* migration might be considered a continuation of this (Hau'ofa 1994). In the post-Second World War period, opportunities for economic and social advancement in other countries led to significant labour and chain migration (Connell 1987). New Zealand's economic boom in the 1950s and 1960s, with its demand for unskilled labour (Ongley 1991), facilitated the migration of Tongans to New Zealand, thereby contributing to the Tongan diaspora (Morton 1998; Morton Lee 2003). Despite restricted immigration imposed in the 1980s, the Tongan population has continued to grow primarily due to the New Zealand born Tongan population. In New Zealand today nearly 50,000 people identify as Tongan (Statistics New Zealand 2002). There are also significant numbers of Tongans in the US, particularly in San Francisco and Salt Lake City, and in Australia, in Brisbane, Sydney and Melbourne. All in all, there are more people of Tongan ethnicity living outside Tonga than there are living in Tonga itself (Morton Lee 2003).

Most Pacific families and communities can be described as transnational, that is, their operation as social units transcends across various national boundaries while also contributing to a transformation of their various locations of residence (Spoonley 2001). What is significant is that there are multidirectional flows across national

---

1 *Pasifika* refers to the Indigenous Peoples of Oceania, their cultures, and world views.

boundaries of materials, people, culture and resources that are key to the Tongan economy and to the development and well-being of families and communities (Vaden 1998). According to Bertram (1999) based on the level of resource flow into Pacific nations from family and community members living in other parts of the world, Pacific Peoples may be understood as having become globalized long before the rest of the non-OECD (Organization for Economic Cooperation and Development) world. Such practices reflect Tongan culture where values around reciprocity and extended family remain central (Evans 2001; Vaden 1998; van der Grijp 2004).

Thus from a culture based in oral traditions and local culturally embedded practices, *Pasifika* knowledge has reached far afield as an increasing number of *Pasifika* people move into and contribute to the socio-economic fabric of Western nations. However, while embracing Western culture, they simultaneously retain their culturally specific economic and social systems which base human well-being principally on reciprocal social relations within extended kinship networks.

Researching Tongan social work practice

The research on which this chapter is based involved 28 Tongan social workers in New Zealand in a qualitative exploration of Tongan values, knowledge, skills and helping processes which formed a basis of their practice primarily with Tongan, but also with non-Tongan peoples. A broad definition of 'social worker' was employed to include those who the Tongan community might perceive as 'community workers'. As such, the participants included those with (12) and without (16) a formal social work qualification, some of whom identified with other human service professions, such as counselling, nursing or pastoral ministry. Participants also included both New Zealand born (six) and Tongan born (21) social workers. The participants had practice experience in a range of fields of practice, including health, mental health, justice, child welfare, community development, alcohol and drug abuse, domestic violence, policy and administration. Data collection involved three stages: 1) an in depth individual interview; 2) four bilingual focus groups; and 3) a final individual interview. The interviews were audiotaped, transcribed, translated where required and were coded and analysed thematically.

Since Tongan 'social work' arises from a set of culturally embedded values and practices, use of a cultural metaphor seemed more appropriate than taking the modernist prescriptivist (criteria) approach frequently used to measure the professional status of Western social work. Grounding Tongan social work in the world views and day to day experiences of Tongan peoples seems appropriate since it facilitates a holistic perspective consistent with Payne's (1997) pragmatic approach. The use of metaphor draws on a Tongan way of knowing and is similar to Payne's assertion that conceptualizations ought to be guided by what is useful in practice.

The use of metaphor draws on the Tongan practice of *heliaki*, that is, to speak ironically, to say one thing and mean another (Churchward 1959: 219). Herda (1995) describes *heliaki* as the unfolding of several layers of meaning; the use of 'metaphors, plays on names or words and poetic or historical allusion' (p. 39). She adds that the complexity of *heliaki* might mean that not everyone in an audience is necessarily able to identify all the meanings and that the layers and narrative change over time. Mahina (2004) states that '*heliaki*, the equivalent of the Greek *epiphora*, can be viewed as an instrument through which qualities of two closely associated objects are exchanged in the event, where the qualities of one point to the real in the other' (p. 20).

The *Pola* metaphor and its suggestion of a 'welfare' value system

Pola is a communal activity that captures and depicts the essence of a Tongan construction of social and community work. It illustrates the four key Tongan values of *fetokoni'aki* (mutual helpfulness), *tauhi vā* (looking after relationships), *faka'apa'apa* (respect) and *'ofa* (love). *Pola* refers to a 'community fishing event' when several villages join together, mainly on the *hihifo* (western) side of Tongatapu (the main island of Tonga),[2] to maximize the fishing yield. This community event is not just about fishing for food; it also contains a festive element. All members of the village participate, including children, adults and older people, men and women alike. Each family makes an *aū* to trap the fish using a type of vine woven into a rope with the finned leaves of the coconut branch wound around it. At low tide the people go to the sea (*toafa*) and form a long line for several hundred meters across the inlet. The *aū* are then tied together and partly buried in the sand. Everyone stands and waits for high tide. As the tide comes in, the *aū* lifts from the sand and its movement and sound in the water directs the fish to remain in small depressions in the tidal flats. It is thus a highly organized event. The key to the success of the *pola* is that individuals cannot move forward to catch the fish ahead of the group or the largest fish will escape and there will not be enough fish for anyone. This is important because the *pola* is relied on to feed all who participate. Acting in self-interest would also take away from the spirit of the event. Leaders ride along the shore on horses to give the cue as to when to proceed. Fish are first taken for the *hou'eiki* (chiefs) and then the signal is given, '*Tufi!*' (gather up the fish) and village members gather fish from the small pools. The *pola* exemplifies the Tongan belief that the well-being of Tongan society depends on collective effort (Helu 1999) involving *fetokoni'aki* (mutual helpfulness), *'ofa* (love), *faka'apa'apa* (respect) and *tauhi vā* (looking after relationships). Thus these values are foundational to the Tongan social system and way of life, and they are consistent with core social work values.

Essentially Tongan social work practice aims to capture and cultivate the cultural value system that has advanced the well-being of Tongans. The *pola* then can be understood as a metaphor for the goal of Tongan social work whereby through collective effort Tongan values and social systems are reinforced to strengthen, protect and promote Tongan culture and its propensity to respond to the day to day needs of Tongan *kāinga* (extended family) even in Western contexts. The values of *fetokoni'aki* (mutual helpfulness), *'ofa* (love), *faka'apa'apa* (respect) and *tauhi vā* (looking after relationships) characterize the type of society which Tongan social

---

2   My father participated in *pola* during his childhood in the village of Te'ekiu.

and community work promotes as well as providing a guide for practice as discussed in the section which follows.

Fetokoni'aki (mutual helping)

Fetokoni'aki means 'mutuality', 'reciprocity' or 'helping and cooperating with one another' (Churchward 1959: 178) within the *kāinga* or the extended family and the community at large. One participant described his role of being the eldest male in his *kāinga*.

> *Fetokoni'aki* means, you know, supporting, caring for one another. Being the eldest, it is expected of you to ... [be a] good role model ... As the eldest, you are expected to care for the rest of the family, in every form and every way. You care for their children, care for the time of celebration. You expect to contribute the most, you expect to organize. You are expected to speak, you are expected to take control and make sure that everything is okay ... And you are supposed to have the most love, hhh ... But I find that the resource does not drain out, because that's your bank as well, the family ... When [it's] your time of need, the family will come around and then you get support as well. You play your role [and] they will do their part as well.

Historically essential for survival in a subsistence existence, *fetokoni'aki* endures in contemporary transnational Tongan communities based on the belief that more is achieved materially, socially and spiritually from collective rather than individual action. Thus *fetokoni'aki* is a 'production mechanism' in everyday community life. As explained by another participant, it means, 'I'll help you today, you help me tomorrow ... It's just the culture and custom of Tonga to help one another'. It leads to collective work for the good of 'others' as illustrated by the village rugby team in Tonga who worked at the copra boats to raise funds for rugby boots; in a spirit of *fetokoni'aki* even those who could afford their own boots worked to raise the funds to help those who could not. When individuals who are part of a group *fetokoni'aki* (help each other), the synergy of their efforts leads to both material achievement and strengthened relationships.

> ... say ten families, for example, contribute ... Little bits and pieces added ... make a richer, spiritually and financially, occasion, than one or two people [who are] really rich and have everything [can achieve] ... because it lacks the spirit and the contributions of *fetokoni'aki*.

One participant talked about the building of their new church[3] in New Zealand, the financing of which was substantially assisted with an interest free loan from another Tongan congregation in the same city.

> ... you'd be more or less paying a quarter of a million dollars just for the interest, and yet you don't have to. It's been helped out, and you build your church, and when its time for

3   Christianity is prominent among Tongans. In comparison to the total New Zealand population a high proportion of Tongans in New Zealand have a religious affiliation (Statistics New Zealand 2002).

us, you'll do ours. We give back their money, no interest, but when theirs come[s] along, there will be a time they will come and ask for some money, and then we lend them the money.

A community support worker in a social service facilitated a community garden project in which families were allocated a plot to grow home produce as a means to improve health and alleviate poverty. So successful was this project that clients of the service delivered food parcels to the agency rather than receiving them. Here *fetokoni'aki* enabled a mutual, two-way resource flow in contrast to the traditional or paternalistic charity model. Such reciprocity characterizes agency practice so that accommodations are made when clients are late for appointments. One participant stated that, from his observations, this was unlike the usual practice of non-*Pasifika* practitioners. In the spirit of *fetokoni'aki* practitioners do not expect immediate or direct personal benefits or rewards for their work. Instead the focus is on the value of sustained and ongoing reciprocal relationships that ultimately benefit the individual in the context of the collective. The value of *fetokoni'aki* is pivotal to the survival and well-being of Tongan culture within a diasporic and transnational context and to Tongan social work practice.

Faka'apa'apa (respect)

Faka'apa'apa or 'respect' is an important part of Tongan culture. The stratification and structure of Tongan society is largely determined by relations of *faka'apa'apa*, and the context specific concepts of *'eiki* (superior) and *tu'a* (inferior). Hence *faka'apa'apa* characterizes social relationships. At the top of the social hierarchy are nobles and royalty. *Kau tu'a* (commoners) show *faka'apa'apa* towards *hou'eiki* (nobles) and *kau tu'i* (royalty). A transgression of *faka'apa'apa* is seen to be a breach of *tapu* (Churchward 1959: 183) or 'social convention' and by implication both individual and collective well-being is undermined when *faka'apa'apa* is disregarded. An individual's status or rank within a given context determines to whom they *faka'apa'apa* and from whom they receive *faka'apa'apa*. Respect is therefore about knowing your status in relation to others within the Tongan social structure, as one participant noted.

> My Tongan values, as a Tongan? It's respect ... The Tongans ... are very structured at home; you have royalty, the nobles, the commoners. I know my position as a commoner. I know what is expected of me, I know my role, and I know how to move around that role. I know how to sneak around that role. I know how to survive in those situations whether it be for the church, in the village or the community.

Within the extended family, *tuofefine* (sisters or female cousins) are *'eiki* (superior) to *tuonga'ane* (brothers or male cousins) (Helu 1999).[4] As noted by James (1995), the

---

4   Helu (1999) argues that by translating *tuonga'ane* and *tuofefine* as brother and sister respectively, misunderstandings emerge as the words brother and sister are distinctive of the nuclear family, focus on sexual categories and emphasize the individual, when Tongan society is about interactions between groups of people and the extended family.

most strongly marked aspect of *Tongan relationships between siblings, especially, is concern for one another's well-being implied in the notion of faka'apa'apa* which means love and reverence but also fear and sometimes even dread. One's status may also be determined by age, so that older people generally have *'eiki* status in relation to younger (but younger sisters will always be *'eiki* in relation to their older brothers).

As regards the social worker's status in the Tongan community, in one sense, social workers are in an *'eiki* position due to their job position, education or statutory power. In another sense, they could also be *tu'a* in terms of their age or their commoner status. Importantly, though, social workers who are aware of their place within the Tongan social hierarchy are able to manoeuvre their practice in a way that honours *faka'apa'apa*. One Tongan social worker stated that, as someone who works in the community, she saw herself as a role model of living according to this principle of respect. Showing respect was as important as having a qualifying degree.

> One of the values and principles of a social worker is [respect] ... If you can't respect them, there is no use. Even though you ... are professional ... if you don't have all those principles on you ... then what is the use of getting there? ... If you ... stand and say, 'I have completed my degree and I'm a professional in this area', that means that you are above others. In doing that, others will not respect you. I must regard myself as starting from a lower rank; then this can go together with my knowledge, love, feelings, and not looking at monetary gains or anything else.

Thus *faka'apa'apa* and *feveitokai'aki* in social work practice are about negotiating one's way around social structures in a way that maintains the dignity of all involved and proceeds from a position of humility (Mafile'o 2004). This is done by taking into consideration the relations of *'eiki* and *tu'a*, which define one's superior (*'eiki*) or inferior (*tu'a*) status in relation to others.

Tongan social workers use *faka'apa'apa* in the construction of social work relationships along with the use of *matakāinga* (behaving like family) (Mafile'o, 2006) or kinship-like roles in relation to clients, thus integrating *'eiki/tu'a* roles. In this way, a young New Zealand born female social worker used *faka'apa'apa* to facilitate her anger management group work with young men. She demonstrates how by coming across 'as their sister' she drew on the *faka'apa'apa* relationship between *tuonga'ane* (brothers) and *tuofefine* (sisters) and was successfully able to engage with the young men she worked with.

> There were lots of things on the program that I implemented that were Tongan, and I guess my values and my character. A lot wasn't Tongan too traditionally, but I wouldn't call that not being Tongan. Like I sat in a forum with six guys for twelve weeks and gave anger management. That's not Tongan. But ... I came across as their sister and they respected me in that sense.

Some participants revealed how *faka'apa'apa* imposed restrictions on the boundaries of their practice, including with whom they could work. As part of her training, a female health worker, for instance, was required to give a talk on reproductive health to a group of Tongan men. She discussed how she was uncomfortable with this expectation and was not able to talk in depth as this was an inappropriate expectation given the value of *faka'apa'apa* that was shared by both herself as a worker and the men's group. Another participant highlighted how the Family Group Conference model prescribed within the Children, Young Persons and Their Families Act (Government of New Zealand 1989) raised issues for practice with Tongan families if sexual abuse was being discussed. In such cases, it was more appropriate to hold separate discussions or to conduct the meetings in particular ways as it was unlikely that aunts and uncles of the child, who related as *tuonga'ane* and *tuofefine*, would attend the meeting if the content were *tapu*, in other words, offensive in terms of *faka'apa'apa*. Great care needs to be taken in regards to meeting preparation and facilitation to ensure issues are discussed in a manner that engages all family members.

In a very practical sense *faka'apa'apa* is also shown by dress and social manners.

> Never wear a miniskirt when you know you are going to see a Tongan family, hhh … For me, I plan when I go and see a Tongan family. I don't wear long jeans, long pants. I wear long skirty looking things … a long dress. For example, this is really short sleeved. I would always, no matter how hot I was … wear my jacket because it's short sleeved. So it's like respect for them as well …

All cultures have social conventions regarding the way people dress hence this is important when working cross-culturally. Thus, says Egan:

> While comments about attire may appear 'old hat', sexist and possibly not relevant to this new millennium, these considerations are part of being sensitive to the differing cultural milieus in which we practice. How we dress conveys respect and power. It can impact on the way we are able, or not able to engage with clients, especially during the first meeting (Egan 2004: 80).

Notions of *faka'apa'apa* or *feveitokai'aki* arise from within a Tongan world view and gain meaning from within Tongan social kinship structures. In social and community work settings *faka'apa'apa* depicts a way of relating and defining relationships.

'Ofa (love)

Derivatives of *'ofa* (love) include *loto'ofa*, which translates as 'kind-hearted, of a kind or loving disposition' (Churchward 1959: 305), *'ofa fakatonga* (Tongan heart), and *fe'ofo'ofani* (to be friendly with one another). Kavaliku (1961) concluded that *'ofa* is the philosophy underpinning Tongan society. Tongan behaviours, customs, and ceremonies are often explained in terms of *'ofa* as one participant explained.

> I think it is important that you have a love for people … For example, if someone has got no money and they're on the unemployment I don't charge them to help them get their residency. They get their residency. If they're working, I give them a nominal fee, $100 or $200 depending on how many things I have to do and how much time I spend. It's never in proportion to what it should be.

Another stated:

> *Loto'ofa* means … not just to look at yourself, what you get out of it … Often my family … made an extra dollar to do something that's nice, but there was a family there that needed it more. *Loto'ofa* is, to me, giving it to that family that needs it, [rather] than giving an extra luxury to my family … It's an unselfish giving of one's self, possession[s], time, everything, and never thinking that I'm going to get anything good out of it.

The proverb *'Tonga mo'unga ki he loto'* (Tonga's mountain is in their heart) highlights that we make courageous decisions with our hearts. *'Ofa*, however, is more than feeling and emotion. Rather it is similar to the Christian notion of 'charity' and implies 'self sacrifice' for the benefit or good of another, or other centeredness.

Within social work practice the value of *'ofa* (love) infers a compassionate attitude and selfless action. Social work is then seen as a suitable career for one participant because she was said to be a *ta'ahine 'ofa*, that is, a young woman who showed love towards her family and community. Another participant recalled how *'ofa* determined the way in which she provided support to a younger woman who was being held in custody for a stabbing.

> I was in … the jail for eight hours with one of the clients. They said, 'What about your safety? … Aren't you scared?' I said, 'No'. I said to them, 'If you go there because you really love them, they won't mind because they can tell the feeling'. … if you don't have the feeling you can't … go inside, [its] no place for you. Here is … your mind together with your heart and then you can do the work properly … If not, you just come here to work for money.

For Tongan social workers, *'ofa* meant that their practice was not about money (income).

> The more successful social workers are the ones who can convince the people that you are not doing it for a job; you're doing it because of your personal passions … It's something that you … really love to do and it's not money … The people in the helping professions, I believe that they are people who have a genuine love for people.

Tongan social workers referred to *'ofa fakatonga* (Tongan heart) as fundamental to their practice. As one participant put it, 'I think it's just my Tongan heart … I just did it from my heart. I think that's another thing that is Tongan'. Another noted that *'ofa fakatonga* (Tongan heart) was the principle underlying her choice to help clients with transport if she were aware that this would enable them to get to important appointments. Thus she said while it 'is not in my contract to take people to doctors and things like that … because of the Tongan heart … I've got, I can do it. As long as I have the time, I can do it'. One participant said that she would show *'ofa* in her practice even if it were not part of agency policy. Another acknowledged that while *'ofa* might not be perceived as good social work practice, it remained an important aspect of Tongan culture and helping practice.

> I have to actually get quite involved emotionally otherwise I don't feel like I'm doing justice to the people that I am trying to help. So that would be very Tongan … As

Polynesians we have a real depth of feelings for other people that I'm sure is just a part of our upbringing that we can't separate when it comes time to perform in a profession. So *'ofa fakatonga* would be something that would be obviously a part of how I operate.

In short *'ofa* is a Tongan concept that implies selflessness, use of feelings, commitment and charitable action.

Tauhi va (Nurturing relationships)

Tauhi vā refers to maintaining or nurturing relationships. *Tauhi* means 'to take care of, keep safe and look after' and *vā* literally refers to the 'intervening space' between people. Therefore, *tauhi vā* refers to looking after the space between people, that is, the relationship. Tongans are enmeshed in a matrix of multiple and complex relationships, especially within the extended family system, and there are strict principles to guide interpersonal relationships and social well-being.

Mahina (1993, 2004) notes that notions of *vā* (space) and *tā* (time) are central organizing concepts in Tongan culture, language, art and history. Ka'ili (2005) has demonstrated that *tauhi vā,* the nurturing of socio-spatial ties, provides a framework within which to understand Tongan transnationality. Based on his research and experience with Tongans in the US, Ka'ili shows how *tauhi vā* occurs among Tongans in the form of church membership, genealogy, market dealings and the sharing of food. He theorizes that 'vā is creatively organized by Tongans to construct connecting spaces within the "alienated" spaces of capitalism' (Ka'ili 2005: 112). Mila-Schaaf (2006) proposes a *vā*-centred Pacific approach to social work in which *vā,* as a socio-spatial concept, offers a code of conduct and a pathway to healing. She explains that *vā* is the space that 'relates' rather than 'separates'. She likens it to a garden which if tended is fruitful and if neglected is 'barren and unsafe' (Mila-Schaaf 2006: 10).

The value of nurturing and looking after or attending to relationships (*tauhi vā*) is important for Tongan well-being and is central to effective Tongan social work practice where the emphasis is on *maintaining* relationships. Thus the notion of 'termination' or the prescription of a definite ending phase in relationships common in social work practice is alien to Tongan culture. In Tongan social work, the nature of the relationship may change from being one of 'regular contact for a specific purpose' to an ongoing relationship with a different purpose. In other words, relationships are cemented rather than ended. It just means that when one aspect of the social work process has come to a conclusion, another follows. In essence, relationships are ongoing and nurtured (or fed). Accountability towards clients is an important Tongan ethic. Within Aotearoa New Zealand, Tongan *kāinga* and community may not be in close geographical proximity, but Tongan transnationalism means that close community networks remain an ever-present reality. It is within this reality that *tauhi vā* (looking after relationships) becomes an important Tongan social work concept. Thus Ife's (2002) community development approach, wherein the worker is 'internal' and thus available to the community, is more consistent with Tongan practice.

A Tongan centred framework: Streams and mainstream

The Tongan values of *fetokoni'aki* (mutual helping), *faka'apa'apa* (respect), *'ofa* (love), and *tauhi vā* (nurturing relationships) are core to Tongan social work practice. The metaphor of the *pola*, or community fishing practice outlined at the outset, provides a picture of a Tongan centred approach to social work. The *pola* depicts a system of values for human relations based on collectivism and collaboration. In practice, when Tongan communities uphold and live out these values, wherever they are located, a Tongan system of welfare and a particular construction of social work are perpetuated. When Tongans operate within formal, paid, professional social work positions, they draw from values, skills, knowledge and processes that are embedded within this cultural value system; they draw from a Tongan world view.

One might see this Tongan centred approach as a 'stream' of social work which contributes to the 'mainstream'. Clearly, there are shared values in Tongan and New Zealand or Western culture, such as respect, but it is important to recognize that these can be claimed and framed from a Tongan point of view and contribute to a specific Tongan construction of social work. While *fetokoni'aki* (mutual helping), for instance, resonates with collectivist principles which are central to community development in Australia and New Zealand (Ife 2002; Kenny 1994; Munford and Walsh-Tapiata 2000), this is not the dominant mode of social work practice in these contexts. Nevertheless, social development theory and community development as a method of practice are particularly suited to Tongan and other cultures affected by the historical and social consequences of colonialism (Kaseke 2001; Mafile'o 2005). In post-colonial contexts, Indigenous Peoples are often the most disadvantaged part of the population. In such contexts, *fetokoni'aki* holds particular meaning for Tongan populations and practitioners. While respect is seen as a universal social work value, along with social justice and tolerance of diversity, the particular meanings associated with *faka'apa'apa* (respect), for example, the *'eiki/tu'a* distinctions and *tapu* between brothers and sisters, bring about a specific Tongan understanding of respect that is then transferred into, and underpins, culturally appropriate professional social service practice.

Thus Tongan centered social work highlights three lessons for 'mainstream' social work or social work in non-Tongan contexts. First, Tongan ethnicity and culture is the foundation of the Tongan approach; it explicitly sees social work as a culturally embedded activity. A Tongan construction of social work, therefore, destabilizes assumed and dominant Western constructions of social work where the ethnic and cultural foundations of social work theories and models are not always acknowledged or made explicit. Tongan social work emerges from within a Tongan world view – both in its conceptualization and its practice – and it thus embodies alternatives for mainstream social work development. The challenge for social work internationally is to at once validate and be transformed by the contributions of 'Indigenous' or culturally relevant contributions to the field (Graham 1999, 2002).

Second, cultural diversity within social work cannot be adequately accounted for solely within national contexts, particularly if we take globalization to be an important phenomenon for social analysis and for the social work profession (Dominelli 2004; Pieterse 2004). This discussion illustrates that location is not synonymous with culture.

Tongan social work cannot be captured by merely understanding 'Tonganness' in the Kingdom of Tonga. Ironically, it is Tongan transnationalism and the existence of a Tongan diaspora that has given rise to the very question of what constitutes a Tongan construction of social work. This shows that cultural relevance is a domain of resistance to social work's colonizing or universalizing leanings (Gray 2005). Theorizing must capture the tension between our increasing interconnectedness and our need to maintain distinctiveness. It is a tension that, if grappled with, enables us to respond appropriately to various local and cultural contexts. I contend that the only appropriate route to identifying universals – that is connections – is via an articulation of cultural specifics and not a dismissal of them. Similarly, the purpose for any concern with universals must be the realization of justice and prosperity for diverse groups on their own terms.

Finally, the synergistic interaction of diverse cultural systems becomes a focal point in notions like 'Tongan social work' that exemplify the interface between Indigenous Tongan and other cultural or Western knowledges. Qalo proposes that:

> We must fashion our cognitive cultural crafts to ride the wave of globalization surfing the tunnel, the crest or suffer the mauling of the waves on corals that could end our existence. In doing so we must interface our indigenous and the expanding global knowledge ... to get the best ride (Qalo 2004: 8).

Indeed, cultural constructions like Tongan social work create innovative waves or 'streams' where long existent diverse local cultural knowledges are brought to the attention of the 'mainstream'. Important to such innovation, however, is that Western and other cultural knowledges, rather than being imposed from outside – in claims of 'universal' or 'global' social work – might be incorporated if they were deemed culturally appropriate via negotiation within particular local cultures. In the process herein described, Tongan knowledge occupies a central position and the weaving of other knowledges into Tongan practice was negotiated from *within* Tongan sensibilities.

A Tongan centred framework for social work contains themes that are both familiar to 'mainstream' social work and those which bring in new streams of thought and action. Tongan centred practice, represented by the *pola*, gives priority to collectivist philosophies that are embedded in the social work tradition. Yet for Tongan social workers, collectivist philosophy and values underpin practice that is firmly rooted within a Tongan cosmology and world view. Our concern with culture in social work is challenged to go beyond a concern to deal appropriately with clients from diverse cultural groups within Western contexts. Rather, our concern should extend to transform the very roots of our constructions of social work knowledge, theories, and models by including diverse Indigenous and cultural foundations in the development of social work more generally, that is, the 'mainstream' is transformed.

Chapter 10

Critical Reflections on an Aboriginal Approach to Helping

Michael Anthony Hart

The *mino*-pimatisiwin – pronounced mino pi maa ti si win – Aboriginal approach to helping was initially developed in 1997 as part of my Master's thesis (Hart 1997). It was first published in 1999 in *The Native Social Work Journal: Nishnaabe Kinoomaadwin Naamaadwin* and later as a chapter in an introductory social work text by Tuula Heinonen and Len Spearman (2001) entitled *Problem Solving and Beyond*. More recently, I wrote the most thorough outline of the approach as the basis of a book entitled *Seeking Mino-pimatisiwin: An Aboriginal Approach to Helping* (Hart 2002). The approach has changed little throughout this period. While I welcomed critical feedback and read reviews, I only received positive commentary that provided no suggested considerations to develop the approach further. As such, I have spent a significant amount of time reflecting on this approach on my own.

During this time of critical reflection, I have found that the changes that I have undertaken in the way in which I present my ideas have brought out some points I want to raise in relation to this Aboriginal approach. More specifically, I have found myself challenged by the cautious manner in which I tend to operate. Being an individual who has faced oppression, specifically colonial oppression in many forms, I have found that when I am clearly outnumbered or overpowered I would rock the boat warily, introducing ideas selectively and cautiously. It was in this manner that I *tentatively* introduced my 'Aboriginal Approach to Helping' in 1997, however, while I remain at risk of facing further oppression, I also recognize the need to speak out loudly, directly and of course judiciously. I am thankful to Indigenous writers like Taiaiake Alfred, Marie Battiste, Gregory Cajete and Linda Tuhiwai Smith, to name a few, who speak in a manner worthy of emulation. I am also thankful to some dear colleagues, including Lorne Clearsky, Bob Mullaly and Susan Strega, who have encouraged and supported me in voicing my more critical opinions. By opening myself up and putting my ideas in the public domain, more precisely, by standing up for what I believe in, I am ever mindful of the particular context in which my ideas arise, the debt I owe to my people and my responsibility as an Indigenous person.

When I wrote my thesis, I spoke briefly about colonial oppression, although I was well aware of its disastrous effects and had been teaching about colonization since 1993. However, as I reviewed my initial writing, I realized that, to some extent, I had tried to compensate for the apolitical nature of mainstream social work approaches, such as the ecological systems model, and had given little attention to colonial oppression and the politics of disadvantage. I had done this despite my knowledge of the reality of Indigenous Peoples who continue to face oppression and in spite of knowing that colonialism is not dead or receding but alive and kicking and growing in new forms. Whether stemming from Spanish, British, French, American or Canadian colonialism, many Indigenous People of Turtle Island, in colonial words North America, still face the same oppressive issues as they have for the past several hundred years. Always someone else is determining our lives, most often to our people's detriment. Whether these people are colonialists or settlers of several generations matters little for us, the people oppressed. Whether we speak about the new imperial order (Stewart-Harrawira 2005) or the ongoing internal colonialism faced by Fourth World Nations (Manual and Posluns 1974), we are discussing the same overt and covert oppression of Indigenous Peoples and our ideas and practices.

This context of colonialism and imperialism, and Indigenous resistance to such forces is the critical lens through which I have been reviewing this Aboriginal approach to helping. I believe it is important that the approach be seen in light of, and as a contribution to, Indigenous resistance to ongoing colonialism. These ongoing events are giving rise to a 'radical Indigenism' and anticolonial social work. To reaffirm this Aboriginal approach of Indigenism and anticolonialism, I reflect on the *mino-pimatisiwin* Aboriginal approach and its roots in an Indigenous world view, particularly in the way in which the Indigenous People of Turtle Island view their world.

Critical reflection

In my original work, I had begun by reviewing material on Indigenous world views and developing my approach both from the Indigenous literature and by speaking to Indigenous People directly. I collected and compared information from several Indigenous People using the Indigenous practice of the 'sharing circle' and found remarkable similarities in the data thus collected. However, as these people were all from a small territory in central Turtle Island, I thought that further confirmation of the *mino-pimatisiwin* Aboriginal approach was needed. In the following section, I seek further grounding for this approach in the Indigenous social science literature and provide an overview of Indigenous world views. Further, I highlight aspects of the *mino-pimatisiwin* approach before reflecting on its synergy with these Indigenous world views and its implications in the present colonial context.

World views

The concept of world views is a translation of the German concept *weltanschauung*. Many people from various perspectives have defined it in various ways. Sue and Sue (2003), in writing on culturally diverse psychology, defined a world view as the way in which 'a person perceives his or her relationship to the world (nature, institutions, other people, etc)' (p. 267). From a philosophical perspective, Redfield (cited in Gill 2002) gave us this definition:

> That outlook upon the universe that is characteristic of a people ... a worldview differs
> from culture, ethos, mode of thought, and national character. It is the picture the members
> of a society have of the properties and characters upon their stage of action. Worldview
> attends especially to the way a man [*sic*] in a particular society sees himself [*sic*] in relation
> to all else. It is the properties of existence as distinguished from and related to the self. It
> is in short, a man's [*sic*] idea of the universe (p. 15).

In his writing about Native American world views, Gill (2002) noted that the concept
of 'world view' is used in anthropology, philosophy, specifically in metaphysics and
in religious 'doctrine', to mean 'belief systems' or 'conceptual frameworks'. Simply
put, he noted that world views indicate the way in which particular people in particular
cultures understand the world in which they find themselves. The implication is that
we are defined by, and embedded in, our culture, which moulds our world views and
which, in turn, determines the way in which we make sense of the world. Thus in
relation to multicultural counselling and psychotherapy, Ivey, D'Andrea, Bradford
Ivey and Simek-Morgan (2002) suggested that world views reflect the ways in which
'individuals construct meaning in the world' (p. 4).

Our world views reflect our understanding of the world, our ideas about the
universe, our perceptions of our relationship to the world and ways in which we
construct meaning (Olsen *et al*. 1992). Sue and Sue (2003) suggested that individual
world views comprise a person's attitudes, values, opinions and concepts, and affect
the way in which individuals think, define events and make decisions. Since people
behave in keeping with the way in which they perceive and evaluate situations based
on their world views, they make decisions and take appropriate action based on
such appraisals. Ivey *et al*. (2002) emphasized that world views include the various
beliefs, values and biases individuals develop as a result of *cultural* conditioning.
Olsen *et al*. (1992) noted that they are composed of our beliefs, belief systems and
social values. They defined belief as, 'a specific idea about some aspect of life that
its holders are convinced is true, regardless of any disconfirming evidence' (p. 14);
belief system as, 'a set of interrelated beliefs dealing with a broad social condition
or type of activity' (p. 15); and social value as that which society discerns as 'good
and bad, or desirable and undesirable, in social life' (p. 16). Beliefs are the building
blocks of world views and beliefs systems are their central framework. A world view
contains countless beliefs and belief systems that are interrelated, unrelated, and
even contradict one another and people work hard to make them congruent. Social
values are tightly linked to beliefs and belief systems in that beliefs are expressions
of how people think things are, while social values are expressions of how people
think things should be, based on their socialization.

From their sociological perspective, Olsen *et al*. (1992) highlighted that world
views are 'mental lenses' formed by habituated or entrenched ways of perceiving the
world. As such they are cognitive, perceptual and affective maps developed through
socialization, which determine the way people make sense of the social and cultural
landscape and the opportunities available for the goals they seek. From this point of
view, they are all-encompassing and have a pervasive influence. People do not easily
let go of their world views even when there are discrepancies between their world
views and observed events, or inconsistencies in their beliefs and values within their

particular world view. More often than not, we are unconscious of our world views, unless we deliberately reflect on them; we uncritically take them for granted in our everyday interactions. The way we view the world rarely alters in any significant way, though world views can, through ongoing reflection and awareness, slowly change over time.

Olsen *et al.* (1992) noted that in any society there is a dominant world view that is held by most members of that society, even though most societies today comprise diverse cultures. A society normally establishes culturally accepted definitions of social reality and, in turn, the dominant world view is constantly reinforced by the majority culture of that society even though alternative world views do exist. Thus an essential question relating to social justice is the way in which societies deal with minority interests.

The notion of world view is helpful in intercultural dialogue. Indeed, Bishop, Higgins, Casella and Contos (2002) believed that 'understanding worldviews of both the targeted community and ourselves is imperative if we are going to do more good than harm' (p. 611). Sue and Sue (2003) believed that 'it is very possible for individuals from different cultural groups to be more similar in world views than those from the same culture' (p. 287). Individuals are not necessarily caught within one world view, but can adapt and use behaviours associated with other world views (Sue and Sue 2003).

However, considering that the Western individualistic world view dominates the planet (Clark 1998) and that 'any analysis of social behaviour is ultimately shaped by the *weltanschauung* (world view) and basic culture postulates about the nature of human and his/her place in the world and society' (Sinha 1998: 18), I believe work with Indigenous Peoples often requires us to act against the dominant individualistic world view found in social work internationally, particularly on Turtle Island. This is particularly evident when one considers the point that Western and Indigenous world views differ fundamentally and might even be conflicting. The former extols individualism and the latter collectivism (Williams 2003) where there are strong regulatory norms within Indigenous culture, which encourage respectful individualism, as we shall see.

World views of the Indigenous Peoples of Turtle Island

Before discussing the world views of Indigenous Peoples, particularly the Indigenous People of Turtle Island, attention needs to be drawn to the fact that several terms other than 'Indigenous' are used here. Self-identification, or what we call ourselves, is particularly relevant in this context. While there is no *one* Indigenous world view, there are many similarities and overlaps between Indigenous world views from different societies to the extent that there appear to be more commonalities than differences among Indigenous world views (Gill 2002; Rice 2005). However, using Olsen *et al.*'s (1992) notion of 'belief system', one could conclude that overall in Indigenous Peoples' world views collectivism is valued over individualism, and this collectivist 'belief system' includes Indigenous Peoples' beliefs – building blocks – about harmony with nature; a present time orientation; a collateral relational orientation that includes kin and extended family; an active orientation to 'being' and 'being in becoming' where attainment of inner fulfilment and serenity with one's place in the community and the universe is the focus; and the 'goodness' of human nature (Sue and Sue 2003). Sue and Sue noted that while it is difficult to ascribe a set of values that encompass all American Indians' world views, there were several discernible general values, including sharing, cooperation, non-interference and observation, a present orientation, a strong focus on nonverbal communication and a spiritual focus where the spirit is interconnected with the body and mind. Rice (2005) added respect, reciprocity, sharing, balance and harmony. Little Bear (2000) identified wholeness as a key value from which several others emerge, including strength, sharing, honesty and kindness, and Weaver (1997) stresses community.

Gill (2002) noted that a Native American world view of the cosmos involves a vertical layering of realms and horizontal expansions related to the cardinal directions – north, south, east and west. At the centre of the vertical and horizontal dimensions stands the space of the community where 'the people' live anchored in the world. This 'horizontalism' is also evident in understandings of time that connect to kinship and clan structures where temporal evolutions of life within the family and community from birth to death are focused on through regulations of rites of passage and family and community rituals. Similarly, ceremonies are very important to Native Americans not only as a means for supporting the relationship between family and community members, but also for participating in the patterns and processes of the world around them. Most importantly, in this collectivist world view, the welfare of the individual is intricately bound to the well-being of the community and its relationship with the more than human world. Thus the notion of 'all my relations' (Francis 2000; Little Bear 1998), which denotes that everything is connected, and thus the symbol of the 'circle' as illustrative not only of connection but also of life's cyclical nature always moving towards harmony and balance. Balance between mind, body, spirit and heart is essential to individual and community well-being. It is implicit in Native Peoples' non-dualistic inclusive 'both-and' rather than 'either/ or' thinking. Indigenous People view the cosmos as being in constant motion or flux, where everything is forever changing, combining and recombining. Many of us believe that most everything is or may be animate, with spirit, including such entities as trees and rocks. As Leroy Little Bear (1998) observes, 'if everything has spirit, then everything is capable of relating. In the Native view, all of creation is interrelated' (p. 18). McKenzie and Morrissette (2003) explain that the Aboriginal world view emerges from people's close relationship to the environment and the six metaphysical beliefs that shape this relationship.

> All things exist according to the principle of survival; the act of survival pulses with the natural energy and cycles of the earth, this energy is part of some grand design; all things have a role to perform to ensure balance and harmony and the overall well-being of life; all things are an extension of the grand design, and, as such, contain the same essence as the source from which it flows ... and this essence is understood as 'spirit', which links all things to each other and to Creation (p. 259).

Rice (2005) notes that many Aboriginal people believe that there are various realms of existence that interconnect with times and special places where spiritual energies are present in the universe, in the human and more than human world. Thus people's spiritual ties with the cosmos. Similarly, Aboriginal people see the world holistically through these ties. People have relationships with the earth world, the plants, the animals, other people and the environment as well as with the spirits and 'sky world'. Aboriginal 'ways of doing' are guided by moral principles embedded within these spiritual constructs and expressed in individual and community action. This 'is crucial to understanding Aboriginal cultures as these spiritual beliefs promote behaviours [*sic*] within society that maintain stability, harmony, and balance' (Rice 2005: 73).

In the following section, I further develop three key characteristics that I see as pivotal to this *relational* world view and to extend the Aboriginal approach I developed, namely, respectful individualism, communalism and spirituality.

Extending an Aboriginal approach to helping with a relational world view

From the brief overview of Indigenous world views, it is evident that respectful individualism, communalism and spirituality are core features of the ways Indigenous Peoples of Turtle Island live. I suggest that these concepts are also central to the Aboriginal approach to helping I outlined (Hart 1997, 1999, 2002, 2006). This Aboriginal approach to helping is based on the 'medicine wheel', an ancient symbol of the universe that reflects the cosmic order and unity of all things, variously interpreted by Aboriginal people from different societies. Generally it symbolizes wholeness, harmony and balance, nurturing relationships, growth, healing, and *mino-pimatisiwin* – the goal of the good life – as well as respect, sharing and spirituality. Briefly:

- The concept of *wholeness* is about the incorporation of all aspects of life and the giving of attention and energy to each aspect within ourselves and the universe around us.
- *Balance* reflects the dynamic nature of relationships wherein we give attention to each aspect of the whole in a manner where one aspect is not focused on to the detriment of other parts.
- All aspects of the whole, including the more than world, are related and these *relationships* require attention and *nurturing*; when we give energy to these relationships we nurture the connections between them. Nurturing these connects leads to health while disconnection leads to *dis*ease.
- *Harmony* is ultimately a process involving all entities fulfilling their obligations to each another and to themselves.
- *Growth* is a life long process that involves developing aspects of oneself, such as the body, mind, heart and spirit, in a harmonious manner.
- *Healing* is a daily practice orientated to the restoration of wholeness, balance, relationships and harmony. It is not only focused on illness, but on disconnections, imbalances and disharmony.
- *Mino-pimatisiwin* is the good life, or life in the fullest, healthiest sense. *Mino-pimatisiwin* is the goal of growth and healing and includes efforts by

individuals, families, communities and people in general, in fact, all living forms, including the more than human world.

Grounded in these central ideas are the core values of the *mino-pimatisiwin* approach:

- *Respect* or the showing of honour, esteem, deference and courtesy to all, and not imposing our views on others.
- *Sharing*, including the sharing of all we have to share, even knowledge and life experiences, which show that everyone is important and helps develop relationships.
- *Spirituality* is the recognition that there is a non-physical world. It is all-encompassing in Aboriginal life and is respected in all interactions, including this helping approach, and is demonstrated through meditation, prayer and ceremonies that guide good conduct.

These core values mould the helping approach wherein people are seen as *inherently good* and where growth towards *mino-pimatisiwin* – the good life – means overcoming negative attitudes and behaviours and involves a connection to something greater than self; to those who have lived before, to other life forms, to nature and to the broader community. This is the route to the attainment of inner fulfilment and serenity with one's place in a community and broader universe of which Sue and Sue (2003) speak. People are first and foremost *social beings*; helping relationships focus on the person or people being helped, and on the helping relationship itself. Those offering help are not experts but speak from the heart, drawing honestly on their personal emotional experience and intuition. The helping process is a shared experience moulded by the life experience of the person seeking help as well as the person offering help and the helping process within this broader understanding of the world.

Respectful individualism

Respectful individualism captures the *relational* values of Aboriginal culture and the spiritual, healing aspects of helping relationships. Respectful individualism allows individuals to enjoy freedom of self expression and to ensure that 'the individual takes into consideration and acts on the needs of the community, and does not act on the basis of selfish interest alone, so the community is willing to grant a given individual great leeway in personal expression' (Gross 2003: 129). Respectful individualism recognizes and supports individual growth and healing while giving individuals leeway to determine what that means for them. People seeking help are supported to address their concerns and to find their direction in life. Helpers offer thoughts, model options and share stories relatable to the people seeking help. In situations in which people are putting others at risk of harm or imposing their will on others and trying to control them, helpers work to give them a sense of their individual responsibility; a respectful individualism implies that individual responsibility is everyone's collective responsibility rather than individuals being free to determine and control their own lives without thought for others. The notion of self determination is more often used in relation to Indigenous People's right to self governance as a nation. At the individual level, respect means we show honour, esteem, deference and courtesy to all and that we accept our central responsibility in all relationships, to nurture people's potential for growth and to help them find meaning and belonging (spirituality) through respectful individualism.

Communalism

Communalism is an orientation towards sharing and doing for one another by all members of a community. As Morrisseau (1998) says, 'I speak of *community* as if it were a living entity, and rightly so, for a community has a life of its own. It is made up of many individuals tied together through a collective desire to live in a type of harmony' (p. 48). Aboriginal epistemology derives from individuals reaching into their inner being to tap into the life force to gain insight and direction *for the benefit of the community* (Ermine 1995). This process, referred to as *mamatawisiwin*, is supported by community. Indeed, many Indigenous nations have developed the means, in other words ceremonies, which facilitate this process. This Aboriginal approach recognizes that all entities, including people, are connected as part of a single whole and the need to balance each of the parts within the whole. Balance implies that each part of the whole requires attention in a manner where one part is not focused on to the detriment of the other parts. When all entities are fulfilling their obligations in this manner, harmony occurs. Indeed, all relationships need to be nurtured, as connections between people lead to health. One of the ways we nurture relationships is by sharing. These fundamental concepts of wholeness, balance, harmony and relationships, and the value of sharing all, sit at the heart of communalism.

Spirituality

Spirituality, as distinct from religion, is a defining feature of Indigenous ways of life and concerns the relationships between people and the land and their surrounding environment as well as between one another and the self. It is a way of being in the world. Spirituality is central to an Aboriginal approach to helping and distinguishes it from Western social work where it is seen as marginal and thus as less important than psychological, behavioural, cognitive, social, emotional and other factors. By way of contrast, 'the Indian world can be said to consist of two basic experiential dimensions which, taken together, provide a sufficient means of making sense of the world. These two concepts [a]re place and power, perhaps better defined as spiritual power or life force' (Deloria 1991: 10). Spirituality is implicit in all aspects of Indigenous life, including our ontologies, epistemologies and axiologies (Deloria 1991; Ermine 1995; Garroutte 2003); our social, political and economic interactions (Alfred 2005; Cajete 1994; Cardinal and Hilderbrandt 2000; Wastesicoot 2004); and our personal health and development (Anderson 2000; Long and Fox 1996;

McPherson and Rabb 1993; Young *et al.* 1989). It truly encompasses our world view and is a pillar to this Aboriginal approach to helping.

The outcome of my critical reflections

In extending the notions of respectful individualism, communalism and spirituality, I acknowledge that these ideas were not fully developed in my previous writing on the *mino-pimatisiwin* approach. For example, although I emphasized the significance of spirituality, I did not accord it central importance. I wrote, 'Aboriginal philosophy and ways of knowing encompass spirituality to such a degree that it almost dictates the necessity of including spirituality in this approach' (Hart 2002: 46). On reflection, I skirted the topic of spirituality partly because I was concerned about crossing the line, in both mainstream academic social work and Indigenous camps.

From my academic perspective, I was operating in a context where spirituality had a very separate place in higher learning in subjects like anthropology and religious studies. Outside these domains it was seen as anti-intellectual and unscientific given the common positivistic empiricist practice of negating the spiritual. Little did I realize how much I was caught in this Euro-American perspective fearing the potential wrath of working against it!

From an Indigenous perspective, I was concerned that discussions on spirituality did not belong in the realm of academic texts. And I did not want to move beyond what I thought Indigenous communities were prepared to offer outsiders – or make public – since I was mindful of the concern of some Elders that so much has been taken from our people that we need to hold on dearly to our spirituality as one of the final realms of 'Indigeneity'. Hence, I acknowledged our ceremonies, and identified Elders who were key supports in addressing issues in culturally appropriate manners, which included the spiritual, yet I still did not present spirituality as central in the book. Perhaps it is semantics, in that I identified spirituality as a value thinking that this explained its central importance. Here I am mindful of Dale Turner's observation that:

> … the second role a philosopher *can* play in reconciling the indigenous and European traditions has to do with addressing a concept I have tried to avoid in this book: the spiritual dimension of our indigeneity. From an indigenous [*sic*] perspective, when we think about thinking it is impossible for us to avoid the centrality of the spiritual in how we perceive the world. Midé philosophers possess privileged forms of knowledge, and this knowledge is grounded in profound *spiritual* relationships with the world—how quickly our language becomes muddied! I am indigenous [*sic*], yet I am *not* an indigenous [*sic*] philosopher; and therefore I ought not to place myself in the privileged position of explaining the *meaning* of indigenous [*sic*] spirituality. In a European philosophical context, having invoked a term like 'spirituality' I must then explain how this normative term is to be used in its rightful place—and do so in the English language. It is this step that can be paralysing [*sic*]. Wittgenstein's famous imperative stops me in my tracks: 'Whereof one cannot speak, therefore one must be silent' (Turner 2005: 114–5).

Like me, Turner was caught in a Euro-American perspective yet he succinctly raises the question of whether 'indigenous [*sic*] intellectuals who possess the privileged form of indigenous [*sic*] knowledge' (Turner 2005: 72) have the right to speak about Indigenous culture. I am an Indigenous academic and I am driven to help people as best I can, including my own people and those who want to learn about Indigenous culture. Academia forces us to become 'word warriors' (Turner 2005). We are educated in the legal and political discourses of the dominant state whose primary function it is to engage in the legal and political discourses of the state. My obligation as a word warrior is to know what can and cannot be said in the dominant culture and to know this I need to remain close to, and be guided by Indigenous philosophers, our Elders who are knowledgeable of our ways and understanding of the world (Turner 2005).

The persistence of colonializing forces compels us into a 'radical Indigenism' (Garroutte 2003) and forces us to become political so my position as an academic is a political one. My overriding political goal is to support Indigenous causes in a manner which maintains Indigenous community identity, world views, and cultural practices in the face of ongoing colonial oppression. Radical Indigenism requires scholars to stop studying tribal philosophies from without and rather to enter into them. It requires the abandonment of any notion of the superiority of dominant academic philosophies, interpretations and approaches based on them. It requires that scholars accept tribal philosophies as containing 'articulateable' rationalities and that they give themselves to these philosophies so that they can look through the lens of traditional ways of knowing. To develop such a view requires a level of devotion, commitment and intellectual flexibility in which scholars do not just read or think about these philosophies; instead they trust them, practice them, and live within them. Operating in this manner would enable scholars to raise topics for discussion, contribute information and insight for discussion and play a part in carrying forward the collective projects of acquiring knowledge. However, Garroutte (2003) warned that such actions do not mean that scholars can then impose their own conclusions on the community or become self-appointed spokespersons for their people. Radical Indigenism requires genuine respect that may make it:

> … even harder for scholars to agree … (and) to observe the community's values in deciding what is discussed publicly. The value of Native communities often regulate the circulation of certain kinds of knowledge outside the community. In practice, this means that communities may prohibit scholars from researching or writing about some topics (Garroutte 2003: 109).

I want to be infinitely more than a word warrior; for me these topics are not merely academic. Immersed as I am in my traditional ways of seeing and being in the world, I respectfully seek the guidance and direction of our Indigenous philosophers – our Elders – on what to say and how to say it. I want to make a difference in the world. While reflecting critically, I can act politically, and exert my influence both as an Indigenous scholar and a committed social worker.

Conclusion

Clearly these reflections are only a start. Much more needs to be addressed. Indeed, even this review of an Aboriginal approach within an Indigenous world view is questionable as the concept of world view stems from German philosophy and has been carried mainly by non-Indigenous academics. Through such an origin and evolution, the concept of world view can easily be seen as individualistically based and within the realm of the mind reflecting the Cartesian mind–body separation. Hence, even my critical reflections are limited by non-Indigenous thought. This clearly emphasizes the paradoxical nature of this review. I am not alone in such a stance for it is also evident in the writings of such individuals as Fanon (1967) who used concepts stemming from individuals like Marx and Freud, however, it does demonstrate that Indigenous People need to continue to reflect critically on all work, including that of an Indigenous author.

Chapter 11

Home-made Social Work: The Two-way Transfer of Social Work Practice Knowledge between India and the USA

Jayashree Nimmagadda and Diane R. Martell

Social work practitioners in developing countries have difficulty in comprehending and applying Western knowledge to their day to day practice (Huang 1978; Nagpaul 1972; Nimmagadda and Balgopal 2000; Nimmagadda and Cowger 1999; Roan 1980). In its survey of social work training in 1971, the United Nations originally used the term 'Indigenization' to describe the inappropriateness of Western theories of social work when applied to non-Western and 'third world' societies (Midgley 1983, 1992). Since then, the concept has been widely used in relation to issues surrounding technology transfer and the goodness of fit of 'Western social work knowledge'. Midgley (1983, 1992) questioned the appropriateness between social work roles and the needs of different countries as well as the suitability of social work education to social work practice in non-Western countries. In this chapter, we use the term 'localization' to refer to the 'west to the rest' approach rather than the term 'Indigenization' which frequently appears in the literature.

Discussions of technology transfer have thus far focused primarily on the one-way transmission of Western social work practice knowledge to non-Western countries and cultures. In this chapter, the authors present an alternative approach of 'two-way transfer of knowledge'. We discuss how a local, culturally appropriate model of social work practice was developed in India and then applied to a practice setting in the United States. In addition, the dialogical process that facilitated the transfer of knowledge between a non-Western and a Western social worker is described. It is our hope that this example will generate discussion about the ways in which non-Western approaches may serve to inform Western social work practice and the processes by which the two-way transfer of knowledge can occur.

This chapter first summarizes the literature related to the development of local, culturally relevant social work. Second, we illustrate the process by which the conceptual framework of 'home-made' social work developed, and outline the ingredients of localized practice in India. Third, we describe how the home-made social work framework was applied to a community programme for Southeast Asian youth in the United States. We end by commenting on the dialogical process that supported the two-way knowledge transfer and assert that the development of good and effective culturally relevant and locally appropriate social work practice should be a two-way process between non-Western and Western worlds.

Knowledge transfer and 'localization' of social work practice

Social work knowledge was transferred from the 'developed' to the 'developing' countries in the early half of the twentieth century. This transfer was based on the premise that social work practice theories and models were relevant universally and applied equally in all contexts (Midgley 1983, 1992), however, Midgley (1983) warned that this smacked of 'Western imperialism' especially in the 'third world'.

There have been many consequences of this one-way technology transfer. Several researchers have argued that models designed for Western environments are often unsuitable for other environments, especially in Africa where a distinct brand of social work already existed among field level practitioners (Bar-On 2003b; Gray and Allegritti 2002; Jacques 2000; Osei-Hwedie 2002a). In Hong Kong, social workers have also gradually distanced themselves from Western models unsuited to their local context (Yip 2001).

The development of effective culturally relevant practice is a highly desirable though complex and multidimensional process (Gray and Allegritti 2002; Gray 2005; Yip 2001). For example, when social work education was reintroduced in China in the late 1980s, there was a great deal of tension between social work education and social work practice within the government bureaucracy (Tsang and Yan 2001; Yuen-Tsang and Wang 2002). The ways in which Taiwanese and Chinese clinical social workers 'localize' their knowledge has been explored by Chang (2002) and Lee (2001). Chang, for example, proposed a 'golden mean relationship building model' where Chinese characteristics were combined with Western ideas and, through creative integration, a 'middle of the road' approach emerged. Focusing on Chinese women, Cheung and Liu (2004) and Wong (2002) deconstructed Western feminist social work approaches to develop culturally relevant practice interventions. For example, when working with Chinese women, they reported that it was important for the social worker to consider women's personal interests and their families' interests simultaneously as Chinese women do not separate their personal and family lives. Also, cultural expectations relating to help seeking required rethinking the concept of self-determination as in Chinese culture directive counselling, including advice giving, was seen as culturally appropriate practice (Cheung and Liu 2004).

Few researchers have explored and documented the methods by which 'localization' occurs in practice and how the diffusion of knowledge has taken place between Western to non-Western practitioners and vice versa. Although Yip (2005a) and Ferguson (2005) discussed the need for the transfer of ideas between countries, and proposed dynamic, circular and globally interactive models for knowledge sharing, the profession as a whole has yet to explore and educate practitioners about 'localization' in day to day practice. Given the current era of rapid globalization, it seems appropriate for social work to study this process and encourage the development of conceptual frameworks to assist in the generation of culturally relevant social work practices.

Social work in India

India has an ancient tradition of social service. Serving the needy is greatly valued in Indian culture. In the ancient and medieval periods, assistance was provided primarily in the form of charity. These efforts were centred in religious institutions, such as temples, *maths* (religious places where one can stay) and *dharmashastras* (places to stay that are free) (Kulkarni 1993). In the villages, the joint family, caste system and the *panchayat* (committee which looked after the affairs of a village) catered to the basic needs of the poor, disabled, ill, aged and all those in distress. During the British period, 1658–1947, social work activities were greatly influenced by the political and social conditions of the times and largely concentrated on colonialist social reform (Wadia 1968).

The first professional training school of social work was established in 1936. Initially known as the Sir Dorabji Tata Graduate School of Social Work, it later became and remains the Tata Institute of Social Sciences. Known to most people as the Tata Institute, it has offered a Master's degree in social work since 1964. Since schools of social work in India were chartered by Americans, the curricula of these programmes mirror those in the United States (Kulkarni 1993; Nagpaul 1972). Nagpaul rightly points out that social work knowledge in India could have evolved from an analysis of the techniques used by the social reformers who waged battles against *sati* and child marriage, and for alcohol prohibition and widow remarriage. Instead, he says, graduates learned about Freud, the traumatic implications of overly strict toilet training, and other theories that were irrelevant to the Indian experience.

More than a decade ago, the *Indian Journal of Social Work* (1993) published a special issue related to the status of the social work profession in Asia. The guest editor (Drucker 1993) noted that 'Indigenous' social work knowledge generated from Asian countries was not being disseminated successfully. In the same issue, Nanavathy (1993) discussed the factors blocking the 'Indigenization' of the profession in Asian countries. As the large cities became more industrialized, Western influences became more pronounced. Consequently, the use of local knowledge was de-emphasized and support for professionals to engage in the development of 'Indian' knowledge was negligible.

In the last decade there have been some efforts to discuss how social workers in India 'localize' their Western knowledge. Narayan (2000), Nimmagadda and Balgopal (2000) and Nimmagadda and Cowger (1999) have all discussed the applicability of Western notions of social work practice within the diverse cultures of India and the particular skills that emerge as 'best practice'. Further, Nimmagadda and Balgopal (2000) examined the 'Indigenization' process; Nimmagadda and Cowger (1999) studied 'Indigenized' casework; Nimmagadda and Chakradhar (2006) examined the 'Indigenization' of Alcoholics Anonymous; and Venkataraman (1995) looked at 'Indigenization' from an urban to a rural setting.

Indigenization of social work practice: An example from India

The TT Ranganathan Clinical Research Foundation – hereafter referred to as the Foundation – in Chennai, South India, provided an ideal opportunity for the study of the 'localization' of practice knowledge. The Foundation was founded in 1980 by a social worker who replicated an American model of intervention for alcoholism (Hazelden Foundation at Minneapolis, USA) in India. An inpatient treatment programme was developed to address rising alcohol abuse among men in India.

There is no reliable data on the extent of alcohol, tobacco, and drug use and abuse in India despite several studies since the late 1960s (Deb and Jindal 1974; Dube and Handa 1969; Lal and Singh 1978; Mohan *et al.* 1978; Sethi and Trivedi 1979). In a multicentre study, Khan and Krishna (1982) found that alcohol, tobacco and painkillers were the most commonly abused drugs. Collecting data in 1995–96 from 471,143 people in India over the age of ten years, researchers from John Hopkins School of Medicine estimated that 4.5 per cent of the population regularly used alcohol. Men were found to be nearly ten times more likely use alcohol on a regular basis than women. Those belonging to the lower-castes were also significantly more likely to report regular use of alcohol, smoking and tobacco chewing. Overall, poor people were most likely to consume alcohol despite social and religious prohibitions (Neufeld *et al.* 2005).

Analysing the impact of globalization and economic liberalization policies, Benegal (2005) reported a major shift in Indian attitudes towards normalization of the consumption of alcohol. He found that the age of initiation to alcohol had significantly lowered and that alcohol sales had registered a steady growth rate of 7–8 per cent over a three year period, especially in South India. He called for policy changes in response to these macro environmental shifts.

Within this context, the TT Ranganathan Foundation, with 25 years of experience in the treatment of addictions, expanded its services and gained recognition as the regional training centre for Southeast Asia. In addition to an inpatient treatment programme, the social workers train professionals from Southeast Asia; run rural outreach and employee assistance programmes, and halfway homes; and engage in addiction research (see Cherian 1986, 1989; Ranganathan 1994; Ranganathan and Ranganathan 2003).

Adaptation of the Hazelden model was necessary for social workers at the Foundation to effectively support their Indian clients. In the mid-1990s, research began, using focus groups and interviews, with social workers and founding members of the treatment centre, to identify how this Western practice model was being applied in this local clinical setting (Venkataraman 1996). The social workers were frustrated because aspects of the Hazelden model did not fit their practice context. Local cultural practices were clearly at odds with the Western world views and treatment approaches that had been developed. For example, the Hazelden model advocated 'tough love' for families of alcohol dependent individuals – mainly men – whereby the spouse should, if necessary, leave her alcoholic husband so that he would realize the error of his ways and come to his senses. Clearly this was completely out of sync with Indian culture where arranged marriages were the norm and where leaving one's spouse would meet with strong social disapproval. Leaving was certainly not an option as it was against the wife's *dharma* or duty towards her husband. Instead, the social workers developed a supportive family programme where attendance by family members became mandatory and in which they assumed the role of 'pseudo counsellors'. The strong social pressure that was brought to bear on the alcoholic spouse was highly effective and family members could easily be involved in the programme because this was their *dharma*. Directive practice of this nature is culturally appropriate in Indian culture with its strong collective family values. Self-determination rests very much on the well-being of all. Further this family centred approach corrected the highly individualistic style of Western treatment models and built in an essential dimension of family group support.

Social workers also quickly realized that in India every hospitalized client has numerous visitors during their stay in hospital and this offered another valuable opportunity for intervention. They developed a social support programme involving a half day workshop in which the client's friends and relatives were informed about alcoholism and ways in which they, as well wishers, could help the alcoholic family member or friend in the recovery process. These social support programmes were creative and innovative but, more importantly, they were culturally relevant and drew on cultural strengths – family and community support – and the collective values of Indian culture.

There is a great deal of cultural diversity in India and in order to intervene effectively in alcoholic families, it is necessary to understand the meaning of alcohol in their lives. Social workers talked about this in relation to the complex caste system in India, which is very foreign to people from Western cultures. The caste system is one of the primary structural foundations of Indian society and has the following hierarchy: The *brahmins* are the highest caste, followed by the *kshatriyas*, the *vaisiyas*, the *shudras* and the *harijans*, who are outcasts or untouchables. Despite constant attempts to change discrimination against *harijans* since India's independence in 1947, they still experience insurmountable social and economic barriers in this highly unequal society. This raises severe dilemmas for Western practitioners schooled in a culture of human rights and social justice to whom the practice of social exclusion is unjust.

Social workers found that attitudes towards alcohol abuse varied greatly depending on the client's caste, and learned that they could work effectively with these cultural differences. For a *brahmin*, the social worker used the client's guilt, since drinking was a sin and considered to be morally and socially repugnant for *brahmins*. On the other hand, the *shudras* or *harijans* would not experience guilt as drinking was sanctioned within their communities, especially with *harijans* where excessive drinking on certain occasions was considered the norm. Thus only social pressure, as outlined previously, could counter this practice.

Also important was local wisdom, beliefs and practices; faith in shamans or local healers and astrology as well as observance of religious festivals. Superstition is rife as is the belief of external intervention in people's lives. Indians commonly believe horoscope readings, which hold that misaligned planets lead to tumultuous life events and frequently attribute alcohol addiction to such causes. Hence social workers actively engage with the family and participate in rituals to minimize the impact of the misaligned planets or angry gods. Some social workers included the family astrologer in the recovery process and provided updates on the client's progress.

Western group work approaches presented a particular challenge. Clients were frequently not supportive of one another and always focused attention on the social worker. They were reluctant to confront one another and wanted the social worker to give them advice and direction. Thus social workers developed an Indian group work approach in which there would be a topic for discussion, chosen by the social worker, for each session. The social worker would take a directive role, inviting group members to talk, commenting on what they said, reinforcing positive contributions, initiating discussion, answering questions and confronting group participants if necessary. Thus the groups were simultaneously educational and therapeutic, following the Western-style, but nondirective therapeutic group work done the Western way was clearly not culturally appropriate.

A conceptual framework was developed called 'home-made social work', a term first used by Crawford (1994), to explain the way in which social workers localized Western ideas to make them culturally relevant. Key areas were the importance of context; the relationship and connections not only between clients but also between clients and their families and communities; the centrality of culture; and the validation and active use of local knowledge.

Home-made social work

Conceptual frameworks inform practice. They are tools social workers use to organize their perceptions and thoughts about the reality with which they are dealing. In other words, they are tools social workers use to explain how we make sense of what we are doing and the processes involved. Frameworks are lenses, or perspectives, or angles of view, through which social workers view their practice reality. The metaphor of framing reality implies that we set boundaries in the way in which we view phenomena; frequently we don't always see the whole picture as only the things that we choose to focus on are considered. Thus our framework sets the parameters for our understanding and the activities in which we choose to engage (Alasuutari 1992; Gray and Powell forthcoming). In 'localizing' social work, practitioners use their cultural framework, which focuses attention on the local meaning of the client's experience and the context in which it takes place, to shape intervention and generate possibilities and solutions. This 'local' emphasis is pivotal to home-made social work practice, which draws on the creative and innovative use of culturally relevant local knowledges.

Home-made social work views things from the client's social world. It is context-specific. 'It is home-made in the sense of emerging from where I found myself and from [my] ... reading of that particular context. Home-made in the sense of my deciding what is to be done given the purpose of my engagement in the [local] setting' (Crawford 1994: 58). There are four essential ingredients to home-made social work: cultural authenticity, use of local knowledge, creativity and connectedness.

1. Cultural authenticity: Home-made social work originates with the client in the local community. It draws on longstanding social work principles, such as 'being with the client' and 'starting where the client is' and requires 'attentive listening' so that social workers 'tune into' the context, meaning, and culture of the client. Though central to social work, these guidelines can become clichéd and, in practice, lack substantive meaning if the social worker is not familiar with the client's culture. Within Indian culture the social worker is seen as an authority figure and it is a cultural expectation that they will offer clients direction and guidance. Thus advice giving is culturally appropriate and is seen to help the client take responsibility for his or her behaviour. Respect for social work concepts such as self-determination requires 'cultural faithfulness' rather than a more literal textbook application.

2. Use of local knowledge: Authentic cultural practice must be built on local knowledges and in particular, on diverse local cultural knowledges. Home-made social work recognizes that there are differences even within local cultures and makes space for everyone's voice to be heard. It attempts to generate local solutions for local needs and avoids 'social control' measures. Its style is participatory, working 'with' rather than 'for' clients. This requires that practitioners remain open minded and listen to their client's voice (Hartman 1992). In the examples given above, local knowledge overrode Western practice knowledge about the treatment of alcohol abuse and resulted in culturally appropriate interventions.

3. Creativity: Home-made social work is creative and innovative. It requires that social workers think 'outside the box' – outside their normal frames of reference – and actively use their imagination to develop culturally authentic interventions. Creativity involves intellectual inventiveness, flexibility, the use of intuitive or tacit knowledge and sound practical judgement.

4. Connecting: Home-made social work challenges orthodox ideas about professionalism. Indians living in villages do not need regular office-based appointments with timed fifty minute sessions for social work to happen! Effective social work intervention can happen with these client groups, however, the method and style of connection between the social worker and client must fit with the reality of the client's world. In India, people are oriented to the present and do not make appointments – clients just stop by – nor do they enter into written contracts – they make verbal or tacit agreements. Thus home-made social work focuses on the development and maintenance of culturally authentic relationships, which means discarding the trappings of professionalism.

To summarize, home-made social work is a conceptual framework developed by Indian practitioners to generate knowledge and support effective practice. It is a framework of 'localized' social work, which draws on 'original knowledge' – on local wisdom – and describes the practice that emanated from local cultural beliefs and practices; however, the framework also serves a broader purpose. It makes a political statement that the best practice is home-made rather than imported and it provides a useful structure for conceptualizing culturally authentic practice when working with diverse cultures in other contexts, particularly practice settings in which 'localization' is necessary and 'cultural relevance' is an issue. The following case example illustrates how the lessons from India encapsulated in the home-made social work framework were used to inform practice in the United States.

How lessons from India informed practice in the US

The Socio-Economic Development Center for Southeast Asians (hereafter referred to as the Center) is a non-profit, community-based organization that serves the Southeast Asian community – mainly immigrant families from Cambodia, Laos, Vietnam and members of the *Hmong* ethnic group – in a large metropolitan city in the New England area. The Center offers a diverse array of services, including early childhood intervention, domestic violence counselling, pregnancy prevention, services for the elderly, health education, English as a second language instruction, an international language bank, after school violence prevention and youth substance abuse prevention. The authors have been consultants at the Center and active in programming and evaluation. The funding parameters for this programme stipulated the use of a particular empirically-based Western intervention for substance abuse prevention. This posed a practice dilemma for the social workers as they had the task of implementing this culturally inappropriate programme.

The home-made model of social work based on the experience of designing culturally appropriate interventions for alcoholics in India was presented. Consequently, a series of conversations took place with the Center's caseworkers about culturally appropriate practice for their client group and gradually the programme was modified accordingly.

1. Cultural authenticity: In Asian cultures, collectivism is highly valued. Thus programmes based on individual goal attainment are often overshadowed by people's sense of duty and obligation to their family (Nimmagadda and Cowger 1999). Hence what was needed was a programme which affirmed non-Western practices, chief among them being connection through material assistance to the family of the youth, which the caseworkers provided informally, outside their normal duties. They routinely translated clients' mail into their native language so they could understand its contents; they assisted with translating application forms, helping clients fill them in; they took clients to doctor's appointments, and so on. In this way, they had gained the trust of clients and developed strong relationships with families in the migrant community.

With regard to the content or curriculum of the substance abuse prevention programme, the young people had difficulty understanding that using alcohol or drugs 'was their own individual choice'. Rather than an individualistic self-deterministic approach, the caseworkers suggested that a 'mentoring approach' – which fostered interdependency between young adults and younger school children – would be more culturally appropriate and effective in preventing young people from using alcohol, tobacco and drugs. Additionally, the caseworkers emphasized their role as mentors to the young people and began working on the development of a more expansive youth mentoring project at the Center.

The important lessons learned about the inappropriateness of self-determination when working with Asian cultures resonated with the caseworkers' experiences with their young clients (Ezaz 1991; Mathew 1981; Neki 1973; Nimmagadda and Bromley 2006; Nimmagadda and Cowger 1999). The idea of choosing for oneself had to be more closely related to the spiritual belief of *karma* and the 'law of harvest' versus material benefit. *Karma* is a spiritual philosophy embedded in Asian cultures which holds that the inner character of a person is the driving force behind their behaviour and its consequences (Yang and Martell 2006). The 'law of harvest' refers to the belief that people 'reap what they sow'. In other words, positive actions in the world generate positive life situations whereas negative behaviours bring about negative outcomes. The caseworkers used these concepts to encourage the young people to think about the kind of values they wanted their personal character to reflect and how their choices about alcohol and drug use could impact either positively or negatively on their moral character. Thus the goal of the Western model, to help them understand the consequences of high risk behaviours, was discussed within the context of *karma* and its impact on their moral character.

Storytelling is a culturally appropriate therapeutic strategy in Asian cultures. Stories offer an indirect way to address and attend to sensitive matters (Venkataraman 1996). The caseworkers found the young people to be more responsive to storytelling than role playing and revised the programme accordingly. The caseworkers collected stories from their family and relatives and incorporated these 'ethnically authentic' narratives into the curriculum and in their interventions with the young people.

The caseworkers also adapted the questionnaires that were used as part of the programme to make them more culturally authentic. For example, the youth were asked to complete a form in which they were asked to identify 'positive qualities' in other group members in terms of predetermined categories, such as 'who is the coolest person in the group' and 'who is the most serious'. These items were replaced with 'who is the kindest person in the group', 'who is the most modest' and 'who is the most peaceful', all of which were personal characteristics valued within their culture.

2. Use of local knowledge: Learning from the experiences of the Indian social workers who had explored their clients' meaning of alcohol abuse, the author and the Southeast Asian caseworkers used a similar approach to understand the meaning of substance use for Southeast Asian youth. Much of the Western prevention literature places an emphasis on risk and protective factors that propel youth toward or deter them from alcohol and drug use (MacKinnon *et al.* 1991). To determine whether these factors made sense to the Southeast Asian experience, a focus group was held in which the young people discussed the things that would deter or propel the use of drugs among themselves and the people they knew. Protective factors identified included a sense of belonging to their ethnic group and cultural pride. Thus the workshops were adapted to include positive histories about Southeast Asian countries and ethnic groups, and respected cultural symbols were incorporated. For example, in the Western programme, emphasis was placed on the way in which

life had changed with technological advancements over the past century and the young people were asked to discuss how life was different now from a hundred years ago. For many of the Southeast Asian youth, their countries of origin are largely agricultural and many of the technological inventions familiar to American youth would be foreign to them. Since the students had talked about their cultural heritage as a protective factor, the sessions that were to focus on the changes from past to future were modified to explore how the past links to the present. Focus was placed on how their parents came to migrate to the United States, what their parents' dreams might have been during this transition, and where they – the children – fit into their parents' dreams. This gave them a strong sense of their background and origins, and also incorporated the Asian valuing of the past rather than only the Western value of future progress (Spiegel 1982). The collectivistic culture was also validated through discussion of their parents' dreams and how they, as a family, envisioned their life in America. This collective focus was incorporated later into the curriculum when students were asked to create an ideal future city, one they would like for themselves, their family and their friends, instead of identifying aspects of their ideal personal future.

Regarding the use of cultural symbols to represent ideals, the Western curriculum used American symbols found on an American dollar bill to demonstrate this point. These symbols were replaced by the peace symbol – to emphasize the Southeast Asian value of peace and tolerance – and the Yin and Yang, an Asian symbol representing the two primal opposing but complementary forces, which create balance in all aspects of life and nature.

3. Creativity: The creative approach of the Southeast Asian caseworkers was vital to the programme's success. For example, the Western programme included Socratic circles that were used to foster debate and to encourage the young people to be more assertive in presenting their points of view. This was not favourably regarded by Southeast Asian cultures, especially from children, and would be a mark of disrespect to their mentors and Elders, to who silence signalled respect. Thus Socratic circles were replaced by 'peace circles' that draw on Indigenous Peoples' tradition of the 'talking circle' and which offer an alternative to win-lose approaches to discussion and problem solving. Participants sit in a circle, share their thoughts and feelings about a particular issue or concern, and use a talking tool to identify the person who has the floor. This allows all of the youth to have the opportunity to share their thoughts without interruption or argument. A small statue of Buddha was used as the talking tool in the youth substance abuse prevention programme.

4. Connecting: The Indian social workers' emphasis on leaving professionalism 'at the door' resonated with the Southeast Asian caseworkers' experience. The empirically-based Western prevention intervention emphasized inviting parents of the youth to attend workshops aimed at strengthening their relationships with their children. Historically, parents' attendance at the workshops was poor and the staff realized that Southeast Asian parents would respond better to informal and personalized discussions during home visits than to a formal workshop on child development and

substance abuse. Caseworkers made home visits to all of the participants' homes and this personal connection with parents led to family involvement in the programme.

The Western model had a strict rule that if a child missed three sessions of the programme they would be excluded. The caseworkers felt that this rigid professional approach would backfire with the Southeast Asian youth since family duty was the first priority for them. Thus if a child had to baby sit younger siblings or accompany their parents as interpreters to banks or medical appointments, they would miss sessions of the programme. Staff chose to incorporate attendance flexibility into the programme, providing individuals with private catch-up sessions, as inclusion was central to staying connected with the Southeast Asian youth and their families.

Dialogical Process: A tool that helped in this transfer of knowledge

How we understand and make sense of the world around us is always influenced by our historical and present day environment and the context in which knowledge is generated and integrated. Given these complex issues, the transfer of practice knowledge from a non-Western to a Western practitioner requires more than a shared language and good communication skills. A dialogical process is needed to facilitate mutual understanding and to navigate the potential minefields of cross-cultural exchange.

Dialogical process is seen as the ongoing and vibrant, interactive exchange of reflections – private thoughts, questions and reactions – regarding what occurs over the course of the knowledge transfer. A dialogical process is an exchange of verbal and nonverbal interactions that occurs over time and builds understanding, respect and trust between the parties involved. Ideally, both parties gain knowledge from the exchange and the exchange of knowledge facilitates professional and personal growth.

Such a dialogical process is essential to the two-way transfer – or cultural exchange – of social work practice knowledge. Given the historical hegemony of Western culture it is not surprising that relationships between Western and non-Western social work practitioners often lack authenticity. Differences in world views, social position, and life experience typically result in distrust on the part of non-Western social workers and tunnel vision on the part of Western practitioners.

We identified four factors that supported our dialogical process. First, the development of a respectful and honest relationship is essential though it requires time and effort. All participants must prove their trustworthiness for a meaningful exchange to occur. Second, both parties must believe that there is something of value to exchange. Both non-Western and Western practitioners must desire the transfer of non-Western knowledge and hold this knowledge in high regard. Third, willingness to engage in a pedagogical process is the key to information exchange. Non-Western social workers should be prepared to share their knowledge and be comfortable with taking on a teaching role to support the development of Western competency. Western practitioners must be willing to be learners and to enter unknown territory, letting go of the need for superiority in whatever form it manifests itself. Finally, a dialogical exchange needs to occur within an affirming environment. The transfer of knowledge will be most successful in a supportive, respectful atmosphere, an environment in which all parties feel comfortable enough to express themselves honestly and fully.

Conclusion

In this chapter, a new conceptual framework, home-made social work, is presented to suggest key elements of local, culturally relevant social work practice with people from non-Western cultures. This framework was used to support the two-way transfer of knowledge, that is, the sharing and application of social work concepts and practice methods generated by social workers in India to an American social worker and Southeast Asian caseworkers in a Western setting. As a result of this two-way knowledge transfer, Southeast Asian youth in the United States were able to participate in a culturally appropriate intervention relating to substance abuse prevention.

The transfer of knowledge from non-Western to Western practitioners will not occur in a regular and systemic manner until the profession of social work comes to recognize and validate the importance of 'two-way exchange'. Western social workers need to gain knowledge and understanding of non-Western perspectives and experience with Western social work practice models. To support two-way transfers, the social work profession must first acknowledge that the development of current social work knowledge and practice models has been dominated by Western ethnocentric thinking and experience. It is our hope that our comments will serve as a catalyst for future debate and discussion among professionals from diverse countries regarding the meaning and practice of 'localized' culturally relevant social work and the benefits of two-way social work knowledge transfers.

Chapter 12

Localizing Social Work with Bedouin-Arab Communities in Israel: Limitations and Possibilities

Alean Al-Krenawi and John R. Graham

The process of rendering social work culturally relevant to the international communities in which it occurs has been fraught with problems of terminology. While some understand 'Indigenization' to mean that same localization process that occurs only within Indigenous communities worldwide, of which the Bedouin-Arab are one community, others see the term to be a synonym for localization, with application to communities whether Indigenous or not. Other terms, such as 'authentization' appear to us as too awkward and too uncommon for daily parlance (see, for example, Bradshaw and Graham 2007). Because 'Indigenization' has conflicting meanings, we have preferred the term 'localization' to describe our work with Arab communities in the Middle East.

This chapter, on localizing social work with Bedouin-Arab communities in Israel, has three objectives. The first, and most important, is to provide insight into social work's limitations. As our research demonstrates, localization processes with the Bedouin-Arab in Israel may be insufficiently oriented to political and social change. Social work's potential in this area is therefore mixed. And most might agree that social work in this region is constrained, and its mandate is limited, by the broader contexts in which it operates. The second objective is to outline how social work nonetheless can use case vignettes as a modestly useful tool in localization efforts. Third, as the conclusions point out, spirituality is also a useful means for localizing social work. This chapter begins by looking at the political and cultural realities that dominate this part of the world.

Two stories

Stories are essential to the development of community and national consciousness, and this chapter begins with two, sometimes competing, narratives of the peoples claiming rights to the same territories. The first involves the Jews. One of their holy books tells of humanity created by God, from which His chosen people emerged. The Jews – the descendants of Jacob – were thereby among the world's first to worship a single God, the creator of the universe. Under the patriarchs of the Israelites – Abraham, his son Isaac, and grandson Jacob – the Jews lived in Canaan, later known as the Land of Israel. Jacob's 12 sons spawned the 12 tribes that developed into the nation of Israel. The story continues with the Jews held as slaves in Egypt, but escaping around 1300 BCE under the leadership of Moses. They received the Torah and the Ten Commandments, and after forty years in the wilderness, they finally returned to a land of milk and honey: Israel, the place promised by God to the descendants of the patriarchs, Abraham, Isaac and Jacob. The generations that followed King David made Israel's capital Jerusalem, and his son Solomon built that city's first temple. In 587 BCE the temple was destroyed, and the Jews were exiled to Babylon. They returned many years later, built a second temple, but were ruled by a succession of occupying forces. The last of these, the Romans, destroyed the second temple in 70 CE.

The second destruction was a calamitous event leading to the Jews being exiled. Here began a 1900-year period of Diaspora across the world. Suffering was commonplace; the Jews experienced pogroms in places like Russia, were banished from many European countries and as minority communities around the globe, they suffered much discrimination. For example, it was not uncommon for Jews to be excluded from owning property. Here also, however, is a story of Jews also contributing markedly to the countries in which they emigrated. Among their progeny were many impressive people, and their achievements, in culture, economics, politics and other aspects of life, are profound. How commensurately diminished would the world be without the likes of Disraeli, Einstein, Freud, Marx or Mendelssohn, to cite five of myriad names. But in the twentieth century, perhaps the greatest horror to be visited upon the Jews occurred: the Holocaust. Six million Jews perished during the Second World War. In that aftermath came the 1948 creation of the modern state of Israel. At last, the Jews were finally able to return to their Promised Land. Hebrew, a language long consigned to written and scholastic activities only, was rejuvenated in spoken form and is now the country's lingua franca, cohering diverse communities that had emigrated from countries across the world. A political democracy and modern society rapidly unfolded and many continue to think of the emergence of present day Israel as a miracle.

A second story sees 1948 with vivid difference. Among many Palestinians, Al-Nakbah – disaster – is the common name for Israel's 1948 creation. Arabs made up the majority of inhabitants of Palestine prior to that year, but as a result of the war of 1948 and the establishment of the state of Israel, 84 per cent of the Palestinian population was exiled and became refugees (Kanaana 1992). Those Palestinians who remained were a minority in what had become a Jewish state. Of a pre-1948 Palestinian population of 950,000, two categories of Palestinian refugees were created. Approximately 800,000 Palestinians were expelled from the country and forced to become refugees in the Arab states; 150,000 Palestinians remained within the boundaries of the new state of Israel. Close to 25 per cent of those who remained within the state were displaced from their homes to other locations, thus becoming internal refugees (The Arab Association for Human Rights 2003; Wakim 1994). The right to return for the 800,000 and their offspring seems elusive and is certainly contested by many, including such leading Israeli peace advocates as Amos Oz. In Israel, Palestine and neighbouring countries in which the Palestinians now live, the psychosocial and economic consequences have been severe. Most Palestinians lost their homes and livelihood, and all experienced remarkably reduced political power. Families were displaced and separated as communities were destroyed. Al-Nakbah is the moment when a large part of the Palestinian people became homeless, a state that is associated with a deep sense of insecurity. In light of it, the house key has become a symbol of the former home: of the return to it and to normality (Sa`di 2002).

Prevailing narratives are, however, invariably in the voice of history's victors. In Israel, dominant interpretations of history have been consciously rewritten in ways that strike many as untruthful. One of the more egregious examples was a 1969 interview with Israeli Prime Minister Golda Meir in which the existence of Palestinians was even called into question: 'It is not as though there was a Palestinian people in Palestine considering itself as Palestinian people and we came and threw them out and took their country away from them; they did not exist' (in Shlaim 2001: 311).

This second story needs to be read in a broader backdrop of colonialism. For centuries prior to 70 CE, outside powers were in control. Palestine was likewise highly contested during the period of the Medieval Crusades. Since the early sixteenth century, foreign rulers permanently occupied the region. First the Ottoman Empire and from 1917 to 1948 the British held Palestine and Jordan, and the French claimed present day Lebanon and Syria. While small populations of Jews had existed in Palestine since at least the mid-nineteenth century, growing calls for an Israeli homeland over the latter half of the 1800s culminated in the 1917 Balfour Declaration, a letter from the British foreign minister advocating a national home for the Jewish people in Palestine. The British Mandate saw a growing, organized political movement for greater Jewish presence in the region, and Arab opposition to the partition of Palestine emerged in counterpoint. The United Nations, created after the Second World War, called for partition of Palestine in 1947, war immediately followed and led to the 1948 creation of Israel.

The period 1948 to 1967 was one of military rule and the post-1967 occupation of Palestinian territory – the West Bank and Gaza Strip – constitutes a continued affront to Palestinians, and indeed to many around the world, the present authors included. Arabs in Israel find themselves in a difficult, complicated reality and they are described as possessing 'dual identity'; they live with family, friends and communities in Israel, but also may have family, friends and feel a strong sense of community with Palestine. Indeed, similar relationships to Palestine may also be felt towards other neighbouring Arab countries (Sagiv and Schwartz 1998). Many perceive themselves primarily as Palestinians. Many have first and second degree relatives in the occupied territories. Most identify nationally and emotionally with the Palestinian people in the occupied lands (Ruhana 1997). A survey of 1,202 Palestinian Israelis conducted by Ganim and Smooha (2001) shows a high level of identification with the Intifada and the struggle of the Palestinian nation. Similarly, findings of a survey conducted by Ben Meir (2002), show a soaring rise in the percentage of Arab Israelis who identify as Palestinians, from 46.4 per cent in 1996 to 74 per cent in 2000, and a plummeting decline in the percentage that identify as Israelis, from 38.4 per cent to 11 per cent during the same time period. Most North American observers, and many in Western Europe, seriously underestimate the degree of opposition within many communities throughout the Arab and Muslim worlds to Israeli and American hegemony in the Middle East. Mainstream media in North America, particularly the CanWest Media Service, CNN and Fox News, typically report on the Middle East without questioning this hegemony. English language readers are better off consulting the BBC or *Manchester Guardian*.

Palestinians in today's Israel

Palestinians are now a minority within Israel, constituting 19.4 per cent, or 1.3 million of the country's total population of 6.7 million. The vast majority resides in all-Arab towns and villages located in three main areas: the Galilee in the north where Palestinians comprise approximately 50 per cent of the population; the 'Little Triangle' in the centre; and the border that separates Israel from the occupied West Bank (Statistical Abstract of Israel 1998). Over 700,000 Palestinians are Muslims (82 per cent of the Arab minority), roughly 150,000 are Christians (9 per cent), and almost 100,000 Druze, Circassian, or other groups (9 per cent) (Nir, 2003).

Arab people are discriminated against in multiple respects. There continue to be huge gaps in the quality of life between Arab and Jewish Israelis (Israeli Government 2002). Over 100 Palestinian Arab villages in Israel lack official government recognition. More than 70,000 Palestinian Arab citizens live in villages that are threatened with destruction, prevented from development and are not shown on any map (Statistical Abstract of Israel 1998). Infant mortality rates among the country's Arab minority are 8.4 infants per thousand, contrasted with the Israeli majority's 3.4; medical specialties and access to medical services are lower among Arab communities; workforce participation rates amongst Arabs in 2002 was 39 per cent compared to 57 per cent among Jewish Israelis; among families headed by a salaried worker, 56 per cent of Arab households are in the country's bottom income quintile compared with 16 per cent of Jewish Israeli households; 45 per cent of Israel's Arab population live in poverty, compared with 15 per cent of Jewish families (The Association for the Advancement of Civic Equality 2004). Despite the achievements of Israel's education system, there are great disparities between Arabs and Jews in facilities, funding allocations, number of pupils per class and academic achievement. A 2004 national social security report reveals that high school drop out rates in Arab communities are more than double the national average, and of the 50 localities which receive the lowest government allocation for education, 41 are Arab (National Security Report 2004).

Within this Arab Palestinian minority, there are specific communities called Bedouin. Bedouin-Arab is the generic name for all Arabic-speaking tribes in the Middle East. The Bedouin-Arabs are distinct to the Arab world because they have a nomadic tradition and inhabited deserts, but this should not infer a unified racial, ethnic, or national group or a homogeneous-style of life. They are present in Egypt, Israel, Jordan, Saudi Arabia and Syria among other countries (Hana 1984; Yosef 1991). In Israel, many Bedouin-Arab live in the Negev region, in the south of Israel, constituting 25 per cent of this region's population. They are undergoing a rapid and dramatic process of sedentarization; 56 per cent of the Negev's 180,000

Bedouin-Arab population now live in villages, and the remaining 44 per cent live in unrecognized villages.

With the 1948 establishment of the state of Israel, the Negev Bedouin-Arab have been radically transformed. The state has precipitated this process of sedenterization, and has determined what sites the Bedouin-Arab may settle. For millennia, the Bedouin-Arab had been a nomadic people relying on travel, the ownership of camels, sheep and other animals, and their involvement in trade, as the principle forms of livelihood (Al-Krenawi and Graham 1996a, 1997, 2000; Marks 1974). The transition to settlement and modernity accompanies a struggle between cultures – both experienced among individuals and between Israeli and Bedouin communities. A myriad of social problems prevail, including poverty, family problems, school dropout, delinquency and substance abuse (Savaya 1995). Women in particular may face limitations of geographic mobility, stresses relating to lack of education, transformation of their way of life from traditional to modern, as well as the everyday stresses associated with many social problems that are prevalent within the community.

A good portion of geography is contested by the Israeli state and the Bedouin; those areas that are 'officially' recognized by the state are described as recognized villages, those that are not, are unrecognized, although both are populated by the same people and culture. Since the Israeli state does not provide unrecognized villages funding for health, education, social service or other urban infrastructures, those living in unrecognized villages must go to recognized villages to receive such services. These are often far away – sometimes over an hour by vehicle – and it is especially difficult for women or people in poverty, to access services over these distances (Al-Krenawi and Graham 2006; Al-Krenawi *et al.* 2000).

Localizing social work

How, then, to provide effective social work services for Palestinian communities on both sides of the Green Line; in Israel and Palestine, the West Bank and Gaza Strip? How should social work be conceived for the Bedouin-Arab in particular? Should one practise political social work, and be committed to genuine social change and to the emancipation of Palestinian Peoples in general, and the Bedouin in particular? One organization that is dedicated to many of these principles is Hamas, the twenty year old Islamic Resistance Movement in Palestine. Indeed, until early this decade, people in countries such as Canada could legally donate money to this organization, which is dedicated to community development, social and health services and political rights for Palestinians. The Hamas Movement is also associated with political violence towards the Israeli state, and its refusal to recognize the state of Israel as a legal entity. And here lies an example of the difficulties in developing genuinely emancipatory and radical social work in Palestinian contexts. How does one promote individual well-being and social change peacefully and without supporting violence?

The ongoing political conflict led us to write studies on the psychosocial impact of violence on widows, sons and daughters of the Hebron massacre, and a 2004 study on psychosocial services for victims of political violence in Palestine (Al-Krenawi *et al.* 2002, 2004) as well as a study of psychological symptomatolgy among Palestinian adolescents living with political violence (Al-Krenawi *et al.* in press). But there remain profound difficulties in carrying out genuinely emancipatory social work at the level of communities and Palestinian society. True, allying with peace efforts is significant. And the work we have done has been genuinely committed to, and we hope has contributed to, the social development of Palestinian and Bedouin-Arab communities. However, we clearly understand that these are no panacea for genuine human rights and we hope there is fertile ground for peace.

Case vignettes

One particular approach to social work practice and education has been the use of case vignettes. Indeed, we think that case vignettes highlighting particular approaches to Indigenization are potentially fruitful venues for generating a more sophisticated theory and method. Case vignettes have long been used in social service, medical research and practice, and are perfectly well established means of helping to assess the quality of care that may be available (Dale and Middleton 1990; Gibelman 2002). As previous work in the area points out, providers can be presented with vignettes of case material and asked to indicate what they would typically do in such situations. Vignettes are easily administered, inexpensive and account for case mix because everyone sees the same case. Case vignettes can be altered to differ by race or gender to examine disparities in service delivery. They can be used in social services research wherever there are accepted practice guidelines (Fihn 2000; McMillen *et al.* 2005; Peabody *et al.* 2000). We suspect, too, that they can be used as a viable tool for generating knowledge in transregional, transcultural contexts, particularly if analytical points may be extrapolated from one culture or context to another's unique culture or context.

The following paragraphs outline four examples from our own work; polygamous family formation, blood vengeance, cultural mediation, and traditional healing. Practicing with clients from polygamous families can present challenges for many social workers. Based on a study of 25 cases, Al-Krenawi *et al.* (1997) identified a number of ways in which social work practice in this context can be more effective. The first consideration for improving practice is for the social worker to become knowledgeable about the cultural and personal significance of polygamy to family members. The women in polygamous marriages face unique life transitions, for example from sole wife to second wife, or from junior wife to intermediate wife, which may be traumatic. In many Muslim Arab communities, men may favour the most recent wife and her children with differential instrumental and emotional support afforded to them. These dynamics lead to significant relationship implications between wives, who may also live with their children in separate accommodations from the other wives and their children.

Blood vengeance is most significant to the field of child welfare practice. Say, for example, that a man has been put on death row because a third cousin within his tribe killed a member of a different tribe. The aggrieved tribe seeks vengeance against the man, who with his family flees his immediate community and with his family lives in the most extreme form of isolation and poverty. Blood vengeance therefore puts children at risk (Al-Krenawi and Graham 1997). The role of social work is particularly significant within a blood vengeance situation. Based on a case vignette, Al-Krenawi and Graham (1999) outlined a number of strategies for clinical and child welfare practice that include 'non-authoritarianism, strategies to form a positive helping alliance, and culturally sensitive assessment and (in their various forms) intervention' (p. 283). It is difficult to not be, and not be construed to be, an authority figure. It would be helpful in developing a positive helping alliance to base the relationship on acceptance, respect, trust and validation of the family's current situation. Cultural sensitivity in appreciating the ecological context of and significance to family members of blood vengeance is important for building a constructive working relationship with family members. It is also important to consider family members' perceptions of their circumstances, problems and resources. Social workers should be very responsive to the needs of children, who may be under considerable psychological distress. Encouraging an identification and positive helping alliance with children of vengeance families will increase the effectiveness of any intervention. To that end, playing games with children is a powerful way of connecting and establishing trust. It is important that the practitioner not impose culturally inappropriate techniques; for example, insisting that the family make office appointments rather than continuing to make home visits. It may be useful to use mediators within Arab communities to resolve or reduce tensions associated with blood vengeance conflict, and as discussed in the preceding section. Providing concrete services for meeting the family's basic needs may also be very useful (Al-Krenawi and Graham 1997, 1999).

Based on the wasit tradition, we explored a model of cultural mediation in child welfare; a demonstration project using the assistance of approximately 35 senior male Elders in a large Arab city over an 18 month period, none of whom had any social work training but all enjoying community respect and all having skills in traditional mediation. Research suggested that when social workers undertook various child welfare interventions collaboratively with a select mediator, interventions were rendered more culturally appropriate, gaps between the cultural and professional canons were bridged, social work's role was promoted in a society that had a limited understanding of, and experience with the profession (Al-Krenawi and Graham 2001). The importance of cultural mediators in the community is their ability to encourage the empowerment of different groups that are deprived of access to the power centres in society (Schellenberg 1996). Thus cultural mediators are not perceived as a neutral third side but rather are expected to operate for the sake of social justice in the community and for the sake of cultural sensitivity. The community mediators were important teachers to social workers, conveying culturally appropriate ways of interacting with people in their community, and helping social workers, many of whom were from the community, to unlearn some of the problematic assumptions they had picked up in their social work training. The community mediators also became important ambassadors of social work, learning from practitioners and conveying to the community various principles related to women's health, children's health, and healthy family functioning (see Al-Krenawi and Graham 2001).

A final case vignette example is traditional healing. We looked at various ways of understanding traditional healing in the Middle East, among Dervish and Koranic healers, among others, in relation to social work and other helping professions. Different healers occur in different Arab countries (Al-Issa 2000; Al-Krenawi and Graham 1996b; El-Islam 1982; Okasha 1999). Their names may vary but their functions may be similar, among them dealing with such psychosocial problems as depression, anxiety or problems with interpersonal relationships. They often recommend rituals for helping people; these, as research has concluded, often have strongly therapeutic components. Examples include the Zar ritual, the Dhkir, or visiting a saint's tomb (Al-Issa 2000; Al-Krenawi and Graham 1996a; Boddy 1989; Crapanzano 1973; Kennedy 1967).

The work that we have undertaken in traditional healing leads to some implications. Given that informal and formal sources of help may be intertwined in Muslim Arab cultures, it is desirable to promote a mutual understanding between social work and traditional healers, however, caution should be exercised in how this occurs. There can be a great deal of variability in the ways and levels at which an individual engages with a traditional healer. Whether the precipitating problem is somatic, psychosocial, psychiatric or a combination of these elements, the presenting problem will be the primary level of engagement between the individual seeking help and the traditional healer. However, beyond the problem is a shared level of understanding and connection between them. One level of shared understanding is cultural, since the healer incorporates rituals familiar to the community. This shared cultural background promotes trust and enhances the helping process (Al-Krenawi and Graham 1996a). The interpersonal is another level of connection, as the healer is known personally or by reputation. Some rituals enjoy community sanction or are related to rituals that are known to promote wellness. Informal discussions between modern practitioners and traditional healers could provide insight into their respective roles (Al-Krenawi and Graham 1996a). Creating opportunities for mutual referrals between traditional healers and social workers could provide opportunities for client good. Social workers should be vigilant in respecting the domains appropriate to traditional healing, however, opportunities exist for professionals to learn from traditional healers about how to create and sustain effective helping alliances (Al-Krenawi and Graham 2000).

As these latter examples highlight, spirituality has been a major theme in the localization work we have undertaken. Of particular importance has been understanding traditional healers; learning from them, applying their methods and theories to social work in an effort at cultural sensitivity, and understanding the worlds we have worked in on the spiritual (emic) grounds on which they often function. For example, understanding the spiritual roles of Islam, collective ways of knowing, and the roles of healers among other things (Al-Krenawi and Graham 2000). Attending to spirituality is a viable source of engaging with a recently rejuvenated movement to render social work relevant to the international communities in which it occurs, to localize social work's knowledge base (Graham 2006).

Conclusion

Such diverse and loosely defined social groupings as 'Arab', 'Bedouin-Arab', 'Muslim', 'northern', 'southern' or 'western' are fraught with dangers of reductionism, simplification and essentialism. Their advantage, on the other hand, is the possibility of considering broad patterns at this early stage in the literature's evolution. And so the generalizations that we present are intended as nothing more than a beginning point (as one scholar describes such enterprises, as 'signposts for future research rather than as definitive conclusions' (Salem 1997: 11)) for further reflection and for application in more precise and defined geographic, historical, national and other contexts. Insofar as generalizations may occur, we provide evidence that social work epistemology, with its profound roots in the global north, is nonetheless beginning to add space for other perspectives, including the Bedouin-Arab communities. Historically, many aspects of social work have fit poorly with Bedouin-Arab cultures and social structures. Polygamy and blood vengeance are excellent examples of culturally embedded practices for which social work theory and methods had, until recently, little to say. As well, there are other important areas where social work in the Arab world has been enhanced: conflict resolution, collaboration with religion and with traditional healing and strategies for working with families. Our observations lead us to conclude that there are benefits for practitioners to integrate social service theory and methods as they are presently conceptualized in the Bedouin-Arab communities, with principles derived from local cultural and religious practices; this process may lead to a more locally responsive, culturally appropriate model of professional intervention.

A cursory tour of recognized and unrecognized Bedouin-Arab villages of the Negev provides ample evidence of how helping professional structures can reproduce broader, societal inequalities. The extent to which helping professions can be instruments of community and individual empowerment is closely aligned to how professional and cultural ways of knowing intersect. Is the former hegemonic over the latter? Can alternate ways of knowing assist helping professions to work with communities in order to deliver services in culturally respectful and inclusive ways? To what extent do helping professional practices impose principles that are external to communities and that ultimately alienate community members from their communities, contexts and potentials? In an era of globalizing communication technologies, the transfer of knowledge between the global north and global south is paradoxical. Bedouin-Arab Peoples own television sets, satellite dishes, telephones, computers, can access the Internet and may have a ubiquitous experience of culture from around the globe. At the same time, there can be profound dissonances between Bedouin-Arab cultural traditions and values that are transmitted through the structures of globalization. Local cultures around the world simultaneously experience and resist these broader forces. The rise of political Islam is one example of cultural resistance that has been occurring in the Arab world over the past thirty years. Any Bedouin-Arab consumer of helping professional services is ipso facto a part of these broader processes.

Helping professionals in communities such as the Bedouin-Arab, as throughout the global south, straddle two mutually contradictory spheres. On the one hand, they are a product of global processes of colonialism. Globalization, in that sense, appears to prevail. On the other hand, their practitioners may seek to ally with social movements that are allied with those communities that often have the least to gain, and the most to lose, from the forces of globalization that have produced increasing income and social inequalities within and between societies. The neologism 'glocalization' has been coined to capture those local forces at work, throughout the world, that are deliberate attempts to resist the worst forces of globalization and to capitalize on the best.

In Israel and Palestine, Arab Peoples may be suspicious of the helping professions, and the professions' tenuous relationships with Arab traditions introduce an imperative of localizing knowledge bases. Social work and its allied disciplines may be useful conduits for a clearer understanding of social problems, for developing a social conscience within Bedouin-Arab communities for their resolution and for the development of social services for vulnerable peoples. But has social work been a tool of profound political resistance, or of profound emancipatory social change? Could it be?

PART 4
Culturally Relevant
Social Work Education

Chapter 13

Reconfiguring 'Chineseness' in the International Discourse on Social Work in China

Rick Sin

The international community needs to foster mutual exchanges of experiences and information between social workers in different societies. More opportunities for the representation of Third World social workers at international gatherings are needed, and publication sources should provide a forum for disseminating Third World experiences ... It is time to challenge the one way international flow of ideas and practices and to learn from the Third World (Midgley 1990: 300).

The modern notion of culture thus becomes problematic. Problematizing culture, critiquing essentialist ideas about culture, focusing on the diversity and subordination of the Other under the conditions of late capitalism, all contribute to debate on the production and reproduction of welfare discourses and practices (Leonard 1997: 61).

In the new era of economic globalization, the success and sustainability of the coexistence of humankind hinges on how much we respect and learn from one another within and across cultural, geographical and political boundaries. In the field of international social work, practitioners and scholars in the north passionately call for learning from the south (Hartman 1990a; Midgley 1990). Their previously silent or silenced southern counterparts were eager to bring their perspectives into international intellectual debates. As Dei, Hall, and Rosenberg (2000) observed, more and more people have come to realize the urgency of 'promoting multiple and collective readings of the world ... and [of] exploring multiple and alternative knowledge forms' (p. 70). The major challenge is to find ways in which these theories and practices are transferable across contexts (Gray and Fook 2004) while avoiding the imperialistic imposition of Western notions of social work (Gray 2005; Midgley 1981). At the core of these debates and dialogues is the question of how to identify, understand and respect cultural difference within and between national and regional borders (Gray 2005). An examination of the literature on cultural difference, particularly in relation to the so called 'Indigenization' of social work theories and practices within the *International Social Work* (ISW) journal between 1986 and 2006 revealed that 'culture' is used as a 'relational demarcator' (see also Park 2005) inscribing differential positions and hierarchical identities. The limits of universality and the need for adaptation rest on how we deal with 'difference' between the west, where social work originated, and the rest.

However, as noted in Chapter 1, culture is a fussy term. In his much celebrated book *Orientalism*, Said (1978) warned that knowledge of cultural difference can be deceptive. Culture is not a pre-existing thing to be known, but a product of the knowing process that involves an uneven relationship of power between the dominant knower and their culturally different 'other'. The uncritical use of the term 'culture' might pose a danger, weakening issues of 'hierarchy' and 'power' in the imagination and articulation of difference (Bilik 2002). Also, it runs the risk of obfuscating contextual factors that require political and intellectual intervention, as in the case of Indigenous Peoples, reifying otherness and making excuses for neglect or domination, as the case may be, in local and international social welfare discourse (Razack 1998).

Based on observations in the field of cross-cultural psychology, Kim (2000) identified several common problems when 'adaptation to local cultural contexts' was called for: 1) Often the texts cited in justification were developed several thousand years ago mostly within philosophical or religious school of thoughts, like Confucianism, Buddhism and Daoism in East Asia, where their nature and use were very different from the empirical orientation of Western social theories; 2) Within a particular culture, only a small percentage of the population had direct knowledge of the texts from which their cultural practices derived; 3) While people were cautious about cross-cultural impositions, there was a tendency to neglect social pressures towards conformity 'within-cultures'; and 4) Despite the consequent cultural unity thus engendered, systemic analysis of the texts from which cultural practices originated revealed numerous contradictions, inconsistencies and conceptual leaps of faith. The essential point is that there is diversity even within cultures but unity becomes a political force of resistance when a culture is threatened from without.

The post-structuralist scholar Avtar Brah (1996) says that to fully understand the meaning of culture in particular contexts, it is important to ask how the notion of difference is used to designate the culturally different 'other' and what the consequences of this are. Clearly, the presumed norms which mark a population as different depends on who is defining difference and on the way in which boundaries are drawn or constituted, maintained or challenged. More important for our purposes, however, is whether or not this 'othering' discourse is helpful in intercultural exchanges.

Since cross-cultural social work and the global application or transfer of social work have been major themes in *International Social Work* over the last 20 years, it seemed an appropriate place to start in examining social work's construction of the notion of 'Chineseness'. Being a Canadian social work researcher of Chinese descent, my ethnic background provides me with an entry point to look at the construction of 'Chineseness', to explore its complexity as a marker of cultural and political identity and to open a discursive space for critical thinkers to interrogate social relations, cultural identities and individual subjectivities in their ongoing struggle for global social justice and the recognition of human rights across diverse socio-political and cultural contexts. However, Chineseness in this context is also a metaphor for 'Indigenous' and the discussion that follows raises issues that are paralleled in the experiences of Indigenous Peoples everywhere. Who constructs Indigenous identities and who determines what Indigenous People need? Who is interpreting

Indigenous culture and deciding on the nature of Indigenous social work? While this chapter examines these questions through the lens of 'Chineseness', the lessons and observations have a much wider import and relevance.

As a result of a keyword search to identify articles which dealt with issues relating directly to Chinese populations, communities and cultures, 98 articles were downloaded and reviewed to determine the following: 1) the way in which 'Chineseness' was constructed; 2) the way in which the 'West' was imagined and projected as the backdrop against which 'Chineseness' was juxtaposed; and 3) the 'nativity' evoked and performed to provide writers with 'discursive authority'. As in the case of Indigenous Peoples, questions were raised as to who had the authority to speak on this subject: Chinese people living in China or Chinese people living in other parts of the world. Does Chineseness signify the same to Chinese people in China and in Chinese Diasporas? By the same token are there different forms of Indigeneity depending on where in the world one lives or on whether one is a first, second or third generation First Nations person? In his book *Songman*, Bob Randall (2003) talks about his shock and sadness when many of his reservation friends and family refused to participate in any of the cultural activities he was organizing. 'They told me', he recalled, 'We are "coloured people" not Aborigines ... It was as if a whole new race had been created because they did not want to be considered Aboriginal' (p. 90).

Culture as a site of domination and resistance

In his most influential work, *Orientalism*, Edward Said (1978) provided a convincing argument relating to the way in which 'European culture gained ... strength and identity by setting itself off against the Orient as a sort of surrogate and even underground self' (p. 3). However, he emphasized that:

> This is not to say that Orientalism unilaterally determines what can be said about the Orient, but that it is the whole network of interests inevitably brought to bear on any occasion when that peculiar entity 'the Orient' is in question (Said 1978: 3).

In and through a web of power relations, people in the West discussed the Orient and developed a set of discourses on Orientalism to establish an allegedly superior 'Western self' in relation to an inferior 'non-Western other'. Philosophically speaking, Orientalism begins with the assumption that there is a radical distinction between the east and west, and then proceeds to treat everything as evidence in support of this 'two worlds' division. One of the major criticisms levelled against Said's work is that he characterized colonial discourse as a homogenous group of texts, which bore a monolithic message about the colonial 'other' (Mills 2004). Bhabha (1994) criticized Said's suggestion that colonial power and discourse was possessed and constructed entirely by the 'colonizer' as this was an historical and theoretical oversimplification. Said implied that Orientalist knowledge was all powerful and his notion of the homogeneity of culture has been challenged (Spivak 1988).

Fifteen years later in *Culture and Imperialism* (1993), Said's sequel to *Orientalism*, he introduced the idea of 'contrapuntal reading' as an analytical method to examine the perspectives of both the colonizer and the colonized thus accommodating both accounts of history by addressing 'imperialism and the resistance to it ... by extending our reading of the texts to include what was once forcibly excluded' (pp. 66–7). In short, Said recognized that what was not said might be as important as what was said. Thus he claimed that textual analysis required the deconstruction of the structural and historical components of texts and the reconstruction of their internal logic from the perspective of the present.

Edward Said's *Orientalism* revolutionized Western understanding of non-Western cultures by showing how Western projected images shaped the occidental view of the Orient, however, Carrier's (1995) and Chen's (1992, 1995) work pushed the theoretical edge further and led people to reflect this understanding back onto Western societies, that is, onto what they called 'Occidentalism'. Carrier (1995) saw Occidentalism as 'styled images of the West' (p. 1). It showed the way in which images of the west shaped people's conceptions of themselves and others, and how these images were, in turn, shaped by members of Western and non-Western societies alike. It led people to examine the dualism of essentialized images of the Orient as well as of the west.

Chen (1995) saw Occidentalism as a product of Western imperialism. She forced people to see beyond the imperial west and subjugated 'other' and to recognize that forces of domination and resistance also came from within the east and west respectively. In her book *Occidentalism: A Theory of Counter-Discourse in Post-Mao China*, Chen (1995) demonstrated that Chinese Occidentalism was not simply imposed from afar, but was constantly and creatively changed by Chinese concerns with adapting constructions of Orientalism and Occidentalism to their own political purposes. What interested her most was how Occidentalism as a discursive construct was imported into China and became an instrument of the communist government and intelligentsia. Chen defined Chinese Occidentalism as:

> ... primarily a discourse that has been evoked by various and competing groups within Chinese society for a variety of different ends, largely, though not exclusively, within domestic Chinese politics. As such, it has been both a discourse of oppression and ... of liberation (Chen 1992: 688).

Chen argued that Chinese Occidentalism constituted two related yet separate appropriations of the same discourse for strikingly different political ends. The first was 'official Occidentalism' in which the Chinese government used 'the essentialization of the West as a means for supporting a nationalism that effect[ed] the internal suppression of its own people' (Chen 1992: 688) such that anything opposed to the dominant Maoist political discourse could be labelled 'Western', bourgeois or pro-capitalism and thus be subject to strict censure and prosecution. For example, intellectuals who studied things 'Western' were accused of promoting the notion that 'that the Western Other was ... superior to [the] Chinese Self' (Chen 1992: 691). Either by virtue of their cultural status or their perceived political sympathies to the west, alongside the official Occidentalism there arose an 'anti-official Occidentalism' that was contingently and strategically employed by the Chinese intelligentsia to articulate what was otherwise 'politically impossible' and 'ideologically inconceivable' (p. 692). To her, excessively positive evaluation of Western civilization by some Chinese scholars could be seen as a 'potent anti-official discourse' in contrary to the anti-Western official Occidentalism (Chen 1995: 28). Thus she stressed that all discourse was *local* and contingent and therefore must be judged not just in terms of its content but also by its political effects or consequences. The First Nations discourse might be seen in the same light (see Chapter 6).

In a nutshell, Orientalism and Occidentalism must be seen as theories or signifying practices without essential content. To Chen, it was the use to which they were put by those who articulated them, and by those who heard and received them, that determined 'their social—and literary—effects' (Chen 1992: 710).

Clearly then culture is a site of domination and resistance. The construction of culture, in this case Chineseness, and cultural difference rests on the operation of power relations in 'discursive spaces' whether writers are silencing or making 'marginalized voices' heard. In the international arena that is dominated by English language, writers can only but write from their privileged position – educated and Westernized. Their proficiency in English equips them to engage in the study of Western ideas and theories and their proficiency in Chinese enables them to serve as intercultural interlocutors. How does one assess the 'accuracy' of such translations of cultural meaning and (re)configurations of Chineseness? Until Chinese texts are translated into English, rather than the other way around, we have no empirical or concrete grounds on which to engage in mutual intercultural dialogue. At the rate with which Western social work is being introduced into China, it is unlikely that such a grounded approach is possible.

(Re)configuring 'Chineseness': Who and what is Chinese?

Smith optimistically noted that having 'had a unique past, the Chinese will have their own unique future' (Smith 2003: 403). To be sure, China has a unique 6,000 year history which predates the emergence of Western history with the Ancient Greeks two thousand years ago. But what makes Chinese social work unique if it is being imported from the west? What implications arise from the importation of Western social work into the People's Republic of China (PRC)?

Without exception, the writers believed that social work in China or within the Chinese diaspora had unique 'Chinese characteristics' that defined it as non-Western, however, there were differing opinions on the nature of these characteristics and their relevance to the development and understanding of social work theories and practices. Given the domination of communist ideology for over half a century, writers struggled with the extent to which so-called 'Chinese characteristics' were rooted in traditional Chinese culture or whether they were constituted by the contemporary political regime. Although Chinese leaders continue to maintain the essential socialist character of the country (Ngan and Hui 1996), there has never been a fixed, unified, dominant interpretation of its socialist ideology (Tsang and Yan 2001). Those who insist that knowledge of Indigenous culture rests on the 'identification of genuine and authentic roots in the local system' (Ragab, in Cheung and Liu 2004: 112) need to argue which roots are indeed local, original and authentically Chinese.

Writing from an in between space as Chinese-Canadians, Tsang and Yan (2001) in their paper entitled 'Chinese corpus and western application' challenge their Chinese colleagues to recognize the immense diversities within their country along *inter alia* ethnic, rural-urban, gender and class lines. Nevertheless, as they observed, the discourse on the development of social work in China assumed that there was an essentially 'Chinese corpus' – a body of knowledge and structure of social institutions, cultural traditions and Chinese values – grounded in Confucianism (see also Becerra and Chi 1992; Chan 1992; Chan 2006; Cheung and Liu 2004; Kilpatrick and Zhang 1993; Yan 1998; Yao 1995; Yip 2005b). In this social work discourse, Confucianism is used to explain the importance of family to individual identity (Cheung and Liu 2004), the centrality of harmony and integration (Chow 1987; Kilpatrick and Zhang 1993), students' lack of creativity (Chan and Chan 2005), children's submission to hierarchy and authority (Kwok and Tam 2005) and the primacy of benevolence over rights in Chinese society (Yao 1995).

Among these texts, Chow's (1987) paper on 'Western and Chinese ideas of social welfare' was repeatedly cited by other writers to articulate their notions of Chinese culture, or to support their view of the differences between Western and Chinese welfare systems. Interestingly, Chow cautioned that ideas about social welfare were 'no more than shadows of prototypes which can at best show how people think, but cannot account for how they behave' and 'it is almost impossible ... to treat each belief system as a separate entity developed autonomously and unaffected by others' (p. 32). Likewise, Tsang warned that it was a 'mistake to assume homogeneity among people within the same culture' saying that both 'intercultural and intra-cultural heterogeneity' (Tsang 1997: 141) must be carefully examined. Still, it is not uncommon to see writers turning these philosophical 'ideas' about 'ideal or prototypical states' into explanatory tools for empirical inquiry into Chinese help seeking and caring behaviour. Consider the following examples from academics in Hong Kong:

Generally speaking, traditional Confucian concepts of mental health still have a very strong influence on the thinking and behavior of Chinese. For those Chinese coming from or in Mainland China, Taiwan, Hong Kong, its impact is still strong. Traditional Chinese concepts of mental health encourage Chinese people to restrain their emotion, avoid interpersonal conflict and suppress individual rights so as to maintain harmony with others and with the law of nature (Yip 2005a: 395).

Under the guidance of *li*, they are conscious of their performance and judgements by others. Doing things in a right and proper way is important, and they will feel a loss of face if they fail. The culture discourages experimentation. Chinese students tend to avoid taking risks by trying new ideas. Too much consciousness of performance and others' judgements discourages people from being creative and adventurous in their knowledge building (Chan and Chan 2005: 385).

[T]he Chinese sayings 'do not give what one dislikes to others', or 'restrain oneself and respect the rule of propriety' became guiding mottoes of the Chinese in their human interactions. It is only that one could gradually work towards the ideal of being *ren*, that is being virtuous. With such an understanding, it would not be difficult to understand why the Chinese tended to avoid conflicts and maintain harmony as far as possible (Yuen-Tsang 1999b: 368).

These writers try to apply normative schema to interpret, explain and justify what Chinese people do or do not do. Since social work as it is known in the west is completely foreign to China, it has to be introduced from the west and acculturated for a Chinese audience. Given the way these cultural characteristics are articulated, it is almost impossible to dispute or affirm the extent to which they match reality. At best they may be described as theoretical or normative. Nevertheless, they convey and are creating and influencing, a distinct 'discursive current' in the discourse on China in the international social work literature.

Arif Dirlik (1987) referred to this as 'culturalism', an 'ideology which not only reduces everything to questions of culture, but has a reductionist conception of the latter as well' (p. 14). While he acknowledges the centrality of culture in international discourse and the importance of people's world views, he believes that 'culturalist' assertions of the autonomy of culture as exemplified in the international social work literature need to be critically examined. This literature reduces the 'whole of experience' to questions of culture through an artificial intellectual exercise whereby those constructing the discourse are not those engaged in confronting everyday problems in China. Real 'cultural engagement', as Bhabha (1994) points out, whether antagonistic or affiliative, is produced performatively through cultural practices; intercultural dialogue or discursive interaction constructs interpretations of practice or normative schema of what practice requires. In the international social work discourse, Chinese perspectives can only be introduced through a Western lens because they must be articulated in English to reach a Western audience. Thus, as Bhabha notes,

> The representation of difference must not be hastily read as the reflection of pre-given ethnic or cultural traits set in the fixed tablet of tradition ... The 'right' to signify from the periphery of authorized power and privilege is resourced by the power of tradition to be inscribed through the conditions of contingency and contradictoriness that attend upon the lives of those who are 'in the minority' (Bhabha 1994: 2).

The minority here might be educated Chinese writers involved in introducing social work to China and interpreting China's needs and struggles to the west. Their 'culturalist analysis' is filled with the possibility of liberating Chinese people from oppression, masking the hegemonic nature of the Western theories and practices they are introducing.

However, culturalist discourse could never gain full legitimacy if it were at odds with the official storyline of the Chinese authorities. The question is whether this discourse of traditional values could also serve the interests of the ruling regime. As some writers argue, the reawakening of the Confucian tradition comes right in time to fill the ideological void resulting from the erosion of socialist ideals over the past two decades (Chan 1992; Karl 2005).

The Chinese government would seem to be at a crossroads. After decades of economic reform, the socialist system has been replaced gradually with a market economy. State enterprises started to vanish, as did the public welfare functions tied with these production units. The need for welfare and the dilemma of providing social care without overburdening the profit making potential of the newly emerging capitalist market presents the government with a dilemma. And the ideological basis of contemporary welfare philosophy being promoted in China is unclear. Thus Chan (1992) questions whether it is based 'on Confucianism, Marxism or Darwin's "survival of the fittest"?' (p. 352).

Under communism, all aspects of life in Mainland China could be politicized and the possibility remains that the cultural discourse reaching the ears of the communist leaders is becoming part of its new political armoury. This was evident in President Hu Jintao's policy framework for 'Building Harmonious Society' introduced during the 10th Annual Meeting of the Chinese National People's Congress in March 2005. It would seem that the Confucian ethos is being used as a lever as the government seeks to maintain its legitimacy through economic reform, that is, the introduction of Western capitalism and Western ideas to China.

Bringing a 'new rationality to old values' (Chau and Yu 1998: 17), the communist leaders have downplayed revolutionist solidarity and class struggles and attempted to make traditional Chinese culture, socialist ideology and the market economy work together. As Chau and Yu observe, 'traditional values such as family and self-care, interdependence, and emphasis on informal care still form part of the backbone of the new welfare system. Current reforms demonstrate the resurgence of these values' (p. 17).

The fantasy of an authentically 'culturalist China' serves as an 'anti-politics' (Karl 2005) while ruling elites join swiftly and smoothly with the rest of the world economically simultaneously clinging to political authoritarianisms. Chinese social workers, whether professionally trained or not, have rarely or 'at least not publicly' (Tsang and Yan 2001: 442) questioned the move to capitalist economic reform and the linking of social stability with the achievement of wealth and prosperity. Nevertheless, it is doubtful whether they, as participants in this 'culturalist discourse', deliberately or consciously wish to promote the interests of the government and its ostensible intention to nurture social stability and social harmony through self-reliance at the grassroots level and centralized control of resources.

Indeed, certain 'culturalist' analyses could easily be adopted by political elites to justify denial of the government's caring responsibilities. For instance, in her study on mental health services in China, Pearson (1989) pondered whether Chinese people indeed favoured family care over hospital care or whether this was merely a cover for the lack of medical services. Through interviews and field observation, she maintained that Chinese people had no choice but develop alternative ways of looking after the mentally ill because the government failed to provide the formal hospital care they would otherwise have liked. In fact, there are frequent reports of demands to provide more inpatient facilities (Pearson 1989: 60).

Ngan and Hui (1996) suggested that social workers should be more vocal in advocating for progressive social change and enhanced social justice and they should expand social work's role in policy development. In a haze of nostalgia, they recalled that social workers in Hong Kong had played an active role in advocating for macro level social policy initiatives but unfortunately, this role was not part of the existing discourse. Unfortunately, little will change while 'culturalists' extol traditional Chinese values like family allegiances, self-reliance, and submission to the power hierarchy (Chan and Chan 2005; Yao 1995).

Reconstructing the west: Where and what is the west?

The 'idea of "the West" … [which] was essential to the … formation of [Western] … society' (Hall 1996: 187) seems to pervade Western social work knowledge and practice where it is seen as a monolithic and homogenous entity (Tsang and Yan 2001). In much the same way, the idea of a unique stable 'Chinese corpus' seems to characterize the international literature on social work in China. Thus it presents Chinese society and cultural traditions, even within the Chinese diaspora contra the monolithic west. In his seminal paper, 'The West and the Rest: Discourse and Power', cultural theorist Stuart Hall (1996) identified four ways in which the concept or idea of 'the West' functioned: 1) it allowed the creation of the binary categories of Western and non-Western; 2) it led to images of Western, urban, and developed countries set against non-Western, non-industrialized, and underdeveloped ones; 3) it resulted in comparisons between Western and non-Western societies; and 4) it functioned as a standard of evaluation against which other societies were ranked. Hall saw the 'the west and the rest' discourse as destructive since 'it draws crude and simplistic distinctions and constructs an over-simplified conception of "difference"' (p. 189). It represents things that in reality are fluid and diverse, as fixed and homogeneous. In short, the idea of the west plays a powerful role as China seeks to establish a post-socialist identity.

Science is an aspect of Western culture that some Chinese scholars seek to emulate. Thus 'Western scientific approaches to social work' are valued highly even though aspects of Chinese culture are seen to be incompatible with scientific enquiry:

> The hierarchy of teacher and student is defined by *li* (rites). For a student the two golden rules are to respect the teacher and to honor truth. A teacher's role is highly respected, as he or she owns knowledge and truth. Challenging a teacher's ideas is deemed to be impolite. The stereotype of the Chinese student is that he or she displays an almost unquestioning acceptance of the knowledge of the teacher or lecturer (Chan and Chan 2005: 383).

> In Western teaching the main focus is on the development of creativity. The Chinese method focuses on memorization and students are expected to memorize the classics. In ancient China, advancement was based entirely on examinations and the only subject in the curriculum was classical literature (Chan and Chan 2005: 385).

> In Western society the main purpose of obtaining knowledge is to control, manipulate and change the natural and the social worlds. Positivism is the dominant paradigm that guides research themes and methodologies. In contrast, the Chinese hold a harmonious attitude towards nature (Chan and Chan 2005: 385–6).

To make scientific enquiry work, Chan and Chan (2005) believe that some of those cultural elements that are incompatible with scientific enquiry should be eliminated. On the other hand, they also consider that the strengths of Chinese culture must be retained if Mainland China is to develop its own Indigenous methods of enquiry. In this discourse, 'Western' and 'Chinese' are seen as two divergent traditions. While the cultural difference between Western methodology and Chinese ways of knowing is emphasized, the diversity among Chinese is not. Concepts, interventions and practices developed in one Chinese community, such as Canada, are often seen to be equally relevant in the UK, US and Australia, for example:

> Although the discussion in this article is in the context of the Chinese community in Canada, the implications for social work practice could be relevant to other Chinese communities in western countries … where legislation prescribes social workers with a statutory role in child protection (Kwok and Tam 2005: 341).

This notion of ontological sameness and global knowledge transfer overshadows the 'intersecting diversity' within and between Chinese societies (Tsang and Yan 2001). Thus Tsang and Yan challenge social work scholars in the west to 'resist the temptation of prescribing a single, comprehensive approach to our Chinese colleagues' (p. 448).

Interestingly, none of the writers ask, 'Where is the west?' In the discourse, Toronto, the city where I live, is part of the west while Hong Kong, the place where I was born, is in the east even though each time I fly over the Pacific to visit my family in Hong Kong I go in a westerly direction. The west signifies liberal democracy and capitalist society, rather than the Marxist–Leninist politics of China even though they have their roots in Western philosophy. To the extent that the PRC idealizes the work ethic, egalitarianism, social justice, the class struggle and proletarianism, it embodies the values Western Marxists extol (Chan and Tsui 1997). China has been a socialist 'welfare state' since 1949 and its modernization project continues to follow the Four Cardinal Principles: socialism, the dictatorship of the proletariat, the leadership of the party and the ideology of Marx, Lenin and Mao (Chau and Yu 1998). The only difference in Deng's social reforms, which began in the 1970s, is the hegemonic force of global market economics and capitalist ideology but it has not replaced the Marxist–Maoist modernist logic that prevails in the PRC. Still the culturalist discourse seems optimistic about the possibility of developing culturally relevant Indigenous social work in China despite these hegemonic Western forces (Ngai 1996). In fact, Cheung and Liu (2004) contend that the kind of social work that develops in China will have 'a ripple effect' in the international discourse 'on the definition of social work' (p. 123). In similar vein, Chi believes that it will have an impact on social work in developing countries:

> China could learn from the experiences of developing social work in the developed countries and at the same time take the initiative to develop social work that is more appropriate for the developing countries. China has no real burden of historical established social work structure, so it can take any direction it likes to develop its own social work theories and practices to meet the needs of its society. This opportunity would not only benefit China itself but also contribute to global social work development (Chi 2005: 379).

Relocating the tellers of the tales: Who are the speakers and who is missing?

The tales tell more about the tellers than the story told (Hall 2000). So who are the tellers of the Chinese tales? The majority of the authors of the selected texts were scholars of Chinese descent living and teaching in Hong Kong. There were also ten authors writing from the Chinese diaspora in Australia, New Zealand, Canada and the United States. Meng Liu is the only scholar who is teaching social work in China. With few exceptions, the non-Chinese contributors co-authored papers with their Chinese colleagues or students. Both Smith (2003) and Pearson (1989) referred to themselves as Westerners and acknowledged the effect of their Western viewpoint on their research. For example, Pearson noted that, 'Westerners sometimes tend(ed) to romanticize the idea of the closely knit Chinese family and community, comparing it with our own (western) isolationist and alienated existence' (p. 60).

The established authority of Hong Kong scholars is evident as most of the articles published in English language journals, including those submitted to ISW, come from authors in Hong Kong rather than Mainland China or Macau. Indeed, Hong Kong is a major player in the development of social work education and practice in China (Chi 2005; see Chapters 14 and 15). As early as 1986, the Asian Pacific Association of Social Work Education established the Committee on Relationships with China to explore possible future relationships with the PRC. The members of this committee were predominantly from Hong Kong (Chamberlain 1991). It comprised Angelina Yuen and Paul Lee from the Hong Kong Polytechnic and Nelson Chow from Hong Kong University with Janet George from the University of Sydney and Edna Chamberlain, the President of APASWE ex-officio, from Australia. It was chaired by Foo Tak Nam from the Hong Kong Polytechnic and its mandate was to maintain ongoing dialogue with members of the Peking University which had received approval from the PRC Department of Education to develop a social work programme in China.

Having been a colony of the United Kingdom until 1997, the colonial influence which characterized social work education and practice in Hong Kong *inter alia* the English language as the medium of instruction and communication of research findings, was extended to China by social work academics, as is evidenced in the international discourse already discussed (Chi 2005). One might question whether Hong Kong scholars are 'qualified' to represent the interests of people in Mainland China. Are they the authentic voice of Chinese people living in Mainland China? What information are they privileging and what are they leaving out of this discourse? Is it in their interests to claim success and progress in developing social work in Mainland China? If 'Indigenization' comes from within (Cheung and Liu 2004) and reflects the multiethnic, multilingual and multicultural nature of China, can knowledge transferred from Hong Kong be Indigenous (Wang 2000)? Interestingly, scholars who are writing from an in-between position seem to be more eager to address the issue of internal diversity among the Chinese in their communities and across the globe (Kung 2005; Sin and Yan 2003; Tsang and Yan 2001).

In anthropology, nativization – or Indigenization – is complex and political:

Scholars in China talk about 'nativization' in similar terms, but differing overtones. Han colleagues talk 'nativization' meaning China versus the West. Mongolian scholars advocate 'nativization' hinting at Mongol versus Han and the West ... Within the Mongolian scholarly community, 'nativization' can mean mother-tongue or even dialect-based scholarship. The checklist has to stop here, though further fragmentation is still possible (Bilik 2002: 137).

As Bilik illustrates, particularism in China, as in the rest of the world, is hierarchically ordered. Each higher order can use 'universalism' against the 'particularism' of the lower order(s), and theoretically the latter can also use the 'particularism' against higher orders. In reality, the hierarchy of difference is maintained through differential access to discursive spaces; language and access to publication and computer technology is available for a privileged minority. Thus as well as calling for 'Indigenization' from within (Enriquez 1993), one also needs 'Indigenization' from below. Ethnic minorities outside the cities and metropolitan areas where most scholars reside fall beyond the reach (Bilik 2002) of the social work being introduced in Mainland China. Only Smith's (2003) study explored the social development of ethnic minorities in China. As Wang (2002) observed in relation to minority issues, scholars who have benefited from their cultural and ethnic affiliation and Western educational background form a new breed of local cultural promoters who simultaneously extol cross-cultural competence from the north and 'Indigenization' from the south.

Conclusion

Despite the extreme diversity of the Chinese population, the international literature conveys the idea that there is a single 'Chinese corpus' that operates in the same way as the idea of the monolithic west. Those constructing the international discourse on social work in Mainland China come mainly from Hong Kong and the Chinese diaspora, which raises questions as to whether they are the authentic voice of the people of Mainland China. This discourse tends to simplify complex political issues by constructing a 'culturalist' image of 'Chineseness' based on universal values rooted in Confucianism which the creators of this discourse justify on the basis that it has outlasted socialism. In reality, Chinese leaders are appropriating this culturalist discourse while clinging to socialist ideology despite economic reforms. Thus it is important to use a critical lens that is sensitive to power relations and the need for multiple voices to be heard in this international discourse (Wong 2002).

Chapter 14

A Journey of a Thousand Miles begins with One Step: The Development of Culturally Relevant Social Work Education and Fieldwork Practice in China

Angelina Yuen-Tsang and Ben Ku

There is an old Chinese saying that 'a journey of 1,000 miles begins with one step'. Though the path of social work's development in China has not been smooth and it still has a long way to go, our older generation started by taking the first step. Today what we have accomplished is only part of the marathon of social work's development in China, which is traced in this chapter. Specifically, we describe the development of an MSW programme in China undertaken in partnership with Hong Kong Polytechnic University. A characteristic feature of social work education in China is its close relationship with the Central Government which has played, and is still playing, a pivotal role in the planning and development of social policies and social services in China. The voluntary sector is only just emerging and its contribution to social welfare development has been relatively insignificant in the past. Moreover, the fact that most social work graduates are employed by the various government ministries means that social work education has to work closely with the Central Government in both its educational and service development endeavors. In recognizing the reality of the central role of the government in social welfare policy and service development, the social work curricula of most Chinese social work training institutions place a heavy emphasis on knowledge and skills pertaining to working with or within the government bureaucracy. The managerial and administrative roles expected of social work graduates are, therefore, much more prominent in China than in most other countries, and the qualities expected of the graduates are developed accordingly (Lu 1996; Xiong 1999).

In order to build a partnership between social work education institutions and government organizations, social work educators are actively involved in government projects as honorary advisors, consultants and trainers. Social work educators realize that they must maintain this close partnership with the government both out of necessity and because of the need to keep abreast of developments in the field. Therefore, with the exception of the first few years when social work education was still groping for its direction, social work educators in China have made a conscious effort to discard their 'ivory tower' image by actively reaching out to government departments both centrally and locally, and in the main, we have managed to establish a good relationship with the government enabling us to facilitate the development of social work education and practice in China.

Our MSW graduates actively provide training and consultation to government ministries, local government and NGOs. Our MSW programme has developed a critical mass of dedicated social work educators who are actively involved in the China Association of Social Work Education established in 1994 by the Ministry of Civil Affairs (MOCA), and are playing a leading role in the development of social work education in China. The programme's curriculum also provides an education model which emphasizes theory–practice integration, critical reflection, action learning, culturally sensitive practice and commitment to social change and development.

The history of social work education in China

Social work in China, in the form of philanthropy, dates to earlier times. It has included all kinds of social relief and social services provided by the government and private and religious organizations and had a strong flavor of 'paternalism'. It was only in the early part of the 1920s that social work was first introduced to China's academy by overseas trained expatriate social work and sociology scholars as a sub-branch of sociology. They returned to China to start social work training programmes in many renowned universities, such as the Yanjing University (now the Peking University), Jinling University, Lingnan University, Fudan University, Qili University, Tsinghua University and Furen University. Since most of these programmes were housed in sociology departments, and were strongly influenced by the Chinese sociological tradition, the 'applied sociology' approach was used in teaching and learning, emphasizing the importance of social inquiry and field research and the applied nature of knowledge (Lei and Shui 1991). With the advent of the socialist government, social work was seen as a capitalist academic discipline and all social work and sociology programmes were eliminated shortly after the formation of New China (the People's Republic of China or PRC) during the 'restructuring of institutions of higher learning' in 1952 in line with the government's 'leftist guiding principles' and claims that a socialist society 'had no social problems and therefore had no need of education on social work' (Yuan 1988: 8). China adopted the Soviet model of socialism and created a centralized planned economy in which the government provided its people with a comprehensive cradle to grave welfare package. Thus social work became redundant and was eliminated from all universities.

In 1979, soon after the introduction of the Open Door Economic Policy in the PRC, the discipline of sociology was restored to the university curriculum. Social work subjects were reintroduced largely through the dedicated efforts of several elderly social work educators who had been educated in the west during the pre-liberation days and who had been instrumental in the early development of social work education in China in the 1920s. Observing the problems brought about by rapid social change and realizing the immense need for social services and the corresponding need for high-level social welfare manpower, they, together with the PRC's Ministry of Civil Affairs (MOCA),[1] zealously advocated the reintroduction of social work as a university-based discipline. Thus in 1986, the PRC's State Education Commission formally established 'Social Work and Management' as a recognized university discipline. In 1988 the government gave approval for four universities to offer social work programmes. In 1989 Peking University launched its social work programme at both the undergraduate and post-graduate levels. It was gradually followed by other universities and training colleges in China (Yuan 1998).

However, the number of programmes remained small in the early 1990s because of the lack of trained teachers, a lack of interest from students and poor job prospects for graduates. The most serious problem was the lack of social work educators with expertise and experience in curriculum planning, and the absence of teaching material and other resources. Worse still, the social work educators who had been recruited to teach social work in the designated universities were not trained in social work and had neither the professional knowledge nor the practice experience in social work necessary for effective teaching (Ku *et al.* 2005; Yuen-Tsang 1996). The few social work academics who had been trained in the pre-liberation days were already in their late seventies and eighties and although they could offer advice and guidance they could hardly provide much concrete support.

Through trial and error and much painstaking toil and labor, the Chinese social work educators managed to overcome numerous obstacles and gradually their own unique pattern of social work education evolved. The China Association of Social Work Education (CASWE) was established to coordinate and facilitate the development of social work education in the PRC. After 1999, the number of social work programmes expanded dramatically because of the rapid growth in higher education in China. At the same time, the demand for professional social work services also increased because of the demise of the welfare system traditionally provided by *danwei* (work units) in urban China and by the *gongshi jiti* (collective commune); the rising public demand for quality social services as a result of rising incomes and aspirations; and the impact of quality services provided by international and Hong Kong NGOs.

To date, more than 172 universities formally offer social work programmes at the degree level. Together with post-secondary and cadre training colleges, there are over 200 social work programmes in China (Wang 2005), signifying that social work education has gained increasing popularity and recognition in the PRC. Now that China's social work education is entering a stage of consolidation and professionalization, the CASWE has firmly established its leadership. Its membership and geographical coverage, its degree of representation and the breadth of its activities have led to its recognition and visibility both within China and international professional bodies. The CASWE is taking active steps to provide

---

1   During the past decade, the Ministry of Civil Affairs, the China Association of Social Work Education and numerous social work training institutions in Mainland China have extended repeated requests to the Department of Applied Social Sciences (APSS) at Hong Kong Polytechnic University (PolyU) to offer a training programme at the Master's level for mainland social work educators.

training, and to develop culturally relevant teaching materials and local textbooks. The Ministry of Education is beginning to limit the growth of social work programmes and has invited the CASWE to take part in reviewing the standard of social work programmes. However, while we consider the development of our MSW in China a great achievement, there are many questions and issues concerning curriculum content and the relevance of social work education in China. Thus the invitation to participate in the development of an MSW programme in partnership with one of Mainland China's leading universities, the Peking University, provided an ideal opportunity for reflective assessment on the rapid expansion of social work education and for the development of culturally appropriate social work in China.

The context of the development of culturally relevant social work education in China

We soon realized that there was a serious disjunction between the rapid expansion of social work education institutions and the lack of social service related job opportunities. Most importantly, all the social work educators who had been assigned to teach social work were transferred from other disciplines within the university, such as history, anthropology, sociology and philosophy. They had no 'professional training' and no background in social work whatsoever. Thus social work was being reintroduced into universities by academics with neither the professional expertise nor the practical experience to develop this newly introduced professional discipline. Furthermore, there was tremendous internal and external competition among those wanting to offer social work education in China and conflicting options about the direction it should take. To compound this situation, these academics were being trained to teach social work when there were no jobs available for the graduates of their programmes. Our assessment was that there were three main forces shaping or impacting on the development of social work education in China when our programmes were engaged: Professional colonization, bureaucratic constraints and the commodification of higher education.

Right from the start, when social work was reintroduced in 1988, it was seen by the Chinese government and key stakeholders as a pragmatic solution to social problems and as a way to stabilize society following the introduction of the open door economic policy and the market economy which brought about rapid economic and social change and a host of social issues and problems. The state tried to appropriate the social work profession, expecting it to develop effective approaches to meet the changing needs of Chinese society. During the opening ceremony of the 1988 Seminar on Social Work Education in the Asian and Pacific Region organized by Peking University, the officer in charge of social work education in the State Education Commission issued the challenge to social work educators to 'start from the practical needs of China' and to build and develop education programmes 'to suit the Chinese practical context, and the needs of the Chinese society' (Xia 1991: 6). Likewise, Peking University senior social work professor, J.Q. Lei asserted that 'social work education must suit the needs of the modern society ... and the reality of China' (Lei and Shui 1991) indicating that it had to be simultaneously locally relevant and globally competitive.

Thus social work education was not only an academic matter but also a political issue. Despite the lapse of just over thirty years, caution against Western liberalization was still very much alive in the late 1980s in the official guise of *heping yanbian* – peaceful evolution and transformation. Key stakeholders involved in service provision did not want the social work profession to be too closely associated with the west such that it became a medium for the ideological transformation of China by Western powers to Western ways. It was in this historical context that Chinese psychologists, sociologists and anthropologists drawn into social work education began to reflect on the need for 'sinolization' or 'Indigenization' of the social and behavioural sciences in the late 1970s. Resistance about the direct borrowing of theories and methods from the west also dominated discussions among Chinese social work academics in the late 1980s. They saw the importance of grounding social work theory and practice firmly in the local sociocultural context in which it was embedded. There was a strong sense that it should not be directly transplanted from other countries. Yuen-Tsang and Wang (2002) highlighted the pivotal tensions relating to the mission and purpose of social work education. Should it be about individual treatment or social reform given that there wasn't a history of psychologization in China and social work had historically been aligned to sociology within the university? And with regard to curriculum design, should it follow international social work standards or local contextual needs? Should a professional or populist model be pursued given China's strong collective culture? Concerns about relevance, expressed in discussions about localization, contextualization and Indigenization, ran the danger of being overshadowed by professional colonization from the internationalizing and universalizing social work practiced in North America and Europe.

We noticed that professional colonization was already evident in at least two respects. First, when social work was reintroduced in the early 1980s it was classified as a sub-branch of sociology. While the influence of sociology as a discipline for analyzing social problems had diminished, social work was seen as a tool for solving social problems. Unlike Europe and North America, in China the foundation disciplines of social work, such as sociology, psychology and political science, were still being developed and consolidated and thus social work's Western theoretical foundation was nowhere to be found. The 'scientific and systematic professional social work knowledge' from developed Western societies, like the United States and Britain, or its Westernized neighbours, Hong Kong and Taiwan, had become a role model Chinese society wanted to emulate. Second, China's higher education system was already being influenced by globalization though unevenly. Those with money to support the rapid growth of higher education in China sought to import global knowledge systems, like Western social work models taught in the United States and Britain, and used by aid programmes involved in international development.

These professional colonization processes were hemmed in by politics and bureaucratic constraints. Under the socialist system, helping activities similar to those of social work were shared by organs of state, such as the civil affairs administration, local administration in the sub-district and resident committees, as well as state sponsored mass organizations, like the Communist Youth League,

Women's Federation and labor unions. These bureaucracies competed for their share of control over social work activities. While the professional model of social work advocated by the universities in the west that we were emulating called for autonomous professional status supported by a monopolization of professional credentialization, these bureaucracies feared that this would jeopardize their sphere of influence. Thus they favored a statist approach and the human services model embedded in existing mass organizations.

Amid the restructuring of higher education towards 'market demands', the 'market obsolete' disciplines, such as philosophy and history, were looking for ways to transform themselves into disciplines with 'market value', like economics, business administration and management. Fortunately or unfortunately, social work, in its quest for professional status while being dogged by bureaucratic politics, was chosen as a 'shelter' for academics from these obsolete disciplines. Thus social work flourished even though its academics had no social work training or professional status, and despite the non-existence of a career related job market for social workers.

Nevertheless, China's social work educators, with the help of its older generation of social workers, have struggled relentlessly over the last ten years to develop local, culturally appropriate programmes, while constantly torn between the conflicting tensions of professionalization and bureaucratization. They struggled with adapting Western social work knowledge as they sought to borrow and apply social work theories developed in the west to local Chinese contexts believing that Western theories were applicable and adaptable to the needs and characteristics of different societies. Despite attempts at a critical reflective and selective approach to the adoption of these Western theories, methods and approaches, to a great extent, their philosophical underpinnings went unchallenged and they were adopted wholesale despite some realization that they did not fit local sociocultural contexts. Few attempted to engage actively in critical reflective dialogue with local service users and, in effect, there was little practical concern with cultural appropriateness in local contexts. Many lacked the creative ability to reconceptualize Western social work theories and to experiment with innovative culturally appropriate approaches. Thus it was mainly students who generated innovative, culturally appropriate practice theories relevant to local contexts during their field practica.

When we entered the picture, our stance was that relevant social work should derive from the 'lived experience' of Chinese people. Thus we began by mapping existing approaches, constructing a working framework, experimenting with its implementation, reflecting critically upon it and reconceptualizing its theoretical foundations, which initially were largely sociological. We focused on developing employment prospects for social work graduates and the contexts in which their services might be deployed, such as NGOs or local government administrative offices. This is where the field practicum became pivotal. To identify appropriate practicum sites and to develop appropriate community-based projects, we engaged students in research on the problems faced by various disadvantaged groups and looked for gaps in government administration and service delivery where social work intervention might be possible. Below we describe the process followed by our group, based in Hong Kong, and its involvement in developing an MSW programme to train social work educators drawn from obsolete disciplines at Peking University and in creating social work services, through the field practicum, in Mainland China.

Case study: MSW programme

As part of the international social work community, our approach involved exporting Hong Kong's Western social work education model to China, and adapting and integrating it in local cultural contexts. This was a demanding undertaking since none of our Chinese MSW students, that is, the social work educators drawn from obsolete disciplines, had an undergraduate degree in social work nor did they have any grounding or experience in social work whatsoever. In terms of international professional standards, they were 'not qualified' to teach or practice social work. Essentially our task was to develop a critical mass of social work educators to lead the future development of social work education and practice in China. In short, we had to 'train the trainers'. We received financial support from MISEREOR and the Keswick Foundation, and developed the MSW programme in collaboration with Peking University.

Pedagogic approach and course content

Our role was to 'train these trainers' to teach 'advanced generalist social work practice and to produce social work practitioners capable of responding to escalating social problems within China's rapidly changing cultural and socio-political context. Given the aforementioned bureaucratic restraints, graduates had to be able to provide high quality 'scientific–professional' services and work flexibly and realistically within severely constrained organizational contexts. Thus we had to train these non-social work trained social work educators to develop a future generation of critically 'reflective social work practitioners' (Yuen-Tsang 1999a: 2–3) who adhered to the universal core values of social work, namely respect for human dignity, mutual help and support, social justice and human rights. But how were we to teach that 'all people have a right to share equally in the world's resources and to be masters of their own development' in a country without a human rights culture? Would our students understand that the rejection of human rights lay at the heart of poverty and suffering? How would we introduce a culture of individual autonomy and an understanding that individuals have the capacity to determine their own values and priorities, and to act on these? How would we introduce the notion of personal development?

First we had to create a culture in which students took responsibility for their own learning and knowledge building processes. This, in turn, required strengthening the students' capacity to understand that their values and priorities are self-determined and their actions freely chosen. We decided that 'capacity building' was central to our programme since essentially we were building the capacity of these educators to train Chinese social work students to adopt professional social work values built on individual autonomy, that is, the ability to determine one's values and knowledge building endeavors. Related to this was the realization of their capacity through personal development training. We did this by drawing on their 'lived experience' and 'existing capacity' as experienced, though non-social work, academics. Some held senior positions and were professors and heads of the academic departments from which they had been recruited. They came from geographically diverse areas of China, including the more remote and deprived southwest provinces of Yunnan, Guizhou, Sichuan, Qinghai and Xinjiang. This was intentional to ensure that social work education would spread far and wide and have maximum social impact on local communities. We had to teach these students that relationship development is central to social work and encourage them to cultivate relationships with local people.

Thus the MSW took the form of a three-year part-time in-service programme since our 'students' had to continue with their teaching responsibilities while they were studying. Students were required to take seventeen subjects including ten required subjects, one elective, Social Work Practicum I, II and III and Dissertation I, II and III. The programme was taught jointly by academics from Peking and Hong Kong Polytechnic (PolyU) universities. Most of the social work subjects and practica were carried out in diverse locations on the Chinese Mainland but during intensive study period, students came to Hong Kong to study at PolyU for a semester in order to gain an understanding of social work in Hong Kong. We encouraged students to develop their own theory and practice of social work grounded in the lived experience and institutional context of Chinese people. In other words we wanted them to adapt our Western models to their local context and thus develop new culturally relevant models through their field practica.

We used an interdisciplinary approach involving academics from different disciplines and backgrounds from PolyU and Peking University to broaden the students' theoretical perspective. Our teaching staff comprised scholars from philosophy, psychology, sociology, anthropology, social work and social policy and administration. We saw this approach as critical to countering inappropriate Western social work approaches, like micro or clinical practice (Haynes 1998). While we taught 'micro skills' and direct practice, we encouraged our students to focus on community development and policy analysis or 'macro social work' and we strove to give them a broad understanding of China's development in relation to the spread of global capitalism. Professor Wang Sibin of Peking University has been a leading proponent of 'social development and poverty alleviation ... [as] the primary focus of social work education in China ... [arguing that] individualized practice should only constitute a supplementary and secondary role in the social work curriculum' (Wang 1994: 13). We were bent on 'producing social work graduates with a macro perspective to social issues and problems and with the generic skills necessary to engage in multi-level intervention' (Yuen-Tsang and Wang 2002: 379). Professor Wang Sibin's involvement helped shape our culturally appropriate curriculum. In short, our innovative interdisciplinary approach integrated well with our capacity building pedagogy.

Practicum as an experiment in culturally appropriate social work

The practicum extended our capacity building approach into the community. Its objectives were to:

1. Help students adapt their generalist social work practice skills and approaches in local communities in Mainland China.
2. Increase students' sensitivity to competing values, develop their ability to make ethical decisions, and strengthen their capacity to deal with tension, uncertainty and conflict.
3. Enable students to synthesize and integrate knowledge from a number of disciplines, enhancing their learning and practice competence.
4. Encourage students to articulate a coherent personal perspective of and approach to social work practice in Mainland China.
5. Strengthen students' capacity and interest as active learners and to encourage their continuing development as reflective practitioners in social work and social development.
6. Develop students' capacity to continue to develop social work education and to train professional social workers in Mainland China.
7. Prepare students for their professional responsibilities as educators of social work practitioners who were simultaneously shaping professional, scientifically-based social work practice in Mainland China.
8. Develop students' competence in applying research methods to the analysis of problems and to articulate the process and results of their empirical investigations.

As already mentioned, given that our students had not had any prior grounding or experience in social work when they joined our programme, the field practicum was challenging especially when they had to play the non-expert role of 'community developer'. Particularly challenged were their preconceptions of poor and deprived people as uneducated, backward, uncivilized and in need of help from outside experts. Given the lack of social (work) services these community development projects developed important sites for social work intervention. For example, the practicum in Beijing developed social support networks for unemployed women workers and urban families undergoing social and economic transition. The practicum in Shanghai, in collaboration with the legal department, developed a home-school-community delinquency prevention project. The Wuhan project focused on the elderly and families with special needs, including families in poverty experiencing violence and abuse. In Kunming of Yunnan province, the hospital-based practicum focused on micro clinical and community-based mental health practice. In Harbin, students developed a factory- based 'quality of work life' project helping workers to deal with the pressure and difficulties of the state enterprise reform process.

Thus far we have enrolled three student cohorts and have developed three practice programmes. In the first and second practica, students selected an agency or government unit for their placement and each was matched with a teacher-supervisor.

Intensive skills training workshops were held prior to, during, and at the end of the practicum to prepare students and monitor their progress in their placements.

The second practicum was the most critical and also the longest involving 400 hours in one location supported by a supervisor and teaching assistant who was a graduate of the first cohort. We also insisted that some students undertake at least one placement in a rural setting to introduce them to underprivileged areas of the country where the vast majority of China's population lives and to give them the opportunity to appreciate the nature of the problems that marginalized people face. Two rural practica were developed in Yunnan and Hunnan where students created a community development and community health project for rural disabled people respectively.

The third practicum was conducted in Hong Kong. Students were grouped in pairs and undertook placements in social work organizations where they gained an understanding of professional social work practice in Hong Kong. Students kept practicum portfolios that became pivotal documentations of the processes involved in developing culturally relevant social work theory and practice models.

Research as social praxis

In many of their practicum projects, students adopted an integrated action research approach, using participatory research methods, applying ethnographic methods to collect oral histories and to generate local knowledge and relevant practice models in partnership with local communities. Students tested their evolving intervention models thus generating grounded practice knowledge. Some teachers and students continued to participate in the projects beyond their practica. In some cases, local networks and small groups formed during the practicum gained support from overseas foundations. Students were encouraged to develop innovative practice models in collaboration with local universities and government units to serve as demonstrations of local initiatives, which could be used by local universities as examples of sustainable development.

Participatory action research bridged the theory and practice divide through familiarization with the needs of local communities and enhanced the students' ability to respond to local problems. It enabled students to listen to client voices and to understand their life circumstances. It also generated valuable 'theory' and well documented case studies for teaching. Students covered diverse topics in their research dissertations, including elder support networks, women's issues, youth work, rural development and the plight of migrant workers. They provided a unique insight into China's social problems, ways in which social work might respond, and pointed to directions for future professional development. The first student cohort's work was compiled into a book entitled *Research, Practice and Reflection of Social Work in Indigenous Chinese Context*. It has become an example of social work research and teaching material for social work programmes in China's universities. Some of the students' research also informed policy makers about the impact of policy on local communities.

The students' practicum experience was transformative as they discovered that poor people were neither powerless nor passive and as they unleashed local people's and their own capacity. Local communities participated willingly in the student practica and learned to organize themselves to accomplish their goals. People centred community development has led to the transformation of local communities. The students were encouraged by the process of discovering their own values; developing a strong sense of confidence and competence; and the capacity to rethink issues of power and domination in China's development. One student stated:

> Peasants are not as stupid as we thought before. Actually, they're full of wisdom. They have their local knowledge. They don't need our supervision and imposition, but they need encouragement and support.

And another:

> All of a sudden, I gained a sense of satisfaction (from the villagers being able to make decisions), because I could observe the changes in the villagers in these seven weeks, while their potential was being realized. In the beginning, they considered us to be playing, and observed us from afar. Later on, they began to get close to us, to chat and to sing with us. And finally, they started working with us (doing oral history), and organized themselves to plan their own future. How encouraging! There were a few girls in particular, who were so shy at first that they would not even lift their heads. After working with their own groups, they became bold enough to sing some ditties at evening gatherings and participate in group discussions. What an amazing change!

Another wrote:

> We began to ask about development for what, for whom. Actually, we found that the village secretary, the head of the village and the director of the Credit Co-opt were the actual beneficiaries of the development in the tourism industry, while such benefits lay beyond the reach of the ordinary villager.

Critical thinking and self-reflection

In the MSW programme, we emphasized critical thinking and self-reflection to get students to examine their values and attitudes towards the social and political structures within which they were working and to deepen their understanding of how these affected practice with culturally diverse clients. We encouraged students to engage in critical reflection throughout the learning process and to engage in critical dialogue with their teachers and with service users. Thus we endeavored to enhance their capacity as independent and active learners able to construct, deconstruct and reconstruct their professional practice and knowledge in the Chinese context.

Teachers modeled the non-directive, non-expert role in the classroom and encouraged students to take responsibility for their own learning; teachers, coming from Hong Kong, were also learners. Such humility prepared students to work collaboratively with local communities to search for possible paths to local community development. Our student or learner centred approach helped students discover their own worth and to develop a strong sense of confidence in their own capacity and competence. As one student said:

In the process, I felt myself to be like a teacher ... What are we to do? How to do it? We had to make a decision all by ourselves. Now the villagers had also become a subject themselves; they therefore had to make a decision as to what to do and what not to do in community development.

Reflective learning also developed their awareness of their position and role in local development. As another student said:

Our ideals (of development), if not handled with care, could possibly become an invasion to others. It is indeed noble to fight for our ideals, but we should also pay more attention to realities, and experience them more.

The capacity for self-reflection enabled students to examine and consider the limitations of their professional social work role and the need for cultural sensitivity. A student shared this thought with us:

Now I realize what we believe in, and no matter what position we are in, it is irrelevant, for the most important thing is whether or not we have re-examined ourselves enough, understood our limitations and advantages, and become adequately alert. It is important to acknowledge the co-existence of different values, and to approach issues from an all-embracing aspect.

The practicum experience forced students to reconsider the rational foundations on which social work is based and the messy reality of everyday lived experience and to see learning as a lifelong process of constant self-examination and construction, deconstruction and reconstruction of knowledge in relation to life experience. Students learned to see their professional power and authority. One student bravely talked about the hypocrisy of professional social workers who were fond of taking the moral high ground in the classroom and at conferences.

Once in a real-life situation, however, these professional social workers more often than not separated themselves from the theories, giving people the impression that they do not live up to their words.

To them, the values social workers espouse should be congruent with their behaviour and actions.

At the beginning, I didn't understand that self-growth and becoming an active learner is so important to a social work educator. I thought I was a teacher in any case, I taught others, learning is none of my business. However, this program helped to understand myself, through unceasing reflection, I found self-growth is so important.

In these three years, through the solid training and learning, I found that I was more confident to grasp the social work professional knowledge, new theories, and professional techniques and accumulate rich practicum experiences. However, most important, this program cultivates my professional value and enhances my reflection capacity, makes ... It changed my life path, renewed my life. It doesn't only help me to learn professional social work, but also to learn what the meaning of life is. Therefore, I should be very thankful to my *liangshi yiyou* (good teachers and helpful friends in the class)!

> The fifty days of fieldwork in the village is something I will not forget for the rest of my life, for it has given me inspiration and has had a great impact on me. I have made new discoveries with regard to myself, others, and to villages in China as well as the peasants. I have been made to rethink and reflect on the idea of social work as a profession, the conventional theories of rural development and, in particular, my character as well as that of others …

The practicum experience became the important locus of reflection as students brought these experiences back to the classroom and discussed the relationship between textbook theories and practice realities. Such discussions enabled us to assess students' critical reflection skills and their capacity to apply their learning to concrete social work processes. Students also critically reflected on the programme and their teachers' performance. As one student said:

> We didn't have any formal social service organization here; when we were required to select an agency or government unit for our first placement, it was difficult to find a suitable one. But some of the fieldwork I just didn't understand, some activities, like governmental fund raising activities, I participated in were not counted as practicum work. They told me that it was not professional social services.

Another stated:

> Some of our Hong Kong teachers didn't have enough knowledge of the China Mainland situation. In their teaching, they couldn't give us examples which we were familiar with.

The students' comments helped us to reflect on the benefits and limitations of our programme and were especially helpful to those who were encountering students from a socio-political context which, though also Chinese, was different from Hong Kong. Critical reflection proved important to students and staff alike.

Supportive learning network

Within the MSW programme, we endeavored to develop supportive networks, such as peer tutoring groups through which students provided mutual support to one another. Students in the second and third cohorts were engaged as teaching assistants and supervisor trainees as part of their training to become trainers. Students from different geographic regions were grouped in regional clusters to form strategic partnerships for future collaboration.

We also established the Center for China Research and Development Network as a platform to host and advance research collaboration with academic institutions and MSW graduates. Together with the Department of Sociology at Peking University, we have established a Research Center for Social Work Theory and Practice in China and with the Department of Social Work at Yunnan University a Research Center for Rural Social Work and Development in China. These two centres will collaborate with MSW graduates and local universities to develop relevant social work theory and practice in China.

The social impact of the MSW programme

The most outstanding social impact of our MSW programme is its commitment to the development of social work education, and social change and development in China. Our students have gradually positioned themselves as catalysts for community improvement and social development via actively developing participatory action research and community development projects through the fieldwork practicum in different parts of China. They realize that social work education is a vehicle for the production of future leaders and policy makers who can contribute to community and social development by dealing with critical social issues in contemporary China, such as unemployment, street children, poverty, marital breakdown, an aging population, and so on. Thus deliberate efforts have been made to equip these students with knowledge and skills both in working with individuals and families as well as in relating individual and family problems to social change and development in the larger social context. Conscious efforts have also been made to introduce social policy analysis and macro level intervention strategies into the social work curriculum. Some of our students are actively collaborating with local NGOs and governmental organizations and use them as practicum sites for their students. For example, our graduates in the Department of Social Work in Yunnan University sent their students to World Vision China and worked with them to develop services for street children. Their students also do their practicum in the drug treatment and rehabilitation centre of Daytop China and learn how to help drug addicts and prevent HIV and AIDS transmission.

Another characteristic feature of the impact of social work education in China is its close partnership with the government. The government of China has played, and is still playing, a central leadership role in the planning and development of social policies and services in China. Most of the MSW graduates, being university professors, are commissioned by government ministries as honorary advisors, consultants and trainers and their participation is shaping social policy. For example, one graduate, the department head of social work from Changsha College of Civil Affairs works with the Hunan Provincial Disabled Persons' Federation to provide services for the disabled in rural Hunan. This work has been recognized by the public and the government and in 2005 was named in the Top Ten Public Charitable Affairs in Hunnan Province. The department of social work was named as the National Advanced Unit for Disable Services jointly by the China Disabled Persons' Federation and the Central Communist Youth League.

Finally, in collaboration with MOCA, CASWE and some of our graduates, we conducted research on the professionalization of social service personnel in MOCA that led to a policy decision to professionalize its social service workers. This was a major achievement and an important step in developing standards and procedures for professional accreditation and licensing in China.

Chapter 15

Re-envisioning Indigenization: When *Bentuhuade* and *Bentude* Social Work Intersect in China

Miu Chung Yan and A Ka Tat Tsang

In the original manuscript presented at the writers' workshop, we subtitled our presentation: 'When the Indigenous and the Indigenized in social work intersect in China'. The word 'Indigenous' led to rigorous, forceful and sometimes emotional debate among the participants. Details of the debate are important and provide useful material for another book on this subject and we cannot do it justice here! However, what we want to do is to report why we decided to change the subtitle by using two Chinese terms – *bentuhuade* and *bentude* – instead of *Indigenized* and *Indigenous*. There are three reasons. First, to decentre the 'Western domination' of social work discourse, we should try to use terminology developed by people who are involved in the process of social work development in their own unique local context. Second, translation inevitably leads to a distortion of meaning. For instance, in our case *bentuhuade* bears the meanings of Indigenized, localized, contextualized, recontextualized, and so on. Similarly, *bentude* can be understood at least as Indigenous, local, native, home-made or home-grown, just to name a few senses in which the concept is used. Since we are describing a social process taking place in China, we think it is fair to use Chinese terminology to contextualize our discussion. Last, but certainly not least, we are conscious of the discursive consequence of any choice of words. One of the debates during the workshop regarded the political implications of the word 'Indigenous'. As pointed out by some Aboriginal colleagues, the word 'Indigenous' has a significant meaning to the identity and history of Indigenous Peoples who have suffered from the continuous colonialization of their land in North America and elsewhere. They expressed strong concern over the usage of this word in the discussion of Indigenization. We have not come to the conclusion that this term should bear one fixed meaning. Nonetheless, with respect to our colleagues present at the workshop, and to avoid confusion and potential distraction from their political agenda, we have decided to stay away from the term 'Indigenous' in this discussion. More than respecting our Indigenous colleagues, there is a recurring caution against professional imperialism and the universality of Western[1] social work values, knowledge and technology (Gray 2005;

---

1   The authors are fully aware of the diversity of the Western social work knowledge. In this paper, to magnify the focus of discussion, we deliberately use a capitalized 'W' to

Hugman 1996; Midgley 1981) which has gradually drawn people's attention to the issue of Indigenization in the international social work literature. In the literature, Indigenization is generally understood as a process of adapting, adjusting and modifying imported knowledge – theories, values and technology – mainly from the West to fit the local context – cultural, social, economic and political – of a developing country (Ferguson 2005; Gray 2005; Nimmagadda and Cowger 1999; Walton and Abo El Nasr 1988). While this understanding recognizes the function of 'agency' – the autonomy to adapt and modify – of scholars and practitioners of local social work communities in the importing countries, there are still underlying problems with it.

First, Indigenization is understood as a filtering process through which components of the imported knowledge that do not fit the local context will be excluded based on clear criteria, such as incompatibility with local culture. Whereas local relevance and cultural appropriateness can be seen as the major selection and exclusion criteria, the *bentuhuade* practices, namely, the modified imported approach, are still expected to be commensurable within this dominant (Western) paradigm (Coates *et al.* 2006; Gray 2005). Apparently, this assumption still privileges the social work paradigm of the Western, or more specifically the Anglophone world (Haug 2005). Using the Chinese metaphor *jiegui* (connecting the track), the Western paradigm is the track to which the trains in the developing world must connect regardless of how local trains are originally designed.

Second, it assumes that the indigenizing process is a linear and unidirectional process (Ferguson 2005). Appeals are made to the need for interdependence and dialogue among diverse social work communities (Healy 2001, 2002; Hokenstad and Midgley 1997). Attention, however, is mostly put on the interaction between local and foreign agents; both are seen as monolithic and homogenous (Tsang and Yan 2001). The internal diversity and dynamics among local agents are seldom mentioned. Such dynamics may tie closely with the existing conditions of local society, including the native social helping system and the local knowledge upon which that system is built. Local knowledge and practices are often construed in terms of cultural difference and are, therefore, inherently diverse and in almost all cases have a distinct political dimension (Yan and Cheung 2006).

In this chapter, examining the process of Indigenization of social work in China, we try to problematize the meaning of Indigenization. We concur with Ferguson's (2005) argument that Indigenization is not just a linear importing–adapting process. Furthering her argument, we assert that Indigenization is a political process involving a complex interaction between agents who represent the *bentude* (native and local) and the *bentuhuade* (imported and adapted) knowledge and practice and derive benefits from them (Yan and Cheung 2006). These two interest groups[2] will draw on different sources of power and resources to compete for the framing of what

---

signify the assumed monolithic set of knowledge from different social work communities in the Western world.

2   We divide these agents into two groups for analytical purposes only. As reflected in the following discussion, the boundary of these two groups is not clear-cut and they also work closely together on some issues. The authors are also aware of the internal diversity and

Chinese social work is. We also want to demonstrate that social work Indigenization in China is not a rational modification process undertaken by a singular agent but a *selective assimilation* process involving multiple agents or players. The state, being the most powerful agent, plays a key role in the selective assimilation process, while other players, such as academics, including those from the West, and practitioners are finding their own niches and respective roles. Together, but not necessarily working in concert with one another, the Chinese players selectively assimilate parts or components of the so-called Western social work system according to their relevance and utility in serving the political agenda of the state, and the respective interests of the other players involved. They are not adopting Western social work *en masse* though Western influences sometimes obstruct rather than facilitate the development of Chinese social work. One wonders what would happen if Chinese people were allowed the space to develop their own grounded social work without Western interference or 'noise'.

The Indigenization discourse in China

Tsang and Yan (2001) report that concern with Indigenization has a long history among Chinese intellectuals dating back to the late Qing Dynasty. Since the early re-inception of social work education, social work educators in China have been exploring how to *bentuhua* (which literally means Indigenize, localize or contextualize) Western social work to their local context. Given existing political conditions in China, the notion of *zhongti xiyong* (Chinese corpus and Western application) has always dominated the discussion. For instance, as quoted in the *Economist* (2006), when commenting on China's recent development of high-speed trains, the Minister for Railways in China said, 'Our technology is a re-innovation on the basis of *assimilating* advanced technologies of foreign countries' (p. 69, emphasis added).

The idea of assimilation signifies the unwillingness of China to passively accept the domination of Western technology as well as its skepticism and caution regarding values and ideologies embedded in Western technology which may threaten its current version of socialist ideology. There are at least two principles of selection: 1) the weak test – how useful it is to keep the country stable and prosperous (*anding fanyou*), and 2) the strong test – the extent to which or whether or not it is likely to jeopardize the Chinese Communist Party's reign. The political reality is that the latter always overrules the former. The most noticeable example of how these two principles are played out is perhaps the so called 'socialist market economy', a market economy serving a socialist ideology. To assure that these two principles are observed, the central government conducts its social reform with great caution. A social engineering approach, as demonstrated in the recent community construction movement, has been employed (Yan and Gao 2005). In other words, the Chinese government always owns, operates and controls the process through its various

---

contestation between these two groups, however, the description and analysis of their internal dynamics are beyond the scope of this chapter.

ministries and organizations to make sure that imported technology will support the country's economic development, while social stability is maintained and the reign of the Communist Party remains unchallenged and unquestioned.

Modernization is a national policy. In China, the idea of modernization has always been understood within the notion of 'science' which has been a major theme in political discourse in China since the May Fourth Movement of 1919, when leading intellectuals and student activists, including founding members of the Chinese Communist Party, advocated that science, among other things, is a key solution to the country's crises. The notion of science is very visible in Chinese public discourse. Being scientific means being rational and methodical and it is strongly associated with being advanced and authoritative. Being unscientific, in contrast, carries negative connotations of being irrational, backward and unworthy.

Bentuhuade social work: An academic construction

The meaning and significance of the Indigenization discourse, however, has to be assessed within the Chinese context. Closely related discourses in social work's development relate to science and professionalization (Yan and Tsang 2005; Tsang *et al.* 2001). These discourses illustrate the dynamics of Indigenization and the significance of contextualized understanding. To date, China has more than 200 post-secondary social work programmes ranging from technical diplomas and undergraduate baccalaureate degrees to a handful of Master's degree programmes. Since its re-inception in 1986, social work educators, the majority of whom have no social work training or practice experience whatsoever, have struggled to grapple with the foreign and complex system of Western social work knowledge and practice. They have received a great deal of help and support from their counterparts in Hong Kong's higher education system as well as from the professional social work community there. The establishment of the China Association of Social Work Education in 1994 was a milestone in the development of social work education in China. Since then, the association has been working hard to improve professional standards through a variety of training courses, mainly delivered by social work academics and senior members of the professional community from Hong Kong. An increasing number of social work educators in China have received their MSW or PhD degrees from social work schools in Hong Kong.

In keeping with the Chinese nation's desire to be global players, social work educators in China believe that *bentuhuade* social work, which frames Chinese social work as scientific and professional, will connect them to the international social work community and strategically increase their credibility (Wang *et al.* 1999).[3] This credibility has critical political and practical significance. Given the high concentration of power within the government system, and the lack of an

---

3   We notice that in the 2004 version of this book, this point of view is not found, at least not in the same chapter. We also note that reflective engagement with the scientific discourse is taking place within academia. Many schools of social work have incorporated post-modern and critical theories in their academic courses, and the application of some of these critical perspectives to both local and international discourses and practice is gradually growing.

alternative organized voice, the discourse of science and professionalization helps create a site of power, or at least an alternative authority. The claim of scientific and professional authority, located in the civic sites of academia and professional structures, counterbalances the hegemonic discourses of the state and its various instruments, including the ministries and offices that are major employers of social workers and similar social service personnel. Given the official endorsement of the scientific discourse as part of the government's modernization agenda, this articulation has not met with any major interference from the government, but has legitimized an alternative voice in the public debate over social issues and ways to address them.

Meanwhile, the ideological commitments of Western social work, which are grounded in Western values, such as democracy, individual rights and freedom, are politically sensitive. To desensitize the liberal and democratic values inherent in Western social work, many social work scholars in China tend to emphasize the scientific and technological aspects of Western social work knowledge and practice that they are trying to import and promote. Whereas the idea of science, especially understood in a positivist–empiricist framework, has been subjected to critical scrutiny and challenge in Western social work discourse in the last few decades, Chinese social work scholars promote the use of scientific methods by professionally trained workers or evidence based practice as a defining feature of social work (Yan and Tsang 2005). This rhetoric presents social work as a scientific and apolitical form of helping. Members of this new profession are thus equipped with technical knowledge in the *science* of helping and are, therefore, less likely to be seen as advocates and practitioners of a subversive value system.

To fulfill the mission of Indigenization, namely, constructing a system of social work with Chinese characteristics, social work scholars in China have made continuous efforts to filter and adapt Western social work knowledge. Building on the accumulation of almost two decades of teaching experience among its members, the professional association launched the first standardized set of core social work curricula and eleven textbooks as the *Textbook Series for 21st Century*, published by Higher Education Press in 2004. This book series is seen as the first standardized material for teaching *bentuhuade* social work (Wang *et al.* 2004). Nonetheless, as reported by Yuen-Tsang and Wang (2002), there have been questions about the academic content of these published materials among those who debate the standards to be formalized; whether they should adhere to international universal or global standards or be based on local Chinese cultural context specific standards. As reflected in the published version of the textbooks, a compromise was made. In the master preface the chief editor of the book series, Professor Wang Sibin from Peking University, highlighted the prescribed, guiding principle: To integrate imported social work theories with local experiences. In other words, the test of utility is the main criterion for cross-cultural integration (Wang *et al.* 2004).

To examine how this principle worked, we reviewed three direct practice books in the series including: *Social Case Work* (Xu *et al.* 2004), *Group Work* (Liu *et al.* 2004) and *Community Work* (Xu *et al.* 2004). Our observations were as follows: 1) most introduced Western theories and approaches; 2) there was limited coverage of local practice; and 3) there were only sporadic comments on how to integrate the imported theories with local Chinese practice experiences. The content revealed the huge gap between imported theory and local practice. Thus far social work educators in China have not articulated a model or framework of *bentuhuade* social work in China nor has there been any documentation of successful cases of Indigenization. This led us to conclude that, in effect, theories and methods were being adopted wholesale from Anglo-American countries.

For instance in *Social Case Work* the authors spend two pages reporting on the history of casework in China, two pages on value differences, and less than a page on the code of ethics of social work in China. Some case examples are used. Compared to the other two books, *Group Work* presents more local case examples. Even with its long history in organizing people and the recent massive community construction movement, the authors of *Community Work* only spend 32 of the book's 250 pages describing issues related to Chinese contexts. We believe that variations in presenting local experience are due to: 1) the experience and orientation of the individual authors of the books, and 2) the pace of development of different practice methods in China. In short, it is probably accurate to say that Western social work, primarily in its Anglo-American varieties, still dominates the content of this set of books. At this stage of development, Chinese social work scholars are preoccupied with quickly establishing a body of knowledge and practice principles, which is critical in justifying their social role and credibility; and there is relatively little time and resources devoted to systematic Indigenization, which demands rigorous critical reflection and extensive practice and experimentation.

Conceptually, social work scholars in China have summarized at least two possible strategies to *betuhua* (Indigenize) Western social work which they are trying to import (Wang *et al.* 2004). The first one is to examine the applicability of Western social work through practice or using Deng Xiaoping's famous principle 'let practice verify the truth'. In other words, through the *practice* of Western social work in China, local and *bentuhuade* experiences would be accumulated and recontextualized. The second is to examine the applicability of Western social work through *critical intellectual engagement*, and then use the results to compare with and hopefully inform *bentude* helping practices. In turn, new ideas and insights could be generated and the development of a hybrid *bentuhuade* form of practice could benefit from the simultaneous use of both strategies. While the points of entry of these two strategies might be different, both would require field practice to test theories and ideas. Ironically, 'the field' is exactly what social work educators and students in China lack since professional social work practice, as it is known in the West, is still in a very rudimentary stage of development. There are only a handful of professional social work practitioners in the country, and the vast majority of social work students cannot find practicum settings where the professional social work to which they aspire is actually practiced. Upon graduation most of these students become part of an embarrassing situation where social work job postings are very rare and, in all likelihood, there will be no employment prospects for these graduates. With reference to the rapid development in social work education and the proliferation of academic discourse and publication, *social work practice in China exists mostly in the virtual world of academic discourse*. Social service functions, however, are still performed by the state, mainly in their administrative executive mode. On the ground professional social work practice, whether as characterized in the West or as imagined in China, is still a rarity.

Bentude social work: A state controlled field

So who has the field? Or what is the field? China started developing its own system – *bentude* social service programmes, corresponding policies and legislation, institutional structures, personnel and material resources – in 1949 (Dixon 1981; Wong 1998). In China the government's stake in social service and social work is entrusted to several ministries, including Civil Affairs, Education, Labor, Health and Environment, and the State Commission of Population and Family Planning, as well as state sponsored organizations like the All China Women's Federation, The Communist Youth League and the Trade Union. Most personnel working in these ministries and organizations have not received any formal training and the nature of their work is largely administrative and policy oriented. Therefore social work educators in China describe these *bentude* services as administrative and semi-professional in order to distinguish them from the virtual imported scientific and professional practice that they are vigorously trying to *bentuhua* (Indigenize) and promote (Wang 2000).

In response to the national agenda of modernization, in the last two decades or so all these arms of government have been pursuing their own strategies of modernization. While implementing the policy directions of the Central Government, however, these ministries and units have their respective agendas and mandates, organizational cultures, administrative and executive powers, spheres of influence, strategic priorities, share of state resources, and so on. Most importantly, *each also has its own institutional interest to serve and protect*. Therefore, in order to strengthen their capacity to compete under the slogan of modernization, many have solicited help from outside the government. To the Ministry of Civil Affairs (MOCA), the major ministry in charge of social welfare services, professional social work practiced in Western countries is seen as one of the ways to help the country 'modernize' its massive social service machinery.

To import foreign knowledge, MOCA first turned to academics. Therefore, it played a notable role in reintroducing social work into China in the 1980s, hoping that social work academics would be instrumental in selecting Western ideas and practices for local use. In line with the approach adopted by the Central Government, MOCA's idea was not to transfer Western social work knowledge and practice *en masse* – it especially did not want its ideological and value base – but rather to selectively assimilate components which supported its existing mandate and functions. Under the modernization banner government ministries like MOCA and most Chinese social work scholars did have a common agenda and language, endorsing the notion of 'science' as mentioned before, and some social work principles deemed to fit national objectives, like the mantra of 'helping people to help themselves' (Yan and Tsang 2005). This notion shifted social welfare responsibilities from the state to the citizens, and could hardly be seen as subversive or critical of the failures and shortcomings of government policies and programmes. It is little wonder, then, that 'helping people to help themselves' is now the mantra of bureaucrats and academics alike.

'Cultural fit' is another criterion of selective assimilation that is unevenly applied since not all cultural differences are treated in the same way and it is interesting to see which cultural differences assume importance. For instance, drafting its first comprehensive charity law is an institutional expression of China's acceptance of the modern form of charity, which is initiated, supported and operated by non-government organizations, as a possible measure to alleviate increasing social problems. Of significance too are the values and practices considered 'foreign' and 'culturally incompatible'. A good example is liberal individualism, which most Chinese social work academics identify as a key feature of Western social work. Hence they caution students and colleagues against it, usually without any exploration of the historical development of the idea, the possibility of its early introduction in China, or its potential connection to contemporary values and aspirations among the Chinese population.

Although MOCA and the social work academics appear to share certain positions, their partnership is not without challenges. One of the reasons may be that the development of social work education in China has grown out of the control of MOCA. In the early 2000s China's higher education reform aimed to massively expand its higher education capacity in response to the demand for skilled labor in its rapidly growing economy. Whereas the Central Government expects all its ministries and organizations to work in concert with one another to achieve its policy objectives, in practice there are situations of communication failure, non-cooperation, competition and rivalry (Yan and Cheung 2006). By encouraging the expansion of new disciplines, the Ministry of Education indirectly encourages the development of social work programmes. As a result, the number of social work programmes has increased from about forty in the late 1990s to more than 200 today (see Chapter 14).

A critical mass of social work educators has been established and their existence has led to tensions with MOCA. First, the notion of *professionalizing bentuhuade* social work as preached by the social work educators poses threats to MOCA by claiming an alternative site of authority. It challenges the ontological security of this massive *bentude* social service machinery. It posts doubts regarding the appropriateness and effectiveness of their services. As a *bentude* service system employing a cadre of almost two million non-professionally trained workers, MOCA's interest is the job security of this massive troop of foot soldiers.[4] The primary goal of importing Western social work is to upgrade, not to replace, this mass of non-trained personnel. The original thinking was to pick and choose components from Western social work, particularly the technological, for use in the *bentude* field.

This new critical mass not only threatens the interests of individuals in MOCA but also the socio-political functions assigned to MOCA, a large part of which relies on millions of volunteers at the community level. Many of these volunteers not only provide services but also perform critical political functions, particularly at the

---

4   MOCA is also the department that absorbs the most veterans retiring from their military service every year. Most of these veterans have very low skills and little training.

grassroots level, such as rural and urban residents' committees. In other words, the *bentude* social service system is also a governmental apparatus serving the political agenda set by the Central Government. Recently this system has been assigned an economic function. For instance, in the last two decades a massive development of community services in China has been used not only to 'download' the welfare burden of the government but also to provide an economic buffer for the government to employ tens of thousands of workers laid off from state enterprises. These former employees are hired as low paid community workers to operate the hundreds of thousands of community centers and residents' committees (Xu *et al.* 2005). The *bentude* social service system, therefore, not only serves social needs but also more importantly the economic and political interests of the state.

To counter the discourse of 'professionalism' claimed by social work academics, MOCA tried to control the framing of the social work profession in China by establishing the China Association of Social Workers under its own auspices. While this association is a member of the International Federation of Social Workers, and dialogues with other professional social work bodies globally, members of this association are largely MOCA staff members who have not been trained in Western social work practice. In other words, both MOCA and the IFSW recognize this *bentude* body of largely non-(Western)-social work trained personnel as part of the international social work community, whereas the majority of its international member organizations comprise professionally trained social workers. In turn, MOCA has discursively controlled the field in which social work can practice in China through this association, while at the same time maintaining material control over most of the actual sites where social services are delivered.

MOCA has adopted several strategies to maintain its control of the field. First, it selectively engages social work educators in areas where help is needed. Many social work teachers are currently doing policy research, much of which has been commissioned or financed by different levels of government. They are involved in government advisory committees and panels, and are often invited to deliver in-service training programmes for civil servants at all levels in the various ministries and organizations. Such active engagement and involvement can be read as the government's endorsement of the development of social work both as an academic discipline and a professional area of practice and it certainly creates a critical space for social work academics to advance their own agenda and make a difference in government policy and practice. On the one hand, from a developmental perspective, it is probably fair to say that the relative power of this elite group of social work educators in Chinese society is increasing, when measured by the resources it commands, its expanding discursive space, and the continual expansion of its roles and spheres of influence. On the other hand, by controlling the research agenda, MOCA is still tightly controlling the advancement of the Indigenization process in a way that will not jeopardize the gradual modernization of its mandate and personnel.

Second, MOCA controls the field by gate keeping; it decides on the admission of social work graduates into the social service workforce. Given that most social work educators in China have no direct practice experience and are burdened with heavy teaching loads and administrative duties and obligations, they need to rely on their students to test Western theories and techniques through internships and direct practice in the field after graduation. Most social work programmes in China, however, do not have a formal and well designed field education component. In analysing the qualitative data collected from 50 graduating social work students, we found that none had undergone any formal fieldwork education. This is unlikely to change as there are simply not enough jobs for social work graduates and, therefore, no supervised fieldwork sites despite the fact that the country and its population probably needs hundreds and thousands of social work graduates. This has led to the disheartening finding that almost all of these fifty students do not see themselves finding a social work job in the near future. Many have given up the idea of a social work career. The job situation not only disappoints most graduates but it also poses a major challenge to social work scholars who need fieldwork practice to *bentuhua* Western ideas in local communities, not to mention favorable employment statistics to justify their role and existence in Chinese society.

There is recent evidence that the door is slowly and cautiously opening. In 2004 social work was listed in the National Occupation Standard, however, social work as a job or position in the government structure is still in its rudimentary stage, awaiting cautious implementation and experimentation. Taking the lead in opening the social work job market, Shanghai is the first municipal jurisdiction to employ professionally accredited social workers in selected social services. A registration system, which would take most Western countries almost a century to establish, is already in place.[5] To date, 1,658 social workers have successfully passed the registration examination in Shanghai (*Shanghai Social Work*, 17 May 2006). The Shanghai experience is gradually spreading to other cities. This development, however, lags far behind the expectation of the thousands of social work educators and students from the more than 200 post-secondary social work programmes. Only a handful of graduates have been hired to work in the social services. Meanwhile, since the examination-based registration system is not limited to people who have been trained in social work, it also provides an opportunity for non-social work trained MOCA staff to gain a professional title.

Conclusion: Indigenization re-envisioned

In conclusion, the Indigenization of social work in China is not merely a rational process through which knowledge – and values, theories, and techniques – is selectively imported or transferred in terms of its adaptive or cultural fit. Rather it is a political process in which different interests compete. Despite the common notion of importing Western knowledge, practitioners of *bentude* social helping systems

---

5   On 20 July 2006, MOCA officially announced a Provisional Measure on Assessment of Occupational Level of Social Workers and Operational Measure on Examinations for Occupational Level of Junior Social Worker and Social Worker effective from 1 September 2006. Since this is a recent development, this chapter will not further elaborate on the impacts of this development on social work in China, however, the measures signify official recognition of the emerging profession and the social engineering approach of MOCA in controlling the development of social work in China.

and members of the newly established social work programmes are engaging in a tug of war competing to frame 'what Chinese social work is going to be'. This competition is, however, dictated by the rules of the socialist State whose main concerns are the stability of society and economic prosperity, the two prescriptions that ensure the ontological security of the regime. Therefore, instead of an abrupt transformation through critical intellectual invention, a gradual evolution through careful social engineering and renovation is the approach for change. The Minister of Railways' statement may indicate a clear direction of social work Indigenization, that is, Indigenization of social work in China is a selective assimilation of bits and pieces from Western knowledge into the *bentude* system and practice which has a clear socio-political assignment. After all political utility, rather than cultural fit, may be the ultimate selection criterion. As shown above, the discursive management of what constitutes *bentude* and foreign, and which cultural differences should be carefully monitored or guarded against, is a politically driven process. A lot of changes in traditional cultural practices resulting from exposure to Western culture are well tolerated and even welcomed in China, and certain ideas are selectively targeted for critical engagement.

In the process of social work Indigenization in China, the competition between the *bentude* and *bentuhuade* contenders is always connected to the notion of internationalization, a process which tends to favor the transfer of knowledge from the developed north (or the West) to the underdeveloped south (Yan 2005). Therefore, coming back to the supply side of the equation, perhaps when discussing indigenization, we also need to understand that Western social work is not monolithic or static (Tsang and Yan 2001). Western social work is embodied by heterogeneous institutional structures, including practitioners, professional bodies, unions, academics, researchers, employing agencies, funding bodies and government departments and offices. These institutional entities are differentially associated with the intersecting discourses in the profession regarding political ideology, epistemology, substantive theories, policy frameworks, service models, practice methods and the like. There are also considerable differences along these dimensions across countries. And even within a given country, there can be significant change over time. The United States, for example, has very different policies and practices in its pre- and post-9/11 periods, especially where international development and exchange is concerned. International exchange, which encompasses the transfer of social work knowledge and methods to China, is often a function of foreign policy and the funding arrangements of specific countries or groups of countries, like the European Union. The plurality of foreign policy agendas is almost inevitably tied to other policy imperatives, such as trade, economic interests, diplomacy, political or military objectives, which also condition the actual procedure and format of knowledge transfer.

Recognizing this diversity, any analysis of the issue of Indigenization and recommendations made cannot be a singular, standardized articulation but can, at best, be a set of contingent principles facilitating a more sensitive and well informed engagement not only between local and foreign agents but also among local agents. The imported entity inevitably modifies *bentude* practice and the interests embedded in it. *Indigenization is, therefore, not only a rational experimentation of new ideas in local contexts but also a political competition among different interests*. The agenda of Indigenization is never as straightforward as making the imported fit the local context. It is a process of negotiating and rebalancing power between contenders of the *bentude* and *bentuhuade* models. Perhaps the case of China is not unique with regard to its political situation. So far, little has been reported in the literature regarding how existing local social welfare systems and their vested interests engage politically with imported concepts and practices. Future study on social work Indigenization may need to consider these dynamics of political engagement.

Chapter 16

Developing Culturally Relevant Social Work Education in Africa: The Case of Botswana

Kwaku Osei-Hwedie and Morena J. Rankopo

The debate on using local knowledges to develop non-Western societies is not new. In the case of social work, the concept of localization is linked to the processes of developing culturally appropriate education and practice models to meet the unique needs of diverse cultures in local contexts. The search for appropriateness emerged as social work expanded to non-Western countries, and scholars began to question the relevance of Western social work in developing countries. Criticisms of Western imperialism were spearheaded *inter alia* by scholars including Branscombe (1961), Brown (1957), Clifford (1966), Dunning (1972), Hoey (1954), Midgley (1983), Robertson (1963), Shawky (1972) and the United Nations (1971).

Since the 1960s, many authors, sympathetic to the plight of developing countries, have joined the search for appropriate social work practice (Almanzor 1967; Khinduka 1971; Nagpaul 1972; Nimmagadda and Cowger 1999; Osei-Hwedie 1993b, 1995). In addition, several authors, especially in developing countries, have added their voice to the debate, advocating for the development of relevant social work methods that take into account a country's culture, socio-economic, political, environmental and other factors (Elliott 1993; Gray *et al.* 1996; Hutton 1992, 1994; Louw 1998; McKendrick 1998; Midgley 1983; Midgley *et al.* 1986; Mupedziswa 1992, 1993, 2001; Muzaale 1987; Mwansa 1996; Ntusi 1998; Osei-Hwedie 1995, 1996b, 2002b; Rankin 1997; Silavwe 1995; Walton and El Abo Nasr 1988). These writers argue that social work must be relevant to the needs of local contexts, and that social work education must fulfil the demands that are placed on the profession by the unique sociocultural factors in non-Western countries. The need for culturally relevant social work practice was made more urgent by social workers in Latin America who became disillusioned with Western theories and practices. They found Western models of practice incongruent with the structural social problems embedded in their regions (Ferguson 2005).

In this chapter we discuss our attempt to make social work culturally relevant in an African country. Specifically, we discuss the processes and outcomes in which we engaged to make the social work curriculum at the University of Botswana appropriate to the local sociocultural context. We also examine attempts by practitioners to make their interventions appropriate by the use of local examples. These attempts were identified through discussions with practitioners who are currently students in the

Bachelor of Social Work (BSW) and Master of Social Work (MSW) programmes at the University of Botswana.

Before colonialism, most sub-Saharan African societies were ethnic nationalities, organized around kith and kin, with authority exercised through a system of chieftaincy, clan Elders and heads of households. In regards to social welfare, this was generally adequate to meet most requirements – from housing and the storage of food to personal support in times of bereavement – based on the exercise of mutuality and accepted reciprocity (Osei-Hwedie and Bar-On 1999). Colonialism negatively affected this social support system due to a variety of factors, including the introduction of capitalism and money as the medium for the exchange of goods and services, the acceptance of a distinction between the homestead and the workplace, and the associated reduction in the importance of mutual reciprocity as the basis of welfare (Osei-Hwedie and Bar-On 1999; Ouma 1995).

Throughout the colonial period, the colonialists sidelined Africans and promoted the sociocultural supremacy of Europeans. Thus developmental activities focused on Europeans to the neglect of Indigenous populations (MacPherson 1982). The practical implication of this was that the welfare of Africans was made subordinate to that of the colonialists, so that African knowledge and skills were seen as inferior and unnecessary, and consequently neglected. Independence and nationalist governments in sub-Saharan Africa were associated with high socio-economic expectations for social development. Among the priorities were the guaranteeing of free education and health services for all, the improvement of housing and the provision of other amenities, such as electricity, running water and roads. Equally important were the promise of popular participation in the identification of needs and the establishment of programmes to address them. Thus the prospects were good although African countries suffered considerable economic hardship (Osei-Hwedie and Bar-On 1999).

African governments often argue that their primary concern is with social and not personal development. This is partly because independence found much of the development efforts and related structures wanting. For one thing, to establish their development policies, colonialist governments built an institutional capacity for providing services that required an expansive civil service bureaucracy rather than intensive informal helping networks. Thus after independence the members of this service bureaucracy had to be dissociated from the previous colonial administration. This called for the localization of the administration. Mechanisms had to be put in place to give the people an effective voice in running their civil affairs. The mechanism introduced to tackle the socio-economic problems was to revive the village as the basic unit of administration and to establish town councils in urban areas, making them the effective units for development. These were linked to the centre through a string of similar development organizations at the district and provincial levels. This was a process of decentralization.

In Botswana's model of decentralization, policy formulation begins when problems come to the attention of different village level committees, popularly elected at the *Kgotla* or its equivalent village-based organ. The *Kgotla* is the central decision making agency of a village, presided over by the local 'chief', and serves as the village's administrative and judicial centre. All adult members of the community are supposed to attend to discuss public affairs. Decentralization has also meant that families and communities must be far more extensively involved in meeting their social and economic needs, both in symbolic and practical terms (Osei-Hwedie and Bar-On 1999; Silitshena 1989). It is within this sociocultural context that the search for appropriateness in social provision must be understood.

The context of Botswana

Botswana is a landlocked country located at the centre of southern Africa. It is bounded by Namibia, South Africa, Zambia and Zimbabwe. It attained independence from Britain in 1966. It is a multiparty democracy, and a multiracial country that maintains freedom of association, freedom of the press, freedom of speech and the rule of law. It has a parliament, a strong executive president, and *Ntlo ya Dikgosi* (House of Chiefs) that advises parliament on matters affecting tradition and custom (Republic of Botswana 2003).

When Botswana attained its political independence from Britain in 1966, it was among the world's poorest countries. Botswana's economic growth began shortly after independence and has been sustained ever since. The economic growth was the highest for any country in the world from 1966 to 1986. With high mineral revenues, the government has made considerable strides in the provision of social services, especially in education and health. Citizens have access to universal basic education up to junior secondary school. Health services are provided within reasonable reach of all communities for a nominal fee (Republic of Botswana 2003).

However, a major challenge facing the country is HIV and AIDS. According to the Botswana AIDS Impact Survey II (CSO 2004), the national HIV and AIDS prevalence rate is 17.1 per cent. The impact of HIV and AIDS is visible through the increased mortality rates, reduced life expectancy and high occupancy rates of hospital beds by AIDS patients (Republic of Botswana 2003). Due to the government's efforts to address the pandemic through research, early detection and treatment therapies, the Sentinel Surveillance Study of 2005 showed that the HIV prevalence rate among pregnant women aged fifteen to forty-nine years decreased from 37.4 per cent in 2003 to 33.4 per cent in 2005. At the same time, the prevalence rate among the group aged fifteen to nineteen decreased from 22.8 to 17.8 per cent. The government has been able to provide antiretroviral treatment (ARVT) for a large number of people who are HIV positive. In 2005, for example, 54,378 were under ARVT compared to 32,835 in 2003. In addition, Botswana has the biggest programme in sub-Saharan Africa with respect to Prevention of Mother to Child Transmission where 73 per cent of pregnant HIV positive mothers are covered (Republic of Botswana 2006). Despite these achievements, the HIV prevalence rate is still very high.

To a great extent, Botswana is a homogenous society with the majority of its citizens from the *Tswana* group. This includes the *Bakwena*, *Bangwato*, *Bangwaketse*, *Bakgatla*, *Batawana*, *Batlokwa*, *Balete* and *Barolong* ethnic groups. At independence, these were recognized constitutionally as the 'principal tribes' and, in effect, the ruling elite. The other ethnic groups, including *Bakalanga*, *Batswapong*, *Basarwa*, *Bakgalagadi*, *Bayei* and *Baherero*, were historically regarded as ethnic minorities.

The *Basarwa* and other semi-nomadic groups are the most disadvantaged, and the poorest among these ethnic groups. In an effort to promote ethnic equality, the government has expanded the *Ntlo ya Dikgosi* (House of Chiefs) to include some of those previously excluded. The official languages are *Setswana* and English with the latter being the language in government. Despite these different ethnicities, they have the same world view with regard to socio-economic and political life, that is, the relationship between humans, between humans and the spiritual world, as well as between humans and the natural environment. These relationships define individual and societal beliefs and values, obligations, roles and rights, the distribution and use of power and authority, and the acquisition, distribution and use of wealth and resources. All these occur in a communal context, and it is this *communalism* that makes the African unique and different from people of the west.

Theoretical definitions and concepts of cultural appropriateness

Developing nations, Botswana included, seek solutions to poverty, disease, ignorance, inequality and lack of opportunity. Despite massive investments in socio-economic and political development aimed at modernization, however, about 36 per cent of the population are poor and remain economically deprived, politically marginalized and generally ill fed, ill housed, undereducated and extremely vulnerable to preventable diseases, such as HIV and AIDS and malaria. The government and other stakeholders are constantly searching for better and more effective ways to tackle these problems to improve the welfare of the people. Osei-Hwedie (2005) contends that, until recently, Western values, ideas, theories and models were seen as the only source of development despite the fact that other values, ideas, theories and models have always been evident. Mangaliso (2005) emphasizes that in a globalizing world, societies must develop their own unique knowledge, values and resources that they can use as their source of comparative advantage and the basis of their own development. In the case of Botswana, qualities and values embedded in the culture, and connected to social provision, represent an intangible resource that can lead to social development.

The idea of appropriateness or relevance of social work education and practice among African scholars was probably first clearly articulated by Midgley (1983) who defined it as 'appropriateness, which means professional social work roles must be appropriate to the needs of different countries and social work practice' (p. 170). It refers to the appropriateness of knowledge, values, norms, philosophies and procedures which underlie practice and lead to the type of development that both professionals and client systems can understand, relate to and control (Osei-Hwedie 1996b). Making social work appropriate is critical and has, in the past years, increasingly received international recognition such that the International Federation of Social Workers (IFSW) has included the concept in its revised definition of social work where the term 'Indigenous knowledge' refers to 'the critical importance of shaping social work to suit economic and cultural realities, particularly in developing countries' (Hare 2004: 416). However, the IFSW seems unaware that use of this term is offensive to the Indigenous Peoples of the world (Hughes 2003). The emphasis therefore, should be on a locally determined and culturally relevant social work practice rather than a homogenized 'one size fits all' social work practice that may not satisfy all cultural contexts and solve unique socio-economic problems. This is the priority of contextualized social work practice. For example, social workers in Botswana and other developing countries provide basic health and social care to patients on home-d care, especially for HIV and AIDS and other terminal illnesses. They are also involved in other activities, such as organizing for community infrastructural development, drought relief programmes, public education on social and community health issues, orphan care and nutritional programmes. Such activities are consistent with the needs of the people and social workers qualify as legitimate providers.

Deciding that social work must be appropriate is a very different matter from agreeing on how this can be achieved. Apart from *indigenization*, many concepts, such as authentization, reconceptualization, conscientization and radicalization (Alfero 1973; Costa 1987; Kendall 1973; Osei-Hwedie 1996b; Resnick 1976; Walton and Abo El Nasr 1988) have been used to describe culturally relevant social work or processes for its realization. *Indigenization* was a concept coined to mean the incorporation – with imported Western knowledge – of local knowledges, ideas and processes of problem solving, and service delivery as well as the adaptation of external ideas and practices to fit *local* contexts. Essentially it is a process of *localization* that is more easily achieved from the ground up rather than from top down imposed Western models that are totally foreign to local cultural contexts. *Authentization*, on the other hand, focuses on local knowledges and resources, and processes rooted *solely* in the local system and, therefore, authentic approaches are original and *vice versa*. According to Osei-Hwedie, authentization:

> ... emphasises the creation ... of social work practice and education which are original domestic models in the light of society's political, economic and religious structures and conditions. Hence, responses to (local) social conditions must be the force behind the development of theory and practice. Foreign ideas, theories and practices are not totally neglected, they just become secondary to local ones (Osei-Hwedie 1996b: 216).

Reconceptualization relates to a radical review and reframing of Western social work models and processes. Rooted in Freire's (1970) application of the Marxist notion of conscientization in adult education within Latin America's broader liberation theology approaches, it emphasizes the reformulation of knowledge, concepts, values and philosophies to be in line with developmental and empowerment efforts of the poor and marginalized. 'Practice is to be based on local experience from which new "constructs" are then created' (Osei-Hwedie 1996b: 216). According to Mupedziswa (1993), reconceptualization emphasizes rethinking, restructuring and strengthening of social work practice in the context of adapting and modifying old *local* ideas and the emergence of new ones. *Radicalization* calls for social work in non-Western countries to shed its liberal character for a radical approach that allows comprehensive transformation of oppressive systems (Mupedziswa 1992; Mwansa 1992; Osei-Hwedie 1996b).

These concepts are mutually inclusive and irrespective of where one begins, whether with indigenization, authentization, reconceptualization or radicalization the end result must be cultural appropriateness. However, all of them fail to understand the importance of people's cultural embeddedness and the difficulty of the cross-cultural transportation of ideas and practices. Because of the tendency towards 'outside in' approaches 'from the west to the rest', it is difficult for scholars to agree on what exactly is relevant to social work in Africa. The importation of ideas results in the need for local processes where local stakeholders discuss 'restructuring' and 'repositioning' in terms of external ideas rather than their own. Thus the question of 'relevance' becomes a tug of war among academics with very little input from local practitioners. Instead of discussing local realities we discuss abstract and foreign concepts. Thus Bar-On (2003a) observes local social workers' discomfort with terms like 'appropriateness' and 'relevance'. He sees this from his perspective, wherein localization runs counter to individuals' and society's wish to modernize, industrialize and to be generally competitive in the globalizing world. Even the notion of 'cultural relevance' comes from social work's humanistic, homogenizing tendencies and its assumption that as a science of professional practice it can be globalized and thus that the same content can be taught and practised across diverse cultures.

> This (dominant social work) idea does not mean that all people are equal but that their nature is. It follows, therefore, (on this view) that human predicaments are similar and hence can be managed by employing similar theories, principles, and techniques (Bar-On 2003a: 30).

On ideological grounds, Bar-On (2003a) argues that since societies are at different levels of development there is a need for universal standards of social work education and practice to ensure the promotion of some standard of equality and social justice. Also, he contends that the search for appropriateness has expanded social work unnecessarily into development issues that distort the original focus of the profession, magnify the risk of encroaching into other occupations and basically distort social work as a unique profession. He thus argues, most confusingly, that in Africa generally, and Botswana in particular, there is no need to search for culturally relevant practice because what passes for social work is fundamentally different from that of the west because social workers engage in fields that bear little resemblance to those of their Western counterparts. By implication then it is already 'culturally different'.

Despite Bar-On's (2003b) paradoxical argument, we find the notion of 'cultural appropriateness' helpful in developing social work as an 'idea' whereby we can think of problem solving even in non-Western societies as we search for culturally relevant local models of social work practice in Africa. We say this even though current imported Western practice models have not been effective thus far in Africa with its unique cultures, needs, institutional structures and patterns of social relationship. Like many 'native' or 'original' cultures found in most developing nations and countries, Botswana's people are *communalistic* and find fulfilment in the context of the group. Its social work focus is on communities rather than on individuals and within these communities the 'more than human' realm carries a great deal of

import. Thus the domain of social work is *local communities and cultures* and these
determine the norms and values and social processes and relationships of Batswana
people (Osei-Hwedie 1996b) (see Figure 1).

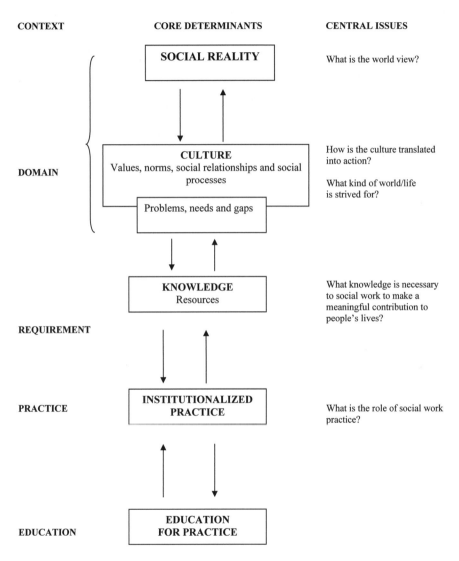

Figure 1 A framework for culturally relevant social work practice
Source: Osei-Hwedie (1996b).

The term *culturally appropriate* is used throughout the chapter in place of *Indigenization* or *Indigenous* because of the controversy surrounding the interpretation of these two concepts across cultural contexts. In *Setswana* language, *Indigenizing* means *go nyalanya/amanya* – to blend or fit in, relate to or with – or *go lebanya* – to align – while *Indigenization* refers to *kamanyo le ngwao* or *tetlanyo* – blending of different ideas to achieve one acceptable position. We see the creation of culturally appropriate social work as a process that requires dialogue – *dipuisanyo* – among diverse stakeholders, especially when the idea originates from an external source. This may be expressed as *go baya letlhaku le lesha mo go le legologolo* – literally translated as adding new branches to reinforce an old wooden fence. In the same way, the idiom of 'the baby and the bathwater' – retaining the best of the past and discarding what is no longer appropriate – serves as an analogy for using relevant concepts, norms and mores as a base for the consolidation of a new philosophy. When the modern element is externally generated the process is a particularly sensible one requiring mutually respectful discourse and empathic communication. Positive change is the *raison d'être* of the profession of social work and its mandate for clients and this can be achieved through dynamic cultural appropriateness. In this sense, therefore, the issue of blending new and old ideas or making new ideas work in a particular manner and context is reinforced.

Social work becomes 'context-specific' (Jinchao 1995) not by proclamation in international definitions and standards but when its values, principles, strategies, education, knowledge and practice are *local*, when it is responsive to *local* economic, political, sociocultural and psychological realities. Culture defines peoples' daily life and patterns of interactions. Local cultures, therefore, have the greatest influence on the manner in which social workers make their decisions and interact with their clients (Nimmagadda and Cowger 1999; Taylor 1999). However, even in local – and African national – contexts, there is a great deal of cultural diversity. For example, Nigeria alone has over 250 languages and Ghana has about 76. In the southern African region alone, Mozambique has 33 languages, Botswana 28, Namibia 26, South Africa 23, Zimbabwe 17, Swaziland four and Lesotho two. This demonstrates the diverse cultures even in the African context.

Experiences of making social work culturally relevant in southern Africa: The case of Botswana

Influences from South Africa

In the southern African region, developing culturally relevant social work practice became more urgent in the new economic and socio-political dispensation and the Reconstruction and Development Programme in South Africa in the 1990s. This programme was aimed at fulfilling basic needs, developing human resources, improving the economy and creating a democratic, just and open society. In this case, development was to be equitable, integrated, sustainable, redistributive and people focused in the context of peace and security. Thus, social work in South

Africa redirected its focus to social development, social security, social welfare (with a strong emphasis on social security) (see Gray *et al.* 1996), and the general socio-economic well-being of all people (Patel and Midgley 2004).

South Africa, like most countries in the developing world, has not been spared by the new wave of calls for culturally relevant social work. Social work in the new South Africa faces dynamic challenges. Mamphiswana and Noyoo (2004) observe that in the old South Africa, social work education was tilted towards the maintenance of the status quo of discrimination in every sense of the word, at the expense of social problems of the highly marginalized majority African population. They contended that social work education and practice should be localized through deliberate attempts to mould it in accordance with prevailing Africanizing culture and philosophy in democratic South African society.

The case of South Africa can be considered unique given its history of apartheid, which inflicted racial discrimination and consequent socio-economic deprivation and underdevelopment on the majority of African people. South Africa can be said to be moving towards culturally relevant social work to suit the post-apartheid times. Since the end of apartheid, South Africa has been undergoing rapid social change which, according to Gray and Simpson (1998), called for 'developmental social work' that acknowledges the structural causes of social problems and contributes to the process of social, economic and cultural reconstruction and development. In the new dispensation, therefore, social work educators and practitioners need to modify and redefine their theory and knowledge to redress social injustice, poverty and racism. Essentially, social work curricula should reflect local South African needs and problems from an Afrocentric perspective.

Culturally relevant social work education in Botswana

The debate on culturally relevant social work education in Botswana started at the same time as it did in South Africa in the early 1990s. It was influenced by the global emphasis on social development and on local experiences of the (in)appropriateness of Western development models in African societies; however, the process was not as nationalized and as political as the South African one. Academics at the University of Botswana reflecting on the then predominantly Western social work curriculum saw the need for change. With the debate on the new direction of social work in South Africa in the post-apartheid era, academics in Botswana had a reference point and a support base for a new social development orientation. During this period, these academics wrote about their experiences of the process of making social work education culturally appropriate (Hutton 1994; Hutton and Mwansa 1996; Mwansa 1992; Osei-Hwedie 1990, 1993b, 1996b). This led to the adoption of 'community' as the organizing precept for social work and to the emphasis on 'social development' as a priority for social work practice. In this case, social work translates into social development where the emphasis is on social and community needs and resources that then subsume those of individuals and small groups. Individual problems find expression and solution in relation to social conditions. Thus, in our context, we argue that social work is especially meaningful when it aims at social development. Most of the issues that social workers address begin in the community where limited resources suggest the need to focus on socio-economic development and prevention rather than individualized casework interventions. This was consistent with national values of development rooted in the cultural concept of humanness or *botho* which is similar to *ubunthu* in South Africa and emphasizes *inter alia* respect, acceptance, compassion, cooperation, equity, social justice and socio-economic integration as integral to social development.

Prospects of localizing social work in a developing country

Our path to developing a culturally appropriate social work curriculum has not been smooth. While Western social work has not proved relevant to the needs of African societies, it is almost impossible to avoid its reach. As demonstrated by Osei-Hwedie, Ntseane and Jacques (2006), paradoxically the exercise is influenced by the very thing it is trying to avoid. It is clear that developing a relevant, appropriate or necessary social work knowledge, skill set, outlook, philosophy and theory is not as easy as it seems. Pressures towards Western models come from university authorities who want their programmes to be internationally competitive, from academics who want international recognition and from students who want their skills to be internationally marketable. To cite one example, in the early 1990s lecturers endeavoured to ground their courses for both the Diploma (DSW) and Bachelor of Social Work (BSW) degrees in what students knew from their personal and practical experience. However, they were soon forced to change their approach because the students revolted arguing that they had come to university to learn, not to reflect on their life experiences, so lecturers must teach them. In addition, they wanted teaching to conform to Western notions of social work contained in the Western texts in the library. The confrontation was so intense that some lecturers, even Westerners, had to be reassigned to different courses while others resorted to traditional methods of teaching using the same 'irrelevant' Western texts. Nevertheless, we persevered in developing a curriculum in tune with local needs and culturally appropriate teaching materials. This meant identifying local needs by involving local stakeholders – practitioners, policy makers and organizational managers – but it also required appeasing the university's objective of developing academic programmes that were 'relevant to, and consistent with, the needs, aspirations, and vision of the country, the southern Africa region, and the continent as a whole' (Osei-Hwedie *et al.* 2006: 8).

The university's vision was to become a centre of excellence in Africa and internationally and this meant that the programme could not be wholly localized or inward looking but also had to have a comprehensive international dimension. Thus internal university processes looked set to compromise our lofty ideals of a culturally appropriate social work curriculum. It was unavoidable that those with a vested interest would examine our proposals from their particular intellectual and professional perspectives. Most of those involved did not think that social work warranted special treatment and thus selling culturally relevant social work to this diverse group of academics and other professionals was no mean feat. We had to do our homework well.

We undertook extensive research and widespread consultation with stakeholders in government, parastatal and private, nongovernmental organizations (NGOs), including individual practitioners, managers and members on the social work school's advisory board. Thus the process involved people both in and outside the university working together in a committee chaired by the Dean of the Faculty of Social Sciences. Internally the committee included social work academics, the Director of Career and Counselling Services, representatives from academic services and the departments of sociology, psychology, population studies, as well as the health and wellness centre. To ensure that the curriculum would conform to regional and international standards, we researched programmes from around the world. There was no avoiding this international outlook despite our primary concern with local needs.

While the impetus for the curriculum review was initiated by the social work department, it soon began to take on a life of its own (Osei-Hwedie *et al.* 2006). The social work team deliberated on course content and titles, and after approval of its advisory board, it took its proposal to the faculty executive, which made comments and recommendations to the faculty board which is responsible for ensuring that the process is collaborative and involves widespread participation from related university disciplines and services and that it adheres to faculty rules and regulations and broader university objectives. From faculty it went to the university's Academic Policy Review and Planning Committee whose task it is to ensure compliance with university and national requirements. From there it went to the university senate, which assessed its intellectual and professional quality. Finally, it went to the university council, the highest governing body, which approved the implementation of the programme.

What then were the compromises we had to make? To satisfy regional and international requirements we had to change some course titles and content to reflect broad needs and knowledge interests. For example, the course in the MSW on 'Death and Dying in Africa' had to be renamed since it was argued that death and dying in Africa cannot be fundamentally different from that of other societies, this despite our counter argument that the circumstances of dying; the organization of death with its associated rituals before, during and after death; and the relationship between the living and the dead in African societies make death and dying in Africa very different from the experience in other societies. Thus we called the course 'death and dying' and, on paper anyway, it looked like any Western social work course on the subject.

The battleground extended to our home turf for there were differing opinions among the social work team members on the desirability of local content and the importance of cultural relevance (Bar-On 2003a, 2003b). Thus the course on 'African Centred Helping and Counselling Strategies' approved as part of the MSW in 1999 has been taught differently by various lecturers under the pretext that psychoanalytic theories of helping and counselling from the west may not necessarily be inapplicable in Botswana. Thus our original intention of teaching the course based on African values, norms, notions of relationships and general experiences of helping and problem solving has not been wholly implemented. Lecturers find Western theories and techniques comfortable, not only because of their own social work training but also because of the ready availability of Western textbooks and teaching materials.

Curriculum development is a political process in which people have vested interests and power plays are inevitable. Right from its inception, social work has debated the issue of cultural relevance and even then identified the need to change the programme's heavily clinical focus where psychology and home economics featured prominently to a more developmental orientation. Within the department there were fierce battles as to whether a Westerner – a Canadian head of department – could lead a process to develop culturally appropriate social work in an African country. The debate had nothing to do with her qualifications and professional integrity but was rather a resistance to the ongoing stream of Western departmental heads, first a Briton, followed by an American and a Motswana – in acting capacities – then a Canadian, a Ghanaian and a Zambian. It was only in 2006 that the substantive head came from the familiar Motswana culture. The cultural diversity of the social work team has been a source of ongoing tension over the years and right up until 2004, all the senior academics were expatriates – one professor, three associate professors and two senior lecturers.

Even within the broader faculty, senior academics were unconcerned about our internal struggles. They argued that all we were trying to do was substitute the remedial focus with a developmental one when, in fact, there was only one social work and it was Western. Thus there was little support for all this 'fuss' about 'appropriateness' when the old Western-style programme was seen as adequate for Botswana's purposes. Because of this, many of our proposed changes were not fully supported at faculty level. Fortunately the university accepts that programmes should be internationally acceptable while simultaneously encouraging academics to take a critical perspective on Western models modifying them for local use. Thus, to some extent, it supports authentization and localization. The challenge, however, was to blend local and international content and in the process avoid Western dominance. Even within social work there are those who believe that it is an international profession that must include both local and international content (Razack 2002). Advocates of appropriateness, like us, remain marginal to territorializing Western social work. Global interdependence and cross-fertilization advocated by Nagey and Falk (2000) are being vigorously pursued to the disadvantage of 'local cultures' as the following practice examples show.

Examples from practice

Our main focus has been on social work education, however, our research involved focus group discussions with social work practitioners who were also third- and fourth-year students in the BSW programme. Those involved in the focus group discussions had at least five years' practice experience in the welfare context. What emerged from these discussions was the degree to which social workers had to adapt Western models creatively and innovatively, similar to Nimmagadda and Cowger's (1999) experience in India. Thus, in practice, social workers expend a great deal more energy making Western models fit than they do inventing new local, culturally relevant practice models.

Counselling and support

Western textbooks view counselling as a one-to-one relationship involving the counsellor and the client, wherein the client is helped to come to grips with their situation, and through understanding the problem, to make their own decisions or choices. However, what is happening in the field is very different. As Nimmagadda and Cowger (1999) found in India, social workers in Botswana were expected to give advice, and regularly engage in a very directive form of social casework practice which is rooted in cultural expectations where Elders or those deemed knowledgeable are required to direct and guide others. Such practice is supported by the local saying, *motho fa ana le mathata o gakololwa gore a fedise jang* – a person who has a problem must be advised on how to solve it.

The practice, however, does not end with advice. In a counselling situation, it is not unusual to find a client going into a session with a relative, and two or three of their best friends for moral support. Again, collective or non-individualistic African culture demands that a person in trouble is supported and made to feel that they are loved by and belong to their community. In this case, social workers are compelled to include those accompanying the client in the helping process, giving their advice alongside the social worker and being witnesses to the decisions taken and agreed to. They also have to ensure that the client adheres to their decisions. Even when the client has gone alone for help, they are expected to report back to significant others and friends for ongoing support. This is not a monitoring or policing function but a genuine desire to help another who is struggling to cope.

Referral processes

Usually, social work professionals are supposed to refer clients to appropriate services provided by other professionals when they cannot offer these themselves or when it is necessary due to particular circumstances. In many situations, especially those involving domestic issues such as family violence, inheritance, childcare and divorce, social workers routinely refer these back to the extended family. Normally social workers want to deal with cases that have officially gone through the extended family lest they be blamed for interference and disregard for cultural protocol. This process is followed even in some of the domestic cases referred to social workers by the police. The main reason for this is that the extended family is the primary agent for resolving personal and family matters before being referred to the chief and the Elders. Thereafter the issue is allowed to enter the public domain where professionals, such as social workers and 'other strangers', can attend to the matter.

Informal support as an extension of the formal provision of services

The wisdom behind the provision of social services, when they are not provided under the institutional model, is that they are an extension of the family and the public domain. In this view, the family is deemed to have failed to provide for its members and therefore the state must step in. However, what pertains culturally is a reversal of this situation. The family and the community are seen as an extension of public provision. For example, in community home-based care for HIV and AIDS and other terminally ill patients, the family and the community volunteer support and other inputs for the care of their terminally ill members. The package of care and associated resources is made available by professionals – social workers, nurses, doctors and health educators – but it is implemented by family and community members who volunteer to ensure that necessary psychosocial, material and spiritual needs are provided. Along the same lines, the Revised National Policy on Destitute Persons (Republic of Botswana 2002) uses the extended family members' inability to provide needs as a basis for defining individuals as destitute and, therefore, in need of care. These demonstrate the recognition of the importance of the family and the community as the basis of social provision. This is not an abrogation of state responsibility as in Western welfare critiques but culturally appropriate intervention.

Social development

Social development in rural Botswana emphasizes self-reliance and *botho* – humanness exhibiting compassion, love, and caring. It is in this context that social workers involved in social development activities encourage kinship and community systems to support and work with each other for the common good. Thus the development of community infrastructure, such as schools, health clinics and houses for village level civil servants has been undertaken on the basis of communal cooperation or kinship bonds. Similarly, small communities with a population of less than 2000, which usually have kinship bonds, are encouraged to work together on projects for their mutual benefit. This has become important in the context of government policy whereby only a population of circa 10,000 may have a government school. In this case, social workers may convince four smaller communities with kinship ties living near each other to organize themselves and come together to have one shared centrally located government school.

As these communities are mobilized to cooperate, there are cultural factors that come into play. These relate to the connection between the living, the dead and those yet to be born. Thus, those living are entrusted with ensuring that wealth and resources are guided and used judiciously for posterity. Also, rituals associated with death, dying and mourning, and birth all ensure that people are sent off and welcomed in the other and this world properly. The slaughtering of animals, pouring of libation and the offering of food and drinks, among other rituals, reinforce these. The connection between the living and the dead also emphasizes the importance of spirituality in everyday life. This is underlined by the belief that the ancestors have the capacity and indeed the obligation to intervene in the lives of the living and that this must be taken into account by social workers. In this respect, social work is not so much about independence, self-determination and individual rights but more about collective self-determination and rights, mutual cooperation, obligation and responsibility, and social and economic inclusion. Thus, whereas the individual is not neglected, they are not the core focus of intervention.

Conclusion

In this chapter we have discussed our experiences in trying to develop culturally relevant social work. We have written extensively on the importance of this (Osei-Hwedie 1993b, 1995) since we have observed that Western social work is not relevant and is not working in Africa where it has little of value to intervene in situations of widespread poverty and social deprivation where people are living with HIV and AIDS, and other curable diseases because of a lack of social and health resources. If social work wants to be context based it must draw on and respond to the values and norms of *local cultures*. While adapting Western knowledge, skills, theories and principles to suit local conditions is a possibility, we believe that social workers could spend their time more productively developing localized knowledges, skills, theories, principles and problem solving strategies relevant to African cultures, world views, and ways of life. Culturally relevant social work is good social work.

Despite our concerted attempts to develop culturally relevant social work in Botswana, it remains elusive. We have discussed some of the difficulties we have experienced and, when all is said and done, our dividends have not matched our investments. Nevertheless, we continue to publish in this area to share our experiences and to enlighten others about culturally appropriate social work practice in Botswana. The focus on 'community', 'developmental social work', 'culture' and 'integrative fieldwork practice' are first steps and we believe they are in the right direction. More needs to be done, however, to ensure that cultural relevance becomes the organizing precept for social work practice not only in our university and country but also within international social work.

Chapter 17

Missing the 'Flight from Responsibility': Tales from a Non-Indigenous Educator Pursuing Spaces for Social Work Education Relevant to Indigenous Australians

Susan Gair

Rather than abandoning the field altogether in an intellectual and political climate that contested whites' roles in writing Aboriginal histories, I felt a new way of understanding and writing … had to be found (Cole *et al.* 2005: xv).

We give the impression that we have been moved by Aboriginality, but our response to it, in reality, is merely decorative, externalist and literal (Tacy 2000: 141).

In this chapter I discuss my thoughts, feelings, critical reflections and new learning acquired through conversations, literature reviews, community engagement, mentoring and supervision. In particular, I reveal how learning from Indigenous People within the academy and in the community has provided essential teaching for me in my quest to provide safer learning spaces and more appropriate curriculum content for Indigenous social work students at James Cook University in North Queensland, Australia.

In the last decade the Commonwealth Department of Education, Science and Training (2002) identified an urgent need for initiatives aimed at increasing Indigenous Australian degree completions. Since 2000 there has been a reversal of engagement of Indigenous Australians in higher education after growing numbers of Indigenous students in the 1980s and 1990s (Brabham *et al.* 2002). This reversal may be due to a range of factors, including changes to eligibility for ABSTUDY (an income benefit for tertiary Indigenous students), and a lack of adequate peer and academic support for Indigenous students who find themselves in this foreign environment. Consequently, recent evidence suggests that the retention and completion rates of Indigenous students at a tertiary level continue to be disappointing (Indigenous Higher Education Advisory Council 2006; Krause *et al.* 2005). Indigenous and non-Indigenous educators agree that Eurocentric curricula are a factor, noting that they are foreign to, and exclude and discriminate against Indigenous students and there have been calls for urgent changes to teaching and learning in Australia (Christensen and Lilley 1997; Commonwealth Department of Education,

Science and Training 2002; Gair *et al.* 2005b; Herbert 2000; McConville 2002; Nakata and Muspratt 1994).

A growing body of literature points to cultural imperialism within the academy and identifies barriers and deterrents for Indigenous Peoples in higher education. First, they point to the inadequacy of Eurocentric education for Indigenous Peoples at primary, secondary and tertiary levels (Herbert 2000; Lampert and Lilley 1996; McConville 2002; Nakata and Muspratt 1994; Ruwhui 1999). Leading the way in addressing this inadequacy, literature emerging from Canada and New Zealand calls for resistance against Eurocentric teaching and promotion of foundational learning from an Indigenous perspective (Graveline 1998; Hart 1999; Nash *et al.* 2005; Ruwhui 1999; see also Chapter 10). Second, Indigenous scholars like Smith (1999) and Atkinson (2002) expose the damage caused by the scientific knowledge claims of white researchers, implicating such claims in the worst excesses of cultural imperialism and colonialism. Third, many writers challenge the authority and legitimacy of non-Indigenous academics to teach and write about Indigenous history and contemporary social issues, including racism (de Ishtar 2004; Hart 1999; Rigney 1997; Smith 1999; see also the Postscript). Within this higher education environment, where colonialist discourse reigns, Indigenous students must somehow perform without sufficient academic support to help them survive this foreign cultural terrain.

The James Cook University social work curriculum includes some subject content on Aboriginal history and the devastating aftermath of colonization for Indigenous Australians but it could be increased. For example, content is incorporated from Indigenous literature (Aboriginal Deaths in Custody Secretariat 1997; Bringing Them Home Report 1997; Gilbert 2001; Human Rights and Equal Opportunity Commission 1997; Langton 2002; Pearson 1994, 2000). As well, relevant social work theory is taught, including anti-racist, anti-oppressive and anti-discriminatory practices (for example, the work of Dominelli 1997; Thompson 1997) along with associated critiques (for example, Moreton-Robinson 2000; Wilson and Beresford 2000). However, these inclusions do not provide relevant content from which Australian Indigenous social work students might build knowledge and skills for practice; current social work education may predominantly assume that (white) workers need a certain body of (white) knowledge and skills to work with a range of clients, including Indigenous Australians. Indeed, Sinclair (2004) writes that, 'for Aboriginal social work students, engaging in studies on how to become an effective cross-cultural worker ... verges on ludicrous because ... they are required to perceive of themselves and their people as "other"' (p. 52).

Pioneering research undertaken with Indigenous social welfare practitioners highlighted Aboriginal and Torres Strait Islander helping styles (Lynn *et al.* 1998) and revealed a 'Murri Way' of Aboriginal helping (Lynn 2001). This research provided the impetus and first steps toward a more informed approach to teaching Indigenous students at James Cook University (JCU). Yet the numbers of Indigenous students in our School and in the social work profession remain well below the proportionate numbers of Indigenous People in our community and this disproportion is reflected nationally and internationally. It may be that the intergenerational damage and stolen generations resulting from past, destructive child welfare policies in Australia and other colonized countries make social work unattractive to Indigenous Peoples (Sinclair 2004). Nevertheless, we were concerned about the decrease in Indigenous student numbers and joined the throng of voices calling for increased opportunities for the education and employment of Indigenous Australians in social work and welfare education and practice (Gilbert 2001; Lynn *et al.* 1998; Ruwhui 1999; Youngblood Henderson 2000). The first hurdle was to decide *who* could and would undertake curriculum development as we waited for Indigenous People to study, graduate and become employed as social welfare practitioners and educators. While we had encouraged applications for academic positions from Indigenous People, there were no Indigenous educators in our School.

A related concern was that even if we did get new Indigenous staff members, we could not place the full responsibility for the School's curriculum development on the shoulders of new Indigenous recruits when this was not required of other educators. This would be tantamount to what Dominelli (1989) called 'dumping', that is, the *expectation* that Indigenous educators and students can and will be cultural experts and help raise awareness about Indigenous cultures. Notwithstanding this inappropriate *expectation*, Indigenous staff and students may welcome the opportunity to counter prejudice and correct ignorance in this potential 'teachable moment' (Jensen 2005: 56). Nonetheless, Tripcony (2004) reminds us that the responsibility for successful completions of Indigenous students is 'everybody's business' (p. 1).

The ongoing damage perpetuated by white people in the name of welfare and education, in particular by 'white women', has been debated in the literature. Various writers position white women as 'bystanders' in colonization and as 'catalysts for increased racial divides' (Cole *et al.* 2005: xxii) not least through their expectation that Indigenous women, from a 'maid service position' would help white women 'unlearn their racism' (Huggins 1998: 61; see also Bush 1998; Gilbert 2001; hooks 1981). Other writers identify the 'civilizing' missionary work of white women in the early twentieth century (Cole *et al.* 2005) and the activism of some who attempted to join Aboriginal Peoples in their 'rights struggle' from a place of common humanity (Bush 1998; Cole *et al.* 2005; Maynard 2005). Moreton-Robinson (2000) is critical of the privileged position of white women educators who teach about racial oppression but have not engaged with their own unnamed 'whiteness' (p. 131).

Whiteness, white guilt and white confessional literature have become prominent in the last decade (see, for example, Anderson 2002; Bonnett 1996; Jensen 2005; Tannoch-Bland 1998), although groundbreaking work is evident from the 1960s onwards (Baldwin 1998; McIntosh 1988). Overall the literature identifies the value for non-Indigenous Peoples of interrogating the invisibility, power, privilege and guilt of whiteness (Jensen 2005; McIntosh 1988). Baldwin (1998) identifies that the *force* of history is that it informs 'our frames of reference, our identities and our aspirations' (p. 723). He asserts that white people are 'impaled' (p. 725) on their history and are unaware of how to release themselves from it, however, he suggests that we all can assess our history and enter 'into battle with that historical creation, to attempt to recreate' (p. 723) ourselves in spite of our history. Also debated in this literature is the unhelpful paralysis of white guilt and the inherent dangers associated with essentializing and centralizing whiteness in a way that does not recognize and resist its own reproduction (Baldwin 1998; Bonnett 1996; Jensen 2005). 'Recreating' myself in order that I became skilled in facilitating learning for Indigenous students was of great interest to me.

Baldwin (1996) argues that anti-racism can and should be taught by white social work educators and he condemns the 'flight from responsibility' by white, mainstream tertiary educators. In agreement with Baldwin (1996) and others (for example, Dominelli 1989), I considered curriculum review as the work of all academics. Given this critique, the anxiety and illegitimacy I felt as a white, female educator seeking to increase numbers of Indigenous graduates through an improved – 'Indigenized' – curriculum was confusing (Baldwin 1996; Larson and Brown 1997; Lee 1995). According to Dissanayake (1995), transitions from one place to another often provoke anxiety or heightened emotion because they mark the end of something known and the beginning of something unknown. I considered that my anxiety could be reframed as a space of opportunity for transformation of my own and others' learning.

Creating spaces for growth and learning

Building on the work of Eliade and van Gennep, Victor Turner (1974, 1982) developed the concept of 'liminal space', an in-between imagined place where boundaries dissolve as we stand on the threshold or horizon, ready to move beyond previous boundaries into a transitional space. Liminality is conceptualized as 'a state of being betwixt and between, neither here nor there, in a sort of limbo – fraught with the unease of not being one thing or another' (Dissanayake 1995: 70). Leggo (1997) promotes the creation of safe liminal spaces in schools where students can linger in the margins to develop new narratives. Specifically, with regard to social welfare education and practice, Lynn (2001) drew on the work of Turner (1982) to ponder ways to create a liminal 'space of possibility' (p. 903) in tertiary education.

Relevant here, Lee (1995) speaks of difficulties, contradictions and tensions for writers of colonialist heritage who live within a disputed civil space, for example where there is a lack of recognition of Indigenous rights, where treaties are not upheld and reconciliation has yet to be accepted on the political agenda. A transformation occurred for Lee when he accepted his responsibility to highlight hidden yet contested issues between the colonized and the colonizer. Gelder and Jacobs's (1998) refer to this 'post-colonial "uncanny"' (p. 23) place where, through dispossession 'the familiar (*heimlich*) is rendered unfamiliar (*unheimlich*)' (p. 23). These concepts aptly described the unfamiliar space in which I was located as a non-Indigenous educator trying to change dominant colonialist curricula in the academy. It seemed to me that I had stepped into an unfamiliar – liminal – space where my knowledge and frames of reference were inadequate (Gelder and Jacobs 1998) and new, negotiated ways needed to be found.

Framing my learning

I was aware of Crawford's (1996) work on 'auto-ethnography' as a mode of inquiry and an educational tool in which through 'use of self' one could move reflectively between academic theory and practical engagement thus 'weaving together practice, research and theorising' (p. 75) in social work education. Similarly, Clark (2000) had outlined the usefulness of an 'interpretive ethnographic' approach to social work practice and education, including the simultaneous stance of self as learner. Arnold (2005) described an exceptional educator as someone who was attuned to their own and others' 'thinking and feeling processes' (p. 12) and, as such could use empathy or empathic intelligence to 'mobilise deep shifts in consciousness' (p. 12) to transform understanding of self and others. Using an empathic, ethnographic approach I framed and tracked the advancement in my learning and transformation as I asked myself how I could improve my own teaching of culturally relevant social work education for Indigenous Australians.

Beginning the journey

I considered that what was needed was a space for dialogue and learning. I wanted to advance my own understanding and awareness and to introduce strategies that would move our social work curriculum beyond Eurocentrism and tokenist inclusions of Indigenous material. I identified a need to critique pedagogy and knowledge building which furthered the image of Aboriginal people as victims of colonization and positioned them as 'other' from a white perspective, and which did not advance practice knowledge for Indigenous students derived from their own cultural context (see Chapter 16). Further, such pedagogy could engender a victim rescuer mindset in non-Indigenous students thus compounding Indigenous disadvantage (Bennett and Zubrzycki 2003; Heron 1992; Pearson 2003; Ruwhui 1999; Sinclair 2004; Youngblood Henderson 2000; see also Chapter 6). I considered what was needed was innovative, meaningful, heartfelt ways of learning, teaching, working and writing with collaborators who could share the learning space.

Action to 'Indigenize' the curriculum

In 1999 I asked an Aboriginal educator within our university whether she could mentor me as I sought to make curriculum changes. Simultaneously, I submitted an application to our University's Teaching and Learning Committee for a small grant (unsuccessful in 2000, but successful in 2001) to fund this mentoring. Through the resultant action research project to 'Indigenize' the curriculum we recruited an Indigenous consultant who advised interested non-Indigenous staff, there being no Indigenous educators in the School at the time. Together we planned, implemented and evaluated changes to our social work curriculum (see Gair *et al.* 2005a). Despite the positive outcomes, for me it highlighted significant gaps in my knowledge as a social work educator.

Corben and Thomson (in Elson-Green 2002) recommend that what is needed for excellence in teaching is 'a passion to facilitate learning; a commitment to reflection and improving on practice; a commitment to the teachers' own learning and professional development; and a commitment to maintaining professional currency' (p. 6). I realized that I had some knowledge *about* Aboriginal Australians, less *about*

Torres Strait Islanders and little professional currency in that I did not have advanced understanding, skills and knowledge of Indigenous helping. Thus I was eager to learn *from* and *with* Indigenous Australians on their terms. While many social work educators might have these skills and this knowledge, I realized I had to address this deficit in my own knowledge.

Teacher as learner in the community

In 2003 I successfully negotiated, after initial introductions from a community member – a student and friend – to spend three months living in a small town in northern Queensland working as a volunteer – learner – at an Aboriginal, traditional owner organization. Some of that time was spent visiting a small Aboriginal community northwest of the town. While this time was relatively brief, it had a profound, transformative effect on me. Each day I accompanied the male manager as he attended meetings between Elders, staff, government departments and community members. I attended staff meetings, sessions on health and social issues and accompanied workers on fieldwork activities. I increased my knowledge substantially about Native title through reading and discussion with my teachers and supervisors.

I also talked with Elders and community members about ways through which to increase Indigenous student numbers. They suggested we needed Indigenous educators and support staff, flexible community-based course delivery and increased support for Indigenous students. We talked about how to improve course content and delivery and how to encourage non-Indigenous students and graduates to work more respectfully with Indigenous Peoples. They suggested racism needed to be confronted in the classroom, that non-Indigenous students and graduates needed to learn how to listen deeply, and that students needed detailed, accurate information about Native title and the recognition in Australian law of the rights of the original owners and of the fiction of *terra nullius*. Many community members spoke to me about experiencing racism from white professionals. I too was surprised at aspects of my own hidden racism regarding who the knowledge bearers were, who could teach and who needed to learn. Why was I surprised that Indigenous Elders had such insight into what students needed? Why was I surprised when the chairperson of the Aboriginal organization could quote large sections of the Queensland National Parks and Wildlife policy in relation to Native title when representatives of Queensland National Parks and Wildlife were incorrectly quoting from this source?

I had also underestimated the immeasurable generosity and capacity of Indigenous People to act as collaborators in my learning and to take up the role of teacher. My experiences were often uncomfortable – but sometimes humorous, humbling and emotional. One example was when the male manager exclaimed one day that, 'We had another white woman here once and she was worse than you Sue!' Other occasions when I felt humbled and emotional included when I was permitted to attend an 'Elders talking to young people' meeting, to share and write stories with women on the experiences of family violence, and to attend some planning meetings for a significant community memorial event – for the loss of Aboriginal lives previously unacknowledged—and a commemorative opening. In return for my learning, I provided assistance with a large grant application and other writing, such as a draft strategic document, draft survey and minutes of meetings.

During my time in the community I gained a much more comprehensive understanding of the limited nature of Indigenous content within subjects I had developed and taught. Notwithstanding the inclusion of Aboriginal and Torres Strait Islander helping styles and working with families and communities – for example, the work of Bessarab (2000) and Lynn *et al.* (1998) – I could now identify huge gaps in my coverage of Indigenous knowledge and skills in many practice areas. For example, I identified that a major deficit in the organizational practice subject that I taught was the absence of content on understanding Indigenous community organizations and organizational practices and processes, including decision making; this organization had a management committee of two Elders from each of the nine language groups it represented and these Elders made all the decisions. Examples of Indigenous community work, planning community events and undertaking community research were also limited in subjects I had taught.

Similarly, information and examples of Indigenous leadership, conflict resolution, theories, policy making, ethics, case management, networking, healing, resistance, advocacy and brokerage virtually were absent from, and needed to be included in, my teaching. One observation was that almost all of these processes were collective and, therefore, quite at odds with mainstream content where group work was taught only as one possible mode of practice. Further, I recognized a lack of content on working separately with men and women, on Indigenous women's perspectives on feminism, childcare and child protection, and on examples of Aboriginal women's activism.

Thus it was fortuitous that, as I sought to meet women in the community, one woman asked me whether I could document her stories of family violence and those of family members so that the community, and especially young people, could learn from them. Several women from a nearby town had also spoken to me about similar issues and needs. Initially, I worried about taking control of documenting their stories, not least because of past criticism about white researchers interpreting and misappropriating Indigenous People's stories, and because we had talked about my using their stories in my teaching. Nevertheless, given the lack of understanding of Indigenous women's perspectives, I realized I was being presented with a learning opportunity – perhaps a liminal space – in which to understand more about these women's view and interpretations of their experiences.

Over the next 12 months, we planned and sought funding to cover the costs of travel, refreshments, instruction and materials for the writing workshops – there were two – where the women would write their own stories. It became a joint venture between a regional domestic violence service, a school of social work and an Indigenous publisher and enabled the women to retain ownership and control of their stories and, at the same time, to gain valuable writing skills and experience. The services of a published Indigenous illustrator and a successful author were engaged and each workshop began with sharing stories and concerns about family violence. Thereafter we talked about writing techniques, exercises to get started and beginning to write about lived experiences with particular audiences in mind. I joined in the writing and sharing exercises both as a group member and facilitator. While the small grant we had received was quickly exhausted and the stories were not ready for publication during the time of my involvement, the writing project gave life to other processes.

Aware of the literature on Indigenous story writing as an act of resistance, a way of highlighting injustices, and seeking social justice (Department of Aboriginal and Torres Strait Islander Development 1999; Huggins 1998; Kennedy 1990; Langford 1988; Older Women's Network 2003; Ouellette 2002; Wingard and Lester 2001), I came to realize that this small writing group was a powerful example of activism. This was an act of resistance by women willing to take significant risks in sharing and writing their stories for a wider audience. I had never specifically thought to teach writing as a medium for resistance and activism, for example in, among other things, practice skills and professional helping subjects, nor had I thought of the potential of 'women's writing' for healing, community development and group work in social work education.

Clearly, the inclusion of these culturally relevant topics in the social work curriculum would mean inviting Indigenous guest lecturers and tutors to describe and teach their practice, prescribing readings by Indigenous authors, and encouraging and supporting Indigenous students, community members, practitioners and colleagues to document their stories and practice for sharing, where appropriate, with students. I returned to work with new learning and with a renewed commitment to bringing about change to my teaching and students' learning within our school. Students' evaluations illustrated a mixed response, from something akin to hostility from some non-Indigenous students in response to my apparent pro-Indigenous stance, to appreciation from both Indigenous and non-Indigenous students of stories from local Elders and community workers.

Further action: A dialogue with critical friends

In 2004 I found a colleague from the School of Education who shared an interest in the emerging literature on teaching and learning in higher education for Indigenous Australians. We scheduled a meeting with 'critical friends' to discuss movement beyond colonialism in the academy through legitimate, negotiated conversations and actions. We invited Indigenous and non-Indigenous colleagues within the disciplines of social work and education and a small group of eight colleagues attended the meeting. At this meeting we began by sharing our reflections on our own teaching and students' learning and we aired our frustrations, perceived inadequacies and hopes as educators. We discussed concepts of interest from the literature, including 'Eurocentrism' (Youngblood Henderson 2000), 'dumping' (Dominelli 1989) and 'liminal space' (Turner 1974). We admitted to feeling somewhat immobilized within this new post Mabo[1] 'uncanny' – unfamiliar – place within the academy (Gelder and Jacobs 1998; Lee 1995). In these conversations (see Gair and Pagliano 2006) we

---

1   Mabo refers to the landmark 1992 Native Title case in favour of Eddie Mabo of Murray Island, Queensland, Australia. It confirmed native title and exposed the myth of *terra nullius*.

engaged in an unusual level of respectful dialogue that, more often than not, seemed to have been avoided in our academy. The outcomes from our conversations offered direction and encouragement for us to pursue further conversations and spaces within the academy and confirmed that ongoing conversations would be appropriate and welcomed by Indigenous and non-Indigenous colleagues, and useful for students' ultimate learning within safe intercultural – liminal – spaces.

Moving forward

As noted earlier, recent reports (Indigenous Higher Education Advisory Council 2006; Krause *et al.* 2005) reveal that tertiary level Indigenous students continue to have poor outcomes, and confirm the current, urgent need for an ongoing commitment to tertiary success for Indigenous Australian Peoples. Recent research undertaken within our School confirms that educational outcomes could be enhanced through intensive support – academic, economic and community, recognition of prior learning, understanding of the profound barriers to study for many Indigenous students and curriculum reflecting knowledge broader than 'only the white way' (Gair *et al.* 2005b: 58). Similarly, Bennett and Zubrzycki (2003) report that Indigenous students experience 'a mix of determination to get through the course, isolation and alienation in terms of their perspectives and values, coupled with high expectations from their lecturers that they understood all things Aboriginal' (p. 65), that is, Indigenous students were expected to know Indigenous history, culture and skills for practice even though they might have received little advanced teaching in these areas. Indigenous social work graduates reported needing to work harder to be recognized as professionals and being left to educate their non-Indigenous professional supervisors on 'culturally sensitive practice' (p. 68). On the latter point, Gair *et al.* (2005b) found that Indigenous students on placement were frequently asked to give advice to supervisors on cultural matters about which they might or might not have sufficient knowledge or authority to share.

As noted above, one useful strategy appears to be creating spaces for conversations between non-Indigenous and Indigenous colleagues in the academy. Safe spaces for dialogue between Indigenous and non-Indigenous students and between students and educators seem equally appropriate. The concept of liminal space provided a vehicle for our learning, an opportunity to use simple conversation and stories to develop, revisit, maintain relationships and to suggest a way forward. It indicated to us that together, Indigenous and non-Indigenous tertiary educators – and students – could move beyond Eurocentrism and dumping, and have conversations to improve our own higher education praxis. According to McMaster (1996), an effective means by which a space of possibilities can be kept open is by continually 'engaging in conversations that develop the very space itself' (pp. 150–1). Taking these steps proactively and persistently to create and maintain educational, physical and psychological learning spaces, and to facilitate difficult conversations, seems to us to be useful for respectful academic relationships between Indigenous and non-Indigenous academics and for negotiated teaching and learning.

A second transparent strategy to increase non-Indigenous educators and practitioners' 'cultural' knowledge is located within the realm of mentoring and supervision. Grauel (2002) suggests that the roots of supervision are in medical consultation and psychoanalysis but it is social work that has made an original contribution to the advancement of supervision for professional practice. Hawken and Worrall (2002) suggest that mentoring has favour in business and other arenas and that the process and purposes of mentoring and supervision are very similar. McMahon (2002) discusses supervision as encapsulating three aspects: relationship, developmental process and learning environment. Holloway (in McMahon 2002) identifies this type of supervision, as a 'learning alliance' (p. 18). This alliance develops when the supervisor creates a learning environment but the supervisee is viewed as a self-managed learner who develops his or her own learning goals (see Proctor 1994). This concept of mentoring and supervision as a *learning alliance* is reminiscent, from my perspective, of my experiences during my time in the community as a learner under direction from Indigenous People.

A third useful strategy from my perspective may be exploring the concept of empathy. As noted earlier within the *Framing my learning* section of this chapter, empathy was incorporated to imagine a deeper thinking about learning. In turn, this insight – empathy – can allow educators to be more sensitive to the ways in which students 'might be thinking and feeling' (Arnold 2005: 12) and use this empathic understanding to create purposeful learning experiences. Interestingly, Clark (2000) argues that 'empathy' as defined in social work literature has deep flaws. It is 'identified as a foundational practice principle; (p. 3) and a practice skill which has a therapeutic function and, over the years, there has been little theoretical development of the concept. Following Rogers (in Clark 2000), it is seen as 'a particular type of deep, non-judgemental understanding, distinct from that which comes from external frames' (p. 3) or situated understanding. 'It presumes an ability to enter into the sensibilities of another without first learning the [cultural] context from which those sensibilities arise' (p. 4). Hence there has been little regard for the influence of cultural differences and the impression is conveyed that cultural understandings can be summoned from within us all merely through empathic listening. Rather like didactic teaching and learning, the conventional literature on empathy conveys the impression that it is unidirectional and implies that the practitioner as expert does not need to conceive of the client's – or student's – contribution to the relationship. This view of empathy automatically assumes that the practitioner's perception of the client or student is accurate. Clark (2000) suggests that we adopt the position of learner, rather than expert, and remember that empathy is a two-way or mutual process in which we develop a deep situated understanding of the meaning of the other's experience within the helping – and teaching – relationship. She recognizes the dangers of suggesting that clients can teach practitioners cultural awareness; it is reminiscent of the concept of 'dumping' noted earlier. Rather, she advocates deep listening for advanced understandings of cultural meanings from the clients' frame of reference. Deeper listening and learning as educators will be helpful in advancing meaningful education and practice for Indigenous and non-Indigenous students. A point to begin may be in negotiating, with Indigenous Australian colleagues in the academy and with community members and students, new meanings and definitions of familiar social welfare concepts and terms, perhaps beginning with empathy. Of course this notion is not new and Indigenous writers commonly appeal for new understandings from the non-Indigenous community, through listening and heightened (cultural) awareness of their Eurocentrism (McConville 2002; Moreton-Robinson 2000; Youngblood Henderson 2000).

My learning to date leads me to conclude that it is necessary that, at the very least, Indigenous Australians must undertake some teaching within social work and welfare studies. I believe that I more adequately can facilitate dialogue to advance students' learning from my position of developing insight, but I agree with Larson and Brown (1997) that some reinforcement of oppression will always be present because of my colonizer status within this colonized space.

I wanted to avoid 'dumping', to be respectful and transparent, and to recognize, in a genuine rather than tokenistic way, the cultural capital available to me as a social work educator – and to my students and colleagues and the broader community – in our Indigenous students, colleagues and communities. By seeking mentoring and supervision – paid or reciprocal (see, for example, Hawken and Worrall 2002) as distinct from expecting tuition or exploiting colleagues' or students' knowledge – non-Indigenous educators and practitioners can learn and demonstrate respectful relationships. Curriculum can be developed and taught in collaboration with Indigenous Australians, in ways that model and mirror professional relationships and friendships built on empathy, trust and respect.

Of course, relevant curriculum presenting social work practices inclusive of Indigenous knowledges and world views also is crucial for non-Indigenous students. As noted above, some non-Indigenous students initially could be hostile to, and may need encouragement to embrace, new ways of understanding and learning. Needless to say, these students are not immune to the need for culturally familiar concepts to achieve their own learning. Yet it seems apparent that teaching relevant social work practice in Australia must move beyond victim and perpetrator concepts to encompass wide ranging, culturally relevant practice skills, information, theories, experiences and examples through meaningful, collaborative education processes and dialogue.

Conclusion

Retention and completion rates of Australian Indigenous students continue to be disappointing. As a non-Indigenous Australian social work educator, I have attempted to take my share of the responsibility in facilitating increased Indigenous graduate numbers from our degree programmes. It seems to me that significant responsibility lies with all tertiary educators to undertake the everyday business of the university, providing successful outcomes for all students through relevant, high quality teaching and learning informed by research, critical thinking and reflection. Documented here is my progress as a non-Indigenous reflective educator and learner pursuing ways to better incorporate Indigenous practice into my curriculum. An ethnographic approach frames and gives meaning to the discussion of my thinking, feelings, critical reflection and new knowledge acquired through conversations, community engagement and mentoring and supervision. Learning from Indigenous People within the academy and in the community, and critical conversations with colleagues, have provided essential learning for me and for some of my colleagues, in our quest to provide safe learning spaces and appropriate content for Indigenous social work students. This quest is still in its infancy.

Postscript

In 2005 and 2006 we have reversed the downward spiral of the last eleven years in relation to Indigenous students studying within our School. Numbers of Indigenous students had dropped approximately 60 per cent from 45 to 18 over the decade 1994–2003. Currently we have thirty Indigenous students studying within our School, just over 4 per cent of the student body of 687. While it is difficult to draw any conclusions regarding contributing factors I believe that the actions described above have enhanced our ability to retain students.

Chapter 18

Picking Up What was Left by the Trail: The Emerging Spirit of Aboriginal Education in Canada

Gord Bruyere

One of the things that draw people into human service, especially the fields of social work and education, is the notion of serving something greater than ourselves, of creating change or working for social justice. Recent developments in Aboriginal social work education in Canada, particularly those at the Aboriginal education institute where I serve, can be seen as symbolic of something far greater happening than the work of one or a small group of individuals. Our current work to cultivate an Aboriginal social work programme intends to nurture Aboriginal cultural identities through course and programme curricula that centre Aboriginal cultural values, beliefs and practices and concurrently prepare graduates of diverse identities to work in Aboriginal and mainstream social work settings. It is a complex undertaking but one that feels like a contribution to something broader than itself or ourselves.

Reflection on this work has led me to ponder a number of questions. What makes social work education at an Aboriginal institute different than that in mainstream institutions? What is it that Aboriginal students seek when they attend an Aboriginal social work programme? What are some of the tensions that exist between the non-Aboriginal theories and practices and the re-emerging Aboriginal teachings that Aboriginal students explore at an Aboriginal institution? How do differing, emerging conceptions of social work education interface with prevailing national social work education standards? How does Aboriginal social work education connect to the spiritual renewal of Aboriginal communities in a decolonizing Canada?

'Picking up what was left of the trail' is a metaphor that comes from the Anishnabe teaching of the Seven Fires and connotes the challenges of living within these questions. This chapter discusses these questions and explores the relationships and challenges from the experience of one Aboriginal social work educator in light of his understanding of the Seven Fires teaching. It is my hope that the lessons we can all draw from this reflection are helpful in the broader consideration of Indigenous social work and social work education in other parts of the world, and that it may in some small way inspire others to undertake similar journeys with Indigenous Peoples.

Living in the time of the Seventh Fire

Anishnabe people, also known as Ojibway or Chippewa people, are one of the largest Indigenous nations in North America and can be found in Canada and the United States around the Great Lakes in the centre of the continent. The Seven Fires is a traditional teaching of the Anishnabe people. The Seven Fires is a set of prophecies that are said to have come to the Anishnabe when we were living on the east coast of the continent before we migrated to what we now know as our traditional territory around the Great Lakes. The Seven Fires were given to the people by seven prophets who predicted what would come in the future. Each prophet offered one Fire, and each Fire refers to an era of time in Anishnabe history, spark grown into flame that withers to ash before building again. The first three Fires foretold of the great migration of the Anishnabe from the eastern shores of North America to our traditional territory that we recognized as 'the land where food grows on water' (Benton-Banai 1988: 89) or the land where our traditional staple food, wild rice, grows. This migration was said to last approximately 500 years. The next three Fires told of the coming of 'the Light-skinned race' (Benton-Banai 1988: 89), and presaged the European colonization of the Anishnabe and other Indigenous Peoples, another period often estimated at 500 years. The prophet of the Seventh Fire said:

> In the time of the Seventh Fire, a New People will emerge. They will retrace their steps to find what was left by the trail. Their steps will take them to the Elders who they will ask to guide them on their journey. But many of the Elders will have fallen asleep. They will awaken to this new time with nothing to offer. Some of the Elders will be silent out of fear. Some of the Elders will be silent because no one will ask anything of them. The New People will have to be careful in how they approach the Elders. The task of the New People will not be easy. If the New People remain strong in their quest ... there will be a rebirth of the Anishnabe nation and a rekindling of old flames. The Sacred Fire will again be lit. It is at this time that the Light-skinned Race will be given a choice between two roads. If they choose the right road, then the Seventh Fire will light the Eighth and Final Fire an eternal Fire of peace, love, brotherhood and sisterhood. If the Light-skinned Race makes the wrong choice of roads, then the destruction which they brought with them in coming to this country will come back to them and cause much suffering and death to all the Earth's people (Benton-Banai 1988: 91).

We now live in the time of the Seventh Fire, and it is indeed characterized by a social, political and cultural resurgence of the Anishnabe and other Indigenous Peoples of North America that we can understand as picking up 'what was left by the trail'. Becoming a New People means that we are attempting to shed the impact of colonization and to recreate our relationship with our land, with each other in our urban and reserve communities and society and to recreate our relationships within the body politic of mainstream society. One of the most comprehensive records of the complex challenges and successes of this resurgence for Anishnabe and other Indigenous People in Canada can be found in the Report of the Royal Commission on Aboriginal Peoples. In discussing this resurgence, a friend of mine who works in the field of Aboriginal community economic development said to me, 'We are the contemporary manifestations of our languages, cultures, and ancestors' (Fox 2002: personal conversation).

Since the latter half of the twentieth century, we Anishnabe people have asserted ourselves through reclamation of language, cultural values and beliefs, and the practices that comprise our culture and society. These practices have been reconstituted as institutions that include those associated with social work education and practice.

The developments that Anishnabe people and other Indigenous People across Canada have initiated within social work practice and education can be understood as picking up what was left by the trail because the most successful developments are based on traditional teachings, like that of the Seven Fires, and are guided by our Elders. Picking up what was left by the trail has been a challenge connoted by the teaching of the Seventh Fire, not in the least because of the legacy and current manifestations of colonization that affect the relationships between Aboriginal Peoples and other Canadians (Bruyere 1999: 171). Picking up what was left by the trail to participate in the creation of a New People and to return to the teaching of the Elders who will guide us on this journey has led me to question how we live with the Seventh Fire.

What makes social work education at an Aboriginal institute different than that in mainstream institutions?

The Nicola Valley Institute of Technology (NVIT) was first formed as a private institute in 1983 by the Coldwater, Nooaitch, Shackan, Upper Nicola and Lower Nicola First Nations communities. The Institute was formed in response to the failures of mainstream post-secondary institutions to attract and retain Aboriginal students, and was formed with the vision of creating an environment that Aboriginal students would find welcoming, and which Aboriginal communities would see as responding effectively to their needs.

Working from a basement in the downtown core of Merritt, British Columbia and in three small trailers on the shores of Nicola Lake, three instructors taught thirteen students the basics of what is now our 'Natural Resource Technology Programme'. The programme was taught in an environment that promoted traditional ways and fostered student success, a vision that sticks with NVIT today. Gradually building programme offerings to address Aboriginal community needs, such as socio-economic marginalization, environmental concerns and political issues, NVIT became and remains a unique and important public post-secondary institute in Canada.

In 1995 NVIT was designated as a Provincial Institute under the British Columbia College and Institute Act. This designation as a public institution resulted in a significant infusion of financial resources at a level comparable to other publicly funded colleges and institutes within the province. This means that NVIT can elude the severe financial constraints that affect most Aboriginal institutes in Canada and which can impair growth and development or affect mere survival. It also means that NVIT has a stronger presence in our province than other Aboriginal institutions across Canada, as NVIT entered into a provincial system that recognizes the transferability of its courses and programmes. Hence, NVIT's offerings create opportunities for its students to pursue further post-secondary education. On the other side of the scale, designation as a provincial institute immerses NVIT into a mainstream accountability regime that, without strong governance and diligence, could marginalize our accountability to the Aboriginal communities that we serve and which created us.

The call to accountability to Aboriginal communities is symbolized in our motto 'Education, Strength, Leadership' and in our stated collective vision that NVIT:

1. Becomes the school of choice for Aboriginal students because it has a reputation for producing quality graduates.
2. Offers an extensive choice of programmes relevant to the interests and needs of Aboriginal students and communities.
3. Provides a rich educational and cultural campus environment in which to learn and work.
4. Has the active and dedicated leadership of a First Nation Board of Governors, and a qualified and committed staff, the majority of whom are Aboriginal.
5. Successfully serves as a catalyst to Aboriginal communities in the quest for education, development and greater self-determination (Nicola Valley Institute of Technology 2006).

Although most post-secondary institutions can make similar claims and assertions, part of what also makes us unique are the distinctive values and competencies the NVIT Board of Governors and NVIT Elders Council defined to guide our current work and any developments we undertake (Nicola Valley Institute of Technology 2006).

One of the longest running programmes to arise out of NVIT's vision, values and competencies is the undergraduate Bachelor of Social Work (BSW) degree programme. The social work programme was first offered in 1989 and through a partnership with what was known as the Saskatchewan Indian Federated College (SIFC). SIFC is the most widely known and successful Aboriginal, public post-secondary institution in Canada and is now known as First Nations University of Canada. In many ways, SIFC was the forerunner and model for other Aboriginal post-secondary institutions like NVIT because of their devotion to Aboriginal values, beliefs and practices, the dedication to control and governance by Aboriginal people, and the balancing of relationships with Aboriginal communities and a broader mainstream institutional framework. At the time of writing, First Nations University of Canada and the Nicola Valley Institute of Technology are the largest public Aboriginal post-secondary institutions in Canada.

A partnership to deliver BSW education was struck with SIFC because NVIT is not mandated to offer degree education. Another reason was that SIFC's Bachelor of Indian Social Work programme was – and still is – a nationally accredited programme that respected and included Aboriginal perspectives in its curriculum and its explicit commitment to prepare primarily Aboriginal graduates to work with Aboriginal Peoples. However, limitations of respective institutional capacities led to the conclusion of that relationship and creation of a new partnership with the University of Victoria, School of Social Work in 1993. The current partnership to offer BSW education at NVIT is with Thompson Rivers University in Kamloops, originally known as the University College of the Cariboo and located eighty kilometres from Merritt and NVIT.

Our affiliation agreement with Thompson Rivers University (TRU) is important to understand because of how it has come to allow us to actualize our distinctive vision, values and competencies. When our partnership first began in 1998, NVIT was struggling in many ways. Our first affiliation agreement reflected the need to address the ways in which NVIT and the BSW programme were struggling: Inconsistent application of or non-existent academic policies, a contentious workplace environment, difficulty in attracting and retaining qualified Aboriginal faculty, declining student enrolment, insufficient library resources and a concomitant erosion of the programme's reputation (Seebaran and Johnston 1999: 22). The affiliation agreement that was struck as the relationship commenced was quite detailed and oversight by TRU was cautious and stringent. The relationship at the time was characterized by a statement of the NVIT–BSW programme coordinator who said she felt like 'a butterfly in a jar'.

When the TRU–NVIT BSW affiliation agreement was renewed in 2004, it reflected a shift in the relationship. Gone were the numerous and onerous operational and reporting requirements and these were replaced by guiding principles that respected the mutuality and interdependence of the two programmes. This mutuality and interdependence was due to the huge strides made by NVIT to address the shortcomings identified in the mid-1990s, and the willingness of TRU to recognize and affirm NVIT's growth and development and its own principles of social justice.

The change of relationship captured by comparison of the two affiliation agreements has meant that NVIT has the capacity and freedom to pursue its conception of social work education. This, in turn, has led to the emergence of other qualities that distinguish social work education at an Aboriginal institute which are consistent with the vision, values and competencies of NVIT.

The presence of children and Elders

Having taught in four other social work programmes across Canada, it is my experience that students will bring their children to class or the institution only occasionally. The centrality and sacredness of children is such a strong ethic among Aboriginal people that it is common for staff or students at NVIT to bring their children along with them. It does not happen all the time but often enough that it is normal and such that it is uncommon in comparison to what we may see in mainstream social work programmes. Nursing mothers will simply bring their newborn children to class rather than leave the programme or suspend their studies, and faculty will accommodate them as much as possible to retain mothers as students. Critically analysing child welfare practice takes on a different quality when students and the faculty member hear a child quietly singing while she colours a drawing at a desk in the corner of the classroom.

NVIT is blessed with an Elders Council made up of nearly two dozen Elders appointed by the five local First Nations communities to serve at NVIT. The Elders are a consistent presence throughout the academic term as they create a rotation to ensure that one male and one female elder are always on campus when there are classes. The Elders have their own office centrally located at NVIT where they can see anyone who enters the building, and the Elders' office is one of the first things anyone sees when entering NVIT.

The Elders do not take on one particular role but together the Elders Council fulfils many roles. They are always present at meetings of the Board of Governors or the Social Work Community Advisory Committee and thus serve important roles within the governance and development of the institution and its programmes. The Elders started a food and clothing bank for students, and many students are actually related to the Elders or the Elders may serve as surrogate grandparents for students. As such, the Elders help to create a family-like, supportive environment. Some of the Elders take responsibility for purifying the entire building at the beginning of each week during academic terms, or for saying prayers at the beginning of classes or special occasions. A number of Elders are well known regionally for their traditional knowledge of ceremonies, philosophies and medicines. Though it is an infrequent need, Elders mediate disputes or problems through academic policies related to students and practices entrenched within the collective agreement governing faculty, staff and administration.

Faculty and students are free to ask Elders to attend classes and act as guest lecturers but the presence of Elders goes beyond that. It is accepted practice at NVIT that if a classroom door is open an elder can choose to walk in. It is a common and everyday occurrence that an elder will be conscripted into a small group exercise with students or asked their opinion about a given topic. Elders may also sit silently throughout a class and do their own learning. At other times, Elders will actively take a teaching role. Both students and faculty are accustomed to letting Elders take the lead in how they participate in the learning environment.

The centrality of ceremony

Each year the social work programme orientation begins with a ceremony conducted by Elders. The ceremony begins with a purification ceremony and prayer. The Elders will then welcome visitors to the traditional territory of the Okanagan and Nlaka'pamux Peoples on which NVIT rests. We then facilitate a talking circle among Elders, faculty and students, a practice that carries over to many social work classes as a common pedagogical process.

It is also common, as mentioned above, that sage will be burned by an elder to purify the building at the beginning of the school week and anyone who encounters the elder while this is happening is free to purify themselves. This practice also presages any formal gathering or ceremony at NVIT, including student orientation, career fairs, programme launches, or convocation.

The social work faculty is predominantly Aboriginal and often begins classes with purification and prayer, and uses talking circles as a standard pedagogical practice. The appropriateness and effectiveness of talking circles in social work education has been discussed elsewhere (Bruyere 1997). Suffice it to say that this manner of conducting learning helps to create a particular environment that is spiritually and culturally as well as intellectually grounded. It helps to mitigate power differences and to acknowledge and respectfully include what each student brings to the programme, course or topic.

One of the most important courses in the social work programme at NVIT is Cultural Immersion. In itself it is a ceremony or ceremonies embedded within ceremonies. Cultural Immersion is facilitated primarily by Elders from the local territories and First Nations communities and includes purification, fasting, sweat lodge ceremonies and other traditional teachings that Elders see as critical to personal wellness and to social work practice.

The politics of learning

Given that NVIT is an Aboriginal institute with an Aboriginal conceived vision, values and competencies governed by Aboriginal people, with programmes that seek to serve Aboriginal communities and mainstream Canadians it is not too difficult to understand that colonization and its effects are as much in peoples' hearts and minds at NVIT as are the renewal or resurgence of Aboriginal cultural values, beliefs and practices to address those effects.

Among Aboriginal students, including myself in the past, it is very common that their education is viewed as a part of personal and collective healing. It is my belief that there is not one Aboriginal people that has not been exposed to multigenerational trauma from colonization manifest in the dislocation from traditional territories, residential schools or provincial child welfare practices (Cole 2006). Education is often a step of a healing journey that has seen Aboriginal individuals address personal abuse issues, addictions or the impact of family violence. Of course these issues are not specific to Aboriginal people and similar histories encourage many people to enter social work education. Yet for Aboriginal students there is a sense of urgency that drives them to seek social work education that respects their lived experiences and the desire to exceed or transform those experiences.

For the individual student, education is also often seen as a way to escape poverty; for Aboriginal students that poverty is unfortunately endemic to life on reserves or increasingly to the urban ghettos where Aboriginal people congregate. Often Aboriginal students are the first of their generation to seek post-secondary education, and often those students are financially responsible for the survival of their own children or extended family. Aboriginal students often seek post-secondary education because of leadership roles they already serve in their communities, and regardless of the academic discipline they intend to serve Aboriginal people.

In my experience this notion of service to a family, community or Indigenous nation is something that is unique to Aboriginal people seeking social work education. The individualism that characterizes most post-secondary students is an individualism that serves the collective. Social work education becomes a way to develop innate personal skills, abilities and attributes that are best energized for the betterment of something greater than oneself. An Aboriginal cultural identity is a personal identity but it is an identity rooted in a cultural group with a language, history and schemes of life that organize relationships.

Fostering a social work student's relationship with the land, with family, community, Indigenous nation or Aboriginal Peoples generally, and with self is a means to address the urgency for social work education demonstrated by Aboriginal learners. As feminists would say, the personal is political. I believe this quality makes social work education at our Aboriginal institute a unique experience. It is a unique experience that is crucial to many Aboriginal students and to those students from diverse backgrounds that either want to work with Aboriginal Peoples or who want to learn to work in an Aboriginal centred way.

What is it that Aboriginal students seek when they attend an Aboriginal social work programme?

Through examination of an NVIT BSW programme evaluation from 1999 and from programme proposals for similar kinds of Aboriginal specific social work education at two other British Columbia Schools of Social Work (Green 1999; Harris 2002; Seebaran and Johnston 1999) it is quite easy to encapsulate what Aboriginal students seek from us:

1. Spiritual affirmation, emotional support, physical belonging, intellectual rigor.
2. Development of an Aboriginal cultural identity.
3. Culture-based, culturally safe ways to relate to Aboriginal people and other peoples.
4. A balance of Indigenous and mainstream perspectives.

These are not simply found in books or other instructional resources, nor are they only found in the assignments that students complete, and they are not really reflected through academic policies. These statements of what Aboriginal students seek when they attend NVIT or other Aboriginal social work programmes found elsewhere are a reflection of what students bring with them, what they want, both as lived experiences and unrealized potential. Faculty members, Elders, Social Work Community Advisory Committee members, our degree affiliation partners at TRU and the students themselves co-create these through our will to relate to one another in a good way. These are not just abstractions. These are indications of spirit and life. If we want to call it the Bachelor of Social Work programme at NVIT as if it is a 'thing' that is one way to understand it but these features are signs of a living, breathing, evolving entity. It is one of the distinguishing hallmarks of Indigenous People that we often see as animate what others see as inanimate. This is not only attractive to Aboriginal students but it is also frequently attractive to non-Aboriginal students who seek a different kind of social work education.

What are some of the tensions between non-Aboriginal theories and practices and the re-emerging Aboriginal teachings that Aboriginal students explore at an Aboriginal institution?

Since its inception, the NVIT BSW programme has inherited its curriculum from its degree-granting partners. To varying degrees the curriculum of our three partners has made room for the inclusion of Aboriginal teachings and practices. Yet for thirteen of the first sixteen years of our existence, the one thing that has characterized our most recent partnerships, with the University of Victoria and Thompson Rivers University, is that Aboriginal teachings and practices have been nested in a foundational framework of Western European or Canadian theory and practices and their underlying values, beliefs and ideologies.

I think that the underlying foundation of most schools of social work in Canada is largely unquestioned by its constituents or if it is challenged, such critiques or analyses occur from within that same framework. Analyses or critiques by Aboriginal people that are based on traditional world views and which are informed by an understanding of colonization come from outside the Western European or Canadian theoretical traditions.

If Aboriginal world views and bodies of knowledge are accepted as equal knowledge traditions, and this is by no means certain, Aboriginal ways of knowing and being are usually regarded as marginal to prevailing discourse. Aboriginal social work education is seen, at best, as one interest and usually a minor one within the interests of almost all Schools of Social Work in Canada. As a microcosm of broader Canadian society, Aboriginal interests exist on the periphery except when it suits the broader interests of the majority. I have elsewhere recounted my own experience as a social work student that illustrates the marginalization of Aboriginal ways of knowing and being because of the prevailing theoretical foundations and ways of knowing of social work educators who come from a Western European theoretical knowledge tradition (Bruyere 1998).

This marginalization of Aboriginal ways of knowing and being affects a multiplicity of relationships. Aboriginal students and faculty may hesitate to share what they know with Aboriginal or non-Aboriginal people for fear of being attacked or minimized. Aboriginal people are hesitant or hostile to Aboriginal knowledge because of how they have internalized racism to view such knowledge as mere quaint legend, folklore or stories, rather than complex philosophies, beliefs or practices with their own internal coherence. Students may prefer to unconsciously or uncritically privilege Western or European ways of knowing and being as better. Aboriginal knowledge may be seen as mummified relics of the past rather than vibrant, living systems that are still inherent in the ways of life of Indigenous Peoples. These manifestations of marginalization adversely affect and hinder the development of an Aboriginal cultural identity and the fruition of beliefs and practices that are effective in social work with Aboriginal Peoples and other human beings.

Earlier I asserted that Aboriginal students want a balance of perspectives from their social work education. It is my contention, and our ongoing project at NVIT, that our responsibility and opportunity as an Aboriginal social work education programme is to nest relevant Eurocentric Canadian social work theories, approaches and practices within a still re-emerging bed of Aboriginal vision, values, beliefs and practices. There is a balance to be struck in this regard and if we at Aboriginal institutions or the few Aboriginal social work programmes across Canada do not do it, we certainly cannot rely on anyone else to do it. If we allow someone else to do our work, we stand to have our knowledge appropriated and exploited like a cultural artefact, and if we do not continually breathe life into our ways of knowing and being, we stand to relegate our schemes of life to relics or artefacts.

How do differing, emerging conceptions of social work education interface with prevailing national social work education standards?

NVIT is obviously not alone in creating Aboriginal conceptions of social work education in Canada or around the world. Presently, there are many examples from across Canada where schools of social work have formed partnerships with Aboriginal institutions or communities to deliver social work education. Surveying the respective websites of schools of social work will yield an indication of these partnerships.

Most often these initiatives nest Aboriginal knowledge within prevailing theory and practice frameworks that exert control over the delivery models and who does the instruction. Academic policies and procedures still rest with the mainstream institutions. Schools of social work tend to determine the nature of relationships with Aboriginal communities or institutions based on the school's mission and its interpretation of national social work accreditation standards. In fairness, the prevalence of relationships with Aboriginal communities or institutions that are shaped and controlled by mainstream institutions may be a factor of the limited institutional capacity of Aboriginal communities. It may also be an indication of genuine effort to meet the needs of Aboriginal communities. Or, Aboriginal communities may genuinely desire the brand of social work education available from their mainstream partners. We must at least consider the notion that the issue of the constraints of accreditation standards or the ways in which a school sees its mission, may be – by purpose or accident – effective denial of shared power and control with Aboriginal institutions.

The need for social work education for Aboriginal Peoples is unfortunately not going to go away or ameliorate any time soon given the ongoing impact of colonization. How schools of social work in Canada cast their partnerships with Aboriginal education institutes that are growing in number and capacity will be an issue for these schools to wrestle with.

A critical aspect of addressing the growing demand for culturally competent or culturally safe Aboriginal social workers (Stephenson 2000: 10) will be how the schools of social work make room for stand-alone Aboriginal social work education programmes. Schools of social work are guided in the development of undergraduate and graduate social work degree education by the educational policy and national standards of the Canadian Association of Schools of Social Work (CASSW).

The prevailing interpretation of CASSW policies and standards will likely limit or hinder Aboriginal centred social work degree education at Aboriginal colleges or institutes in Canada without significant debate, discussion or possible revision in the near future. The relevant policy statement concerns social work at the undergraduate or BSW level:

> 2.1 Undergraduate social work degree programmes take the form of professional social work studies within the context of general university education (CASSW 2000: 4).

The most relevant accreditation standard reads:

> SB 2.1 The programme shall be implemented through a distinct unit known as a faculty, a school, a department or a division, which has a clear identity within the university (CASSW 2004: 5).

Those with the power to decide which Aboriginal colleges and institutions may deliver nationally accredited social work degree programmes may use this policy statement and accreditation standard to keep that door closed. It is in the interests of universities to protect their ability to deliver social work education to Aboriginal Peoples, because the Association's Educational Policy Statements call for Schools to respond to the needs of Aboriginal Peoples but not to necessarily make room for Aboriginal institutions:

> 8.1 In keeping with education policy statements 1.1 through 1.5, and where appropriate, schools' education programmes, including admissions, shall respond to the needs of aboriginal students and their communities.
>
> 8.2 Aboriginal Communities affected by the programme shall have an opportunity to participate in the planning and ongoing evaluation of the programme (CASSW 2000: 9).

The prevailing interpretation is that social work degree education can only occur *at a university*, and a university in Canada is commonly understood as those institutions with formal membership in the Association of Universities and Colleges of Canada (AUCC). The only Aboriginal institution in Canada with AUCC membership as of this writing is First Nations University of Canada, perhaps the only Aboriginal institution with the financial means to secure such membership and therefore the approbation of the CASSW to deliver BSW education on its own.

Incidentally, First Nations University of Canada is the only Aboriginal post-secondary institution in Canada to receive ongoing funding from Indian and Northern Affairs Canada to 'maintain a university-level focus on research and development in Indian Education and to deliver special programs' (The Aboriginal Institutes' Consortium 2005: 30). Fifty other Aboriginal institutions across Canada may receive federal funding for university programmes, but since the provinces have the constitutional responsibility to allow institutions to grant degrees and largely do not do that, the conditions by which Aboriginal institutions could be considered 'universities' are not favourable. It also means that the federal funding that Aboriginal institutions receive for degree programmes goes, in large part, to the mainstream institutions that grant the degrees and does little to enhance the capacity of the Aboriginal institution.

NVIT is in a unique situation, similar to that of First Nations University of Canada (FNUC), in that it is already a public institution. While FNUC may be the only Aboriginal institution with degree granting status, NVIT is the only other Aboriginal institution in Canada that offers its own Bachelor of Social Work (BSW) degree programme. That programme is in affiliation with Thompson Rivers University (TRU) and NVIT's BSW graduates receive a TRU degree even though the curriculum of the two programmes differs substantially. The CASSW recognized and applauded the differentiation between the two programmes in its affiliation but the future may push the boundaries.

As mentioned earlier, most Aboriginal institutions in Canada are still private institutions that do not enjoy public funding and either do not have the means or the desire to join AUCC. In addition, regardless of the goals for institutional development, Aboriginal institutions will very likely be limited to private status and ineligible to receive federal funding to become degree granting institutions. So as long as schools of social work dictate that social work degree education can only occur at a university, mainstream institutions will continue to hold the power to limit the development of Aboriginal social work degree education in Canada.

One other option that addresses the development of Aboriginal social work degree education and the usefulness of national accreditation standards is for Aboriginal people to develop and implement our own standards. This option seeks to address the existing limitations in a whole other way, a truly Indigenous way. Aboriginal institutions in Canada are currently making fledgling attempts to explore this idea.

How does Aboriginal social work education connect to the spiritual renewal of Aboriginal communities in a decolonizing Canada?

This is an appropriate point to return to the Seven Fires teaching. Picking up what was left by the trail means that Aboriginal institutions like NVIT have the opportunity to take a leadership role in reinvigorating Aboriginal cultural traditions in a way that nurtures and recreates an Aboriginal cultural identity for the Aboriginal individual, family, community and Indigenous nation.

In addition to Aboriginal cultural identity, Aboriginal social work education that centres Indigenous ways of knowing and being can renew the centrality of Elders within Aboriginal societies and institutions. Aboriginal social work education can offer insight into cultural beliefs and practices that have served Aboriginal people for generations, and which may still be effective in addressing problems facing Aboriginal communities today. These insights can be shared with social work graduates to work more effectively with Aboriginal Peoples. Conventional historical and contemporary mainstream approaches to education, child welfare, criminal justice and governance have had little success in dealing with the multigenerational effects of colonization. Aboriginal people in Canada have consistently advocated for the space and means to use the ways of knowing and being inherent in our cultural traditions to deal with our own problems in the way that we see fit.

That leadership role also invites us to share those traditional values, beliefs and practices in a way that enriches students from all racial and ethnic groups that comprise Canadian society. An Anishnabe elder told me, 'If we have something of spiritual value to share, we should share it. Our teachings are not secret, they are sacred' (Linklater 1993: personal conversation). In addition to developing Aboriginal cultural identities, and preparing Aboriginal and non-Aboriginal graduates to work in Aboriginal communities, we have an opportunity to influence how social work is practiced in diverse settings in British Columbia and across Canada, wherever our graduates find themselves a role. In these ways, Aboriginal social work education can pick up what was left by the trail and help a New People to emerge.

The Seven Fires also speaks to the choice of the Light-skinned race. Most Anishnabe Elders interpret this choice as one between a spiritually oriented path and a materialistic path. Others interpret the choice as one between ways that coincide with the Earth's natural processes or technological ways that harm the Earth. For our purposes, the Seven Fires points to the role of non-Aboriginal students, educators, social work practitioners and social work institutions. That particular choice is to either perpetuate the colonial nature of relationships that are often still in evidence, or to make efforts to re-establish relationships in a way that makes space for Aboriginal ways of knowing and being in social work education for the enrichment and healing of all.

As a means to conclude my discussion concerning the way forward for the Indigenization of social work education in Canada and the potential for Aboriginal social work education, I offer this poem. Its imagery intends to create hope and to illustrate another way in which our shared relationships may be understood as picking up what was left by the trail and a rekindling of old flames.

We are a Ceremony

> We are a ceremony,
> sage coiled through loving hands
> into a sphere into a sphere
> smouldering from inside.
>> We are an offering,
>> beaded feathered stem fit to bowl
>> in a prayer honest prayer
>> Creator-thoughts that we send back.
> We are lusting ancestors,
> cackling stones make water sigh
> conceiving life this changed life
> and we watch their children grow.
>> We are beckoning spirits,
>> calloused palms rasp the skin
>> of that drum that glistening drum
>> a deep and thoughtful pulse.
> We are voices raised in song
> a timid and halting few
> call and response call to response
> each breath stronger and sure.
>> We are certain sacrifice.
>> Unclear days ahead say to

follow our hearts these kind hearts
humbly crawling to the light.
But for now
we are a ceremony
bound and coiled though loving hands
into a sphere into a sphere.

Chapter 19

Indigenous Social Work Education:
A Project for All of Us?

Erika Faith

... to recognise what we are so as to know what we can be, and see where we come from so as to reckon more clearly where we're going ... (Eduardo Galeano 1973: 289).

Introducing myself and my questions

My whole life has been lived at the interface between colonizing and Indigenous ways of being in the world. As a child of missionary parents, I grew up in Nepal where the framework for my parents' presence was the belief that they were benefiting the local Indigenous Peoples with the technologies, systems, values and the Christian religion of the industrialized world. Back in Canada, as a fourth generation newcomer to the land of Saskatchewan, I had neither a sense of my own Indigenous Nordic roots nor the cultures and world views of the Indigenous Peoples of this land. As a result, questions of identity and place, privilege and power, language and voice, harm and healing, have been woven throughout my personal life, and professional and academic work.

Graveline (1998) asserts that 'resurrecting one's own history to find out how it has contributed to the history of the world' (p. 37) is essential to the process of all decolonization work. Decolonization, according to Yellow Bird (2006), 'is the intelligent, calculated, and active resistance to the forces of colonialism that perpetuate the subjugation and/or exploitation of our minds, bodies, and lands, and it is engaged for the ultimate purpose of overturning the colonial structure and realizing Indigenous liberation' (see the Postscript). Imperialism, globalization, patriarchy, fundamentalism and Western rationality have created great imbalance and pain both on a planetary level and in my personal life. My life work involves remembering all that has been fractured by centuries of what Eisler (1987) refers to as 'dominator' ideologies and practices. Decolonization to me means to remember and heal, returning to balance and wholeness the severed connections between body and spirit, between men and women, adults and children, between nations, and between human communities and all our non-human relations. My purpose involves doing my part to reverse the power imbalances in which my life is embedded, and to draw inspiration and direction from Indigenous ways of living in balance and harmony on this earth.

In my Master's thesis I looked at questions of power and privilege, voice and knowledge, inclusion and exclusion, within the discourse of my chosen specialization of 'international social work' (Haug 2001). Although my work explored the interface between colonizing and Indigenous knowledge systems in social work globally (Haug 2001, 2005), I was not grounded in the local context of these dynamics. Then in 2001 my journey brought me back to the land my ancestors had settled on, to teach and learn in the School of Indian Social Work, a unique programme dedicated to Indigenizing social work education and practice. Here the questions I had begun asking in my Master's thesis deepened and expanded. For example, what is social work really? Is it accurate to say that social work is 'Indigenous' to European nation states? Is most of what we know as social work essentially colonialist discourse? Who is served, and who is disadvantaged by, dominant models of social work? If the dominant construction of social work has suppressed Indigenous political, social and cultural systems, what reparations need to be made? What are, or is there a difference between, 'developmental' social work models coming from decolonizing nation states and 'Indigenous social work models' coming from within colonizing nation states? What does Indigenous social work really mean? What is the connection between Indigenous helping traditions and contemporary social work practice? Is there a danger in conflating the two?

From these questions, more questions about voice, power and privilege emerged, such as, who is and who is not Indigenous? Are Indigenous and non-Indigenous either/or categories, a continuum or is Indigenous something we can all claim or reclaim? If Indigenous models are about inner rather than outer knowledge (Ermine 1995), who has a right to speak about Indigenous social work? Who has the right to be an 'expert' on Indigenous social work? Who is Indigenous social work intended for? What are, or is there a difference between, the ways in which Indigenous and non-Indigenous People write about Indigenous social work? What are the impacts and implications of having this discussion in the English language? How do we practice 'right relationship' and recognize power differences within academic conversations? If 'perpetuation of the existing order is perpetuation of the crime' (Galeano 1973: 18), what is the responsibility for those of us who hold privilege within the dominant systems of social work education to 'create space' for Indigenous models (see Chapter 17)? This chapter expresses my learning to 'treasure the questions' as singer/ songwriter Martyn Joseph says; to explore with imagination rather than seeking tidy definitive answers. To begin, I will revisit the first question posed, a question that is as old as our profession: 'What exactly *is* social work?'

What is social work in relation to Indigenous social care traditions?

> … even as we must fully comprehend the pastness of the past, there is no just way in which the past can be quarantined from the present. Past and present inform each other, each implies the other and … each co-exists with the other … Neither past nor present … has a complete meaning alone … [H]ow we formulate or represent the past shapes our understanding and views of the present (Said 1993: 4).

Before the great ruptures of the Industrial Revolution, colonialism, and imperialism, for millennia Indigenous societies around the world had been creating unique systems for taking care of those who were vulnerable, for resolving conflicts, redistributing wealth and building communities. What we know today as 'social work' is a recent and culturally specific manifestation of a societal function that is as old as the human race. It is a specific cultural, political, ideological and historical response to address the social problems of the time and place from which it arose. Folk singer and poet, Utah Philips, states that 'the past didn't go anywhere'; that we are all standing in the 'river of history'. In terms of social work, this 'river' comprises many tributaries that include the emergence of modernist thought in Europe, the Industrial Revolution, colonial imperialism, the rise of commercial capitalism and the ascendancy of the US as a global power. Within this river, many interlinking and mutually reinforcing power relations between and within nation states can be identified and explored.

In response to the economic and social displacement, dispossession, interpersonal conflict, oppression, human suffering and poverty caused by the transition to industrial capitalism, the welfare state was developed across European states, reflecting each nation's ideological, cultural and political context. Social work, in turn, emerged as 'the central and dominant, but not the only, profession involved in staffing the formal social welfare system' (Compton and Galaway 1989: 5). Social work first arose from Holland, Germany, England and the United States, to 'support modern society by largely "helping" those who are unable to support or care for themselves in a manner considered appropriate by social norms' (Coates 2000: 2).

As a product of its time and place, social work's theory-base was mostly derived from the thought of one race, class and gender. As an emerging profession, social work came to replicate the normative and apolitical male defined theories of human development, nature of society and psychological pathologies popular at that time. Freud's psychoanalytic model, Erikson's stages of development and Weber's model of bureaucracy are examples of theories that still influence the profession today. Yet despite the male, modernist bias that much of the theory-based social work adopted, it was an emerging profession mostly founded by women. From its beginning to the present, social work in the northern hemisphere has been mostly practised by white middle class women. Across the different contexts in which the profession emerged, social work remained highly gendered and, as such, lower in pay and profile compared to the male dominated professions, such as medicine, psychiatry, psychology and law (Rossides 1998: 170).

For a time, the Industrial Revolution that gave rise to social work secured the position of economic and ideological dominance of the colonizing nation states over the continents from which wealth had been siphoned during the previous centuries. Rather than due to some inherent intellectual superiority of European people, the Industrial Revolution was made possible through what Uruguayan historian Eduardo Galeano describes as a 'massive haemorrhaging' of natural wealth, and plundering of Indigenous knowledge and technologies over three centuries from South America, Africa and Asia by the European colonial powers (Galeano 1973). As Graveline elaborates:

White society—Westernism—did not rise to prominence because of its inherent superiority, as White historians, philosophers and authors ... would like us to believe. Their success was built on the backs of Indigenous peoples who have been robbed of their lands, their resources and their labour (Graveline 1998: 113).

Economic and political colonization by European powers of the Americas, Asia, Africa and the Pacific Islands, laid the foundation for *intellectual colonization* in which modernist scientific knowledge systems displaced previously established local, popular and Indigenous knowledge systems. In turn, intellectual colonization was linked directly to the *imperialism of aid* of the 'development decades', based on the belief that through assimilation practices, the rest of the world would conform to the industrialized nations. In social work, through *professional imperialism*, modern institutional models of social care replaced the tremendous diversity of pre-existing Indigenous models of social care. Thus, all over the world, social work was a part of the imperialist project of assimilation accomplished by replacing traditional Indigenous social structures, ceremonies and forms of governance with colonial systems and structures. As Yellow Bird asserts, social work is colonization: It was founded on colonization and the exclusion of the well-being of Indigenous Peoples (see the Postscript).

Professional imperialism of social work and resistance from Indigenous Peoples

> Never was it the case that the imperial encounter pitted an active Western intruder against a supine or inert non-Western native; there was always some form of active resistance, and in the overwhelming majority of cases, the resistance finally won out (Said 1993: xii).

Professional imperialism refers to the way in which professional models that emerged from the industrialized nation states were imposed and imported globally. The international dissemination of professional social work mirrored the larger, unidirectional spread to the rest of the world of professional knowledge systems during the nineteenth and twentieth centuries. Under the banner of international development, social work, along with other economic, political, agricultural, health, and educational models and technologies, was transplanted to the emerging colonial nation states in Asia, Africa and the Americas, each with unique world views, political, societal and cultural contexts. In this unilateral transfer, there was little recognition given by the United Nations, or by established schools of social work and nongovernmental organizations, of the existence, never mind validity, of Indigenous methods of social care (Haug 2001; Nagpaul 1993).

Underpinning the professional imperialism of social work was the ethnocentric belief 'that social welfare services in the Third World would develop and conform eventually to western standards' (Midgley 1981: 57). Implicit in this assumption was the belief that the locus of knowledge was the colonizing centres, and that Indigenous Peoples in the colonized lands had no knowledge or expertise, and were incapable of developing their own social care models. Under social work's globalizing drive, the diversity of Indigenous forms of social care, unique to their specific cultural contexts, were silenced, devalued, displaced, ignored and made invisible to the centre.

It is a great irony that models emanating from Europe and the United States, where poverty, crime, social and family violence, and inequality abounded were seen as inherently superior to social care models developed by many highly democratic Indigenous societies where, prior to colonial contact, there was minimal poverty, crime or inequality. Indigenous societies the world over had been built on a deep integration of ties to the community, the spirit world and the natural world (Hughes 2003). The professions, by contrast, were based on the Cartesian split between the physical, mental and spiritual, and between people and the natural world. And yet the superiority of this modernist model was unquestioned, as the following excerpts demonstrate:

> [In view of] the special nature of the problems presented by under-development, little will be lost by those countries in the Third World which use them for the training of their social workers—at least until there is enough local expertise to make their own courses viable (Jones 1990: 194).

> The alternative of local training, in countries where the methods of social work in use are still not very advanced, might well prove to be a case of the 'blind leading the blind' (Friedlander 1975: xx).

With the growth of English as the language of international currency, and with the emergence of the US as a world power, by the mid-1980s American social work hegemony appeared to be virtually complete (Garber 1997). By the end of the twentieth century, social work had a formal presence in 100 of the 176 UN member countries (Garber 1997: 164). From a handful at the beginning of the twentieth century, schools of social work education had reached more than 1,600 around the world by the end of the twentieth century (Garber 1997: 159). A census of social work educational programmes in the 400 plus member schools of the IASSW completed in 2000 found a 'reassuring convergence' between social work curricula globally (Garber 2000). The current search for a universal definition of and global qualifying education standards for social work is one of the latest manifestations of this homogenizing drive (see Chapter 1).

However, just because the US model was broadly exported, does not mean that it was broadly accepted. As Freire (1985) states, 'there is no colonial intervention that does not provoke a reaction from the people about to be colonised' (p. 183). Resistance to the American-European social work model was expressed by Indigenous Peoples around the world, from China (see Chapter 15) to Africa (see Chapter 16) to the various tribal societies across the Americas (see the Postscript). Especially in places where the majority of the population was now living in poverty due to the fallout of colonialism, many Indigenous Peoples questioned, with good cause, the suitability of the formal professional model of social service delivery systems.

For example, Chitereka (1999) states that Western individualism, upon which social work is based, was alien to African culture, while Osei-Hwedie and Rankopo (see Chapter 16) assert that Africa has unique cultures, needs, institutional structures and social relationships which require Indigenous social work models. Similarly,

Gore (1997) records how in India the idea of professional social work was initially considered a foreign import 'and an unwelcome one at that' (p. 447). Prasad and Vijayalakshmi (1997) describe how 'the micro-based practice model adopted in the Indian context (produced) students unsuited to meet the developmental need of the Indian society' (p. 65). Nagpaul observes that:

> US social work education is highly ethnocentric, and its essential elements are inappropriate and irrelevant for India and other developing societies where not only social structures and social problems are different but even human needs, beliefs, myths, values, traditions, goals, roles and the aspirations of people are so divergent that new strategies and solutions need to be developed (Nagpaul 1993: 215).

Not only was the professional model of social work challenged *outside* the countries from which it originated, it was also challenged *within* these same countries by Indigenous Peoples, other cultural minorities, service recipients in general, and by progressive, often left wing, community minded professionals working both within and outside the welfare system (Carniol 2006). Despite ongoing progressive reforms within the profession, the problems with the dominant construction of social work education and practice have remained. Burnout rates are high. Disillusionment, dismay and callousness are occupational hazards. Social welfare systems, derived from the individualistic, capitalist thinking of Western consciousness, often do not benefit those they purportedly 'serve', or those who work for them. Most of the really interesting jobs are to be found on the fringes of social work, rather than in the bureaucracies where job stability and pay are greatest, though job satisfaction lowest.

Professional social work *vis à vis* Indigenous Peoples in Canada

> The white social worker, following hard on the heels of the missionary, the priest and the Indian agent, was convinced that the only hope for the salvation of the Indian people lay in the removal of their children (Fournier and Crey 1997: 84).

In Canada the historical relationship between the social work profession and Indigenous Peoples has been fraught with misunderstanding, abuse, displacement and trauma (Fournier and Crey 1997; Hart 2002). The profession of social work has all too often upheld systems that rather than support, effectively undermine the healing, dignity and autonomy of Indigenous Peoples in Canada. As Hart (2002) says, 'the social work profession's ethnocentric practices and disrespect of Aboriginal[1] cultures have produced anger, distrust and a lack of confidence among Aboriginal Peoples towards the profession' (p. 11). Social work has been just one more form of oppressive, unwelcome outside government intervention into Aboriginal communities.

As the primary profession staffing the social welfare system, social workers played a leading role in the removal of Indigenous children from their homes,

---

[1]   From here on, due to the Canadian context, various terms will be used for Indigenous Peoples including Aboriginal, First Nations and Indian.

families and communities in what is now called the "'60s scoop" in which thousands of children were taken from their communities and placed in non-Aboriginal homes' (Wotherspoon and Satzewich 2000: 90). During this period, '[v]irtually every extended family in every aboriginal village across the country lost a child to "the welfare"' (Fournier and Crey 1997: 86). This pattern of removing Aboriginal children has continued to the present day, so that the term 'baby snatcher' and 'social worker' have become synonymous in many communities.

Today Aboriginal communities across the country are struggling to cope with and heal from the myriad effects of the 'professional interventions' and colonialist assimilation strategies, such as four centuries of Church and State run residential schools that were effectively 'internment camps for Indian children' (Fournier and Crey 1997: 49). 'From the mid-1800s to the 1970s, up to a third of all aboriginal children were confined to the schools, many for the majority of their childhoods' (Fournier and Crey 1997: 50). Despite the harsh and often violent colonial suppression of all forms of traditional educational, social, political, spiritual and justice systems, endorsed by legislation like the Indian Act of 1876, Indigenous communities survived. Although banned until 1960, traditional spiritual ceremonies were carefully preserved, often through great sacrifice and risk and currently these ceremonial practices are undergoing a great resurgence. Across the country the movement toward self-determination is now strong, as First Nations are reclaiming their sovereignty as guaranteed by the international treaties signed at the time of contact. Education is an important site of reclaiming sovereignty of First Nations traditional knowledge, structures and methods of social care.

Case study: School of Indian Social Work, First Nations University of Canada, Saskatoon, Saskatchewan

> Upon initiating a focus on themselves and working to maintain a degree of balance, connection and harmony for healing and growth, helpers are in a better position to follow an Aboriginal approach when helping others (Hart 2002: 106).

While the global project of 'indigenizing' social work curricula has, in some cases, met with resistance by local Indigenous People, as Osei-Hwedie and Rankopo describe (see Chapter 16), in Saskatchewan specifically and in Canada generally there has been strong support from many Indigenous communities to develop culturally grounded social work training based on community healing, as opposed to the dominant social work model that has relied heavily on child apprehension. Today Aboriginal scholars, educators and practitioners are leading the way in reconceptualizing and revisioning the social work profession, child welfare service delivery, community healing and community justice. The Saskatoon-based School of Indian Social Work, operating within the First Nations University of Canada, as Canada's longest standing Indigenous Social Work Programme, has played a significant role in this movement.

While teaching in this programme from 2001 to 2004, I had the opportunity to learn one model of Indigenous social work education and practice, based on the vision and teachings of Saskatchewan First Nations Elders and academics (primarily the Nehiyawak, Anishnabe, Nakota, Dakota and Dene nations). One of my first lessons was the importance of integrating ceremony and the teachings of Elders into the classroom. At their direction, I learned to open each class with a smudging ceremony, led by one of my students – usually someone who was trained as a ceremonial helper – thus creating space to centre and ground ourselves each time we met. Leading by example, my students modelled for me other aspects of Indigenous social work, such as the importance of humour, laughter and personal sharing. In opening their lives to me, they shared their pain and inspiration: Their experiences of various forms of abuse, of the residential schools, of life on reserves, on the streets, of incarceration; as well as their love for their children and grandchildren, their passion for healing, and desire to give back to their communities, the strength of their ceremonial traditions, and what being in the programme meant to them. Inspired and humbled, I, in turn, began to take more risks in sharing from my own life, of being a 'child of the empire' as Chellis Glendinning (2002) says; of being a survivor of sexual abuse; and of my struggle with my identity as a white person. In this way I came to understand two of the fundamental tenets of Indigenous social work practice as discussed by Hart (2002): *reciprocity* and *speaking from the heart.*

Hart (2002) describes personal healing and balance as two key 'foundational concepts' of Indigenous social work. The medicine wheel model is used as an 'assessment tool' for examining both personal and community wellness (Sanderson 1996). From this model I came to reflect on how my own social work training had focused almost exclusively on cognitive or intellectual knowledge, with no attention paid to the spiritual realm. I came to see how the traits that had led to my success in the dominant social work system, represented imbalance according to the medicine wheel teachings. I also came to realize that while in the dominant social work systems I was considered qualified to teach, in the Aboriginal social work model I would be just 'qualifying status', in view of the imbalances I carried within me, including addictions to work and perfectionism, the lack of resolution with my family and cultural identity and my disconnection from the emotional and spiritual aspects of myself.

A central tenet of the Indian Social Work Programme is that 'before you can help others to heal, you have to heal yourself'. Instructors are expected to teach from their own lived experiences, and to model integration of theory with our personal journeys. While in the programme, students are expected to work through their pain, to give voice to aspects of their journey they may never have shared in a group before and, in so doing, gain confidence, discover integration and then be in a position to lead similar groups in the communities they will work with. The basic premise was that we *all* have suffered from living in a society and history steeped in interpersonal violence, including the violence of colonization and, therefore, we *all* have a healing journey to make. This framework creates a sense of shared humanity, egalitarianism and deep empathy. No shame. No silence. No pretence at perfection.

Along with the focus on personal and community healing, the multiple effects of trauma, especially intergenerational trauma, victimization and abuse, were given special attention. Indigenous Peoples, by their very existence, are survivors. Today, within Indigenous communities, the 'survivor movement' is growing exponentially as whole communities gather to talk about healing addictions, sexual abuse, domestic violence and intergenerational pain passed down through the residential schools. These types of community healing processes are unheard of in non-Indigenous communities here, where there is still a strong taboo around identifying oneself as a survivor of any kind, especially for professionals who work in human service fields.

Participation in traditional healing and community building ceremonies is viewed as essential to Indigenous social work training. On a weekly basis, Elders in the programme conduct sweat lodge ceremonies where prayers are made, pain is released and healing shared. In the fall, a powwow celebration is held to welcome students back to school. During the winter months, students, staff and community members hold hands and dance in the spiralling circles of the round dance until the wee hours of the morning. Culture camp in the summer is an intensive ten day course held on reserve land, where students and staff sit together under the shade of a poplar arbour, listening to the teachings of the Elders, participating in sacred ceremonies, learning traditional crafts and survival skills, and cooking meals together. Thus, social work training at the School of Indian Social Work includes personal sharing, training with Elders, a working knowledge of healing ceremonies, a minimum knowledge of Indigenous languages, historical studies of contact and pre-contact societies, and practical skills like making bannock – a popular fried bread – over an outdoor stove!

Indigenizing social work education, a project for all of us?

Aboriginal epistemology is grounded in the self, the spirit, the unknown (Willie Ermine 1995: 108).

Following the completion of my contract at the First Nations University of Canada, I began sessional instructing for the University of Regina's Social Work Programme. Although most of my students were non-Aboriginal, I found myself teaching from the Indigenous model of social work education I had learned, not for 'political correctness', but because I had come to realize that this model optimally serves both my students and myself! Regardless of my class composition, I now integrate Elders' teachings, First Nations' storytellers and ceremonies, such as smudging and give away ceremonies to open and close our circles respectively. I conduct my classes in circles and model self-disclosure and speaking from the heart. I have come to believe that Indigenous models of social work practice and education are good for all of us, whether we identify ourselves as Indigenous or not.

Moreover, in a province where the Aboriginal population is soon to reach 40 per cent, I believe it is my responsibility to reflect this demographic in my course readings, class structure and class content, lest Indigenous content continue to be relegated to elective classes. By integrating aspects of an Indigenous model of social work in my 'mainstream' social work classes, I am doing my part to model the treaty relationship on which this province was founded, without which I wouldn't be here. By sharing my own journey of decolonization, which to me means, in part, transforming all forms of domesticated ways of thinking and being, I create space in the classroom for deeper levels of sharing and community building. I have come to believe that the project of decolonization is global and requires all of us, regardless of where we sit on the colonizer–colonized continuum. It is my hope that through mutual liberation we will be able to find more integrative forms of social work practice that will serve all members of our communities.

Of the mainstream social work programme, one of my former students said to me, 'They don't care at all about life experiences.' This is surely one of the main attractions of the Indigenous social work education model; that life experiences are valued and academic skill in writing papers isn't the sole criterion for assessment. In the real world, social workers don't write academic essays as much as they work with human beings in pain. So how is it that we have a training system that focuses mainly on academic writing? With the insight that I can never know another person's inner world, and led by the Aboriginal social work tenet of self-evaluation (Hart 2002), I have increasingly explored methods for students to self-evaluate their work.[2]

Indigenous Hawaiian author Paul Pearsall asserts that we *all* have 'Indigenous minds' with which we need to reconnect in order to discern new ways of bringing about healing for this world. Part of what I learned during my time at the First Nations University of Canada was how much of my own ancestral tribal knowledge has been lost to me. While storytelling is a powerful and also pleasurable method of education that Indigenous Peoples have used for millennia to instruct and heal (Hart 2002), as Europeans many of us are missing stories that connect us to the land we live in, to our Indigenous mythology. The stories of the bible that many of us grew up with locate the 'holy land' and cultural heroes far away from us. Stories speak to our spirits, to our emotions and to our hearts, and stay in our memories far longer than a lecture! The right story at the right moment can be powerful medicine, instructing in a non-didactic way, and working gently on the soul, over time. For this reason I have come to integrate Indigenous storytellers in all of my classes, and to practice storytelling from our lives in sharing circles. On the whole, my European students have responded positively to the Indigenous model I teach from, whereby our lives are the primary texts and the textbooks are the supplementary texts.

Conclusion

> In a rapidly changing and interdependent world, single models are more likely to go awry. The effort to combine multiple models risks the disasters of conflict and runaway misunderstanding, but the effort to adhere blindly to some traditional model ... risks disaster not only for the person who follows it but for the entire system in which he or she is embedded, indeed for all the other living systems with which that life is linked (Bateson 1994: 8).

On a global level, the world we now live in is very much a product of the hegemony of colonizing knowledge systems, taken to their extreme conclusion. Many of the most pressing problems facing the world, such as the global ecological crisis, stem directly from the modernist scientific paradigm that came to dominate globally (Coates

---

2   I now have students assess their own attendance and participation mark at the end of term, and have also experimented with students self-assessing their class presentations.

2003). In the past two centuries we have moved from the majority of the world living in harmony with the land, to the majority living in unlovely cities, dispossessed from a direct relationship to the land and all the attendant symptoms of post-industrialism. The technology and economics of the modernist model of progress has cost us the meaning and practice of community and, in many ways, has disconnected us from our spiritual connection to the land and all of our nonhuman relations. In sum, the hegemony of colonizing knowledge systems has led to a profound state of imbalance globally. *Koyaanisqatsi* is a Hopi word which means crazy life, life in turmoil, life out of balance, life disintegrating, a state of life that calls for another way of living (Reggio 1982). *Koyaanisqatsi* describes our current global condition.

The profession of social work has been part of this global phenomenon of colonizing knowledge systems being transmitted as monocultures, often obscuring pre-existing Indigenous models. Despite the various forms of colonization, Indigenous Peoples around the world have, against great odds, preserved their cultures, identities and social care practices. Today there are more than 7,000 Indigenous societies comprising about 500 million people identified globally, who maintain their ancient ways of being in relation to the land, human, natural and the spirit world (Hughes 2003: 20). Indigenous practices of social care are coming into the awareness of mainstream social work (see Chapter 20). While in many ways this is a positive development, it is important that the integration of Indigenous knowledge systems be done with great respect, and attention to voice, power and privilege. Einstein observed that no problem could be solved by the same consciousness that created it. Many are now recognizing that the answers, innovations and insights to get us through our current state of *Koyaanisqatsi* will come not from those traditionally seen as the 'experts', but from those 'on the margins' who are maintaining and reclaiming ancient knowledge systems that incorporate the wholeness of creation and of mystery. Rather than a benevolent gesture motivated by guilt, anthropological attraction or political correctness, the incorporation of Indigenous knowledge and methods into professional social work education and practice needs to be viewed as an imperative for all of us, in order to bring our profession into a greater place of balance, harmony and respect for *all* of our relations.

Chapter 20

Hearing Indigenous and Local Voices in Mainstream Social Work[1]

Mel Gray, John Coates and Tiani Hetherington

Social work, like 'sailing, gardening, politics and poetry, law and ethnography are crafts of place: they work by the light of local knowledge' (Geertz 1983: 67).

In this concluding chapter we attempt to counter misconceptions about the silencing of local and Indigenous voices in mainstream social work. Within the mainstream literature notions of difference or diversity have been dealt with in a variety of ways. As we showed in the Introduction, this has spawned several bodies of knowledge or parallel discourses (see Introduction, Table 1) relating to *inter alia* cross-cultural and anti-oppressive social work practice. Culturally and racially sensitive practice models, then, form part of social work's attempt to deal with 'difference'. Critical theorists have been quick to point out the way in which minority and Indigenous voices have been silenced within this dominant social work discourse.

We argued in Chapter 1 that globalizing and universalizing forces continue the profession's colonizing tradition by which Western social work models have supplanted local, Indigenous approaches and practices and argue that these trends are reigniting resistance. At the same time, in those contexts where social workers and local or Indigenous communities have been interacting and working in close proximity with one another, their voices are finding some expression in the mainstream literature, notably in the areas of spirituality and environmental social work. In these contexts, this discourse has progressed beyond multiculturalism, cultural sensitivity, and anti-oppressive practices to embrace Indigenous and non-Western thinking and practices. The examples herein presented – from Australia, Canada, Aotearoa/New Zealand, Tonga, China, Malaysia, Israel, India and Africa – provide evidence of this. They highlight the importance of culture and local knowledge in the development of genuine and authentic social work practices in these diverse contexts.

Like Nimmagadda and Martell (see Chapter 11) we want to promote the fact that Western social workers have as much to learn from Indigenous social workers and social workers from non-Western cultures, as they have to learn from other Western social workers. Thus, for example, the lessons learned in Indigenous contexts have application in Western contexts as well, especially in situations in which social

---

1   Adapted from a paper published as 'Hearing Indigenous Voices in Mainstream Social Work' in the Jan–March, 2007 issue of *Families In Society*, vol. 88, no. 1. Reprinted with permission from *Families in Society* <www.familiesinsociety.org>, published by the Alliance for Children and Families.

workers are dealing with diversity. We want to address the imbalance in the literature on cross-culturalism that is largely directed towards Western social workers practising within culturally diverse client communities in Western contexts where it embraces many of the ideas of anti-racist and anti-oppressive practice. In fact, this literature tends to conflate discussions of race and culture and all forms of discrimination and to subsume it under critically constructed anti-oppressive practice theory. This is not surprising given that most Indigenous groups are minority populations (with few exceptions, for example, black majority South Africans under apartheid) who have historically experienced oppression from colonizing nations that have undermined their efforts at self-government and, therefore self-determination.

While there is much of value in the cross-cultural literature, there is also much to be gained from the Indigenous and international social work literature. If there were to be a single perspective emanating from this book, it would be an appeal for culturally relevant social work and for social workers around the world to be knowledgeable of experiences from 'other' international contexts. Social workers have much to learn from one another's work and each has implications for the other (Gray and Fook 2004; Gray 2005). In this vein, when reading and reflecting on the Indigenous and international social work literature, the central question becomes what might we learn about the cultures of Indigenous and non-Western peoples that might inform mainstream culturally relevant social work practice? Being mindful of our international audience, we believe that the issues raised herein should be of concern to all social workers everywhere, practitioners, researchers and educators alike.

Against this broader political reality, the literature on spirituality and environmental social work – aka 'green' or 'ecosocial work' – articulates and privileges local and Indigenous cultures, to use anti-oppressive terminology, but more importantly it is a countermovement to the universalizing movement in social work and beyond and questions the theory of globalization. Spirituality, a path that seeks greater connection to larger purposes and meaning, celebrates diversity and promotes inclusion. Ecosocial work draws on a deep ecological awareness of our relationship with nature and makes us acutely aware of the importance of protecting and sustaining the natural environment in everyone's interests. It needs to be distinguished from ecological social work, which tends to take an anthropocentric stance focusing on the *social environment* from the point of view of human or *individual interests* (Besthorn 1997; Coates 2003).

The growing acceptance and recognition of spirituality and ecology with their emphasis on alternative world views have brought forth a welcoming and inclusive context enabling the celebration of diversity and the sharing of knowledge. The expanded understanding of *person in environment* to include an awareness of our interdependence and relatedness to the Earth, the importance of place and the openness to more traditional and Indigenous forms of healing and helping offers a refreshing openness as they start from a set of values and beliefs which are similar to many traditional and Indigenous helping approaches. It creates opportunities for social work to make culture an implicit part of professional education and practice and encourages multiple diverse interventions rather than a simplified, modern, universal or homogenized technology. We are mindful that to local and Indigenous

Peoples around the world, globalization – McDonaldization or the trend to promote social work as a homogenized global product – is just a new form of colonialism.

How culturally relevant practice fits with cultural competence

As already outlined, generally the literature on cross-cultural practice in social work flows from the idea that there is a particular body of cultural knowledge, values and skills and 'layers of understanding' (Devore and Schlesinger 1995: 904–5) which the social worker can and must uncover or master (Clark 2000; Lum 1999; Weaver 1998, 1999, 2000) so as to implement 'culturally appropriate interventions' (Boyle and Springer 2001: 56). Within this literature, the development of 'cultural competence', and of 'practice guidelines', is said to aid the process of working across diverse cultures as well as 'transactional learning' (Miller 1998) where the focus is on understanding *other* perspectives and cultures. Lum (1999) refers to the bringing together of culturally specific knowledge, values, and skills as 'bicultural integration' (p. 3) – presumably those of the social worker and client from another culture.

While they are, for the most part, complementary, there are a number of important differences among international, Indigenous and cross-cultural social work literatures. First, the cross-cultural literature is aimed mainly at Western social workers in Western contexts working with people of a *different* culture. The social worker's 'Western' culture is seldom the object of analysis or learning and social work itself is not questioned as a 'cultural construction'. However, the Indigenous social work literature, and much international literature, regards Western social work practice more critically as its main concern is not *professional intervention* but *culturally appropriate helping* embedded in local cultures within particular local practice contexts. As such, culturally appropriate practice is a grounded approach where the point of reference is the local context and cultural practices. The main issue for these diverse contexts is the *relevance* of Western social work models that have been or are being imposed on local contexts by outsiders who, in the process, overlook local cultures (Gray 2005). As we have seen, a constant theme in the Indigenous social work literature and non-Western contexts – as shown throughout this book – is overcoming Western hegemony and searching for authentic, culturally relevant social work practices. Western social work may or may not fit, so its utility must be questioned and what does not fit or prove useful discarded.

At the same time, it is important when reflecting on Indigenous and local cultures and practices not to romanticize the 'traditional' but to question these in relation to the acceptable universals in social work, of which there are few, such as the pursuit of human rights and social justice (Gray and Fook 2004; Gray 2005). As Wiredu (1980) points out, when writing about African culture, modernization and development bring with them a scientific and systematic approach to culture, which is not only about the transfer of technology. In applying scientific thinking to Indigenous cultures, or any other culture, the resultant philosophy of practice must be justified on rational grounds for the continuance of particular cultural practices, *both in Western and Indigenous contexts*. For example, too often belief in the supernatural is attributed to prescientific traditional cultures when, if one were to explore such practices further, one would find more witches in Europe than in Africa, though the myth is perpetuated that traditional Indigenous and local cultures are the main purveyors of supernatural practices.

Second, in all contexts questions arise about outmoded customs or cultural practices. The difference in Western contexts is that Indigenous and non-Western cultures are expected to fit in with mainstream culture in the implicit belief that Western beliefs and practices are superior to traditional ones. Crucial here is the definition of 'culture' being used. Culture is a flexible concept and the process of distinguishing between those aspects of culture worthy of being preserved from those which need to be abandoned is continual in response to historical, social, economic and political changes in the broader society (Dean 2001). Critical evaluation of traditional philosophies is needed as much as critical evaluation of Western thinking, such as the consequences of science and progress and the devastation of the environment. In truth, there is no such thing as pure culture in Indigenous or Western contexts and this is the main weakness of the cross-cultural literature which implies that culture is a static entity such that one can learn about another's culture and practice in a culturally appropriate manner – the culturally appropriate manner being adopting or, at least, accepting the culture of the *other* uncritically (see Sin, Chapter 13). The difference in many local and Indigenous contexts is that many of these societies are in transition from the traditional to the modern and the 'process of modernisation entails changes not only in the physical environment but also in the mental outlook of ... people(s), manifested both in their explicit beliefs and in their customs and their ordinary daily habits and pursuits' (Wiredu 1980: x). Such changes are slow and people do not easily discard their beliefs merely because they have migrated to new places. Thus these issues are important for social workers everywhere, whether they are working with immigrants and refugees in post-industrial societies or with First Nations people in Gabarone, Botswana, Osh Kosh, Wisconsin or Nome, Alaska, as examples.

Third, while cultural identities might be taken for granted in Western cultures, often local and Indigenous People are seeking to reclaim and preserve the best parts of their culture, which is why it is important to find ways to foster development and technological progress so that the best of local culture is preserved (Wiredu 1980). We have much to learn from Indigenous cultures and one area where this is occurring is in the literature on spirituality and ecosocial work (Coates *et al.* 2006).

Fourth, the cross-cultural literature is often silent on the question of language. Language is central to culture as it is much more difficult, if not impossible, to preserve one's culture without retaining one's language. Languages contain concepts, beliefs and ways of understanding that convey particular Indigenous world views; the loss of language is the loss of a foundation for a culture, and this is particularly applicable to Indigenous Peoples (see Chapter 4 and the Postscript). This is one of the reasons why language is highlighted in the postmodernist discourse, and why postmodernists react to the homogenizing effects of universalization. For example, with the dominance of English in global cultural products, local languages – the principal tools of cultural expression – acquire the image of inferiority. More importantly, however, languages are being lost: 'an indigenous language disappears every two weeks. It is estimated that by the end of the 21st century, 5,500 of the current 6,000 languages now spoken will simply be as dead as Ancient Greek and Latin' (Sardar and Wyn Davies 2002: 126). There are words, terms and phrases not available in English that are being lost forever and real voices in real languages are being threatened. Thus even when we hear Indigenous People speaking, it is almost always in a voice, in a language, that is not their own. The loss of language is one of the most pervasively damaging effects of globalization and imperialism. Those whose ancestors spoke in different and dying languages and who had concepts and spiritual impulses not amenable to translation, feel cut off from 'their own kind' when their Indigenous language is lost.

Against this backdrop, we can look critically at social work's enchantment with universal definitions and global standards. We can examine the merits of universalizing trends such as these in light of social work's colonial past and criticisms of its cultural imperialism (Gray and Fook 2004; Midgley 1981; see Chapter 2). We can be sensitive to Indigenous concerns with the perpetuation of colonialism through economic globalization given the fact that in much of the less developed 'Third World' economic indebtedness has supplanted political subordination. In developed 'First World' contexts the move to global standards makes perfect sense in that it is consistent with social work's universalizing and globalizing aims to make its skills transferable across diverse countries and cultural contexts. Nevertheless it shows lack of sensitivity to more pressing concerns in local and Indigenous contexts, such as the preservation of language and the reclamation of the best in their culture against the onslaught of the culturally homogenizing effects of globalization. So while the establishment of national professional standards – competencies – in many countries like Canada, South Africa and Australia (see *Journal of Social Work Education*, 23(5)) might be appropriate as social work and most other forms of knowledge become commodities, there are life and death issues to be dealt with as a consequence of globalization in Indigenous contexts. A profession so avowedly committed to human rights and social justice cannot overlook these issues.

The Indigenous and international social work literature also enables us to take a more critical look at notions of cultural competence and the idea that one can become competent in the culture of another. Cultural competence is a modernist idea that is 'consistent with the belief that knowledge brings control and effectiveness, and, that this is an ideal to be achieved above all else' (Dean 2001: 624). Thus it treats 'cultural categories or groups as ... static and monolithic with defining characteristics that endure over time and in different contexts (and) ... involves learning about the history and shared characteristics of different groups ... using this knowledge to create bridges and increase understanding with individual clients and families' (Dean 2001: 625). More contemporary postmodern views see understanding of culture as individually and socially constructed, as 'always contextual, emergent, improvisational, transformational, and political' (Laird in Dean 2001: 625; see also Dean 2001; Fook 2002); as a dynamic, living thing, constantly being moulded and shaped by diverse influences at play at any one time, which moulds and shapes us as we attempt to understand it (Gray and Allegritt 2003). Hence postmodernists question the notion that social workers can become competent at something as complex as another's culture. The Indigenous social work literature shows how much a person's identity is linked to their culture and how difficult it is to understand culture from the outside. Culture is not something social workers can put on and take off like a cloak. We are *embedded* in our culture and its rituals, practices and ways of doing things. Hence Laird's (1998) observation that we in the global north ought to shift the focus of our discussions on cultural differences to ourselves and find ways to better understand our own culture so as to make us more sensitive to others' cultures. The best mainstream social workers can do is to accept our lack of competence in cross-cultural matters and realize that working across cultures is not so much about 'knowledge' as about 'understanding' (Dean 2001: 624).

> With 'lack of competence' as the focus, a different view of practicing across cultures emerges. The client is the 'expert' and the clinician is in a position of seeking knowledge and trying to understand what life is like for the client. There is no thought of competence—instead one thinks of gaining understanding (always partial) of a phenomenon that is evolving and changing (Dean 2001: 624).

Thus the Indigenous and international social work literature teaches us that it is wise to maintain a healthy scepticism to modernist ideas like cultural competence since it is questionable to assume that 'one can become competent at the culture of another' (Dean 2001: 623) since it is not easy to 'comprehend the perspective of … others differently located' (Young 1999: 127). The postmodern focus on 'the lack of competence' rather than the possibility of cultural competence is a sociologically realistic and fruitful position because it shows that one way of gaining an understanding of the other's culture comes about through the process of communication since 'understanding comes, if it comes at all, only by engaging in a volley of practical dialogue' (Tully 1995: 133). The process of cultural understanding is ongoing and never complete. It proceeds in stages. As we gain an understanding of the other's culture it changes our previous ideas and interpretation, and we redefine our knowledge accordingly. As our understanding changes through cross-cultural or intercultural interaction, communication or dialogue, we then strive to gain further knowledge about the other's culture. It is this emphasis on dialogue, discussion and communication that directs our attention to the fact that *our interactions are intercultural, transcultural, or cross-cultural*, whichever term one prefers. There is an ongoing international debate about intercultural or cross-cultural communication which examines what happens in the process of talking to the cultural *other* (Benhabib 2002; Habermas 1994; Taylor 1994; Tully 1995; Young 1999).

Another lesson from this literature is that culture is not homogeneous, neither is it internally consistent. In fact, 'a culture' is always made up of a number of cultures because historically cultures have not existed alone or in isolation. In many Indigenous communities, Western culture has been historically imposed through colonization and imperialism. Since the beginning of history people from different cultures have interacted in a voluntary capacity. They have *inter alia* exchanged goods, intermarried, fled from religious or political persecution or poverty and emigrated. In the process, there has been a greater blending of cultures than national histories have made out. This is the strength of the postmodernist position. It has discredited the Enlightenment notion of culture and the view that individuals are located 'in independent, closed and homo-geneous' (Tully 1995: 14) cultures and societies. It has introduced the idea that individuals are members of cultures that are 'densely interdependent' and which overlap, interact and are *negotiated* (Tully 1995: 10–11).

The cross-cultural literature tends to look for congruencies, commonalities and similarities rather than to recognize that intercultural interaction, even in professional settings, requires that we leave behind our cultural comfort zones, listen to the different ways, philosophies and practices of the cultural *other* and change and expand our established views on their cultures and, most importantly, keep an open mind (as Gair shows in Chapter 17). One of the starting points in discussing culture from a contemporary, postmodernist position is to recognize that culture is a contested concept or, as Benhabib (2002) points out, 'cultures are constituted through contested practices' (p. viii).

Indigenous social work, ecology and spirituality

The growing acceptance of Indigenous social work has arisen, in part at least, as a consequence of providing services to increasing numbers of immigrants from non-Western countries, the recognition of the value of alternative world views, the development of Indigenous social work literature, the resurgence of interest in spirituality, and growing awareness about environmental degradation. This has been a complex, rather than a linear, process. Recent decades have witnessed the systemic challenge to the social order. This period has seen the intensification of economic globalization, the end of the 'cold war', liberation struggles in many countries, the threat to human well-being due to human initiated environmental problems, a quest for economic domination by the world's most militaristic country, terrorism and the search for security that accompanies such massive changes. In this period of rapid change, which to some appears as chaos, old paradigms, most notably modernism, have been challenged as the guidelines they provide are no longer effective (see Berry 1999). As a consequence, we are witnessing large numbers of people, on all parts of the planet, facing great uncertainty and returning to reactionary beliefs – for example, fundamentalist Islam in the Middle-East and evangelical Christianity in the West. This divide is appearing within professions and academic disciplines, as well as in faith traditions.

However, we have been witness also to the groundswell of social movements that, taken together, argue for significant changes to the current structure of society, for example, movements such as holistic medicine; antinuclear, peace and disarmament; sustainability; process theology; voluntary simplicity; ecofeminism; and goddess worship (Capra 1982; Elgin 1993; Sahtouris 1989; Swimme 1998; Swimme and Berry 1992; Trainer undated). These alternative perspectives have been reinforced by scientific discoveries, like quantum mechanics and evolution, which have shifted our understanding of nature and humanity's relation to it. For example, the concept of nature is shifting from an unchanging mechanistic – dead – universe, to an unfolding, organismic, creative cosmos in which the human can play a significant role. While postmodernism helps to understand this surge to a 'multiverse' of perspectives in which alternative points of view are debated, it will not solve the problems of fragmentation and domination inherent in modernism (see Coates 2003). Postmodernism served to expose the 'soft under belly' of modernism by challenging universalisms, focusing on the social construction of knowledge and drawing attention to the inherent allocation of power that flows from privilege. The challenge to universalism made it possible for the voices of the marginalized to be heard.

The discomfort that the postmodern deconstruction created has contributed to the questioning of foundational assumptions, and the renewal of interest in the search for meaning. The resurgence of interest in spirituality and ecology over the past two decades has arisen, in part at least, to meet this need. It is a consequence of the breakdown of security that has resulted from postmodernism and other challenges, such as postmodernism's critique of metanarratives, the recognition of marginalized voices, the critique of colonialism, the ascent of anti-oppressive practices, environmental degradation and the rise of terrorism. This quest for meaning has led to a search for alternatives to modernism's values and beliefs. It is this quest that has resulted in many scholars – such as Adams (1993), Berry (1999) and Naess (1989) – recognizing the important contribution of traditional and Indigenous beliefs and values.

The environmental movement, with its search for sustainable practices, has gradually gained strength with increasing attention to the scientific evidence indicative of the desecration that human activities, as well as industrial and technological progress and social development, have wrought upon the Earth (see Gore 2006). The search for the causes of environmental destruction has led to a critique of the fundamental assumptions of modern society (Adams 1993; Berry 1999; Coates 2003; Spretnak 1997). These critiques point to the need for a new foundation of beliefs and values, a new paradigm to guide human activity and bring it into harmony with the life processes of the Earth. Thus connectedness and interdependence, harmony with nature, creative unfolding came forth to replace the dualism, domination, and determinism of modernism (Coates 2003). These values are consistent with traditional and Indigenous beliefs and values (see, for example, Four Worlds Development Project 1982; Hart 2002) that place spirituality at the centre of life. While some schools of thought have come to similar conclusions from different paths, for example ecofeminism and deep ecology, some writers have gone so far as to argue that Indigenous beliefs can guide humanity (Berry 1997). As a result, Indigenous beliefs and values, in particular, have gained recognition and credibility among the world views that provide a reconceptualization of the universe and humanity's relationship to it.

In social work this has opened avenues of acceptance toward Indigenous and local approaches to helping along with increasing recognition of the need for alternatives to economic and cultural globalization, like local currencies, community supported agriculture, 'right sized' organizations and ecoregionalism. This is consistent with the centrality of diversity inherent in alternative cosmologies. For social work this can lead to the valuing of diversity and the need to ensure that services are culturally relevant. Such changes can push social work beyond technology transfer and cultural sensitivity, toward the integration of social work principles with Indigenous beliefs, values and rituals, and the corresponding adaptation of its technologies. In Canada, for example, this is reflected in the development of social work programmes that are not only dedicated to First Nations students and services, but also focused on the delivery of services within First Nation communities (see Chapters 18 and 19). There, and elsewhere, as the chapters in this book show, education no longer attempts only to present dominant social work theories and interventions and then discuss how these may be relevant. The focus has shifted to an identification of needs and the application of traditional or Indigenous methods of healing (see Chapters 10, 17 and 18). Greater attention is being given to such traditional practices as healing circles, smudging, sweat lodges and spirit quests, for example. Provincial laws must still be adhered to, and interventions more traditional to social work are adapted when appropriate, but the focus of education for Indigenous social work has shifted. Themes of harmony, balance, connectedness and sufficiency in Indigenous social work literature, as well as the literature on spirituality and ecosocial work, have come to replace exploitation and progress, economism, individualism and consumerism. The case studies in this book show how these Indigenous themes are entering mainstream social work discourse.

Making social work practice authentic to local culture: Some case examples

There is widespread acknowledgement in the social work literature – from both the Western and non-Western worlds – that social work as a profession is a product of culture and that culture plays a critical part in its construction. The discovery – or rediscovery – of the diversity and uniqueness of local cultures has led some academics and practitioners to question the relevance of applying Western models of social work practice to non-Western contexts. Many of the examples presented herein follow from the prior work of our contributors, for example Nimmagadda and Cowger's (1999) qualitative research with Indian social work practitioners in an alcohol treatment centre in India revealed that these social workers had 'distinctive ideas about advice giving, family intervention, confrontation and reassurance that were at variance with Western models of practice and practice behaviours' (Nimmagadda and Cowger 1999: 274). Many non-Western cultures struggle with the Western notions of advice giving and self-determination. Nimmagadda and Cowger found that advice giving was an effective social work strategy used in this context because first and foremost clients expected it. In addition, being more directive also worked in practice due to its alignment with local cultural norms which emphasized self-control and maintaining harmony. Likewise Ling (2003) in Sarawak, Malaysia found that advice giving was a common strategy used in local helping practices, which minimizes problems, avoids conflicts and emphasizes the local cultural values of harmony and stability. Similarly, Cheung and Liu (2004) found that a more directive approach was used by Chinese social workers as clients saw them as having both authority and knowledge and came to them for advice and direction with their problems (p. 121). This approach was applicable due to cultural norms regarding the way in which Chinese people were taught to respect authority and the fact that individuals were not encouraged to make decisions by themselves. It should be noted that in these three contexts authority is not associated with the Western concept of powerlessness, but rather authority is enacted through status, rights and responsibilities as deemed by *dharma* or the social order. In the examples from India, Malaysia and China, social work practice can be viewed as part of *dharma*, working with and through social norms relating to cultural stability and harmony. The involvement of family and community members, or naturally occurring support networks, encourages interdependency and harmony. Thus even though the individual may be the focus of help, the family or community are seen to be intrinsically connected to clients and involved in the helping process either directly or indirectly. This is in line with a culturally relevant Indian world view that emphasizes communal responsibilities and the interconnectedness of people. A similar world view is found among Indigenous Australians (Bennett and Zubrzycki 2003; Collard *et al.* 1994; Thorpe 1997).

Among First Nation groups in Canada, Hart (2002) has articulated an Aboriginal approach to helping which incorporates many elements of an Aboriginal world view and its assumptions about the nature of helping and 'holistic wellness' – wellness in all aspects of life: Physical, spiritual, emotional and cognitive – based on connection, cooperation, collective responsibility, relationship, balance and harmony (see Chapter 10). Mafile'o (2004) writes of similar values – *fakefekau'aki* (connecting) and *fakatokilalo* (humility) – in Tongan social work practice in Aotearoa/New Zealand (see Chapter 9). Tongan society is hierarchical and relationships are not individualized but are governed by one's social position and roles in a network of connections. Similarities to the use of connecting and humility can be found in social work practices in Indigenous Australia, India, Māori/New Zealand, Hawaii, Malaysia and Samoa. Bennett and Zubrzycki (2003) conducted qualitative research with Aboriginal and Torres Strait Islander social workers in Australia and found that the helping relationship and the workers' credibility were enhanced when social workers used self-disclosure during the introduction process, identifying birthplace and kinship ties, shared personal stories and life experiences. The personal nature of the helping relationship was also a theme in Nimmagadda and Cowger's (1999) work in India.

The same is true of Hawaiian culture where an individual is defined in the context of relationships with family, community, the land and the spiritual realm. *Iaulima* (cooperation) and *kokua* (helpfulness) were seen as far more important to harmony and *lokahi* (unity) than self-satisfaction or meeting one's own needs (Ewalt and Makuau 1995). Similarly, writing from earlier research in Malaysia, Hawa Ali (1991) describes the family unit as the foundational social caring system where *gotong-royong* (mutual help) and *kerjasama* (cooperation) keep the community unified. In Samoan culture sharing and reciprocity are pivotal. In short, many Indigenous cultures emphasize the value of the collective over the individual and the strengthening of group cohesiveness and stability as an integral part of life. Individuals are characterized by social relationships and a shared identity that comes from 'sharing food, water, land, spirits, knowledge, work and social activities' (Linnekin and Poyer 1990: 8).

So what might mainstream social work learn from local and Indigenous cultures?

In these case examples, and others presented throughout this book, it can be seen that interventions into non-Western cultures based on concepts like individualism, objectivity and professional distance inherent in Western conceptualizations of social work practice would not be as effective and may even be alienating. While these case examples provide us with demonstrations of genuine, authentic social work practice in that the cultural themes underlying these approaches are compatible with the profession's core values of respect and social justice, they are simultaneously grounded in the beliefs of local people. There is thus a mutuality of world views and the possibility of some aspects of a universal social work emerging, however, to address our question posed at the outset, we end with an enunciation of some important aspects of these local cultures that can enrich mainstream culturally relevant social work practice and thus contribute to its universality:

- *Indigenous approaches remind us of our humanistic goals and the importance, first and foremost, of connecting with the client.* While mainstream social work is replete with models for engaging with clients, for enhancing communication processes and for developing a healthy helping relationship, the most important aspects of connecting with others is grounded in the everyday lives of our clients. If we can reach clients where they eat, live and play, if we can encounter them in the systems that are meaningful to them and understand the relevance of their cultural beliefs and practices, then our practice can be relevant to their needs.
- *Indigenous world views strengthen and enrich social work knowledge and practice.* They remind us that there are many ways of knowing, that science too has limitations and that culture need not be accepted uncritically. These alternative voices draw our attention to our common humanity, to the importance of family and community, to the importance of celebration and ritual, and to the values of humility and compassion. These cultural practices provide some measure of certainty in an otherwise uncertain world.
- *Indigenous and local thinkers question the universality of social work knowledge* but leave open the possibility for shared values and discourses provided that mainstream social work can open itself up to the lessons local cultures have to offer. They remind us not to accept uncritically the idea that Western social work has universally relevant methodologies, that universal standards are desirable and that an international professional identity for social work will necessarily be valued in non-Western countries and contexts. When people think that ideas are being imposed on them without regard for their culture, they will resist, challenging such cultural imperialism. We learn too that there is a need to break free of Western conceptions so that people can recover their own cultural identity (Wiredu 1980). Where else can they find it than in the rediscovery of 'old' Indigenous ways of knowing and helping grounded in the world views and cultures of local contexts? Sifting through this and working out what fits the transition from traditional to modern is a

process from which a new culture emerges, one which is distinctly African or Chinese or Indian or Hawaiian or Malaysian.

- *Non-Western cultures challenge the dualistic notions of Western thinking.* Kissman and Maurer (2002) remind us that:

Eastern and Western healing practices are not opposites but share common attributes … Wellness is enhanced by the emphasis on humility, gratitude, connectedness with self and others, present-moment awareness, sharing and listening to stories … the quieting of the mind to cope with stress and worries, speaking to and listening to a higher power and bridging the gap between mind and body (pp. 35–6).

Much of this thinking is holistic, rooted in place, in harmony with nature, and in preserving the well-being of all life forms. Indigenous approaches remind us of the importance of context.

- *Local approaches demonstrate the importance of valuing both Western and non-Western knowledge* yet of accepting neither uncritically. Concrete practice examples, like those herein presented, release local and Indigenous ways of knowing from preconceptions that they are 'exotic' or romantic. They remind us that we are all grappling with the same questions about the meaning of suffering and hardship. Generally non-Western peoples, particularly from India and certain parts of Asia, may be more accepting of hardship since they take the view that many life events are subject to external control of a transcendental nature. For example, while clients in India may complain about fate (*kharma*), they can also ascribe their problems to it, externalizing the causes of their problems as we do in narrative therapy in Western social work. Similarly the belief in fate also has positive outcomes as it helps clients to accept their problems with equanimity.
- *Indigenous cultures remind us that self-fulfilment can only be realized in group fulfilment.* They help us counter the worst consequences of individualism and draw attention back to the importance of family, of kin and social networks and of community.

In the case examples presented throughout this book, social work practice can be seen to be taking on a distinctive character wherein Indigenous ways are providing mainstream Western social work with new and innovative approaches. In short, there is much for Western social work to learn from Indigenous helping principles and methods.

In conclusion, there are differences and similarities in the ways in which notions of culture are used in the cross-cultural, international and Indigenous literature pointing to the main issues each seeks to address. These include sensitivities in the Indigenous social work literature towards universalizing and globalizing forces which continue the colonization process, and claims in the cross-cultural and anti-oppressive practice literature that mainstream social work silences 'other' voices. We contend that 'alternate' voices are finding expression through the literature on spirituality and environmental or ecosocial work noting that in some contexts where social workers and Indigenous communities have been interacting their discourse has progressed beyond multiculturalism and cultural sensitivity to embrace Indigenous thinking in mainstream practice (Coates *et al*. 2006). In other words, they have proceeded beyond an awareness of culture to making culture explicit in their education and practice. Through case examples, we can draw attention to ways in which Indigenous social work enriches mainstream understanding of culture and how lessons from Indigenous contexts can inform culturally relevant practice. Our aim is to open up these issues, not to prescribe practice or develop models. They offer insights that can shift our thinking on some very important issues in social work about which all social workers should be aware.

Chapter 21

Conclusion

Mel Gray and John Coates

Throughout this book authors have highlighted difficulties with technology transfer, colonization and territorialization, that is, with past and ongoing attempts to introduce social work into their diverse cultural contexts. It was precisely the awareness of these diverse influences that led us to write this book. We were aware that people in very different contexts had distinct concerns with what was generally referred to as 'Indigenization', and that it meant different things to people in different contexts. Those who wrote about 'Indigenization' and Indigenous social work were frequently unfamiliar with the other's work. As well, many Indigenous Peoples took offence to the appropriation of the terms 'Indigenous' and 'Indigenization', as they referred to people's identities as Indigenous Peoples and their struggle to recover from the oppression of colonization. The face to face discussions in our writers' workshop in Canada was thus an eye opening experience for all involved and we all realized that the issues we were talking about were highly political for various reasons: First because for Indigenous Peoples, reclaiming control over their lives involves railing against a system which forever strives to take it away from them under one pretext or another. Second, because the social work profession has an intense interest in claiming a 'global' identity, its desire to be international and to propose international definitions and global standards are yet further attempts at colonization or territorialization. While economic control has replaced the political control of earlier colonial times, we argue that colonization is alive and thriving under the mask of globalization. As we have seen in the case of China, the spread of social work education is big money and proceeds apace even when there are no jobs for the graduates of social work programmes (Chapters 14 and 15). Osei-Hwedie and Rankopo (in Chapter 16) demonstrate how difficult it is to develop culturally appropriate social work education when not only the profession but also universities pressure faculty members into developing internationally recognized education programmes. The profession, through its international organizations, remains remarkably silent on these anomalies and seeks to have a foot in each *wampum*, at one and the same time seeking to be global and culturally relevant. A great deal more discussion is needed on what is universal in social work and what is good for the profession and for local communities. A repeated theme in the discussions was how difficult it is to develop culturally relevant practice when one always has to deal with outside influences. So much energy is expended in warding off such unwanted intrusions that little is left for what must be done at the front lines of practice.

One thing is for certain: The process in which we were all engaged in putting together this book invited us to look at things differently. As we shared diverse views and argued – sometimes heatedly, at times rationally, and at other times in a room charged with emotion – each of us gradually developed a clear understanding of the issues involved and each was changed in a powerful way. We realized then that 'indigenization' and all its derivatives – localization, reconceptualization, authentization, and so on – were all outmoded concepts and the dilemmas of developing culturally appropriate social work practice were, more than anything else, caused by outside influences which were antagonistic to local interests. Nowhere is this clearer than in the history of the Indigenous Peoples of the world. So stark and severe were these experiences that territorializing agendas which continue today can only be met with fierce resistance. For example, one can understand that a Western notion like child *protection* is going to fill people with fear and dread due to a past history where *protectors* were policemen who stole their children (Randall 2003: 6). It is time the international social work profession became sensitive to the reasons for local resistance to its 'taken for granted' assumptions. The cause of the Indigenous Peoples of the world is a just one, as is the cause of all communities and social workers trying to deal with their home-grown problems. If people are indeed the experts of their own lives, then let social work enable people to live their lives and solve their problems in effective and culturally appropriate ways.

Hence we concluded that 'Indigenization' is an outmoded concept and Indigenous social work is a just cause. Not only is the term 'Indigenization' appropriated and, as such, offensive to Indigenous People, there has developed a plethora of terms, such as localization, adaptation, reconceptualization, and so on, to describe this process of adaptation to Western technology. What we are actually talking about is culturally appropriate or culturally relevant social work. We debated the importance of language, and terms like Indigenous, Western, post-colonial, culture and ethnicity. We realized that there is considerable diversity in the use of these terms and that the use of some terms has a negative impact, not only because they convey our lack of understanding of the complexity of the issues involved, but also because they are inherently offensive and misleading. As already explained, the use of the term 'Indigenization' rather than localization has weakened the arguments for social justice and the development of culturally appropriate services for Indigenous Peoples by generalizing their diverse experiences. Awareness of continued pressures and benefits, such as the employment of students and accreditation, to meet international standards and accompanying credibility has resulted in a continuing colonization in the form of US and 'Western' schools setting up or assisting in the establishment of schools of social work in Asian, African and other countries, as the chapters in this book show, and they are driven primarily by financial considerations (see Chapter 15). This practice has had a negative impact on the development and acceptance of local helping practices and local knowledges.

It is important to distinguish the process of developing culturally appropriate social work from 'cultural sensitivity' and 'cultural competence' since both these terms imply 'outsiders' coming in and miss the point that people's lives are embedded in culture, that our beliefs are steeped in culture (as Hart eloquently conveys in Chapter 10). Culture, and spirituality for that matter, is not a cloak we put on or take off as we move from one situation to the next, nor is it a set of techniques or skills we can learn. It is an ingrained thing and people do not easily let go of their values and beliefs.

Also, and receiving less attention in our book, is the importance of using culturally appropriate interventions for minority and immigrant populations within Western countries. This is an area where 'developing' countries, through the cross fertilization of knowledge, may be the source of valuable know-how in local interventions (see Chapter 11). The need for 'Western' social workers to seek wisdom and knowledge from other cultures rather than just applying Western ideas to 'the rest', requires the need to open Western social work to learning from the rest – and to pay this more attention in the international literature, that is, in literature stemming from other contexts. This raises the importance of social workers and social work educators being aware of their own cultural biases and the limitations that the cultural roots of mainstream social work places on the generalizability of its interventions. Further, it poses a serious challenge to the universalization or internationalization, or so called globalization of social work practice and standards. *Perhaps the most important conclusion of our work together on this project is our realization of the centrality of culture in social work services. Mainstream or 'Western' social work is 'Indigenous' to 'Western' societies only and its relevance in other cultures and contexts must be seriously questioned and, if it is transferred, this must be done most cautiously.*

Flowing from the centrality of culture is the reality that social work is not monolithic and, in fact, there may be many 'social works' even in so-called 'Western contexts'. A serious question in need of further investigation and research is exploring what is common or shared among the many varieties and variations of social work around the world: What is *universal* in social work? This is a very important conceptual challenge as it forces social work to explore its foundation in Judeo–Christian and Western traditions, especially as social work develops in Islamic contexts (Chapter 12) and in China where Confucianism is the main value system (Chapter 13). It requires that we explore whether there are indeed universals that are relevant across cultures. It would seem to us that localization or cultural relevance is about responsiveness. What is shared is a desire to help others, variously expressed as seeking social justice for all; a quest to improve people's quality of life; or to empower people to take control of their own lives. This intention is commonly shared but expressed in various ways. Thus calls for cultural relevance and localization are not calls for parochial social work but for a responsive, caring brand of helping and social intervention. And it has implications for social work education. There is no point in teaching an individualistic brand of social work where collectivism is valued. Perhaps it is better to talk about personal responsibility rather than autonomy and self-direction for there are many situations in which the individual's choices are severely constrained culturally, or by values of the family and community. Perhaps community-based interventions are more useful in many contexts than the highly individualistic brand of clinical social work practiced in the US, for example. Yet when US social workers go into Indigenous and local communities that are foreign to them, what are they introducing? Can they introduce community development if all they know is clinical intervention? Fully addressing these issues requires another book, however, from our work, we would like to suggest a few broad and relevant questions and issues for future attention. First, further comparative work is needed on the similarities and differences that attending to culture brings, as exemplified in the chapters of this book. For example, Hart in Chapter 10 and Nimmagadda and Martell in Chapter 11 point to differences in the ways in which respect and sharing, for example, when seen through a non-Western cultural lens, can lead to different and more effective interventions. Second, social work needs to reaffirm its political responsibilities, and its concerns with policy as well as practice. For example, when we are dealing with Indigenous Peoples, social work is a political act as issues of social injustice, loss of control, unresolved land claims and compensation for past and present oppressions become central to the services provided. Political action and attention to policy issues should become a more central part of social work practice in such contexts. Third, the search for culturally relevant social work knowledge and for what is universal within diversity calls for a critical exploration of the foundational values and beliefs of social work. Perhaps, as implied in Chapter 19, new theoretical approaches will emerge that offer a framework within which diversity can be celebrated and domination replaced by interdependence and mutual learning.

We hope that the case studies in this book provide a fair reflection of the diversity of international social work and of the overriding importance of cultural relevance as we work to further the positive contribution that professional social work is capable of providing around the globe. We are grateful to all the contributors for sharing their work and we hope this book will help generate an enhanced understanding of Indigenous and culturally relevant social work practice and education around the world.

Postscript

Terms[1] of Endearment: A Brief Dictionary for Decolonizing Social Work with Indigenous Peoples

Michael Yellow Bird

> In our cultural renaissance there are certain concepts and movements which we should understand and give attention to. The first of these is linguistic imperialism (Adams 1995).

Words have power. They can liberate or oppress, transform or degrade, honour or disparage, acknowledge or ignore and amplify or silence. The manner in which terms are used in the social work profession have important implications for those who work with, and on behalf of, Indigenous Peoples since they describe and direct the moral and intellectual parameters of one's actions, thinking, beliefs, feelings, likes, dislikes, love, hate, ambivalence and commitment. Indeed, in order to form new healthy habits and perspectives, regarding Indigenous Peoples, and shed the old destructive prejudices one has to acquire, understand and use the appropriate language. How words are used to silence, promote, enforce or trivialize what is done in the social work profession is not only critical to helping and understanding Indigenous Peoples, it also reveals much about the intentions, perceptions and health of the discipline and its subject workers. Arguably, there is nothing more important than how and what terms are honoured and employed in the social work profession.

A dictionary is a book written in a language that provides definitions of terms and how they are used. It ensures that words have the same meaning and pronunciation, which is essential for communication between people, and people and other sentient beings. Because of the one-sided history of colonization and oppression, Indigenous Peoples and the social work profession have not developed a compatible language and thus, often, do not find the same meanings in words. While Indigenous Peoples, survivors of colonization, have to be fairly well versed in the language and words of the colonizer, in a colonial situation, the reverse is rarely true; Georg Wilhelm Friedrich Hegel's (1977 [1807]) 'master–slave' paradigm and Robert Phillipson's (1992) notion of 'linguistic imperialism' helps explain why this schism in communication exists.

---

1 Terms, words, and sometimes 'language' are used interchangeably in this postscript.

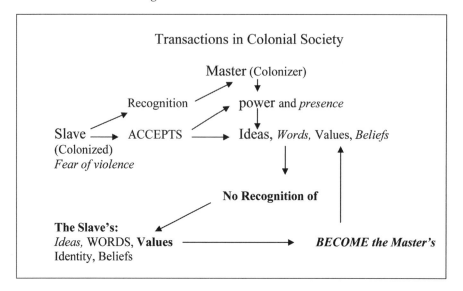

Figure 2 Master-slave paradigm
Source: Hegel (1977).

Hegel argued that in a colonial society the transactions between the master (the colonizer) and the slave[2] (the colonized) represent a one-way relationship where the slave must, out of fear of real or threatened violence, acknowledge and accept the power and presence of the master, which includes his or her words, ideas, beliefs and values (see Figure 2). The master, because of their violently acquired and secure pre-eminent position and status in society has little, if any, obligation to recognize the slave, which means that he or she will have little knowledge or interest in understanding or fulfilling the needs and wishes of the slave. This asymmetrical relationship creates, among other things, a colonizer's vocabulary that is largely based on the status, privilege, respect and power that the colonizer is accorded in society; to advance or survive in this society the slave must learn to accept and adapt to the colonizer's language. The master–slave paradigm helps explain a portion of the current gap in the meaning of words between social workers – the enforcers of the rules of the master's colonial state – and Indigenous Peoples – those who are resisting colonialism and various forms of slavery, which constitute bondage or being under the control of another.

The linguistic struggle between colonizer and colonized, which is born of the master–slave paradigm, can be observed through a hegemonic process where the colonizer deliberately and carefully maintains control of word meaning and discourse in order to enforce the terms and ideas that will ensure his or her control of society

---

2   The use of the term slave does imply that colonized peoples are owned by the colonial state and have no power. It is used to convey the degree to which the colonizer dominates the lives, activities and self-determination of those they have colonized. Indigenous People are constantly resisting colonization and oppression in many different ways.

through the accepted societal language (Phillipson 1992). In this environment almost all social, political and economic transactions between the master and the slave are conducted in the language of the master, who unreservedly maintains a self-imposed right to change, to their advantage whenever they want, the meaning and use of words. Such a situation might be compared to an abusive adult who, in their abuse of a child[3], will control the situation and subject by changing, whenever convenient for the abuser, the meanings of the terms of the rules, rewards and punishments. The outcome of this interaction guarantees the adult (the oppressor) will have all the power and the child (the oppressed) will be forced to exist in a hyper-alert state desperately trying to anticipate and provide what the adult demands of them in order to avoid punishment and obtain rewards.

To offset the savage reality of the master–slave paradigm, to divert attention from their oppression of the colonized, and to convince them, and others, that they have a benevolent and righteous nature, the colonizer creates and uses terms to endear others, such as the oppressed, social workers, and the general public, to their language of caring and 'generosity'. However, upon closer inspection it is easy to see that this language is largely self-serving and, thus, constitutes a 'false generosity' where the oppressor brings further injustice on the oppressed by creating words that disproportionately support their priorities (Freire 2000). For instance, words such as *vulnerable, social justice, empowerment and self-determination*, which are part of the everyday lexicon of professional social work, are often regarded as terms of justice. However, when social workers apply these terms their meaning can vary widely for those who represent and support the colonizers and those – Indigenous Peoples – who struggle against the colonial situation. While some of the language of this discipline may be appropriate and applicable in various contexts when social workers work with Indigenous Peoples, in other situations, especially those that pit the cultural and political interests of Indigenous Peoples against those of the colonial state, many terms quickly become blurred, meaningless and deceptive. Consider the following examples:

1. To a colonizer 'vulnerable' generally means 'susceptible to injury'. To one resisting and interrogating colonization, the term may more accurately be contextualized as 'I am susceptible because of your invasion which stole my lands and dignity and because of your racist policies that destroyed my culture which I depended on for my well-being'.
2. To a colonizer 'social justice' generally means 'a situation where all have the same basic rights, security, opportunities, obligations and benefits' which, at face value seems highly equitable and fair for all. However, for Indigenous Peoples, it is the colonizer who has illegally invaded their lands and advanced this concept after illegally, and sometimes brutally, overthrowing the existing Indigenous order. The term requires the following Indigenous context:

---

3   The use of child in this postscript is in no way intended to imply that Indigenous Peoples are helpless children and that the oppression of the colonizer is pre-eminent and enduring. The use of this example merely points out the depth of struggle faced by Indigenous Peoples against the colonial situation.

'Before colonization our people had our own rights, security, opportunities, obligations and benefits to one another and to other tribal nations. Now we are forced to live with your definitions. My access to your social justice is contingent on my support of your control of our society'.

3. 'Empowerment', one of the most widely used words in the social work vocabulary, means 'the ability to make and act upon one's own choices'. To Indigenous Peoples, empowerment is more likely to mean 'I cannot make choices that are based on my values and beliefs that are in conflict with your values and beliefs and rules and laws. Therefore, my empowerment depends on your generosity, flexibility, and willingness to bend or violate your rules on my behalf '.

4. A common definition for 'self-determination' is 'the ability to formulate any form of government, priorities and courses of action that one wishes to pursue'. For Indigenous Peoples this term often means that 'I can be self-determining if my priorities, form of government and the direction I choose to take do not conflict with, or challenge, your self-determination. This relationship, in which I am forced to disproportionately acknowledge your priorities in order to fulfil mine, has all the elements of the master–slave paradigm'.

These examples help illuminate what are the simplistic, albeit often well intentioned use of various social work terms. These examples are intended to inspire social workers to examine how various words in the professional vocabulary can be imperialistic, falsely generous and self-serving for the colonizer and less than 'empowering' and fair to Indigenous Peoples. To work more effectively with these groups social workers must understand the dynamics of the linguistic struggles between the colonizers and the colonized and how even well meaning language is used to hide the oppression of Indigenous Peoples. Finally, it is important for social workers to learn how Indigenous Peoples experience the language of the social work profession and what words, terms and language must be shifted to if the discipline is to fulfil its mission 'to enhance human well-being and help meet the basic human needs of all people, with particular attention to the needs and empowerment of people who are vulnerable, oppressed, and living in poverty' (www.socialworkers.org/pubs/code/code.asp).

The purpose of this postscript is to provide an overview of several key terms and concepts that are important for working with, and understanding the situation of, Indigenous Peoples. Many of the following words challenge the master–slave paradigm and, therefore, are routinely overlooked, buried deep in extant social work dictionaries or not known or avoided. Using relevant terminology that contextualizes the situation and experiences of Indigenous Peoples is one of many strategies that will help decolonize the imperialistic aspects of social work.

A

Aboriginal means having existed in a territory from time immemorial (the beginning) and before the arrival of European/American colonizers.

Aboriginal culture constitutes the diverse beliefs, lifestyles, world views and values of Aboriginal Peoples. A great deal of Aboriginal culture arises from a group's relationship to their lands.

Aboriginal lands are the territories resided on since time immemorial. Many Aboriginal Peoples in the Western hemisphere continue to regard all the lands of 'Turtle Island' (the 'Americas') to be Aboriginal lands.

Aboriginal Peoples are the descendants of the earliest inhabitants of a place. They are the 'original inhabitants' of the land, hence, *First* Peoples or *First* Nations (see Indigenous Peoples below). Aboriginal Peoples were there before nation states were formed though some Indigenous Peoples, such as Indigenous Peoples in the Americas, were organized as sovereign nations long before European colonial settlement, albeit not nation states as they are known today.

Aboriginal title is a 'possessory right' of the original occupants of the land to use and occupy a territory based on traditional use and residence (Thompson 1982). This title is relevant to all Indigenous Peoples and cannot be extinguished without the consent of these groups.

Aborigine is a term of contempt used by colonizers to refer to Aboriginal Peoples.

Abuse refers to behaviour intended to cause harm. Colonizers have and continue to use symbols, words and policies to abuse Indigenous Peoples.

Acculturation is the process of adoption of culture between individuals or groups. Acculturation can be *voluntary* where agreement to adopt another's culture is mutual or *forced* when one compels another to accept and participate in their culture.

Activist is an individual who is involved in activities to bring about change. In many societies activists have continually been targeted for neutralization for their attempts to change the system to bring about justice for oppressed peoples.

Alienation refers to the feeling or reality of exclusion, non-belonging and separateness.

Allocentric is 'an orientation to the thoughts, feelings, values, and customs of others rather than oneself (opposite of egocentric)' (Barker 2003: 16).

American Indian is an incorrect name imposed by the US federal government on the Indigenous Peoples who reside in what is now referred to as the United States. Some Indigenous Peoples who are engaging in the practice of decolonization do not use this false colonizer's label, while others continue to do so because of their lack of awareness or for the sake of convenience (see Yellow Bird 1999).

America is the name imposed on the lands and the Indigenous Peoples in the Western hemisphere by invading Europeans.

Amnesia is the inability to recall a past experience.

Apology is a formal, public expression of regret and wrongdoing that must be accompanied by appropriate compensation from the perspective of the wronged. One beginning marker of justice in a colonial society is the colonizer admitting to, and formally apologizing for, its wrongdoing against the colonized. In some colonial situations colonizers rarely, if ever, issue apologize for their crimes against Indigenous Peoples or other groups they feel to be inferior to them. For instance, in 1988 former U.S. President George Bush, Sr. said: 'I will never apologize for the United States of America. I don't care what the facts are.' (This comment was made after the shooting down of a commercial Iranian passenger jet by the US warship *Vicennes*, which killed 290 Iranian civilians.)

Autonomy refers to the ability to seek out and make individual (or group) choices.

Autonomy strategies refer to Indigenous Peoples' movements to break away from previous alliances to implement what was learned in these relationships and to pursue their own strategies to bring about their independence from colonialism (Nash 2005).

B

Backlash refers to an opposing, angry, negative, sometimes violent reaction from the members of one group against another who are regarded as disproportionately benefiting from a trend, development or event. The intensity and success of a backlash is determined by how much power a group has in society to resist or perpetuate it. For instance, since Indigenous Peoples throughout the world have the least influence and power in mainstream society, the backlash against them from other groups can be frequent and deadly. Since colonizers have the most concentrated power in their societies they have little to fear from the backlash of Indigenous Peoples. The greatest backlash for colonizers comes from one another.

Biopiracy is the unauthorized, uncompensated and predatory use of the biological resources of Indigenous Peoples, such as genetic materials, plants and knowledge, which are often patented, without permission, by those who have stolen them. Biopiracy is a highly profitable form of theft since there are few sanctions against it, despite loud objections from Indigenous Peoples. Many health products and the knowledge to create them were stolen from Indigenous Peoples. Vandana Shiva (undated) asserts that:

> Biopiracy and patenting of indigenous knowledge is a double theft because first it allows theft of creativity and innovation, and secondly, the exclusive rights established by patents on stolen knowledge steal economic options of everyday survival on the basis of our

indigenous biodiversity and indigenous knowledge. Over time, the patents can be used to create monopolies and make everyday products highly priced (www.globalissues.org/EnvIssues/GEFood/FoodPatents.asp).

Bioprospecting refers to the 'discovery' of new drugs by pharmacological firms, universities and scientist who have 'fanned out across the globe to interview herbal healers and shamans in order to collect plant specimens and test them for biologically active ingredients' (Tedlock 2005: 149). The 1994 Trade Related Aspects Intellectual Property Rights Agreement (TRIPS) allows pharmaceutical firms to claim information they gain from Indigenous Peoples.

> Under this agreement scientists can take a plant hybridized for generations by indigenous peoples and with the agreement of the nation-state, but without the knowledge of the local community, patent it. In so doing they claim ownership of the entire species and receive all future profits from it (Tedlock 2005: 149).

Bioterrorism is the use of biological and chemical agents to terrorize, eliminate or neutralize an individual or group. Bioterrorism was a weapon used against Indigenous Peoples in the United States by military and civilian populations. In 1763, Lord Jeffrey Amherst, commander of British forces in North America during the French and Indian War (1756–63), with the assistance of Colonel Henry Bouquet, sent smallpox infected blankets to hostile tribes. In 1837 smallpox was deliberately brought to the Northern Plains of the United States by a steamboat called the *St Peter.* Despite that the ship's captain, Bernard Pratte, Jr, and several others on board knew that the ship was carrying passengers infected with smallpox and that this disease would be deadly to Indigenous Peoples they would encounter, they proceeded into their territory causing the deaths of tens of thousands.

Brainwashing is 'the use of propaganda, persuasion, and sometimes coercion to influence people to accept new and different beliefs unquestioningly' (Barker 2003: 51). Brainwashing was a common policy used on Indigenous children in government aboriginal boarding schools. It was intended to get the children to abandon (and despise) their cultural beliefs and identity and take on those of the colonial oppressors.

Bureau of Indian Affairs is a federal government agency within the Department of the Interior of the United States that is congressionally authorized through treaties, federal statutes, executive orders and judicial decisions to carry out its 'trust responsibility' to all federally recognized tribes through the provision of social services, education, economic assistance and resource protection. Because of its inability to carry out its mandate and its incompetence in helping Indigenous Peoples it has been called 'the worst federal agency' and 'a national disgrace' (Satchell 1994). Similar government departments exist in Canada and Australia.

C

Callous colonizer refers to an individual who disregards or ridicules the suffering and injustices experienced by Indigenous Peoples. An example would be an individual who deliberately attacks Indigenous Peoples or those who are educating others about, or protesting, the historical or contemporary oppression caused by the colonizer.

Colonialism refers to the event of an alien people invading the territory inhabited by people of a different race and culture, to establish political, social, spiritual, intellectual and economic domination over that territory and people. It includes territorial and resource appropriation by the colonizer and loss of sovereignty by the colonized (Yellow Bird 1999). The term also refers to a set of beliefs used to legitimize or promote this system, especially the belief that the mores of the colonizer are superior to those of the colonized (www.en.wikipedia.org/wiki/Colonialism).

Colonial amnesia is the inability (or unwillingness) of the colonizer to recall the past oppression that they have perpetuated on the colonized. This is generally due to a long history of covering up or minimizing such events. It is also a strategy to prevent the public accounting of crimes and unfair treatment against Indigenous Peoples.

Colonization amnesia is what occurs when Indigenous Peoples don't have any knowledge of how they have been shaped by the colonists because this knowledge has been denied them by their education and even their families (Porter 2005).

Colonial cachexia refers to the weakening of the colonized by the colonial state to a degree of near immobility so that the Indigenous People can no longer take care of themselves or resist the harmful effects of colonization.

Colonized society is a structure through which the state controls and manages Indigenous Peoples. Perhaps the easiest way to oppress the colonized is by keeping them weak, too weak to upset the system, but strong enough to fulfil their lowly role as menial workers to support the economy of corporate rulers (Adams 1995).

Colonizing tendencies are evident in globalizing and internationalizing processes that pursue social work 'as a professional project' (McDonald 2006) and claim a universal core to social work and seek global standards for education and practice. There is a separate literature in social work relating to this 'west *to* the rest' social work which needs to be seen as distinct from the 'rest *in* the west' social work of the cultural competence literature (see below) relating *inter alia* to immigrant and refugee communities and non-dominant or minority cultures in Western societies (also referred to as the developed north). In the 'west *to* the rest' literature there is a theme relating to the 'misappropriation' of terms like 'Indigenous' and the misuse of terms like 'Indigenization' where it is more appropriate to talk about 'cultural relevance' or the relevance of (Western) social work to non-Western and Indigenous cultures. Within the 'rest *in* the west' literature there is the idea conveyed that one can learn about and become competent in other peoples' cultures as though 'culture' were a fixed conglomeration of attributes and practices that can be packaged into 'how to' manuals (see Park 2005). Non-Western and Indigenous cultures, or others' culture in any context, cannot be so easily learned. People are steeped and embedded in culture hence the importance of grounded approaches rather than 'imported adaptation models' which do not fit and often overlook *local* cultures. This is variously expressed as a call for 'Indigenization', localization, reconceptualization, authentization or contextualization, hence our preference for the term 'culturally relevant' (see below) or 'culturally appropriate' social work practice (see Indigenous Peoples).

Compassionate colonizers are individuals who are well intentioned but often unwittingly perpetuate colonial injustices through their commitment to Western doctrines and ideologies and their blindness to the interests of Indigenous Peoples.

Critical consciousness refers to the ability to perceive social, political and economic oppression and to take action against the oppressive elements of society (Freire 2000).

Culturally appropriate social work is another term used in the literature on cultural sensitivity, cultural competence and cross-cultural social work relating mainly to work with people in mainstream Western cultures whose culture is 'different' and where 'other' cultures usually constitute a minority. In the literature on 'Indigenization', or more aptly the spread of social work from the 'west to the rest', in contexts where dominant cultures are non-Western and populations are not of European or American descent (for example, the populations of Africa, Asia and South America, also referred to as the global south), local cultures have been largely overlooked in social work's colonialist past.

Cultural competence and cultural sensitivity are terms which have taken on specific and distinct meanings associated with different timeframes in the theoretical development of working with diverse populations. For example, in the USA as theories and ideas about working with culturally and racially diverse populations evolved there was a movement away from largely segregated services that emerged after the Civil War to a position of colour blindness that was popular in the 1950s and early 1960s. It soon became apparent that colour blindness – treating all clients equally regardless of cultural background – often ignored a key component of 'who clients are' thus the trend toward cultural sensitivity or becoming aware that there were cultural differences. Awareness and sensitivity, however, was not enough. Hence moving into the 1990s there was a push for *cultural competence* which included an ability to build on the sensitivity or knowledge about different populations and incorporate specific skills. Thus cultural competence added an action to the awareness of cultural sensitivity, also sometimes referred to as cultural awareness; it involves the way in which culture is incorporated into social work practices. There is still a long way to go in empirically elucidating the elements of cultural competence with specific populations but clearly cultural competence is a step beyond cultural sensitivity and cultural awareness as it is understood within the US context (Personal communication, Hilary Weaver, 12 October 2006).

Cultural relevance is a more general term than cultural competence and cultural sensitivity expressing a strong sense of the importance of social work's responsiveness to local cultural contexts.

D

Decolonization is a process that begins with the *understanding that one is* colonize (at whatever level that may be) It is *creating and consciously using* various strategies to liberate oneself from, or adapt to, or survive in oppressive conditions. It is the *restoration* of cultural practices, thinking, beliefs and values that were taken away or abandoned but are still relevant or necessary for survival and well-being. It is the *birth and use* of new ideas, thinking, technologies and lifestyles that contribute to the advancement and empowerment of Indigenous Peoples.

Dikephobia is the persistent and unreasonable fear of justice. One characteristic of dikephobia is hiding past action for fear it might spark criticism and calls for justice from others. For instance, colonizing powers such as the United States of America that want to be perceived as just, humane and democratic nations will hide, ignore or trivialize a long history of oppression of Indigenous Peoples.

Dispossession results from the systematic stealing of people's land, history and culture. For instance in 1,500 Indigenous Peoples in the United States owned billions of acres of land. By 1887, despite all the treaties made with the United States in order to retain their lands, their land base had dwindled to 140 million acres and by 1931 it had shrunk to less than 48 million acres (Olson and Wilson 1986).

'Don't blame me, I wasn't here when that happened' is a common saying among social work students from mainstream communities who react defensively when they are exposed to the numerous unjust acts committed by their societies against Indigenous Peoples. It is an expression that protects them from accusations of involvement but also demonstrates a lack of development of empathy and cultural understanding. It is an anti-allocentric statement.

E

Ethics refers to a system of moral principles and values that focuses on what is right and wrong and the standard for proper conduct in a particular society. Ethics in a colonial society are often absent when the colonizer is dealing with Indigenous Peoples. For instance, over a period of almost one hundred years (1778 to 1871) the United States made hundreds of legal treaties with Indigenous Peoples in which it promised to refrain from taking their lands and natural resources, to maintain friendship with them, to respect and honour their nationhood and to avoid making war against them. The US has broken every treaty it made with Indigenous Peoples and has failed to live up to its promises. This is both an ethical violation and a violation of the good faith on which treaties and contracts are built.

Ethnocide refers to the destruction of culture without the physical killing of its members. One form of ethnocide that has been exceedingly effective has been the use of government and Christian boarding schools (see Residential Schools), which legally abducted Indigenous children from their communities and forced them into a foreign formal education programme that brutalized them for speaking their Aboriginal languages, devalued tribal beliefs and values, and forbade them from practicing Aboriginal ways of life.

Eurocentricism is the view that many Europeans and their descendants have of themselves as being culturally and politically superior to all other peoples in the world (Adams 1995).

Exploitation refers to an unfair, selfish and improper act by one who victimizes another by using their resources (land, natural resources, culture and knowledge) for gain.

F

First Nations is a term acknowledging that such persons are the original peoples of the land and hold Aboriginal title to the lands they occupy. The term also has deep spiritual meaning since it was developed by tribal Elders in British Columbia, Canada, who maintain that the traditions of First Nations include a belief in a Creator who placed their Nations on the land to care for and control them (Yellow Bird 1999).

G

Gatekeepers are people in a society who hold decision making positions, control and select the information one receives, and the access one has to different resources. In a colonial society gatekeepers are essential to keeping power in the hands of the colonizers.

'Get over it' is an expression of annoyance used by social workers from mainstream society to prevent Indigenous Peoples from bringing up past injustices perpetrated by colonial societies. It is a phrase that attempts to trivialize the past oppression of Indigenous Peoples (also see 'Don't blame me I wasn't here when that happened').

Genocide is the systematic killing of a people identified by ethnic or racial characteristics. The purpose of genocide is extermination (Trask 1999: 251).

Genocide has two phases: one, destruction of the national pattern of the oppressed group; the other, the imposition of the national patterns of the oppressor. This imposition, in turn, may be made upon the oppressed population which is allowed to remain or upon the territory alone, after removal of the population and colonization of the area by the oppressor's own nationals (Lemkin 1944: 79).

H

Hypergiaphobia refers to the fear of responsibility. A characteristic of hypergiaphobia is the inability to keep agreements. One could say that colonizing powers such as the United States, Canada and Australia meet the diagnosis for a national hypergiaphobia since each has broken numerous agreements or refused to enter into good faith agreements with Indigenous Peoples.

I

Imperialism is a total system of foreign power in which another culture, people and way of life penetrate, transform and come to define the colonized society. The function and purpose of imperialism is exploitation of the colony. Using this definition, Hawai'i is a colony of the United States (Trask 1999: 251). Imperialism was the vicious destruction of everything Aboriginal; its weapons were Christianity, political subversion, violent repression and germ warfare (Adams 1995). What is sacred to Indigenous Peoples is not so in imperialism (Adams 1995).

Indian is a name mistakenly given to Indigenous Peoples in the Caribbean Islands by Christopher Columbus. The name was later imposed on most of the Indigenous Peoples in the Americas (also see American Indian). In Central and South America it is often regarded as a term of abuse.

Indigenous, according to the *Oxford Dictionary*, is a word which comes from the Latin *indigena* meaning born or produced naturally in a land or region, that is, native to the land or region as opposed to exotic, foreign to the land or from outside the region. It is a term that some groups prefer and others avoid.

Indigenous Peoples are diverse populations located throughout the world that constitute between 300 and 500 million people, residing on ancestral lands, sharing an ancestry with the original inhabitants of these lands, having distinct cultures and languages and regarding themselves as different from those who colonized and now control their lands (Stamatopoulou 1994). For instance, 'American Indians' in the United States, First Nations Peoples in Canada, Māori in New Zealand, Sami (Lapps) in Scandinavia and Aboriginal Peoples in Australia are considered to be Indigenous Peoples (see Hughes 2003; Yellow Bird 1999).

Indigenization is the personal and collective process of decolonizing Indigenous life and restoring true self-determination based on traditional Indigenous values

(Porter 2005). This understanding is quite different from the use of the term in social work where Indigenization can refer to the adaptation of Western social work theory and methods to local contexts.

Invasion is a military action consisting of troops entering a foreign land – a nation or territory or part thereof – often resulting in the invading power occupying the area, whether briefly or for a long period (www.en.wikipedia.org/wiki/Invasion). Most Indigenous Peoples throughout the world consider European/American 'discoveries' of their territories to be invasions.

Invasive is the persistent intrusion of external thoughts and practices which result from territorializing forces like colonization, international social work, globalization, and so on. Local cultural beliefs and practices find it extremely difficult to rise to the top without having to ward off external interference.

J

Justice is the righting of wrongs.

L

Land and resource rights refer to Indigenous Peoples' entitlement to these which rightfully belongs to them through historical precedent and occupancy.

M

Minorities are often Indigenous, for example, the Karen of Burma and the Yanomami of Brazil; Korean-Americans and British-Asians are not Indigenous. According to Hughes (2003), there is no international definition of 'minorities' despite the UN Declaration on Minorities and the Minority Rights Group International (MRGI). However, ethnic, religious and linguistic minorities – who are not necessarily numerical minorities and may include Indigenous and tribal Peoples as well as migrants and refugees – are usually the most disadvantaged, marginalized groups in society and lack access to power. The term has many negative connotations (such as suggesting that Indigenous Peoples are less than or 'minor'). Thus, many groups do not approve of this label being attached to them.

Monetary compensation is recompense provided to First Nations Peoples for the loss of their lands or possessions. However, compensation does not necessarily constitute fairness or resolution of past injustices.

N

Neocolonialism is:

> ... a contemporary strain that reveals that the most effective colonizer is often the colonized. In other words, those who accept the yoke and precepts of colonialism often accept the colonizers' assumptions about political/social institutions, contracting theories, and economic beliefs about land, minerals, water, and labor. This group provides the colonizer with the resources and the social control it demands. Control of Indigenous affairs often occurs through the employment of Indigenous Peoples in the colonial structures (Yellow Bird 2006: 229).

Native title is a legal term referring to a legal process of re-establishing Indigenous Peoples' 'traditional ownership' of the land and reaffirming that their 'Native title' continues to exist in a particular location based on proof of continuous habitation. It is a 'reconciliatory' process that acknowledges peoples' rights and affirms a serious commitment to improve the quality of life for the Indigenous People in particular locations.

O

Occupation is the control of a country by a foreign power's military and domestic forces. In order for occupation to cease to exist, colonizers must either leave Indigenous territories or reach mutual agreements with the original land owners (aboriginal peoples) to identify the terms of their continued occupancy.

R

Racism is discrimination against people based on race or skin colour.

Radical Indigenism is a sustained response to persistent colonizing forces (Garroutte 2003). It refers to scholarship in which tribal philosophies are studied from within and requires the abandonment of notions of superiority of dominant academic philosophies and interpretations, as well as theoretical approaches based on them. It requires that scholars accept the rationalities of Indigenous philosophies as offering a lens through which to view traditional ways of knowing (see Hart, Chapter 10).

Reparation is making amends for past injustices.

Residential School or Indian Boarding School generally refers to 'schools' operated by federal governments and various religious organizations in which Aboriginal children in Canada, United States and Australia were sent to receive an education and to assist their assimilation into the larger society. Some refer to these schools as part of cultural genocide (see Ethnocide) as children were separated from their parents for many months at a time, were forbidden to speak their Native language and did not learn Indigenous cultural traditions. While some adults claim they benefited from their experience, in recent years, a great many individuals have come forward with personal and painful stories of neglect, and physical and sexual abuse at residential schools.

Responsibility is accepting and delivering on promises made.

Righteous anger is the emotional and psychological response of victims of racism and discrimination to the system of power that dominates, exploits or oppresses them. Righteous anger is not racism; rather, it is a defensible response to racism (Trask 1999: 252).

S

Social engineering is the process by which a colonizer strategically changes the culture, identity and way of life of a colonized people to align the Native people more closely with the colonizers, with the final outcome being complete assimilation (Porter 2005).

Sovereignty is the power of a people to control their own destiny. A nation's sovereignty is dependent on three things: 1) the degree to which the people believe in the right to define their own future; 2) the degree to which the people have the ability to carry out those beliefs; and 3) the degree to which sovereign acts are recognized both within the nation and by the outside world (Porter 2005). Colonizers rarely understand Indigenous sovereignty. For instance, see US President George W. Bush's attempt to define this term on youtube.com (www.youtube.com/watch?v=oMzHq4qIS0I).

Suppression is the deliberate holding down of people or ideas with the intention of rendering them powerless.

T

Takeover is the deliberate appropriation of other people's land, possessions, ideas, and so on, so that they are no longer the main providers or lineage of such things.

Treaty refers to a process of formal agreement between Indigenous and non-Indigenous Peoples or between Indigenous groups.

Tribal literally means 'belonging to a tribe' which may or may not be descended from the original people of the land. It should be used with caution and is only acceptable when Indigenous People refer to themselves in this way.

Truth and reconciliation is a concept used since the first truth commission was formed in Uganda in 1974 and has developed into an effective strategy used in various countries for dealing with war crimes and other human rights abuses. It has been used extensively in Latin America to investigate patterns of abuse, such as 'disappearances'. Although in most cases truth commissions are sponsored by governments, the focus is on giving victims, witnesses and even perpetrators a chance to publicly tell their stories without fear of prosecution. The approach is one of 'restorative justice', which differs from the customary adversarial, retributive justice. It seeks to heal relations between opposing sides by uncovering pertinent facts, distinguishing truth from lies and encouraging acknowledgement, appropriate public mourning, forgiveness and healing. With an initial $4-million grant from the Ford Foundation, one of the chief architects of South Africa's truth commission founded the International Center for Transitional Justice (ICTJ) in 2001 to advise other nations employing the process. It promotes the belief that confronting and reckoning with the past is necessary for successful transitions from conflict, resentment and tension to peace and connectedness. In advising the first project of its kind in the US, the ICTJ is helping Greensboro, North Carolina, tailor the process, as all who use it must, to its unique circumstances, history and needs (www.gtcrp. org/truth.asp).

W

Western refers to a way of thinking, a history of philosophy, rooted in 'rational' thought where the individual subject is highly valued; where secular humanism prevails and the rational, autonomous, freely choosing individual is highly valued; where democracy and freedom of choice is seen as the most just system promoting human rights and social justice – fairness and equality of opportunity; where neoliberal economics tend to dominate the social terrain and free market economies and free trade are seen as priorities; where the dominant history is that of exploration and conquest, of voyages of discovery in the interests of progress and the development of *Western* civilization; and where social life is highly bureaucratized, impersonal and largely individualistic. 'Western' social work is rooted in these traditions: detraditionalization, secularization, rationalism, cultural imperialism, colonialization, 'west is best', development as progress, and so on.

Western social work does not imply that there is a monolithic entity on which all are agreed. We accept that there is diversity even within Western social work with a variety of theories, approaches, perspectives, world views and ideologies, but all share the epistemological tradition rooted in rational thinking and linguistic media. It is often not recognized that Western social work is itself a cultural construction that arose in Europe and North America, in the so-called developed Western nations and the rich north, compared to the so-called 'less developed' nations of the south. This is a rough and over-generalized division for the sake of understanding 'difference' when we come to reflect on 'cultural relevance'. The challenge is always for non-Western cultures to declare how they differ from 'Western culture' or to declare how 'Indigenous social work' differs from non-Indigenous social work. This is because social work is a Western profession with a knowledge base steeped in rational explanations of reality and a scientific approach. Most importantly, Western social work seeks to have or promote universal values, principles, education standards, and so on and is bent on standardization in every sphere, most recently the formalization of guidelines for research and international exchange, hence our reference to this as the 'Western juggernaut'.

White supremacy is the belief that white people are the supreme and rightful carriers of culture and history.

White tape (as opposed to 'red tape') is a term used by Indigenous Peoples in the United States to refer to white peoples' endless, inefficient, ineffective and racist federal government bureaucracy.

References

Aboriginal Deaths in Custody Secretariat (1997), *Royal Commission into Deaths in Custody: Queensland Government Report on Implementation.* Brisbane: Department of Families, Office of Aboriginal and Torres Strait Islander Affairs.

Aboriginal Institutes' Consortium, The (2005), *Aboriginal Institutions of Higher Education: A Struggle for the Education of Aboriginal Students, Control of Indigenous Knowledge, and Recognition of Aboriginal Institutions.* Ottawa: Canadian Race Relations Foundation.

Abram, D. (1997), *The Spell of the Sensuous.* New York: Vintage Books.

Adams, C. (ed.) (1993), *Eco-feminism and the Sacred.* New York: Continuum Publishing.

Adams, H. (1995), *A Tortured People: The Politics of Colonization.* Penticton, BC: Theytus Books.

Agnew, J. (2005), *Hegemony: The New Shape of Global Power.* Philadelphia: Temple University Press.

Alasuutari, P. (1992), *Desire and Craving: A Cultural Theory of Alcoholism.* Albany: State University of New York Press.

Alatas, S.H. (1972), The Captive Mind in Development Studies: Some Neglected Problems and the Need for an Autonomous Social Science Tradition in Asia. *International Social Science Journal*, 34(1), 9–25.

Alatas, S.H. (2000a), Intellectual Imperialism: Definition, Traits and Problems. *Southeast Asian Journal of Social Science*, 28(1), 23–45.

Alatas, S.F. (2000b), An Introduction to the Idea of Alternative Discourse. *Southeast Asian Journal of Social Sciences*, 28(1), 1 12.

Alfero, L.A. (1973), *New Themes in Social Work Education.* New York: International Association of Schools of Social Work.

Alfred, T. (2005), *Wasáse: Indigenous Pathways of Action and Freedom.* Peterborough: Broadview Press.

Al-Issa, I. (ed.) (2000), *Al-Junun: Mental Illness in the Islamic World.* Madison, CN: International Universities Press.

Al-Krenawi, A. and Graham, J.R. (1996a), Social Work Practice and Traditional Healing Rituals Among the Bedouin of the Negev, Israel. *International Social Work*, 39(2), 177–88.

Al-Krenawi, A. and Graham, J.R. (1996b), Tackling Mental Illness: Roles for Old and New Disciplines. *World Health Forum*, 17, 246–8.

Al-Krenawi, A. and Graham, J.R. (1997), Spirit Possession and Exorcism: The Integration of Modern and Traditional Mental Health Care Systems in the Treatment of a Bedouin Patient. *Clinical Social Work Journal*, 25, 211–22.

Al-Krenawi, A. and Graham, J.R. (1999), Gender and Biomedical/Traditional Mental Health Utilization Among the Bedouin-Arabs of the Negev. *Culture, Medicine, and Psychiatry*, 23(2), 219–43.

Al-Krenawi, A. and Graham, J.R. (2000), Islamic Theology and Prayer: Relevance for Social Work Practice. *International Social Work*, 43(3), 289–302.

Al-Krenawi, A. and Graham, J.R. (2001), The Cultural Mediator: Bridging the Gap between a Non-Western Community and Professional Social Work Practice. *British Journal of Social Work*, 31(4), 665–86.

Al-Krenawi, A. and Graham, J.R. (2003), Principles of Social Work Practice in the Muslim Arab World. *Arab Studies Quarterly*, 25(4), 75–91.

Al-Krenawi, A. and Graham, J.R. (2006), A Comparison of Family Functioning, Life and Marital Satisfaction, and Mental Health of Women in Polygamous and Monogamous Marriages. *International Journal of Social Psychiatry*, 52(1), 5–17.

Al-Krenawi, A., Graham, J.R. and Al-Krenawi, S. (1997), Social Work Practice with Polygamous Families. *Child and Adolescent Social Work Journal*, 14(6), 444–58.

Al-Krenawi, A., Graham, J.R. and Kanda, J. (2000), Gendered Utilization Differences of Mental Health Services in Jordan. *Community Mental Health Journal*, 36(5), 501–11.

Al-Krenawi, A., Graham, J.R. and Sehwail, M. (2002), Bereavement Responses Among Palestinian Widows, Daughters and Sons Following the Hebron Massacre. *Omega: Journal of Death and Dying*, 44(3), 241–55.

Al-Krenawi, A., Graham, J.R. and Sehwail, M. (2004), Mental Health and Violence/Trauma in Palestine: Implications for Helping Professional Practice. *Journal of Comparative Family Studies*, 35(2), 185–209.

Al-Krenawi, A., Lev-Wiesel, R. and Sehwail, M. (forthcoming), Psychological Symptomatology Among Palestinian Adolescents Living with Political Violence. *Child and Adolescent Mental Health Journal*.

Almanzor, A. (1967), The Profession of Social Work in the Philippines. In Council on Social Work Education. *An Intercultural Exploration: Universals and Differentials in Social Work Values, Functions and Practice*. New York: Council on Social Work Education, pp. 123–37.

Amin, S. (1976), *Unequal Development*. New York: Monthly Review Press.

Anderson, K. (2000), *A Recognition of Being: Reconstructing Native Womanhood*. Toronto: Second Story Press.

Anderson, W. (2002), *The Cultivation of Whiteness*. Victoria: Melbourne University Press.

Anttonen, A. and Siplila, J. (1996), European Social Care Services: Is it Possible to Identify Models? *Journal of European Social Policy*, 6(2), 87–100.

Arab Association for Human Rights, The (15–22 July 2003), More House Demolitions in the Negev. *Weekly Review of the Arab Press in Israel*, 126. Accessed 1 August, <www.arabhra.org>.

Arnold, R. (2005), *Empathic Intelligence*. Sydney: University of NSW Press.

Asad, T. (1986), The Concept of Cultural Translation in British Social Anthropology, in J. Clifford and G.E. Marcus (eds), *Writing Culture*. Berkeley: University of California Press.

Asante, M.K. (1987), *The Afrocentric Idea*. Philadelphia, PA: Temple University Press.

Asante, M.K. (1988), *Afrocentricity*. Trenton, NJ: Africa World.

Ashcroft, B., Griffiths, G. and Tiffin, H. (1989), *The Empire Writes Back: Theory and Practice in Post-Colonial Literatures*. New York: Routledge.

Association for the Advancement of Civic Equality, The (2004), *The Sikkuy Report*. Accessed 1 August 2003, <www.sikkuy.org.il>.

Atkinson, J. (2002), *Trauma Trails*. Melbourne, Victoria: Spinifex Press.

Australian Indigenous Health InfoNet (2006), *The Context of Indigenous Health*. Accessed 15 March, <www.healthinfonet.ecu.edu.au/frames.htm>.

Australian Medical Association (2006), *2006 AMA Report Card: Undue Punishment? Aboriginal and Torres Strait Islanders in Prison: An Unacceptable Reality*. Accessed 25 May, <www.ama.com.au/web.nsf/doc/WEEN-6PU8QN>.

Awa, N.E. (1979), Ethnocentric Bias in Development Research, in M.K. Asante, E. Newmark and C.A. Blake (eds), *Handbook of Intercultural Communication*. Beverley Hills: Sage.

Baldwin, J. (1998), *Collected Essays*. New York: Library of America.

Baldwin, M. (1996), White Anti-racism: Is it Really 'No Go' in Rural Areas? *Social Work Education*, 15(1), 18–38.

Barise, A. (2005), Social Work with Muslims: Insights from the Teachings of Islam. *Critical Social Work*, 6(2). Accessed 24 January 2006, <www.criticalsocialwork.com/units/socialwork/critical.nsf/EditDoNotShowInTOC/554026006519AFC38525700F004B57B6>.

Barker, R.L. (2003), *The Social Work Dictionary* (5th edn). Washington, DC: NASW Press.

Bar-On, A. (2003a), Indigenous Practice: Some Informed Guesses – Self-evident but Impossible. *Social Work/Maatskaplike Werk*, 39(1), 26–40.

Bar-On, A. (2003b), Culture: Social Work's New Deluge? *Maatskaplike Werk/Social Work*, 39(4), 299–311.

Barth, F. (1995), Other Knowledge and Other Ways of Knowing. *Journal of Anthropological Research*, 50, 65–8.

Bateson, M.C. (1994), *Peripheral Visions: Learning Along the Way*. New York: HarperCollins.

Becerra, R.M. and Chi, I. (1992), Child Care Preferences Among Low-income Minority Families. *International Social Work*, 35(1), 35–47.

Benegal, V. (2005), India: Alcohol and Public Health. *Addiction*, 100(8), 1051–54.

Benhabib, S. (2002), *The Claims of Culture: Equality and Diversity in the Global Era*. Princeton, NJ: Princeton University Press.

Ben Meir, E. (2002), *Israeli Arabs: To Whom Do They Pledge Allegiance?* Ariel Centre for Policy Research.

Bennett, B. and Zubrzycki, J. (2003), Hearing the Stories of Australian Aboriginal and Torres Strait Islander Social Workers: Challenging and Educating the System. *Australian Social Work*, 56(1), 6–70.

Benton-Banai, E. (1988), *The Mishomis Book: Voice of the Ojibway*. Hayward, WI: Indian Country Communications, Inc.

Berman, M. (2000), *Wandering God: A Study in Nomadic Spirituality*. New York: State University of New York Press.

Berry, T. (1997), *Annual Colloquium with Thomas Berry*. Holy Cross Centre for Ecology and Spirituality, Port Burwell, Ontario, Canada, 13–15 June.

Berry, T. (1999), *The Great Work: Our Way Into the Future*. New York: Bell Tower.

Bertram, G. (1999), The MIRAB Model Twelve Years On. *Contemporary Pacific*, 11(10), 105–38.

Bessarab, D. (2000), Working with Aboriginal Families: A Cultural Approach, in W. Weeks and M. Quinn (eds), *Issues Facing Australian Families* (3rd edn). Sydney: Pearson.

Besthorn, F. (1997), *Reconceptualizing Social Work's Person-in-Environment Perspective: Explorations in Radical Environmental Thought*. PhD Dissertation, University of Kansas. Ann Arbor: UMI Microform 981157.

Bhabha, H.K. (1994), *The Location of Culture*. London: Routledge.

Bilik, N. (2002), The Ethnicity of Anthropology in China: Discursive Diversity and Linguistic Relativity. *Critique of Anthropology*, 22(2), 133–48.

Bishop, B.J., Higgins, D., Casella, F. and Contos, N. (2002), Reflects on Practice: Ethics, Race and World Views. *Journal of Community Psychology*, 30(6), 611–21.

Boddy, J. (1989), *Wombs and Alien Spirits: Women, Men and the Zar Cult in Northern Sudan*. Wisconsin, WI: University of Wisconsin Press.

Bonnett, A. (1996), Antiracism and the Critique of White Identities. *New Community*, 22(1), 97–110.

Bose, A.B. (1992), Social Work in India: Developmental Roles for a Helping Profession, in M.C. Hokenstad, S.K. Khinduka and J. Midgley (eds), *Profiles in International Social Work*. New York: National Association of Social Workers.

Bourdieu, P. (1990), *The Logic of Practise*. Oxford: Polity Press.

Boyle, D.P. and Springer, A. (2001), Towards a Cultural Competence Measure for Social Work with Specific Populations. *Journal of Ethnic and Cultural Diversity in Social Work*, 9(3/4), 53–71.

Brabham, W., Henry, J., Bamblett, E. and Bates, E. (2002), Indigenous Australians' Participation in Higher Education. *Australian Universities Review*, 45(1), 10–14.

Bradshaw, C. and Graham, J.R. (2007), Localization of Social Work Practice, Education and Research: A Content Analysis. *Social Development Issues*, 29(2) (forthcoming).

Brah, A. (1996), *Cartographies of Diaspora: Contesting Identities*. London: Routledge.

Branscombe, M. (1961), Curriculum Planning for Social Work in Newly Developing Countries. *International Social Work*, 4(3), 1–3.

Briggs, C. (1986), *Learning How to Ask: A Sociolinguistic Appraisal of the Role of the Interview in Social Science Research*. London: Cambridge University Press.

Bringing Them Home Report (1997), *Report of the National Inquiry into the Separation of Aboriginal and Torres Strait Islander Children from their Families*. Canberra: Human Rights and Equal Opportunity Commission.

Briskman, L. (2003), *The Black Grapevine: Aboriginal Activism and the Stolen Generations*. Sydney: The Federation Press.

British Columbia (2005), *College and Institute Act*. Victoria, Canada: Queen's Printer.

Brown, M. (1957), Where Do We Go From Here? *Social Service Quarterly*, 31, 112–6.

Bruyere, G. (1997), Finding the Balance: Anishnabe Talking Circles as Alternative Social Work Education, in R.W. Nelsen (ed.), *Inside Canadian Universities: Another Day at the Plant*. Kingston, ON: Cedarcreek Publications, pp. 171–83.

Bruyere, G. (1998), Living in Another Man's House: Supporting Aboriginal learners in Social Work Education. *Canadian Social Work Review*, 15(2), 169–76.

Bruyere, G. (1999), The Decolonization Wheel: An Aboriginal Perspective on Social Work Practice with Aboriginal Peoples, in R. Delaney, K. Brownlee and K. Zapf (eds), *Social Work Practice with Rural and Northern Peoples*. Thunder Bay, ON: Centre for Northern Studies, pp. 170–81.

Bush, B. (1998), Britain's Conscience on Africa: White Women, Race and Imperial Politics in Inter-war Britain, in C. Midgely (ed.), *Gender and Imperialism*. New York: Manchester University Press, pp. 200–23.

Cajete, G. (1994), *Look to the Mountain: An Ecology of Indigenous Education*. Durango, CO: Kivakí Press.

Canadian Association of Schools of Social Work (2000), *Educational Policy Statements*. Ottawa: CASSW.

Canadian Association of Schools of Social Work (2004), *Standards for Accreditation*. Ottawa: CASSW.

Capra, F. (1982), *The Turning Point*. New York: Simon and Schuster.

Cardinal, H. and Hilderbrandt, W. (2000), *Treaty Elders of Saskatchewan: Our Dream is that Our Peoples will One Day be Clearly Recognized as Nations*. Calgary: University of Calgary Press.

Cardoso, F.H. and Faleto, E. (1979), *Dependency and Development in Latin America*. Berkeley, CA: University of California Press.

Carniol, B. (1990), *Case Critical: Challenging Social Work in Canada* (2nd edn). Toronto: Between the Lines.

Carniol, B. (2005), *Case Critical: Social Services and Social Justice in Canada*. Toronto: Between the Lines.

Carniol, B. (2006), *Case Critical: Social Services and Social Justice in Canada* (5th edn). Toronto: Between the Lines.

Carrier, J. (1995), *Occidentalism: Images of the West*. Oxford: Clarendon Press.

Central Statistics Office (CSO) (2004), *Botswana AIDS Impact Survey II*. Gaborone: Government Printer.

Chamberlain, E.R. (1991), The Beijing Seminar: Social Work Education in Asia and the Pacific. *International Social Work*, 34(1), 27–35.

Chan, C.L.W. (1992), New Challenges to the Forms of Welfare Provision in China After a Decade of Economic Reform. *International Social Work*, 35(3), 347–63.

Chan, K.L. (2006), The Chinese Concept of Face and Violence Against Women. *International Social Work*, 49(1), 65–73.

Chan, K.L. and Chan, C.L.W. (2005), Chinese Culture, Social Work Education and Research. *International Social Work*, 48(4), 381–9.

Chan, R.K. and Tsui, M. (1997), Notions of the Welfare State in China Revisited. *International Social Work*, 40(2), 177–89.

Chang, C. (2002), Narrative Analysis of the Experience of Clinical Social Workers in Building Helping Relationships: An Exploration of the Taiwan Experience. *Dissertation Abstracts International, A: The Humanities and Social Sciences*, 62(9), 3186A–7A.

Chappell, R. (2001), *Social Welfare in Canadian Society* (2nd edn). Toronto: Nelson Thomson Learning.

Chau, R.C.M. and Yu, S.W.K. (1998), Occupational Therapy Stations in China: Economic Integration or Economic Stratification for People with Learning Difficulties. *International Social Work*, 41(1), 7–21.

Chen, X. (1992), Occidentalism as Counter-discourse: 'He Shang', in Post-Mao China. *Critical Inquiry*, 18, 686–712.

Chen, X. (1995), *Occidentalism: A Theory of Counter-Discourse in Post-Mao China*. New York: Oxford.

Chenery, H., Ahluwalia, M., Bell, C., Duloy, J.H. and Jolly, R. (1974), *Redistribution With Growth*. Oxford: Oxford University Press.

Cherian, R.R. (1986), Emergence of a Day-care Centre for Alcoholics in India: Its Referral System and Public Response. *British Journal of Addiction*, 81(11), 119–22.

Cherian, R.R. (1989), Towards Freedom: Treatment Approaches to Drug Dependency. *British Journal of Addiction*, 84(12), 1401–7.

Cheung, M. and Liu, M. (2004), The Self-concept of Chinese Women and the Indigenization of Social Work in China. *International Social Work*, 47(1), 109–27.

Chew, D. (1990), *Chinese Pioneers on the Sarawak Frontier 1841–1941*. Singapore: Oxford University Press.

Chi, I. (2005), Social Work in China: Guest Editorial for the Special Issue. *International Social Work*, 48(4), 371–9.

Chin, J.M. (1981), *The Sarawak Chinese*. Kuala Lumpur: Oxford University Press.

Chitereka, C. (1999), Poverty and the Role of Social Workers in Poverty Alleviation: The Case of Zimbabwe. *African Journal of Social Work*, 1(1), 1–14.

Chow, N.W.W. (1987), Western and Chinese Ideas of Social Welfare. *International Social Work*, 30(1), 31–41.

Chow, N. (1996), Social Work Education: East and West. *Asian Pacific Journal of Social Work*, 6(2), 5–15.

Christensen, P. and Lilley, I. (1997), *The Road Forward? Alternative Assessment for Aboriginal and Torres Strait Islander Students at the Tertiary Level*. Brisbane: University of Queensland, Aboriginal and Torres Strait Islander Studies Unit.

Churchill, W. (1991), *Fantasies of the Master Race*. Monroe, ME: Common Courage Press.

Churchward, C.M. (1959), *Tongan Dictionary: Tongan-English and English-Tongan*. Nuku'alofa: The Government of Tonga.

Clark, J. (2000), *Beyond Empathy: An Ethnographic Approach to Cross-cultural Social Work Practice*. Unpublished manuscript, Faculty of Social Work, University of Toronto.

Clark, M.E. (1998), Human Nature: What We Need to Know About Ourselves in the Twenty-first Century. *Zygote*, 33(4), 645–59.

Clifford, J. and Marcus, G.E. (1986), *Writing Culture: The Poetics and Politics of Ethnography*. Berkeley: University of California Press.

Clifford, W. (1966), *A Primer of Social Casework in Africa*. Nairobi: Oxford University Press.

Coates, J. (2000), *From Modernism to Sustainability: New Roles for Social Work*. Paper presented at the Joint Conference of the IFSW and the ISASSW, Montreal.

Coates, J. (2003), *Ecology and Social Work: Toward a New Paradigm*. Halifax, Canada: Fernwood Press.

Coates, J., Gray, M. and Hetherington, T. (2006), An 'Ecospiritual' Perspective: Finally, a Place for Indigenous Approaches. *British Journal of Social Work*, 36, 381–99.

Cole, A., Haskins, V. and Paisley, F. (eds) (2005), *Uncommon Ground: White Women in Aboriginal History*. Canberra: Aboriginal Studies Press.

Cole, N. (2006), Trauma and the American Indian, in M. Tawa Witko (ed.), *Mental Health Care for Urban Indians: Clinical Insights from Native Practitioners*. Washington: American Psychological Association, pp. 115–30.

Collard, D., Crowe, S., Harries, M. and Taylor, C. (1994), The Contribution of Aboriginal Families Values to Australian Family Life, in J. Inglis and L. Rogan (eds), *Flexible Families: New Directions for Australian Communities*. Sydney: Pluto Press.

Collins, P.H. (1991), *Black Feminist Thought: Knowledge, Consciousness and the Politics of Empowerment*. New York: Routledge.

Commonwealth Department of Education, Science and Training (2002), *Achieving Equitable and Appropriate Outcomes: Indigenous Australians in Higher Education*. Canberra: Commonwealth Department of Communication, Information Technology and the Arts.

Compton, B. and Galaway, B. (1989), *Social Work Processes*. New York: Wadsworth Publishing Company.

Connell, J. (1987), *Migration, Employment and Development in the South Pacific: New Zealand*. Noumea: South Pacific Commission.

Cornell, S. (1999), Indigenous Peoples, Poverty and Self-determination in Australia, New Zealand, Canada and the United States, in R. Eversole, J.A. McNeish and A.D. Cimadamore (eds), *Indigenous Peoples and Poverty: An International Perspective*. London: Zed Books.

Costa, M.D. (1987), Current Influence of Social Work in Brazil: Practice and Education. *International Social Work*, 30(2), 115–28.

Cox, D. (1991), Social Work Education in the Asia-Pacific Region. *Asia Pacific Journal of Social Work*, 1(1), 7–14.

Crabtree, S.A. (1999), Exclusion and Stigma: Implication for Community Psychiatric Services in Sarawak, Malaysia. *Asia Pacific Journal of Social Work*, 9(1), 114–26.

Crabtree, S.A. and Chong, G. (1999), Psychiatric Outreach Work in Sarawak, Malaysia. *Breakthrough*, 2(4), 49–60.

Crapanzano, V. (1973), *The Hamadsha: A Study in Moroccan Ethno-Psychiatry*. Berkeley: University of California Press.

Crawford, F. (1994), *Emic Social Work: A Story of Practice*. Unpublished doctoral dissertation, University of Illinois at Urbana-Champain, Urbana, IL.

Crawford, F. (1996), Using Self for Social Work: Doing Auto-ethnography. *Advances in Social Work Education*, 2(1), 75–81.

Dale, J. and Middleton, H. (1990), Factors Influencing General Practitioners' Management of Psychosocial and Physical Problems: A Study Using Case Vignettes. *The British Journal of General Practice: The Journal of the Royal College of General Practitioners*, 40(336), 284–8.

Dean, R. (2001), The Myth of Cross-cultural Competence. *Families in Society: The Journal of the Contemporary Human Services*, 82(6), 623–30.

Deb, P.C. and Jindal, R.B. (1974), *Drinking in Rural Area: A Study in Selected Villages of Punjab*. Ludhiana, India: Pubjab Agricultural University.

de Ishtar, Z. (2004), Living on the Ground Research: Steps Toward White Women Researching in Collaboration with Indigenous People. *Hecate*, 30(1), 72–83.

Dei, G.J.S., Hall, B.L. and Rosenberg, D.G. (2000), *Indigenous Knowledge in Global Contexts: Multiple Readings of Our World*. Toronto: University of Toronto Press.

Deloria, V. Jr. (1991), *Indian Education in America: Eight Essays by Vine Deloria Jr.* Boulder, CO: American Indian Science & Engineering Society.

Denver Channel News, The (2006), *CU to Fire Ward Churchill: Professor Has Vowed to Sue if School Fired Him*. Accessed 7 November, <www.thedenverchannel.com/news/9424240/detail.html>, see also <www.en.wikipedia.org/wiki/Ward_Churchill>.

Department of Aboriginal and Torres Strait Islander Development (1999), *The Aboriginal and Torres Strait Islander (ATSI) Women's Task Force on Violence Report*. Brisbane, Queensland: Department of Aboriginal and Torres Strait Islander Development.

Department of Immigration and Multicultural and Indigenous Affairs (DIMIA) (2002), *Indigenous Australians: A National Commitment*. Canberra: Commonwealth of Australia.

Devore, W. and Schlesinger, E.G. (1995), *Ethnic-Sensitive Social Work Practice*. Boston: Allyn & Bacon.

Devore, W. and Schlesinger, E.G. (1999), *Ethnic-Sensitive Social Work Practice* (5th edn). Boston: Allyn and Bacon.

Diamond, J. (2005), *Collapse: How Societies Choose to Fail or Survive*. New York: Allen Lane.

Dillingham, B. (1977), Sterilization of Native Americans. *American Indian Journal*, 3, 16.

Dirlik, A. (1987), Culturalism as Hegemonic Ideology and Liberating Practice. *Cultural Critique*, 6, 13–50.

Dissanayake, E. (1995), *Homo Aestheticus*. Seattle, WA: University of Washington Press.

Dixon, J. (1981), *The Chinese Welfare System 1949–1979*. New York: Praeger.

Dodson, P. (2005), A Nation Dispossessed. *The Age*, 1 June, p. 21.

Dominelli, L. (1989), An Uncaring Profession? An Examination of Racism in Social Work. *New Community*, 5(3), 391–403.

Dominelli, L. (1997), *Antiracist Social Work* (2nd edn). London: Macmillan.

Dominelli, L. (1998), Anti-oppressive Practice in Context, in R. Adams, L. Dominelli and M. Payne (eds), *Social Work Themes, Issues and Critical Debates*. London: Macmillan.

Dominelli, L. (2004), *Social Work: Theory and Practice for a Changing Profession*. Cambridge: Polity Press.

Drucker, D. (ed.) (1993), The Social Work Profession in Asia: A Look Homeward 1968–1993. *Indian Journal of Social Work*, 54(4), 513–36.

Dube, K.C. and Handa, S.K. (1969), Drug Habit in Health and Mental Disorders. *Indian Journal of Psychiatry*, 11(1), 23–9.

Dunning, D.W. (1972), Limits to the Amount of Noise. *International Social Work*, 15(2), 4–7.

Durie, M. (1998), *Te Mann Te Kawanatanga: The Politics of Māori Self Determination*. Auckland: Oxford University Press.

Durie, M. (2003), *Te Kahmi Pou Launching Māori Futures*. Wellington: Huia Publishers.

Economist (2006), A New Train Set. *The Economist* (Canadian edn, 25 March), 378(8470), 69.

Egan, R. (2004), Introduction to Engagement, in J. Maidment and R. Egan (eds), *Practice Skills in Social Work and Welfare*. Crows Nest, NSW: Allen and Unwin, pp. 69–87.

Eisler, R. (1987), *The Chalice and the Blade*. New York: HarperCollins.

Ejaz, F.K. (1989), The Nature of Casework in India: A Study of Social Workers' Perception in Bombay. *International Social Work*, 32(1), 25–38.

Ejaz, F.K. (1991), Social Work Education in India: Perceptions of Social Workers in Bombay. *International Social Work*, 34(3), 299–311.

Elgin, D. (1993), *Voluntary Simplicity* (revised edn). New York: William Morrow.

El-Islam, M.F. (1982), Arabic Cultural Psychiatry. *Transcultural Psychiatric Research Review*, 19(1), 5–24.

Elliott, D. (1993), Social Work and Social Development: Towards an Integration Model for Social Work Practice. *International Social Work*, 36(1), 21–36.

Elson-Green, J. (2002), What Makes a Great Teacher? *Campus Review*, July, p. 6.

Enriquez, V.G. (1993), Developing a Filipino Psychology, in U. Kim and J.W. Berry (eds), *Indigenous Psychology: Research and Experience in Cultural Context*. Newbury Park, CA: Sage, pp. 152–69.

Ermine, W. (1995), Aboriginal Epistemology, in M. Battiste and J. Barman (eds), *First Nations Education in Canada: The Circle Unfolds*. Vancouver: UBC Press, pp. 101–12.

Evans, M. (2001), *Persistence of the Gift: Tongan Tradition in Transnational Context*. Waterloo: Wilfrid Laurier University Press.

Ewalt, P. and Makuau, N. (1995), Self-determination from a Pacific Perspective. *Social Work*, 40(2), 168–75.

Ezaz, F.K. (1991), Social Work Education in India: Perceptions of Social Workers in Bombay. *International Social Work*, 34(3), 299–311.

Fanon, F. (1967), *White Skin, Black Masks*. New York: Grove Press.

Fei, X. (1998), From Reflection to Self-consciousness and Communication. *Dushu*, 236, 3–8.

Ferguson, H. (2001), Social Work, Individualization and Life Politics. *British Journal of Social Work*, 31(1), 41–55.

Ferguson, K.M. (2005), Beyond Indigenization and Reconceptualization: Towards a Global, Multidirectional Model of Technology Transfer. *International Social Work*, 48(5), 519–35.

Ferguson, N. (2004), *Colossus: The Price of America's Empire*. New York: Penguin Press.

Fernández-Armesto, F. (2000), *Civilizations*. London: Macmillan.

Fihn, S.D. (2000), The Quest to Quantify. *Journal of the American Medical Association*, 283, 1740–41.

Foley, G. (2000), Whiteness and Blackness in the Koori Struggle for Self-Determination: Strategic Considerations in the Struggle for Social Justice for Indigenous People. *Just Policy*, 19/20, 74–88.

Fook, J. (2002), *Social Work: Critical Theory and Practice*. London: Sage.

Forgey, M., Cohen, C. and Chazin, R. (2003), Surviving Translation: Teaching the Essentials of Foundation Social Work Practice in Vietnam. *Journal of Teaching in Social Work*, 23(1), 147–66.

Four Worlds Development Project (1982), *Twelve Principles of Indian Philosophy*. Lethbridge, Alberta: University of Lethbridge.

Fournier, S. and Crey, E. (1997), *Stolen from Our Embrace: The Abduction of First Nations Children and the Restoration of Aboriginal Communities*. Vancouver: Douglas & McIntyre.

Francis, L. (2000), The Shadow Knows: A Native Philosophical Perspective on the Light and Dark Side of the Soul. *Ayaangwaamizin: The International Journal of Indigenous Philosophy*, 2(2), 171–85.

Frank, A.G. (1975), *On Capitalist Underdevelopment*. New York: Oxford University Review Press.

Fraser, H. and Briskman, L. (2005), Through the Eye of a Needle: The Challenge of Getting Justice in Australia if You're Indigenous or Seeking Asylum, in I. Ferguson, M. Lavalette and E. Whitmore (eds), *Globalisation, Global Justice and Social Work*. London: Routledge.

Freire, P. (1970), *The Pedagogy of the Oppressed*. New York: Herder and Herder.

Freire, P. (1985), Rethinking Critical Pedagogy: A Dialogue with Paulo Freire, in P. Freire (ed.), *The Politics of Education: Culture, Power and Liberation*. South Hadley, MA: Bergin & Garvey.

Freire, P. (2000), *Pedagogy of the Oppressed* (30th Anniversary edn). New York: Continuum International Publishing Group.

Friedlander, W.A. (1975), *International Social Welfare*. Englewood Cliffs, New Jersey: Prentice-Hall, Inc.

Frum, D. and Perle, R. (2003) *An End to Evil*. New York: Random House.

Gair, S. and Pagliano, P. (2006), In Search of Spaces to Rightly Teach, Research and Write: Academic 'White Noise' or Beginning Conversations for Possibilities Beyond Colonialism? *Journal of Teaching in Higher Education* (forthcoming).

Gair, S., Thomson, J. and Miles, D. (2005a), Reconciling Indigenous and Non-Indigenous Knowledges in Social Work Education: Action and Legitimacy. *Journal of Social Work Education*, 41(2), 371–82.

Gair, S., Thomson, J. and Savage, D. (2005b), What's Stopping Them? Barriers Hindering Indigenous Students from Completing a BSW at JCU. *Advances in Social Welfare Education*, 7(1), 54–66.

Gaita, R. (1999), *A Common Humanity: Thinking About Love and Truth, and Justice.* Melbourne: Text Publishing.

Galeano, E. (1973), *Open Veins of Latin America: Five Centuries of the Pillage of a Continent.* New York: Monthly Review Press.

Galper, J. (1975), *The Politics of Social Services.* Englewood Cliffs, New Jersey: Prentice-Hall.

Galper, J. (1980), *Social Work Practice: A Radical Approach.* Englewood Cliffs, New Jersey: Prentice-Hall.

Gangrade, K.D. (1986), *Social Work and Development.* Allahabad: Northern Book Centre.

Ganim, A. and Smooha, S. (2001), *Attitudes of the Arabs to the State of Israel.* Accessed 1 August 2003, <www.66.155.17.109/peace/pyblications.asp#academic>.

Garber, R. (1997), Social Work Education in an International Context, in M.C. Hokenstad and J. Midgley (eds), *Issues in International Social Work: Global Challenges for a New Century.* Washington, DC: NASW Press.

Garber, R. (2000), Effects of the Global Economy on Social Work Practice, Education and Research. Paper presented at the Joint Conference of the IFSW and IASSW, Montreal.

Garroutte, E.M. (2003), *Real Indians: Identity and the Survival of Native America.* Berkeley, CA: University of California Press.

Gavazzi, S.M., Alford, K.A. and McHenry, P.C. (1996), Culturally Specific Programmes for Foster Care Youth: The Sample Case of an African American Rites of Passage Programme. *Family Relations*, 45(2), 166–74.

Geertz, C. (1973), *The Interpretation of Cultures: Selected Essays.* New York: Basic Books.

Geertz, C. (1983), *Local Knowledge: Further Essays in Interpretive Anthropology.* New York: Basic Books.

Gelder, K. and Jacobs, J. (1998), *Uncanny Australia: Sacredness and Identity in a Post-Colonial Nation.* Victoria: Melbourne University Press.

Gibelman, M. (2002), Treatment Choices in a Managed Care Environment: A Multi-Disciplinary Exploration. *Clinical Social Work Journal*, 30(2), 199–214.

Giddens, A. (1991), *Modernity and Self-identity.* Stanford: Stanford University Press.

Gilbert, S. (2001), Social Work with Indigenous Australians, in M. Alston and J. McKinnon (eds), *Social Work: Fields of Practice.* Melbourne: Oxford University Press.

Gill, J.H. (2002), *Native American World Views: An Introduction.* New York: Humanity Press.

Glendinning, C. (2002), *Off the Map: An Expedition Deep Into Empire and the Global Economy.* Gabriola Island, BC: New Society Publishers.

Gold, N. and Bogo, M. (1992), Social Work Research in a Multicultural Society: Challenges and Approaches. *Journal of Multicultural Social Work*, 2(4), 7–22.

Good Tracks, J. (1973), Native American Non-interference. *Social Work*, 18(6), 30–5.

Goode, W.J. (1963), *World Revolution and Family Patterns*. New York: Free Press.

Gore, A. (2006), *An Inconvenient Truth*. New York: Rodale Press.

Gore, M.S. (1997), A Historical Perspective of the Social Work Profession. *Indian Journal of Social Work*, 58(3), 442–55.

Government of New Zealand, Children, Young Persons and Their Families Act (1989), accessed 25 October 2006, <www.legislation.govt.nz/libraries/contents/om_isapi.dll?clientID=177008441&infobase=pal_statutes.nfo&jump=a1989-024&softpage=DOC>.

Graham, J.R. (2006), Spirituality and Social Work: A Call for an International Focus of Research. *Arete: A Professional Journal Devoted to Excellence in Social Work*, 30(1), 63–77.

Graham, M.J. (1999), The African-centred World View: Developing a Paradigm for Social Work. *British Journal of Social Work*, 29(2), 251–67.

Graham, M.J. (2002), *Social Work and African-Centred World Views*. Birmingham: Venture.

Grauel, T. (2002), Professional Oversight: The Neglected Histories of Supervision, in M. McMahon and W. Patton (eds), *Supervision in the Helping Profession*. Sydney: Pearson, pp. 3–15.

Graveline, F.J. (1998), *Circleworks: Transforming Ethnocentric Consciousness*. Halifax: Fernwood Publishing.

Gray, M. (1995), The Ethical Implications of Current Theoretical Developments in Social Work. *British Journal of Social Work*, 25(1), 55–70.

Gray, M. (2005), Dilemmas of International Social Work: Paradoxical Processes in Indigenisation, Imperialism and Universalism. *International Journal of Social Welfare*, 14(2), 230–7.

Gray, M. and Allegritti, I. (2002), Cross-cultural Practice and the Indigenisation of African Social Work. *Social Work/Maatskaplike Werk*, 38(4), 324–36.

Gray, M. and Allegritti, I. (2003), Towards Culturally Sensitive Social Work Practice: Re-examining Cross-cultural Social Work. *Social Work/Maatskaplike Werk*, 39(4), 312–25.

Gray, M. and Coates, J. (2006), The Eco-spiritual Perspective: Creating Space for Indigenous Voices. Paper presented at the 33rd Congress of Social Work, *Growth and Inequality: Scenarios and Challenges of Social Work in the XXI Century*. Santiago, Chile, 28 August–1 September.

Gray, M. and Fook, J. (2004), The Quest for Universal Social Work: Some Issues and Implications. *Social Work Education*, 23(5), 625–44.

Gray, M. and Powell, W. (forthcoming), *The Art of Engagement: Rediscovering Meaning in Professional Life*. Chicago, IL: Lyceum.

Gray, M. and Simpson, B. (1998), Developmental Social Work Education: A Field Example. *International Social Work*, 41(2), 227–37.

Gray, M., Mazibuko, F. and O'Brien, F. (1996), Social Work Education for Social Development. *Journal of Social Development in Africa*, 11(1), 33–42.

Green, J. (1982), *Cultural Awareness in the Human Services*. New Jersey: Prentice Hall.

Green, J. (1999), *Final Report First Nations Program Strategy*. School of Social Work, University of Victoria. Unpublished document.

Griffin, K. (1978), *International Inequality and National Poverty*. London: Macmillan.

Griffin-Pierce, T. (1997), 'When I am Lonely the Mountains Call Me': The Impact of Sacred Geography on Navajo Psychological Well-being. *American Indian and Alaska Native Mental Health Research Journal*, 7(3), 1–10.

Groome, H. (1995), Towards Improved Understandings of Aboriginal Young People. *Youth Studies Australia*, 14(4), 17–21.

Gross, L.W. (2003), Cultural Sovereignty and Native American Hermeneutics in the Interpretation of the Sacred Stories of the Anishinaabe. *Wicazo Sa Review*, 18(3), 127–34.

Guha, R. and Spivak, G.C. (1988), *Selected Subaltern Studies*. New York: Oxford University Press.

Habermas, J. (1994), Struggles for Recognition in the Democratic Constitutional State, in A. Gutman (ed.), *Multiculturalism: Examining the Politics of Recognition*. Princeton, NJ: Princeton University Press.

Hagan, E. (1962), *On the Theory of Social Change*. Homewood, IL: Dorsey Press.

Hall, S. (1996), The West and the Rest: Discourse and Power, in S. Hall, D. Held, D. Hubert and K. Thompson (eds), *Modernity: An Introduction to Modern Societies*. Oxford: Blackwell, pp. 184–227.

Hall, S. (2000), Old and New Identities, Old and New Ethnicities, in L. Back and J. Solomos (eds), *Theories of Race and Racism*. London: Routledge, pp. 144–53.

Hana, N.S. (1984), *The Desert Societies in the Arab World* (in Arabic). Cairo: Daar Al-Marif Press.

Hardt, M. and Negri, A. (2000), *Empire*. Cambridge, MA: Harvard University Press.

Hare, I. (2004), Defining Social Work for the 21st Century: The International Federation of Social Workers' Revised Definition of Social Work. *International Social Work*, 47(3), 407 24.

Harris, B. (2002), *First Nations Bachelor of Social Work Curriculum Workshop Report*. Vancouver: UBC School of Social Work and Family Studies. Unpublished document.

Harris, J. and Chou, Y.-C. (2001), Globalization or Glocalization? Community Care in Taiwan and Britain. *European Journal of Social Work*, 4(2), 161–72.

Harris, J. and McDonald, C. (2000), Post-Fordism, the Welfare State and the Personal Social Services: A Comparison of Australia and Britain. *British Journal of Social Work*, 30, 51–70.

Hart, M.A. (1997), *An Ethnographic Study of Sharing Circles as a Culturally Appropriate Practice Approach with Aboriginal People*. An unpublished Master's Thesis. University of Manitoba, Winnipeg, Manitoba.

Hart, M.A. (1999), Seeking Mino-pimatasiwin (the good life). An Aboriginal Approach to Social Work Practice. *The Native Social Work Journal: Nishnaabe Kinoomaadwin Naamaadwin*, 2(1), 91–112.

Hart, M.A. (2001), An Aboriginal Approach to Social Work Practice, in T. Heinonen and L. Spearman (eds), *Social Work Practice: Problem Solving and Beyond.* Toronto: Nelson, pp. 235–60.

Hart, M.A. (2002), *Seeking Mino-Pimatisiwin: An Aboriginal Approach to Helping.* Halifax: Fernwood Publishing.

Hart, M.A. (2006), An Aboriginal Approach to Social Work Practice, in T. Heinonen and L. Spearman (eds), *Social Work Practice: Problem Solving and Beyond* (2nd edn). Toronto: Nelson, pp. 235–60.

Hartman, A. (1990a), Many Ways of Knowing. *Social Work*, 35(1), 3–4.

Hartman, A. (1990b), Our Global Village. *Social Work*, 35(4), 291–2.

Hartman, A. (1992), In Search of Subjugated Knowledge. *Social Work*, 37(6), 484.

Harvey, A.R. and Coleman, A.A. (1997), An Afrocentric Programme for African-American Males in the Juvenile Justice System. *Child Welfare*, 76(1), 197–211.

Harvey, A.R. and Rauch, J.B. (1997), A Comprehensive Rites of Passage Programme for Black Male Adolescents. *Health and Social Work*, 22(1), 30–37.

Harvey, D. (2003), *The New Imperialism.* New York: Oxford University Press.

Haug, E. (2001), *Writing in the Margins: Critical Reflection on the Emerging Discourse of International Social Work.* Unpublished MSW Thesis. Faculty of Social Work, University of Calgary, Canada.

Haug, E. (2005), Critical Reflections on the Emerging Discourse of International Social Work. *International Social Work*, 48(2), 126–35.

Hau'ofa, E. (1994), Our Sea of Islands. *The Contemporary Pacific*, 6(1), 148–61.

Hawa Ali, S. (1991), Western Theory and Local Practice: Implications for Social Work Practice in Malaysia, *Asia Pacific Journal of Social Work*, 1(1), 26–47.

Hawken, D. and Worrall, J. (2002), Reciprocal Mentoring Supervision. Partners in Learning: A Personal Perspective, in M. McMahon and W, Patton (eds), *Supervision in the Helping Profession.* Sydney: Pearson, pp. 43–53.

Haynes, K. (1998), The One Hundred-year Debate: Social Reform Versus Individual Treatment. *Social Work*, 43, 501–9.

Healy, K. (2000), *Social Work Practices: Contemporary Perspectives on Change.* Thousand Oaks: Sage.

Healy, L. (2001), *International Social Work: Professional Action in An Interdependent World.* New York: Oxford University Press.

Healy, L.M. (2002), Internationalizing Social Work Curriculum in the Twenty-first Century. *Electronic Journal of Social Work*, 1(1), <www.ejsw.net> (URL no longer accessible).

Healy, L.M., Asamoah, Y. and Hokenstad, M.C. (2003), *Models of International Collaboration in Social Work Education.* Alexandria, VA: Council on Social Work Education.

Hegel, G.W.F. (1977 [1807]), *Phenomenology of Spirit.* Trans. by A.V. Miller. Oxford: Oxford University Press.

Heinonen, T. and Spearman, L. (2001), *Social Work Practice: Problem Solving and Beyond* (2nd edn). Toronto: Nelson, pp. 235–60.

Helu, F. (1999), *Critical Essays: Cultural Perspectives From the South Seas.* Canberra: The Journal of Pacific History.

Herbert, J. (2000), Getting to the Heart of the Matter: The Importance of the Aboriginal Community Voice in Education. *Queensland Journal of Educational Research*, 16(2), 130–46.

Herda, P. (1995), Hierarchy and the Prerogatives of History-making in Tonga, in J. Huntsman (ed.), *Tonga and Samoa: Images of Gender and Polity*. Christchurch: Macmillan Brown Centre for Pacific Studies, pp. 37–57.

Heron, J. (1992), *Feelings and Personhood*. California: Sage.

Hodge, P. (1980), *Social Work Education, Community Problems and Social Work in Southeast Asia*. Hong Kong: Hong Kong University Press.

Hoey, J.M. (1954), Professional Implications of International Social Work Development, in C. Kasius (ed.), *New Directions in Social Work*. New York: Harper.

Hofrichter, R. (ed.) (1993), *Toxic Struggles: The Theory and Practice of Environmental Justice*. Philadelphia, PA: New Society.

Hokenstad, M.C.J. and Midgley, J. (1997), Realities of Global Interdependence: Challenges for Social Work in the New Century, in M.C.J. Hokenstad and J. Midgley (eds), *Issues in International Social Work: Global Challenges for a New Century*. Washington DC: NASW Press, pp. 1–10.

Hokenstad, M.C.J. and Midgley, J. (eds) (2004), *Lessons From Abroad: Adapting International Social Welfare Innovations*. Washington DC: NASW Press.

Holt, L. (1999), Pssst ... I Wannabe White, in B. McKay (ed.), *Whiteness, Race Relations and Reconciliation*. Griffith University, Brisbane: The Queensland Studies Centre, pp. 39–44.

hooks, B. (1981), *Ain't I a Woman: Black Women and Feminism*. Boston: South End Press.

hooks, B. (1993), *Sisters of the Yam: Black Women and Self-Recovery*. Boston: South End Press.

Hozelitz, B.F. (1960), *Sociological Factors in Economic Development*. New York: Free Press.

Huang, K. (1978), Matching Needs with Services: Shoes for the Chinese Feet. *International Social Work*, 21(1), 44 54.

Huggins, J. (1998), *Sister Girl*. St Lucia: University of Queensland Press.

Hughes, L. (2003), *The No-Nonsense Guide to Indigenous Peoples*. Oxford, UK: New Internationalist Publications in association with Verso.

Hugman, R. (1996), Professionalization in Social Work: The Challenge of Diversity. *International Social Work*, 39(1), 131–47.

Human Rights and Equal Opportunity Commission (1997), *Guide to the Findings and Recommendations of the National Inquiry into the Separation of Aboriginal and Torres Strait Islander Children from their Families*. Canberra: Australian Government Publishing Service.

Husband, C. (1990), Social Work with Australian Multiculturalism: Conceptualizing the Challenge, in M. Clare and L. Jayasuriya (eds), *Issues of Cross Cultural Practice*. Nedlands, WA: University of Western Australia.

Hutton, M. (1992), *Social Work: An Extension of Community*. Professorial Inaugural Lecture Series No. 6. Gaborone: University of Botswana.

Hutton, M. (1994), *Reshaping the Social Work Curriculum: An African Experience.* Paper presented at the Congress of the International Association of Schools of Social Work. Amsterdam: IASSW.

Hutton, M. and Mwansa, L.-K. (eds) (1996), *Social Work Practice in Africa: Social Development in a Community Context.* Gaborone: Print Consult.

Ife, J. (2001), *Human Rights and Social Work: Towards Rights-Based Practice.* Cambridge: Cambridge University Press.

Ife, J. (2002), *Community Development: Community-Based Alternatives in An Age of Globalisation* (2nd edn). Frenchs Forest: Longman/Pearson Education Australia.

Ihimaera, L. (2004), *He Ara ke te Ao Marama: A Pathway to Understanding the Facilitation of Taha Wairua in Mental Health Services.* Unpublished Masters Thesis. Massey University, To Ntahi a Toi, School of Māori Studies: Palmerston North.

Indigenous Higher Education Advisory Council (2006), *Improving Indigenous Outcomes and Enhancing Indigenous Culture and Knowledge in Australian Higher Education.* Commonwealth of Australia: Report to the Minister for Education, Science and Training. Accessed 23 August, <www.dest.gov.au/ sectors/indigenous_education/publications_resources/profiles/improving_indig_ outcomes.html>.

International Association of Schools of Social Work (IASSW) (2004), *Global Standards for Social Work Education and Training.* Accessed 18 October 2006, <www.iassw-aiets.org/>.

International Federation of Social Workers (IFSW) (2002), *Definition of Social Work.* Berne, Switzerland: IFSW.

Israeli Government (2002), *State Comptroller's Report, No. 52B.* Accessed 1 August 2003, <www.mevaker.gov.il>.

Ivey, A.E., D'Andrea, M., Bradford Ivey, M. and Simek-Morgan, L. (2002), *Theories of Counseling and Psychotherapy: A Multicultural Perspective* (5th edn). Toronto: Allyn and Bacon.

Jacques, G. (2000), The Baby and the Bath Water: The Dilemma of Modern Social Work in Africa. *Social Work/Maatskaplike Werk*, 36(4), 361–76.

James, K.E. (1995), 'Rank Overrules Everything': Hierarchy, Social Stratification and Gender in Tonga, in J. Huntsman (ed.), *Tonga and Samoa: Images of Gender and Polity.* Christchurch: Macmillan Brown Centre for Pacific Studies, pp. 59–83.

Jarvis, G.M. (1977), The Theft of Life. *Akwesasne Notes*, September, pp. 30–2. Originally published in the *National Catholic Reporter*, 27 May.

Jensen, R. (2005), *The Heart of Whiteness.* San Francisco, CA: City Lights.

Jinchao, Y. (1995), The Developing Models of Social Work Education in China. *International Social Work*, 38, 27–38.

John, M. (2006), A Message from the Treasurer. *Seneca Nation of Indians Newsletter*, 24 Febuary.

Johnson, E. (1991), *Royal Commission into Aboriginal Deaths in Custody: National Report.* Canberra: Australian Government Publishing Service.

Jones, H. (1990), *Social Welfare in Third World Development.* London: Macmillan.

Ka'ili, T.O. (2005), Tauhi va: Nurturing Tongan Socio-spatial Ties in Maui and Beyond. *Contemporary Pacific*, 17(1), 83–114.

Kanaana, S. (1992), Still on Vacation. *The Jerusalem Centre for Palestinian Studies*, pp. 67–71.

Kandiah, M. (1991), The National Social Welfare Policy of Malaysia, in K.S. Cho and M.S. Ismail (eds), *Caring Society: Emerging Trends and Future Direction*. Malaysia: Institute of Strategic and International Studies.

Karl, R.E. (2005), 'Joining Tracks with the World': The Impossibility of Politics in China. *Radical Philosophy*, 131, 20–27.

Kaseke, E. (2001), Social Development as a Model of Social Work Practice: The Experience of Zimbabwe, in L. Dominelli, W. Lorenz and H. Soydan (eds), *Beyond Racial Divides: Ethnicities in Social Work Practice*. Aldershot: Ashgate, pp. 105–16.

Kavaliku, S.L. (1961), *An Analysis of 'Ofa*. Unpublished Bachelor of Arts with Honors Thesis, Harvard University.

Keesing, R.M. (1981), *Cultural Anthropology: A Contemporary Perspective* (2nd edn). New York: Holt, Reinehart and Winston.

Kehoe, J. (2002), *Mind Power into the 21st Century: Techniques to Harness the Astounding Powers of Thought*. Vancouver, BC: Zoetic, Inc.

Kendall, K.A. (1973), Dream or Nightmare? The Future of Social Work Education. *International Social Work*, 16(2), 56–60.

Kennedy, J. (1967), Nubian Zar Ceremonies as Psychotherapy. *Human Organization*, 26(4), 185–94.

Kennedy, M. (1990), *Born a Half Caste*. Canberra: Aboriginal Studies Press.

Kenny, S. (1994), *Developing Communities for the Future: Community Development in Australia*. Melbourne: Thomas Nelson.

Khan, M.Z. and Krishna, K.P. (1982), Research on Drug Dependence in India. *Bulletin on Narcotics*, 34(2), 20–50.

Khinduka, S.K. (1971), Social Work in the Third World. *Social Service Review*, 45(2), 62–73.

Kilpatrick, A.C. and Zhang, M.-J. (1993), Family Mediation in the United States and China: A Relevant Method in Social Work Education for a Vulnerable Population. *International Social Work*, 36(1), 75–85.

Kim, U. (2000), Indigenous, Cultural, and Cross-cultural Psychology: A Theoretical, Conceptual and Epistemological Analysis. *Asian Journal of Social Psychology*, 3, 265–87.

Kissman, K. and Maurer, L. (2002), East Meets West: Therapeutic Aspects of Spirituality in Health, Mental Health and Addiction Recovery. *International Social Work*, 45(1), 37–43.

Koegel, P. (1992), Through a Different Lens: An Anthropological Perspective on the Homeless Mentally Ill. *Culture, Medicine and Psychiatry*, 16, 1–22.

Krause, K., Hartley, R., James, R. and McInnis, C. (2005), *The First Year Experience in Australian Universities: Findings From a Decade of National Studies*. Centre for the Study of Higher Education, University of Melbourne.

Ku, H.B., Yeung, S.C. and Sung, P. (2005), Searching for a Capacity Building Model in Social Work Education. *Social Work Education*, 24(2), 213–33.

Kulkarni, P.D. (1993), The Indigenous-base of Social Work Profession in India. *Indian Journal of Social Work*, 54(4), 555–65.

Kung, W.W. (2005), Western Model, Eastern Context: Cultural Adaptations of Family Interventions for Patients with Schizophrenia in China. *International Social Work*, 48(4), 409–18.

Kwok, S. and Tam, D.M.Y. (2005), Child Abuse in Chinese Families in Canada: Implications for Child Protection Practice. *International Social Work*, 48(3), 341–8.

Laird, J. (1998), Theorizing Culture: Narrative Ideas and Practice Principles, in M. McGoldrick (ed.), *Re-Visioning Family Therapy.* New York: Guilford Press.

Lal, B. and Singh, G. (1978), Alcohol Consumption in Punjab. *Indian Journal of Psychiatry*, 20, 212–16.

Lal, D. (2004), *In Praise of Empires: Globalization and Order.* New York: Palgrave.

Lampert, J. and Lilley, I. (1996), *Indigenous Australian Perspectives at the University of Queensland.* Aboriginal and Torres Strait Islander Studies Unit, Research Report Series. Brisbane, Australia: University of Queensland Press.

Langford, R. (1988), *Don't Take Your Love to Town.* Victoria: Penguin.

Langton, M. (2002), A New Deal? Indigenous Development and the Politics of Recovery. *Dr Charles Perkins Memorial Oration*, University of Sydney.

Larson, G. and Brown, L. (1997), Teaching Research to Aboriginal Students. *Journal of Teaching in Social Work*, 15(1/2), 205–15.

Larson, K. (1977), And Then There Were None. Originally published in *Christian Century*, 26 January, p. 61. Accessed 27 October 2006, <www.religion-online. org/showarticle.asp?title=1133977>.

Latouche, S. (1993 [1991]), *In the Wake of the Affluent Society: An Exploration of Post-Development* (M. O'Connor and R. Arnoux, trans.). London: Zed Books.

Lawrence, J. (2000), The Indian Health Service and the Sterilization of Native American Women. *American Indian Quarterly*, 24(3), 400–23.

Lee, D. (1995), Writing in a Colonial Space: Cadence, in B. Ashcroft, G. Griffiths and H. Tiffin (eds), *The Post-Colonial Studies Reader.* London: Routledge, pp. 397–401.

Lee, W. (2001), Chinese Counseling Method: Ways to Indigenization. *Hong Kong Journal of Social Work*, 35(1/2), 35–49.

Leggo, C. (1997), Curriculum as Narrative/Narrative as Curriculum: Lingering in the Spaces. *On-Line Issues*, 4(1). University of British Columbia: Centre for the Study of Curriculum and Instruction. Accessed 10 December 2003, <www.csci. educ.ubc.ca/publication/insight/archive/vo4no1/postscri.html>.

Lei, J.Z. and Shui, Z.Z. (1991), The Thirty Years of the Social Work Programme of Yanjing University, in W.S. Chow (ed.), *Status-Quo, Challenge and Prospect: Collected Works of the Seminar of the Asian-Pacific Region Social Work Education.* Beijing: Peking University Press (in Chinese), pp. 10–16.

Lemkin, R. (1944), *Axis Rule in Occupied Europe: Laws of Occupation – Analysis of Government – Proposals for Redress Chapter IX: Genocide a New Term and New Conception for Destruction of Nations.* Washington, DC: Carnegie Endowment for International Peace.

Leonard, P. (1997), *Post-Modern Welfare: Reconstructing an Emancipatory Project.* London: Thousand Oaks, CA: Sage Publications.

Lerner, D. (1958), *The Passing of Traditional Society*. New York: Free Press.

Levitt, T. (1983), The Globalization of Markets. *Harvard Business Review*, May–June, pp. 2–11.

Lieberman, A. (1990), Culturally Sensitive Intervention with Children and Families. *Child and Adolescent Social Work*, 7(2), 101–20.

Ling, H.K. (2003), Drawing Lessons from Locally Designated Helpers to Develop Culturally Appropriate Social Work Practice. *Asia Pacific Journal of Social Work*, 13(2), 26–44.

Ling, H.K. (2004), The Search from Within: Research Issues in Developing Culturally Appropriate Social Work Practice. *International Social Work*, 47(3), 336–45.

Linnekin, J. and Poyer, L. (1990), Introduction, in J. Linnekin and L. Poyer (eds), *Cultural Identity and Ethnicity in the Pacific*. Honolulu: University of Hawaii Press.

Little Bear, L. (1998), Aboriginal Relations to the Land and Resources, in J. Oakes, R. Riewe, K. Kinew and E. Maloney (eds), *Sacred Lands: Aboriginal World Views, Claims and Conflicts*. Edmonton: Canadian Circumpolar Institute, University of Alberta, pp. 15–20.

Little Bear, L. (2000), Jagged World Views Collide, in M. Battiste (ed.), *Reclaiming Indigenous Voice and Vision*. Vancouver: UBC Press, pp. 77–85.

Liu, M. *et al.* (eds) (2004), *Group Work*. Beijing, China: Higher Education Press.

Long, D.A. and Fox, T. (1996), Circles of Healing: Illness, Healing and Health Among Aboriginal People in Canada, in D.A. Long and O.P. Dickason (eds), *Visions of the Heart: Canadian Aboriginal Issues*. Toronto: Harcourt Brace & Company, pp. 239–69.

Louw, L.R. (1998), Changing Social Welfare Policy in South Africa. *Social Work/Maatskaplike Werk*, 34(1), 134–43.

Lu, Z.J. (1996), Thoughts on the Future Development of Social Work in China, in *Development, Exploration and Indigenization: Proceedings of the Conference on the Development of Social Work Education in Chinese Communities* (in Chinese). Beijing: Chinese Peace Press.

Lum, D. (1996), *Social Work Practice and People of Colour: A Process-Stage Approach* (3rd edn). Pacific Grove: Brooks/Cole Publishing Company.

Lum, D. (1999), *Culturally Competent Practice: A Framework for Growth and Action*. Pacific Grove, CA: Brooks/Cole Publishing Company.

Lynn, R. (2001), Learning from a 'Murri Way'. *British Journal of Social Work*, 31, 903–16.

Lynn, R., Thorpe, R., Miles, D., Cutts, C., Butcher, A. and Ford, L. (1998), *Murri Way!: Aborigines and Torres Strait Islanders Reconstruct Social Welfare Practice*. Centre for Social and Welfare Research: James Cook University, North Queensland.

Macedo, D. and Bartolome, L.I. (1999), *Dancing With Bigotry: Beyond the Politics of Tolerance*. New York: Palgrave.

MacKinnon, D.P., Johnson, C.A., Pentz, M.A., Dwyer, J.H., Hansen, W.B., Flay, B.R. and Wang, E.Y.I. (1991), Mediating Mechanisms in a School-based Drug Prevention Programme: First Year Effects of the Mid-Western Prevention Project. *Health Psychology*, 10(3), 164–72.

MacPherson, S. (1982), *Social Policy in the Developing Nations*. Brighton: Wheatsheaf.

Mafile'o, T. (2004), Exploring Togan Social Work: Fekau'aki (Connecting) and Fakatokilalo (Humility). *Qualitative Social Work*, 3(3), 239–57.

Mafile'o, T. (2005), Community Development: A Tongan Perspective, in M. Nash, R. Munford and K. O'Donoghue (eds), *Social Work Theories in Action*. London: Jessica Kingsley Publishers, pp. 125–39.

Mafile'o, T. (2006), Matakainga (Behaving like Family): The Social Worker–Client Relationship in Pasifika Social Work. *Social Work Review/Tu Mau*, 18(1), 31–6.

Mahina, O. (1993), The Poetics of Tongan Traditional History, Tala-e-fonua – An Ecology-centred Concept of Culture and History. *Journal of Pacific History*, 28(1), 109–21.

Mahina, O. (2004), *Reed Book of Tongan Proverbs*. Auckland: Reed Publishing.

Maier, C. (2006), *Among Empires: American Ascendancy and its Predecessors*. Cambridge, MA: Harvard University Press.

Mamphiswana, D. and Noyoo, N. (2004), Social Work Education in a Changing Socio-political and Economic Dispensation: Perspectives from South Africa. *International Social Work*, 43(1), 21–32.

Mandelbaum, M. (2002), *The Ideas That Conquered the World*. New York: Public Affairs.

Mandelbaum, M. (2005), *The Case for Goliath: How America Acts as the World's Government in the 21st Century*. New York: Public Affairs.

Mangaliso, M.P. (2005), Cultural Mythology and Leadership in South Africa. Symposium Presentation at the Organizational Strategy and Operations Domain, Eastern Academy of Management, *International Managing in a Global Economy XI*, Cape Town, South Africa, June 2005, pp. 585–8.

Mankiller, W. (2004), *Every Day is a Good Day: Reflections by Contemporary Indigenous Women*. Golden, CO: Fulcrum Publishing.

Mannes, M. (1995), Factors and Events Leading to the Passage of the Indian Child Welfare Act. *Child Welfare*, 74(1), 264–82.

Manual, G. and Posluns, M. (1974), *The Fourth World: An Indian Reality*. New York: The Free Press.

Margolin, L. (1997), *Under the Cover of Kindness: The Invention of Social Work*. Charlottesville, VA: University Press of Virginia.

Marks, E. (1974), *The Bedouin Society of the Negev* (in Hebrew). Tel-Aviv: Reshafim Press.

Marsden, M. (1990), *Beyond Science*. Unpublished paper, Auckland.

Martinez-Brawley, E.E. (2000), Social Work, Trans-culturality and Etiquette in the Academy: Implications for Practice. *Families in Society: The Journal of Contemporary Human Services*, 81(2), 197–210.

Martinez-Brawley, E.E. and Brawley, E.A. (1999), Diversity in a Changing World: Cultural Enrichment or Social Fragmentation? *Journal of Multicultural Social Work*, 7(1/2), 19–36.

Mathew, G. (1981), The Concept of Self-determination from a Less used Perspective. *Indian Journal of Social Work*, 41, 376–9.

Maybury-Lewis, D. (1997), *Indigenous Peoples, Ethnic Groups and the State.* Boston, MA: Allyn and Bacon.

Maynard, J. (2005), Light in the Darkness: Elizabeth McKenzie Hatton, in A. Cole, V. Haskins and F. Paisley (eds), *Uncommon Ground: White Women in Aboriginal History.* Canberra: Aboriginal Studies Press, pp. 3–27.

McClelland, D. (1964), A Psychological Approach to Economic Development. *Economic Development and Cultural Change*, 12(2), 320–24.

McConville, G. (2002), Regional Agreements, Higher Education and Representations of Indigenous Reality. *Australian University Review*, 45(1), 15–24.

McDonald, C. (2006), *Challenging Social Work: The Context of Practice.* London: Palgrave Macmillan.

McDonald, C., Harris, J. and Wintersteen, R. (2003), Contingent on Context? Social Work and the State in Australia, Britain and the USA. *British Journal of Social Work*, 33, 191–208.

McIntosh, P. (1988), *White Privilege and Male Privilege: A Personal Account of Coming to See Correspondences Through Work in Women's Studies.* Working Paper 189, Wellesley College Center for Research on Women.

McIntosh, T. (2005), Māori Identities: Fixed, Fluid, Forced, in J. Liu, T. McCreanor, T. McIntosh and T. Teaiwa (eds), *New Zealand Identities: Departures and Destinations.* Wellington: Victoria University Press.

McKendrick, B.W. (1998), Learning from the Past, Building for the Future: The Transformation of Social Welfare and Social Work in South Africa. Editorial. *Social Work/Maatskaplike Werk*, 34(1), i–iii.

McKenzie, B. and Morrissette, V. (2003), Social Work Practice with Canadians of Aboriginal Background: Guidelines for Respectful Social Work, in A. Al-Krenawi and J.R. Graham (eds), *Multicultural Social Work in Canada: Working with Diverse Ethno-Racial Communities.* Don Mills, ON: Oxford University Press, pp. 251–82.

McLeod, J. (2000), *Beginning Post-Colonialism.* Manchester: Manchester University Press.

McMahon, M. (2002), Some Supervision Practicalities, in M. McMahon and W. Patton (eds), *Supervision in the Helping Profession.* Sydney: Pearson, pp. 17–26.

McMaster, M. (1996), *The Intelligence Advantage: Organising for Complexity.* London: Butterworth-Heinemann.

McMillen, J.C., Proctor, E.K., Megivern, D., Striley, C.W., Cabassa, L.J., Munson, M.R. and Dickey, B. (2005), Quality of Care in the Social Services: Research Agenda and Methods. *Social Work Research*, 29(3), 181–91.

McPhatter, A. (1997), Cultural Competence in Child Welfare: What is It? How do we Achieve It? What Happens Without It? *Child Welfare*, 76(1), 255–78.

McPherson, D. and Rabb, J.D. (1993), *Indians From the Inside.* Thunder Bay: Centre for Northern Studies, Lakehead University.

Meemeduma, P. (1993), Reshaping the Future Cultural Sense and Social Work. Paper presented at the *National Social Work Conference*, Newcastle.

Midgley, J. (1981), *Professional Imperialism: Social Work in the Third World.* London: Heinemann Educational Books.

Midgley, J. (1983), *Professional Imperialism: Social Work in the Third World* (2nd edn). London: Heinemann Educational Books.

Midgley, J. (1990), International Social Work: Learning from the Third World. *Social Work*, 35(3), 295–301.

Midgley, J. (1992), Is International Social Work a One-way Transfer of Ideas and Practice Methods from the United States to Other Countries? Yes, in E. Gambrill and R. Pruger (eds), *Controversial Issues in Social Work*. Boston: Allyn and Bacon, pp. 92–8.

Midgley, J. (1995), *Social Development: The Developmental Perspective in Social Welfare*. London: Sage Publications.

Midgley, J. and Livermore, M. (2004), Social Development: Lessons from the Global South, in M.C. Hokenstad and J. Midgley (eds), *Lessons From Abroad: Adapting International Social Welfare Innovations*. Washington, DC: NASW Press.

Midgley, J., Hall, A., Hardimann, M. and Narine, D. (1986), *Community Participation, Development and the State*. London: Methuen.

Mila-Schaaf, K. (2006), Va-centred Social Work: Possibilities for a Pacific Approach to Social Work Practice. *Social Work Review/Tu Mau*, 18(1), 8–13.

Miller, J. (1998), *The Holistic Curriculum*. Toronto: Ontario Institute for Studies in Education.

Mills, S. (2004), *Discourse* (2nd edn). London: Routledge.

Ministerial Advisory Committee on a Maori Perspective for the Department of Social Welfare (1988), *Puao-te-ata-tu (Daybreak): The Report of the Ministerial Advisory Committee on a Maori Perspective for the Department of Social Welfare*. Department of Social Welfare, Wellington.

Mohan, D., Thomas, M.G. and Prabhu, G.G. (1978), Prevalence of Drug Abuse in High School Population. *Indian Journal of Psychiatry*, 20(1), 20–24.

Mokuau, N. (ed.) (1991), *Handbook of Social Services for Asian and Pacific Islanders*. New York: Greenwood Press.

Moreton-Robinson, A. (2000), *Talkin' Up to the White Woman: Indigenous Women and Feminism*. St Lucia: University of Queensland Press.

Morrisseau, C. (1998), *Into the Daylight: A Wholistic Approach to Healing*. Toronto: University of Toronto Press.

Morrissette, V., McKenzie, B. and Morrissette, L. (1993), Towards an Aboriginal Model of Social Work Practice: Cultural Knowledge and Traditional Practices. *Canadian Social Work Review*, 10(1), 91–108.

Morton, H. (1998), Creating their Own Culture: Diasporic Tongans. *Contemporary Pacific*, 10(1), 1–30.

Morton Lee, H. (2003), *Tongans Overseas: Between Two Shores*. Honolulu: University of Hawaii Press.

Mullaly, B. (2007), *The New Structural Social Work*. Don Mills: Oxford University Press.

Mullaly, R. (1993), *Structural Social Work: Ideology, Theory and Practice*. Toronto: McClelland and Stewart.

Munford, R. and Walsh-Tapiata, W. (2000), *Strategies for Change*. Palmerston North: School of Sociology, Social Policy and Social Work, Massey University.

Munford, R. and Walsh-Tapiata, W. (2001), *Strategies for Change: Community Development in Aotearoa/New Zealand* (3rd edn). Palmerston North: Massey University.

Mupedziswa, R. (1992), Africa at a Crossroads: Major Challenges for Social Work Education and Practice Towards the Year 2000. *Journal of Social Development in Africa*, 7(2), 19–38.

Mupedziswa, R. (1993), *Social Work in Äfrica: Critical Essays on the Struggle for Relevance*. Draft Manuscript. Harare: School of Social Work.

Mupedziswa, R. (2001), The Quest for Relevance: Toward a Conceptual Model of Development Social Work Education and Training in Africa. *International Social Work*, 44(3), 285–300.

Muzaale, P. (1987), Social Development, Rural Poverty and Implications for Fieldwork Practice. *Journal of Social Development in Africa*, 2(1), 75–87.

Mwansa, L.-K. (1992), *Radical Social Work Practice: The Case of Africa*. Paper presented at the *National Fieldwork Supervisors Seminar* organized by the University of Botswana. Ramatea, Kanye, 27–29 March.

Mwansa, L.-K. (1996), Contemporary Issues Facing the Social Work Profession in Southern Africa. Paper presented at the *Joint Universities Committee Conference*. Magoebasloof, 9–12 September.

Myrdal, G. (1970), *The Challenge of World Poverty*. Harmondsworth, England: Penguin Books.

Naess, A. (1989), *Ecology, Community and Lifestyle* (D. Rothenberg, trans. and ed.). Cambridge: Cambridge University Press.

Nagey, G. and Falk, D. (2000), Dilemmas in International and Cross-cultural Social Work Education. *International Social Work*, 43(1), 49–60.

Nagpaul, H. (1972), The Diffusion of American Social Work Education to India. *International Social Work*, 15(1), 3–17.

Nagpaul, H. (1993), Analysis of Social Work Teaching Material from India: The Need for Indigenous Foundations. *International Social Work*, 36(3), 207–20.

Nakata, M. and Muspratt, S. (1994), How to Read Across the Curriculum: The Case of a Social Sciences Social Investigation Strategy as Ideological Practice. *The Australian Journal of Language and Literacy*, 17(3), 227–39.

Nanavathy, M.C. (1993), Problems Affecting the Indigenization of Social Work Profession in Asia. *The Indian Journal of Social Work*, 54(4), 547–54.

Narayan, L. (2000), Freire and Gandhi: Their Relevance for Social Work Education. *International Social Work*, 43(2), 193–204.

Nash, J. (2005), The Mayan Quest for Pluri-cultural Autonomy in Mexico and Guatemala, in D. Champagne, K. Jo Torjesen and S. Steiner (eds), *Indigenous Peoples and the Modern State*. Walnut Creek, CA: Alta Mira Press, pp. 121–43.

Nash, M., Munford, R. and O'Donaghue, K. (eds) (2005), *Social Work in Action*. London: Jessica Kingsley.

National Association of Social Workers. (1995), *The 1880s Social Work Milestones*. Accessed 15 March 2006, <www.socialworkers.org>.

National Association of Social Workers (1999), *Code of Ethics of the National Association of Social Workers*. Washington DC: NASW, <http://www.social workers.org/pubs/code/code.asp>.

National Security Report (2004), The Public Department of National Security, Jerusalem.

Neki, J.S. (1973), Guru-chela Relationship: The Possibility of a Therapeutic Paradigm. *American Journal of Orthopsychiatry*, 43(5), 755–66.

Neufeld, K.J., Peters, D.H., Rani, M., Bonu, S. and Brooner, R.K. (2005), Regular Use of Alcohol and Tobacco in India and its Association with Age, Gender and Poverty. *Drug and Alcohol Dependence*, 77(3), 282–91.

Newberry Library (2002), Inventory of the Bureau of Indian Affairs Relocation Records, 1936–1975, Bulk 1956–1958. Accessed 4 June 2006, <www.newberry. org/collections/FindingAids/relocation/relocation.html#d0e131>.

Ngai, N.-P. (1996), Revival of Social Work Education in China. *International Social Work*, 39(3), 289–300.

Ngan, R. (1993), Cultural Imperialism: Western Social Work Theories for Chinese Practice and the Mission of Social Work in Hong Kong. *Hong Kong Journal of Social Work*, 27(2), 47–55.

Ngan, R. and Hui, S. (1996), Economic and Social Development in Hong Kong and Southern China: Implications for Social Work. *International Social Work*, 39(1), 83–95.

Nicola Valley Institute of Technology (2006), *Home Page*. Accessed 27 September 2006, <www.nvit.bc.ca/about/default.htm>.

Nimmagadda, J. and Balgopal, P.R. (2000), Indigenisation of Social Work Knowledge: An Exploration of the Process. *Asia Pacific Journal of Social Work*, 10(2), 4–18.

Nimmagadda, J. and Balgopal, P.R. (2000), Transfer of Knowledge: An Exercise of Adaptation and Indigenization. *Asia Pacific Journal of Social Work*, 10(2), 4–18.

Nimmagadda, J. and Bromley, M. (2006), Building Bridges Through Indigenization. *Reflections: Narratives of Professional Helping*, 12(3), 64–72.

Nimmagadda, J. and Chakradhar, K. (2006), Indigenization of AA in South India. *Asian Pacific Journal of Social Work*, 16(1), 7–20.

Nimmagadda, J. and Cowger, C. (1999), Cross-cultural Practice: Social Worker Ingenuity in the Indigenization of Practice Knowledge. *International Social Work*, 42(3), 261–76.

Nir, O. (2003), *Israel's Arab Minority*. Policy Brief: Middle East Institute. Accessed on 15 September 2005, <www.mideasti.org/articles/doc22.html>.

Ntusi, T.M. (1998), Professional Challenges for South African Social Workers: Response to Recent Political Changes. *Social Work/Maatskaplike Werk*, 34(4), 380–88.

Ogunwole, S.U. (2002), *The American Indian and Alaska Native Population: 2000*. U.S. Bureau of the Census. Accessed 4 June 2006, <www.census.gov/populatio/ www/cen2000/briefs/html>.

Okasha, A. (1999), Mental Health Services and in the Arab World. *Eastern Mediterranean Health Journal*, 5(2), 223–30.

Older Women's Network (2003), *Steppin' Out and Speakin' Up*. Millers Point, NSW: Older Women's Network NSW.

Olsen, M.E., Lodwick, D.G. and Dunlap, R.E. (1992), *Viewing the World Ecologically*. San Francisco, CA: Westview Press.

Olson, J.S. and Wilson, R. (1986), *Native Americans in the Twentieth Century*. Urbana, IL: University of Illinois.

Ongley, P. (1991), O\Pacific Islands Migration and the New Zealand Labour Market, in P. Spoonley, D. Pearson and C. Macpherson (eds), *Nga Take: Ethnic Relations and Racism in Aotearoa/New Zealand*. Palmerston North: Dunmore Press, pp. 17–36.

Orange, C. (1987), *The Treaty of Waitangi*. Auckland: Allen and Unwin NZ Ltd (in association with the Port Nicholson Press, Wellington, New Zealand).

Osei-Hwedie, K. (1990), Social Work and the Question of Social Development in Africa. *Journal of Social Development in Africa*, 5(2), 87–99.

Osei-Hwedie, K. (1993a), The Challenge of Social Work in Africa: Starting the Indigenization Process. *Journal of Social development in Africa*, 8(1), 19–30.

Osei-Hwedie, K. (1993b), *Putting the 'Social' Back into 'Work': The Case for the Indigenization of Social Work Practice and Education in Africa*. Special Report, Bulletin E 12.2. Cape Town: Institute for Indigenous Theory and Practice.

Osei-Hwedie, K. (1995), *A Search for Legitimate Social Development Education and Practice Models for Africa*. Lewiston, NY: Edwin Mullen.

Osei-Hwedie, K. (1996a), The Indigenization of Social Work Education and Practice in South Africa: The Dilemma of Theory and Method. *Social Work/Maatskaplike Werk*, 32(3), 215–25.

Osei-Hwedie, K. (1996b), *The Indigenization of Social Work Practice and Education: Vision or Vanity?* Inaugural Lecture, University of Botswana, 25 September.

Osei-Hwedie, K. (2001), Indigenous Practice – Some Informed Guesses: Self-evident and Possible. Paper presented at the JUC Conference, Bloemfontein, South Africa.

Osei-Hwedie, K. (2002a), Indigenous Practice – Some Informed Guesses: Self-evident and Possible. *Social Work/Maatkaplike Werk*, 38(4), 311–29.

Osei-Hwedie, K. (2002b), Indigenous Practice – Some Informed Guesses. Part II: Self-evident and Possible. *Social Work/Maatskaplike Werk*, 38(4), 311–36.

Osei-Hwedie, K. (2005), Afro-centrism: The Challenge of Social Development. Paper presented at the ASASWEI Conference 2005, *Democracy, Development, Delivery: Mapping the Future Contribution of the Social Service Professions*. Stellenbosch: Stellenbosch University, South Africa, 6–7 September.

Osei-Hwedie, K. and Bar-On, A. (1999), Change and Development: Towards Community-driven Social Policies in Africa, in D. Morales-Gomez (ed.), *Transnational Social Policies: The New Development Challenges of Globalisation*. Ottawa, Canada: IDRC, pp. 89–115.

Osei-Hwedie, K., Ntseane, D. and Jacques, G. (2006), Searching for Appropriateness in Social Work Education in Botswana: The Process of Developing a Masters Programme in a Developing Country. *Journal of Social Work Education*, 6.

Ouellette, G. (2002), *The Fourth World: An Indigenous Perspective on Feminism and Aboriginal Women's Activism*. Halifax, Canada: Fernwood Press.

Ouma, S. (1995), The Role of Social Participation in the Socio-economic Development of Uganda. *Journal of Social Development in Africa*, 10(2), 5–12.

Ow, R. (1990a), Social Behaviour in an Asian Cultural Setting, in M. Clare and L. Jayasuriya (eds), *Issues of Cross Cultural Practice*. Nedlands, WA: University of Western Australia.

Ow, R. (1990b), Asian Perception of Interventions, in M. Clare and L. Jayasuriya (eds), *Issues of Cross Cultural Practice*. Nedlands, WA: University of Western Australia.

Ow, R. (1990c), Working with Asian Families, in M. Clare. and L. Jayasuriya (eds), *Issues of Cross Cultural Practice*. Nedlands, WA: University of Western Australia.

Oxfam Australia (2006), *Commonwealth Games Briefing Paper: Aboriginal and Torres Strait Islander Health*. Accessed 15 May 2005, <www.oxfam.org.au/campaigns/indigenous/docs/health_15032006.pdf>.

Park, H. (2005), Culture as Deficit: A Critical Discourse Analysis of the Concept of Culture in Contemporary Social Work Discourse. *Journal of Sociology and Social Welfare*, 32(3), 11–33.

Parliament of the Republic of South Africa (1994), White Paper on Reconstruction and Development, Notice No. 1954, *Government Gazette*, 353(16085). Pretoria, South Africa: Government Printer.

Patel, L. and Midgley, J. (2004), Social Welfare and Social Development in South Africa: Reshaping the Colonial and Apartheid Legacy for a Global Era, in C.J. Finer and P. Smyth (eds), *Social Policy and the Commonwealth: Prospects for Social Inclusion*. New York: Palgrave Macmillan.

Payne, M. (1997), *Modern Social Work Theory* (2nd edn). Houndmills: Macmillan Press Ltd.

Peabody, J.W., Luck, J., Glassman, P., Dresselhaus, T.R. and Lee, M. (2000), Comparison of Vignettes, Standardized Patients and Chart Abstraction: A Prospective Validation Study of Three Methods for Measuring Quality. *Journal of the American Medical Association*, 283(13), 1715–22.

Pearce, T.O. (2001), Human Rights and Sociology: Some Observations from Africa. *Social Problems*, 48(1), 48–56.

Pearson, N. (1994), A Troubling Inheritance. *Race and Class*, 35(4), 1–9.

Pearson, N. (2000), *The Light on the Hill*. The Ben Chiffley Memorial Lecture. Accessed 6 October 2003, <www.australianpolitics.com/news/2000/00-08-12a.shtml>.

Pearson, N. (2003), *On Leadership*. The 2003 Leadership Lecture. Accessed 6 October, <www.leadershipvictoria.org/speech_pearson200.html>.

Pearson, V. (1989), Making a Virtue of Necessity: Hospital and Community Care for the Mentally Ill in China. *International Social Work*, 32(1), 53–63.

Pease, B., Allan, J. and Briskman, L. (2003), Introducing Critical Theories in Social Work, in J. Allan, B. Pease and L. Briskman (eds), *Critical Social Work: An Introduction to Theories and Practices*. Sydney: Allen and Unwin.

Pedersen, P. (1984), Cultural Assumptions of Education and Non-Western Alternatives, in D. Sanders and P. Pedersen (eds), *Education for International Social Welfare*. School of Social Work: University of Hawaii.

Phillipson, R. (1992), *Linguistic Imperialism*. Oxford: Oxford University Press.

Pieterse, J.N. (2004), *Globalization and Culture: Global Melange*. Lanham: Rowman and Littlefield Publishers.

Porter, R. (2005), The Decolonization of Indigenous Governance, in W.A. Wilson and M. Yellow Bird (eds), *For Indigenous Eyes Only: A Decolonization Handbook*. Santa Fe, NM: School of American Research Press.

Prager, E. (1985), American Social Work Imperialism: Consequence for Professional Education in Israel. *Journal of Jewish Communal Service*, 62(2), 129–38.

Prasad, B. and Vijayaslakshmi, B. (1997), Field Instruction for Social Work Education in India: Some Issues. *Indian Journal of Social Work*, 58(1), 65–77.

Pringle, R. (1970), *Rajahs and Rebels Under Brooke Rule, 1841–1941*. Glasgow: The University Press.

Proctor, B. (1994), Supervision: Competence, Confidence, Accountability. *British Journal of Guidance and Counselling*, 22(3), 309–18.

Pugh, R. and Gould, N. (2000), Globalization, Social Work and Social Welfare. *European Journal of Social Work*, 3(2), 123–38.

Pulido, L. (1996), *Environmentalism and Economic Justice*. Tucson, AZ: University of Arizona Press.

Qalo, R. (2004), *Out of Many, One!: Interfacing Indigenous Knowledge and Global Knowledge – A Strategy for Improving Pasifika Students' Achievement*. Suva: Institute of Pacific Health Research and School of Public Health and Primary Care, Fiji School of Medicine.

Quinn, M. (2003), Immigrants and Refugees: Culturally Affirming Practices, in J. Allan, B. Pease and L. Briskman (eds), *Critical Social Work: An Introduction to Theories and Practices*. Sydney: Allen and Unwin.

Ragab, I. (1982), *Authentization of Social Work in Developing Countries*. Egypt: Integrated Social Services Project.

Ragab, I. (1990), How Social Work Can Take Root in Developing Countries. *Social Development Issues*, 12(3), 38–51.

Randall, B. (2003), *Songman: The Story of an Aboriginal Elder of Uluru*. Sydney: ABS Books.

Randolph, S.M. and Banks, H.D. (1993), Making a Way Out of No Way: The Promise of Africentric Approaches to HIV Prevention. *Journal of Black Psychology*, 19(2), 204–14.

Ranganathan, S. (1994), The Manjakuddi Experience: A Camp Approach Towards Treating Alcoholics. *British Journal of Addiction*, 89(9), 1071–5.

Ranganathan, T.V. and Ranganathan, S. (2003), Meeting Challenges in the Field of Addiction, in V. Patel and R. Thara (eds), *Meeting the Mental Health Needs of Developing Countries: NGO Innovations in India*. Thousand Oaks, CA: Sage Publications, Inc, pp. 289–308.

Rankin, P. (1997), Developmental Social Welfare: Challenges Facing South Africa. *Social Work/Maatskaplike Werk*, 33(3), 184–92.

Rao, M. (1990), International Social Welfare: Global Perspectives. *Encyclopedia of Social Work* (18th edn). USA: National Association of Social Workers.

Razack, N. (2002), A Critical Examination of International Student Exchanges. *International Social Work*, 45(2), 251–65.

Razack, S. (1998), *Looking White People in the Eye: Gender, Race and Culture in Courtrooms and Classrooms*. Toronto: University of Toronto Press.

Razali, S.M., Khan, U.A. and Hasanah, C.I. (1996), Belief in Supernatural Causes of Mental Illness Among Malay Patients: Impact on Treatment. *ACTA Psychiatrica Scandinavia*, 94, 229–33.

Reggio, G. (1982), *Koyaanisqatsi AKA: Life Out of Balance*. Santa Fe: Institute for Regional Education.

Republic of Botswana (2002), *Revised National Policy on Destitute Persons*. Gaborone: Government Printer.

Republic of Botswana (2003), *National Development Plan 9*. Gaborone: Government Printer.

Republic of Botswana (2006), *Budget Speech for 2006/07*. Gaborone: Government Printer.

Resnick, R.P. (1976), Conscientization: An Indigenous Approach to International Social Work. *International Social Work*, 19(2), 21–9.

Rice, B. (2005), *Seeing the World With Aboriginal Eyes: A Four Dimensional Perspective on Human and Non-Human Values, Cultures and Relationships on Turtle Island*. Winnipeg, MB: Aboriginal Issues Press.

Riggs, D.W. (2004), We Don't Talk About Race Anymore: Power, Privilege and Critical Whiteness Studies. *Borderlands e-journal*, 3(2). Accessed 3 September 2006, <www.borderlandsjournal.adelaide.edu.au/vol3no2_2004/riggs_intro.htm>.

Rigney, L.I. (1997), Internationalization of an Indigenous Anti-colonial Cultural Critique of Research Methodologies: A Guide to Indigenist Research Methodology and its Principles. In Higher Education Research and Development Society of Australia (HERDSA) Annual International Conference Proceedings, *Research and Development in Higher Education: Advancing International Perspectives*, 20, 629–36.

Roan, S. (1980), Utilizing Traditional Elements in the Society in Casework Practice. *International Social Work*, 23(1), 26–35.

Robertson, J.M. (1963), Observations on Some Aspects of Social Work Education in Developing Countries. *International Social Work*, 6(2), 19–21.

Robertson, J.M. (1980), Two Decades of Social Work Education in Singapore and Malaysia, in P. Hodge (ed.), *Community Problems and Social Work in Southeast Asia*. Hong Kong: Hong Kong University Press.

Rodney, W. (1972), *How Europe Underdeveloped Africa*. Dar-es-Salaam: Tanzania Publishing House.

Rosaldo, R. (1989), Culture and Truth: The Remaking of Social Analysis. Boston, MA: Beacon Press.

Rossides, D.W. (1998), *Professions and Disciplines: Functional and Conflict Perspectives*. New Jersey: Prentice Hall.

Ruhana, N. (1997), *Palestinian Citizens in an Ethnic Jewish State: Identities in Conflict*. New Haven: Yale University Press.

Ruwhui, L. (1999), Ko Tane Pupuke, Te Komako 111. *Social Work Review*, 11(4), 32–7.

Ruwhiu, L.A., Baucke, H., Corrigan, R., Herewini, M., Davis, N. and Ruwhiu, P.T.O. (1999), Whaka-whanau-nga-tanga – A Touch of Class – We Represent.

Paper presented at *Promoting Inclusion, Redressing Exclusion: The Social Work Challenge*, Joint Conference of Australian Association of Social Workers (AASW), International Federation of Social Workers (IFSW), Asia and Pacific Association for Social Work Education (APASWE) and Australian Association for Social Work and Welfare Education (AASWWE), Brisbane, 26–29 September.

Sa`di, A.H. (2002), Catastrophe, Memory and Identity: Al-Nakbah as a Component of Palestinian Identity. *Israel Studies*, 7(2), 175–98.

Sagiv, L. and Schwartz, S.H. (1998), Determinants of Readiness for Out-group Contact: Dominance Relations and Minority Group Motivations. *International Journal of Psychology*, 33(5), 313–24.

Sahtouris, E. (1989), *Gaia: The Human Journey From Chaos to Cosmos.* Toronto: Simon and Schuster.

Said, E. (1978), *Orientalism.* New York: Pantheon.

Said, E. (1993), *Culture and Imperialism.* New York: Knopf.

Salem, P. (ed.) (1997), *Conflict Resolution in the Arab World: Selected Essays.* Beirut: Lebanon, American University of Beirut.

Sanders. D.S. (1980), Multiculturalism: Implications for Social Work. *International Social Work*, 23(2), 9–16.

Sanders, D.S. (1984), Pacific Developments: Implications for Future Directions in Social Work Education, in D.S. Sanders and P. Pedersen (eds), *Education for International Social Welfare.* School of Social Work: University of Hawaii.

Sanderson, J. (1996), *Aboriginal Pedagogy: An Adult Education Paradigm.* Master's Project, Department of Communication, Continuing and Vocational Education, University of Saskatchewan, Saskatoon.

Sardar, Z. and Wyn Davies, M. (2002), *Why Do People Hate America?* Cambridge: Icon Books.

Satchell, M. (1994), The Worst Federal Agency: Critics Call the Bureau of Indian Affairs a National Disgrace. *U.S. News and World Report*, 28 November, 117(21), 61–5.

Savaya, R. (1995), Attitudes Towards Family and Marital Counselling Among Israeli Arab Women. *Journal of Social Science Research*, 21(1), 35–51.

Schaffer, K. and Smith, S. (2004), *Human Rights and Narrated Lives: The Ethics of Recognition.* New York: Palgrave Macmillan.

Schellenberg, J.A. (1996), *Conflict Resolution: Theory, Research and Practice.* Albany, NY: University of New York Press.

Scheurich, J.J. with Young, M. (1997), Colouring Epistemologies: Are Our Research Epistemologies Racially Biased? in J.J. Scheurich (ed.), *Research Method in the PostModern*, ch. 7. London: Falmer Press.

Schiele, J.H. (2000), *Human Services and the Afrocentric Paradigm.* New York: Haworth Press.

School of Indian Social Work, First Nations University of Canada (2005), *Accreditation Self- Study.* Unpublished document.

Seebaran, R.B. and Johnston, S.P. (1999), *Nicola Valley Institute of Technology Social Work Program Evaluation.* Unpublished document.

Seers, D. (1972), The Meaning of Development, in N.T. Uphoff and W.F. Ilchman (eds), *The Political Economy of Development*. Berkeley, CA: University of California Press, pp. 123–9.

Sethi, B.B. and Trivedi, J.K. (1979), Drug Abuse in a Rural Population. *Indian Journal of Psychiatry*, 21, 211–6.

Shanghai Social Work (17 May 2006), accessed on 17 May 2006, <www.shsw.cn/jsp/index.jsp>.

Shawky, A. (1972), Social Work Education in Africa. *International Social Work*, 15(1), 3–16.

Shiva, V. (n.d.), Food Patents: Stealing Indigenous Knowledge? *Genetically Engineered Food*. Accessed 30 October 2006, <www.globalissues.org/EnvIssues/GEFood/FoodPatents.asp>.

Shlaim, A. (2001), *Iron Wall: Israel and the Arab World*. New York: Norton.

Silavwe, G.W. (1995), The Need for a New Social Work Perspective in an African Setting: The Case of Zambia. *British Journal of Social Work*, 25(1), 71–84.

Silitshena, R.M.K. (1989), *Village Level Institutions and Popular Participation in Botswana*. South Africa: Review of Urban Planning, 1 November.

Sin, R. and Yan, M.C. (2003), Margins as Centres: A Theory of Social Inclusion in Anti-oppressive Social Work, in W. Shera (ed.), *Emerging Perspectives on Anti-Oppressive Practice*. Toronto: Canadian Scholars Press Inc, pp. 25–41.

Sinclair, R. (2004), Aboriginal Social Work Education in Canada: Decolonizing Pedagogy for the Seventh Generation. *First Peoples Child and Family Review*, 1(1), 49–61.

Sinha, D. (1998), Changing Perspectives in Social Psychology in India: A Journey Towards Indigenization. *Asian Journal of Social Psychology*, 1(1), 17–31.

Sjoberg, G. and Vaughan, T. (1993), The Ethical Foundations of Sociology and the Necessity for a Human Rights Alternative, in T. Vaughan, G. Sjoberg and L. Reynolds (eds), *A Critique of Contemporary American Sociology*. New York: General Hall, Inc.

Smith, A.E. (2003), Social Work and Ethnic Minorities' Social Development in the People's Republic of China. *International Social Work*, 46(3), 403–19.

Smith, L.T. (1999), *Decolonizing Methodologies: Research and Indigenous Peoples*. London: Zed Books.

Sowers-Hoag, K. and Sandau-Beckler, P. (1996), Educating for Cultural Competence in the Generalist Curriculum. *Journal of Multicultural Social Work*, 4(3), 37–54.

Spiegel, J. (1982), An Ecological Model of Ethnic Families, in M. McGoldrick, J. Pearce and J. Giodano (eds), *Ethnicity and Family Therapy*. New York: Guilford, pp. 31–51.

Spivak, G.C. (1988), Can the Subaltern Speak? in C. Nelson and L. Grossberg (eds), *Marxism and the Interpretation of Culture*. Basingstoke: Macmillan Education, pp. 271–316.

Spoonley, P. (2001), Transnational Pacific Communities: Transforming the Politics of Place and Identity, in C. Macpherson, P. Spoonley and M. Anae (eds), *Tangata O Te Moana Nui: The Evolving Identities of Pacific Peoples in Aotearoa/New Zealand*. Palmerston North: Dunmore Press, pp. 81–96.

Spretnak, C. (1997), *The Resurgence of the Real*. Don Mills, Ontario: Addison-Wesley.

Stamatopoulou, E. (1994), Indigenous Peoples and the United Nations: Human Rights as a Developing Dynamic. *Human Rights Quarterly*, 16, 58–81.

Stanfield II, J.H. (1993), Methodological Reflections, in J.H. Stanfield II and R.M. Dennis (eds), *Race and Ethnicity in Research Methods*. Newbury Park: Sage.

Stanfield II, J.H. (1994), Ethnic Modelling in Qualitative Research, in N.K. Denzin and Y.S. Lincoln (eds), *Handbook of Qualitative Research*. Thousand Oaks, California: Sage.

Statistical Abstract of Israel, No. 49 (1998), *Tables 2.1, 12.7, 5*. Jerusalem: Central Bureau of Statistics.

Statistics New Zealand (2002), Tongan – Population. Accessed 24 March 2003, <www.stats.govt.nz/domino/external...509040bb31fcc256ccf00792fc8?OpenDocument>.

Stephenson, M. (2000), *In Critical Demand: Social Work in Canada: The Occupation of Social Work in Canada – National Sector Study Final Report*. Ottawa: The Social Work Sector Study Steering Committee.

Stewart-Harrawira, M. (2005), *The New Imperial Order: Indigenous Responses to Globalization*. New York: Zed Books.

Streeten, P. and Burki, S.J. (1978), Basic Needs: Some Issues. *World Development*, 6(3), 411–21.

Streeten, P. with Burki, S.J., Ul Haq, M., Hicks, N. and Stewart, F. (1981), *First Things First: Meeting Basic Needs in Developing Countries*. New York: Oxford University Press.

Sue, D.W. and Sue, D. (2003), *Counseling the Culturally Diverse: Theory and Practice* (4th edn). New York: John Wiley & Sons.

Suzuki, D. with McConnell, A. (1997), *Sacred Balance: Rediscovering Our Place in Nature*. Vancouver: Greystone Books.

Swimme, B. (1998), *The Earth's Imagination* [Film]. Available from Centre for the Story of the Universe, 311 Rydal Avenue, Mill Valley, CA.

Swimme, B. and Berry, T. (1992), *The Universe Story*. San Francisco, CA: Harper.

Tacy, D. (2000), *Re-Enchantment: The New Australian Spirituality*. NSW: HarperCollins.

Tannoch-Bland, J. (1998), *Identifying White Race Privilege in Bringing Australia Together: The Structure and Experience of Racism in Australia*. Woolloongabba: The Foundation for Aboriginal and Islander Research Action.

Taylor, C. (1994), The Politics of Recognition, in A. Gutman (ed.), *Multiculturalism: Examining the Politics of Recognition*. Princeton, NJ: Princeton University Press.

Taylor, Z. (1999), Values, Theory and Methods in Social Work Education: A Culturally Transferable Core? *International Social Work*, 42(3), 309–18.

Tedlock, B. (2005), Indigenous, Cosmopolitan and Integrative Medicine in the Americas, in D. Champagne, K. Jo Torjesen and S. Steiner (eds), *Indigenous Peoples and the Modern State*. Walnut Creek, CA: AltaMira Press.

Thompson, N. (1997), *Anti-Discriminatory Practice.* Basingstoke: Macmillan.

Thompson, R. (1982), Aboriginal Title and Mining Legislation in the Northwest Territories. *Studies in Aboriginal Rights No. 6.* Saskatoon, Saskatchewan: University of Saskatchewan Native Law Center.

Thorpe, R. (1997), Indigenous Challenges to the Social Work and Social Welfare Codes of Ethics in Australia: A Critical Issue for Social Welfare Education. *Northern Radius*, 4(2), 9–10.

Tien, J. (1953), *The Chinese of Sarawak: A Study of Social Structure.* London: Department of Anthropology, London School of Economics and Political Science.

Torpy, S.J. (2000), Native American Women and Coerced Sterilization: On the Trail of Tears in the 1970s. *American Indian Culture and Research Journal*, 24(2), 1–22.

Trainer, F.E. (n.d.), *The Simpler Way.* Accessed 6 November 2006, <www.socialwork. arts.unsw.edu.au/tsw/>.

Trask, H.-K. (1999), *From a Native Daughter: Colonialism and Sovereignty in Hawai'I.* Honolulu: University of Hawaii Press.

Trevithick, P. (2005), *Social Work Skills: A Practice Handbook.* Berkshire: Open University Press.

Tripcony, P. (2004), Indigenous Education – Everybody's Business: Implications for Teacher Education. *Report of the Working Party on Indigenous Studies in Teacher Education, Letter of Transmittal.* Presented to the Board of Teacher Registration, Queensland, December 2004.

Tsang, A.K.T. and Yan, M.-C. (2001), Chinese Corpus, Western Application: The Chinese Strategy of Engagement with Western Social Work Discourse. *International Social Work*, 44(4), 433–54.

Tsang, A.K.T., Yan, M.C. and Guo, H. (2001), Positioning Social Work at a Time of Rapid Changes in China: A Scientific Approach to Social Issues. *Shehuixue Yanjiu* (Sociological Research), published in Chinese, 2001(2), 63–7.

Tsang, A.K.T., Yan, M.C. and Shera, W. (2000), Negotiating Multiple Agendas in International Social Work: The Case of China–Canada Collaborative Project, *Canadian Social Work Review*, 2(1), 147–61.

Tsang, N.M. (1997), Examining the Cultural Dimension of Social Work Practice: The Experience of Teaching Students on a Social Work Course in Hong Kong. *International Social Work*, 40(2), 133–44.

Tully, J. (1995), *Strange Multiplicity.* Cambridge: Cambridge University Press.

Turnbull, C.M. (1989), *A History of Malaysia. Singapore and Brunei.* Boston, MA: Allen & Unwin.

Turner, D. (2005), *This is Not a Peace Pipe: Towards a Critical Indigenous Philosophy.* Toronto: University of Toronto Press.

Turner, V. (1974), *Drama, Fields and Metaphors: Symbolic Action in Human Societies.* Ithaca, NY: Cornell University Press.

Turner, V. (1982), *The Ritual Process.* Ithaca, NY: Cornell University Press.

United Nations (1948), *Universal Declaration of Human Rights.* Accessed 23 July 2006, <www.un.org/Overview/rights.html>.

United Nations (1971), *Training for Social Welfare: Fifth International Survey*. New York: United Nations.

Vaden, B.D. (1998), *Kainga: Tongan Families as Agents of Change*. Unpublished PhD (political science) dissertation, University of Hawai'i.

van der Grijp, P. (2004), *Identity and Development: Tongan Culture, Agriculture and the Perenniality of the Gift*. Leiden: KITLV Press.

Venkataraman, J. (1995), These Camps were Different. *Reflections: Narratives of Professional Helping*, 2(2), 33–41.

Venkataraman, J. (1996), *Indigenization of Alcoholism Treatment From the American to the Indian Context*. Unpublished Doctoral Dissertation, University of Illinois at Urbana-Champaign, Urbana, IL.

Voss, R., Douville, V., Little Soldier, A. and Twiss, G. (1999), Tribal and Shamanic-based Social Work Practice: A Lakota Perspective. *Social Work*, 44(3), 228–41.

Wadia, A.R. (1968), History of Social Work in India 1818–1947, in Planning Commission of India (eds), *Encyclopedia of Social Work in India*. Delhi: Planning Commission of India, pp. 393–400.

Wakim, W. (1994), The National Committee for the Defence of the Rights of the Uprooted in Israel. Paper presented at the first *Conference for Human Rights in Arab Society*, Nazareth.

Walker, R. (1996), *Ngo Pepa A Ranginut: The Walker Papers*. Auckland: Penguin Books.

Walton, R.G. and Abo El Nasr, M.M. (1988), Indigenization and Authentization in Terms of Social Work in Egypt. *International Social Work*, 31(1), 135–44.

Wang, M. (2002), The Third Eye. *Critique of Anthropology*, 22, 149–74.

Wang, S.B. (1994), The International Standards on Social Work Education and Our Choice, in T.Y. Lee (ed.), *Proceedings of the Conference on Social Work Education in Chinese Societies: Existing Patterns and Future Development* (in Chinese). Hong Kong: Asian and Pacific Association for Social Work Education.

Wang, S.B. (1997), On the Indigenization of Social Work in China. Public Lecture Delivered in Connection with the Distinguished Chinese Visiting Scholars Scheme of the Hong Kong Polytechnic University, Hong Kong.

Wang, S.B. (2000), A Preliminary Discussion on Indigenization of Social Work in China, in K.L. Ho and S.B. Wang (eds), *An Exploration of Social Work in Chinese Societies*. River Edge, NJ: Global Publishing Co, pp. 173–90.

Wang, S.B. (2005), Work Report of the China Association of Social Work Education (in Chinese).

Wang, S.B. *et al.* (eds) (1999), *Social work: An Introduction*, Peking. China: Higher Education Press.

Wang, S.B. *et al.* (eds) (2004), *Social Work: An Introduction*, Beijing. China: Higher Education Press.

Wastesicoot, J. (2004), *A Cultural Framework for Cree Self-Government: Retracing Our Steps Back*. An unpublished Master's Thesis, University of Manitoba, Winnipeg, Manitoba.

Watson, L. (1988), An Aboriginal Perspective: Developing an Indigenous Social Work, in E. Chamberlain (ed.), *Change and Continuity in Australian Social Work*. Melbourne: Longman Cheshire.

Weaver, H.N. (1998), Indigenous People in a Multicultural Society: Unique Issues for Human Services. *Social Work*, 43(3), 203–12.

Weaver, H.N. (1999), Indigenous People and the Social Work Profession: Defining Culturally Competent Services. *Social Work*, 44(3), 217–25.

Weaver, H.N. (2000), Culture and Professional Education: The Experiences of Native American Social Workers. *Journal of Social Work Education*, 36(3), 415–28.

Weaver, H.N. (2001), Organizations and Community Assessment with First Nations People, in R. Fong and S. Furuto (eds), *Culturally Competent Practice: Skills, Interventions and Evaluations*. Toronto: Allyn and Bacon.

Weaver, J. (1997), Native American Studies, Native American Literature, and Communitism. *Ayaangwaamizin*, 1(2), 23–33.

Webb, S.A. (2003), Local Orders and Global Chaos in Social Work. *European Journal of Social Work*, 6(2), 191–204.

Webber-Dreadon, E. (1999), He Taonga Mo Matou Tipuna (A Gift Handed Down by Our Ancestors). Paper presented at *Promoting Inclusion, Redressing Exclusion: The Social Work Challenge*, Joint Conference of Australian Association of Social Workers (AASW), International Federation of Social Workers (IFSW), Asia and Pacific Association for Social Work Education (APASWE) and Australian Association for Social Work and Welfare Education (AASWWE), Brisbane, 26–29 September.

Wikaira, B., Prasad, P., Davis, J. and Halbert, M. (1999), Inclusion of Cultural Social Work Perspectives within a Monocultural System. Paper presented at *Promoting Inclusion, Redressing Exclusion: The Social Work Challenge*, Joint Conference of Australian Association of Social Workers (AASW), International Federation of Social Workers (IFSW), Asia and Pacific Association for Social Work Education (APASWE) and Australian Association for Social Work and Welfare Education (AASWWE), Brisbane, 26–29 September.

Williams, B. (2003), The World View Dimensions of Individualism and Collectivism: Implications for Counseling. *Journal of Counseling and Development*, 81, 370–74.

Wilson, A. and Beresford, P. (2000), Anti-oppressive Practice: Emancipation or Appropriation. *British Journal of Social Work*, 30(5), 553–73.

Wingard, B. and Lester, J. (2001), *Telling Stories in Ways That Make Us Stronger*. Adelaide: Dulwich Centre Publications.

Wiredu, K. (1980), *Philosophy and an African Culture*. Cambridge: Cambridge University Press.

Wong, L.J.L. (1998), *Marginalization and Social Welfare in China*. New York: Routledge.

Wong, Y.-L.R. (2002), Reclaiming Chinese Women's Subjectivities: Indigenizing 'Social Work with Women' in China Through Post-colonial Ethnography. *Women's Studies International Forum*, 25(1), 67–77.

Wood, E.M. (2003), *Empire of Capital*. New York: Verso.

World Conference against Racism, Racial Discrimination, Xenophobia and Related Intolerance (2001), *Draft Report of Regional Meeting of Indigenous Peoples*, Sydney.

Wotherspoon, T. and Satzewich, V. (2000), *First Nations Race, Class and Gender Relations*. Regina: Canadian Plains Research Centre.

Wright, R. (1993), *Stolen Continents: The New Through Indian Eyes*. Toronto, ON: Penguin Books.

Xia, Z.Q. (1991), A New Start, in W.S. Chow *et al.* (eds), *Status-Quo, Challenge and Prospect: Collected Works of the Seminar of the Asian-Pacific Region Social Work Education* (in Chinese). Beijing: Peking University Press.

Xiong, Y.G. (1999), Problems and Challenges Confronting the Development of Social Work Education in the 21st Century. *Reflections, Choices and Development: Special Issue on Social Work Education: Journal of China Youth College for Political Sciences* (in Chinese), 18(1), 32–7.

Xu, L.Y. *et al.* (eds) (2004), *Social Case Work*, Beijing. China: Higher Education Press.

Xu, Q.W., Gao, J.G. and Yan, M.C. (2005), Community Centres in Urban China: Context, Development, and Limitations. *Journal of Community Practice*, 13(3), 73–90.

Xu, Y.X. *et al.* (eds) (2004), *Community Work*, Beijing. China: Higher Education Press.

Yan, M.C. (1998), Social Functioning Discourse in a Chinese Context: Developing Social Work in Mainland China. *International Social Work*, 41(2), 181–94.

Yan, M.C. (2005), Searching for International Social Work: A Reflection on Personal and Professional Journey. *Reflections: Narratives of Professional Helping*, 11(1), 4–16.

Yan, M.C. and Cheung, K.W. (2006), The Politics of Indigenization: A Case Study of Development of Social Work in China. *Journal of Sociology and Social Welfare*, 33(2), 63–83.

Yan, M.C. and Gao, J.G. (2005), Social Engineering of Community Building: Examination of Policy Process and Characteristics of Community Construction in China. *Community Development Journal Advance Access*. Published 26 October.

Yan, M.C. and Tsang, A.K.T. (2005), A Snap Shot on the Development of Social Work Education in China: A Delphi Study. *Social Work Education*, 24(8), 883–901.

Yang, Y. and Martell, D. (2006), *Building Positive Capacities*. Unpublished curriculum manual.

Yao, J. (1995), The Developing Models of Social Work Education in China. *International Social Work*, 38(1), 27–38.

Yellow Bird, M. (1999), Indian, American Indian and Native Americans: Counterfeit Identities. *Winds of Change: A Magazine for American Indian Education and Opportunity*, 14, 1. Accessed 16 February 2005, <www.aistm.org/yellowbirdes say.htm>.

Yellow Bird, M. (2006), The Continuing Effects of American Colonialism, in R. Fong, R. McRoy and C. Ortiz Hendricks (eds), *Intersecting Child Welfare, Substance Abuse, and Family Violence: Culturally Competent Approaches*. Alexandria, VA: CSWE Press, pp. 229–65.

Yip, K. (2001), Indigenization of Social Work in Hong Kong. *Hong Kong Journal of Social Work*, 35(1/2), 51–78.

Yip, K. (2004), A Chinese Cultural Critique of the Global Qualifying Standards for Social Work Education, *Social Work Education*, 23(5), 597–612.

Yip, K. (2005a), A Dynamic Asian Response to Globalization in Cross-cultural Social Work. *International Social Work*, 48(5), 593–607.

Yip, K. (2005b), Chinese Concepts of Mental Health: Cultural Implications for Social Work Practice. *International Social Work*, 48(4), 391–407.

Yosef, S.A. (1991), *The Sociology of the Bedoiun-Arabs* (in Arabic). Cairo: Daar Al-Marif Press.

Young, D., Ingram, G. and Swartz, L. (1989), *Cry of the Eagle: Encounters with a Cree Healer*. Toronto: University of Toronto Press.

Young, M. (1999), Residential Segregation and Differential Citizenship. *Citizenship Studies*, 3(2), 237–52.

Young, R.J.C. (2001), *Post-Colonialism: An Historical Introduction*. Oxford: Blackwell.

Youngblood Henderson, J.S. (2000), Challenges of Respecting Indigenous World Views in Euro-centric Education, in R. Neil (ed.), *Voice of the Drum: Indigenous Education and Culture*. Manitoba. Canada: Kingfisher Publications, pp. 59–80.

Yuan, F. (1988), *Education on Social Work and China's Socialist Modernization* (in Chinese). Paper presented at the Asian pacific Symposium on Education in Social Work, Beijing.

Yuan, F. (1998), Promoting Social Work Education in China Towards the 21st Century. *China Social Work: Special Issue on the Development of Social Work Education in China, 1998* (in Chinese).

Yuen-Tsang, A.W.K. (1996), Social Work Education in China: Constraints, Opportunities, and Challenges, in T.W. Lo and J.S.C. Cheng (eds), *Social Welfare Development in China, Constraints and Challenges*. Chicago: Imprint Publications Inc, pp. 85–100.

Yuen-Tsang, A.W.K. (1999a), *Social Work in China Stream of the Master of Arts/Post-Graduate Diploma in Social Work Programme*. Revised Validation Document. Hong Kong: The Hong Kong Polytechnic University.

Yuen-Tsang, A.W.K. (1999b), Chinese Communal Support Networks. *International Social Work*, 42(3), 359–71.

Yuen-Tsang, A.W.K. and Wang, S. (2002), Tensions Confronting the Development of Social Work Education in China: Challenges and Opportunities. *International Social Work*, 45(3), 375–88.

Zapf, M.K. (2005), The Spiritual Dimension of Person and Environment: Perspectives from Social Work and Traditional Knowledge. *International Social Work*, 48(5), 633–42.

Zapf, M.K. (2007), Profound Connections between Person and Place: Exploring Location, Spirituality and Social Work, in J. Coates, J.R. Graham, B. Swartzentruber and B. Ouellette (eds), *Spirituality and Social Work: Selected Canadian Readings*. Toronto: Canadian Scholars Press, pp. 229–42. See also Critical Social Work, 2005, 6(2). Available online, <www.criticalsocialwork.com/units/socialwork/critical.nsf/EditDoNotShowInTOC/62C3C075C4133F288525701900280CFB>.

Index

Page numbers in bold indicate illustrations.